10/21/01

Dear Ashadstvart.

It is horrible like you
who have let the Jewell phone
and melt it burning.

Thanks for that
and for being real great
friends — made that relatives —
for all my 40+ years.

Love,

Lang

ALSO BY LARRY TYE

The Father of Spin

HOMELANDS

HOME LANDS

Portraits of the New Jewish Diaspora

LARRY TYE

HENRY HOLT AND COMPANY   NEW YORK

Henry Holt and Company, LLC
Publishers since 1866
115 West 18th Street
New York, New York 10011

Henry Holt® is a registered trademark of
Henry Holt and Company, LLC.

Library of Congress Cataloging-in-Publication Data

Tye, Larry.
  Home lands: portraits of the new Jewish diaspora / Larry Tye.
    p. cm.
  Includes bibliographical references (p.) and index.
  ISBN 0-8050-6590-3 (hb)
  1. Jewish diaspora.   2. Israel and the diaspora.   3. Jews—Identity.
  4. Social integration. I. Title.

DS134.T94 2001
909'.04924—dc21   2001016918

First Edition 2001

Designed by Paula Russell Szafranski

Printed in the United States of America

1   3   5   7   9   10   8   6   4   2

To the two Shmuels, my great-grandfathers,
who laid such a solid foundation for my family's
Jewish life in the American diaspora

Contents

HOMELANDS

Introduction

CHARTING THE JOURNEY

Diaspora. The word itself suggests an existence as unsettled as it is unsatisfying. It describes a homogeneous people uprooted and dispersed from their native land by unstoppable armies or irreversible social forces. It bespeaks a yearning to go back. The Irish know all about having to abandon their homeland, and the loss that creates. So do Armenians and Chinese, Kurds and Kosovars. But the oldest diaspora of all is that of the Jews. It dates back at least 1,900 years, to when Rome toppled the Second Temple in Jerusalem and Jews were scattered across Asia, Africa, and Europe. Each time they settled somewhere new, a new persecutor— the inquisitors of Spain, the Russian czars, Hitler and the Holocaust he unleashed—reminded them they were strangers, with the perils that implied. For not just centuries but millennia, Jews have vowed to make their community whole again by returning to the homeland, the Holy Land. Each year at the Passover Seder, parents and children end by reciting a solemn vow: "Next year in Jerusalem!"

That metaphor of a people longing to go home is compelling.

It also is outdated.

There is a new definition of diaspora. If there are many who have slowly come to sense it, it remains a vision not yet articulated. This book sets forth that story. It tells of Jews who are forever rooted in Israel but no longer need to live there. It describes a heterogeneous people who thrive in secular societies as far-flung as the former Soviet Union and Argentina, but continue to embrace a core of beliefs and practices that defines them as Jews. It presents a Judaism that, after centuries of dispersion, marks a race as well as a religion, a culture as well as an ethnicity. It shows that the diaspora is no mere curiosity of history, but rather the reality of today and tomorrow.

The foundation of the Jewish future is an understanding that the diaspora is here to stay. After nearly 2,000 years of living outside their ancestral homeland, diaspora Jews finally can say that they have new homes. And they can know that those homes are secure in a world that, for the first time, is more promising than problematic for Jews. There are substantial threats posed by a slow shrinkage of diaspora population and its concentration in fewer lands, by a watering down of belief and a rising up of hate groups. But there is even more reason to celebrate as Jewish communities once presumed dead or dormant are being reborn from the old Eastern bloc to the jam-packed shuls of Los Angeles and Manhattan.

What about the Zionist dream of rebuilding the biblical birthright in Palestine that has inspired the last six generations of Jews? That, too, is being transformed. Israel today is a settled society made up mainly of native Israelis. It is inwardly focused, multifaceted, and increasingly prosperous, though also subject to the volatility of a faltering peace process. It still has a Law of Return that welcomes all diaspora Jews, but these days Israel is a refuge mainly for those who have nowhere else to go. It is experiencing air and water pollution, along with too much private construction and too little public transportation, environmental problems that would only get worse if many more Jews of the diaspora accepted its offer to immigrate. Most Israelis see their nation as complete even if it is not home to all the world's Jews, just as most diaspora Jews are coming to see themselves as complete even if they do not sign up and move to Israel.

All of which suggests the evolution of a new relationship between Israel and the rest of world Jewry as part of the new definition of diaspora. *Eretz Yisrael* will remain the nourishing center of Judaism, a place where diaspora Jews go for everything from replenishment to relaxation and research. But much as grown children do not have to live with their parents to maintain family ties, Jews need not immigrate to Israel to experience its lifeblood. And much as parents must acknowledge their children's self-worth to forge a lasting relationship, so too must Israel accept that diaspora Jews have something rich to offer in their own right.

What is left, then, is not your grandfather's or even your father's diaspora. This new Jewish diaspora has a novel way of looking at itself: as something permanent and positive. It is forging a new partnership of equals with Israel. Its wide-ranging communities are coming to see that they have even more in common with one another than with the Jewish state as they search for spiritual and religious meaning in a largely non-Jewish world.

*   *   *

My first clue that something extraordinary was unfolding in the Jewish diaspora came as I traveled the world for the *Boston Globe*. I might have been in Moscow to cover the surge of Pentecostalism, the planet's fastest-growing religion, or in Warsaw to see how forty years of socialism devastated Eastern Europe's environment—but what really intrigued me was the reawakening of those cities' long-repressed Jewish communities. So long as I wrote the stories they wanted, my editors let me write an extra one on the Jews of Moscow and Warsaw, along with those of Hong Kong, Belfast, Buenos Aires, or whatever other city I was visiting. The more communities I got to see close up, the clearer it became that the Jewish world was being revitalized and reshaped in ways that, for reasons that still puzzle me, were not reflected in all the books I was reading about the disappearing diaspora and the vanishing Jews of America.

That sense of Jewish renewal fed into a decades-long debate I have been having with my oldest and closest friend, Philip Warburg, who after years of going back and forth to Israel moved there with his family in 1994 and became an Israeli citizen in 1999. He says that living in Israel finally puts to rest, for him, the vicariousness of a diaspora identification so premised on the return to a historical homeland. I have been equally insistent that the diaspora offers as compelling an identity for a Jew like me, who grew up and is back living in Boston, but has experienced Jewish life from Washington, D.C., to Alabama and Kentucky.

This book, then, is born out of personal passion and a quest to understand my own Jewish context. I know that, like my parents and many other Jews, I love to attend services and explore Jewish communities wherever I go in the world. It is as if I am seeing myself in different forms at each stop, and each adds to my sense of how strong we Jews are, how diverse, how faithful, how true. I feel that I—we—belong in Birmingham and Belfast and all the other places. But I needed to understand whether, centuries after we had shared a birthright in Russia or Germany, Babylonia or Jerusalem, there was anything more than a sentimental bond that united me to the more than 8 million Jews who populate the diaspora. What does a Jew in Hong Kong, who celebrates the High Holidays at the Arts Center using a Torah tiny enough to fit in the briefcase of his itinerant rabbi, have in common with one in Buenos Aires, who celebrates in a stately synagogue surrounded by four-foot-high barrels of concrete designed to deter suicide bombers? Is there really anything that an utterly American Jew like me shares with either of them?

Even more, I wanted to know whether it was okay for me to feel at home as a Jew in Boston, or anywhere else in the diaspora. Like most diaspora Jews, I grew up with a sense of being deeply rooted in my surroundings, of being a Bostonian and an American, and feeling comfortable with those identities. But at the same time the pride of belonging to an ancient people left me with an unsettled sense that, no matter how firmly grounded I felt in America, I belonged somewhere else. Those feelings of uprootedness were reinforced every Sabbath when we recalled the messianic vision of a return to Zion—and they were dredged up anew each time I thought of the decision my friend Philip and his American-born and -raised wife, Tamar, had made to become actively involved in today's challenging and perplexing Israel.

The best way to answer those questions was to see what actually is going on in today's diaspora. I resolved to digest the unsettling numbers that the scholars of doom were citing on intermarriage and assimilation, then to weigh their evidence against what I found on the ground, as would any journalist. I would determine for myself whether the dying out of the Holocaust generation, and the easing up of anti-Semitism, were erasing the only compelling reasons for Jews to hold on to their Jewish identities. I wanted to find out whether there really were links among the diverse communities of Jews, and to see where I fit in with them.

My first challenge was to map out my rendering of the diaspora. I had to select a sufficient number of cities to get a representative cross section, but set limits that would let me tell in full the story of each city's origins, its evolution, and, most important, its current situation. I consulted historians and demographers, rabbis and leaders of Jewish organizations, asking each to list ten Jewish communities. I ended up with dozens of compelling choices from Melbourne to Montreal and Moscow, all convincingly argued by their advocates and all of which I was eager to explore. I did library research and live interviews on each, finally narrowing the list to seven that I felt had appealing stories, reflected the wider situation in the diaspora, and balanced one another. Dnepropetrovsk (Ne-pro-pə-'trofsk) is representative of the whole of the former Soviet Union. It suggests how difficult it is for Jews to reclaim traditions stifled during a century of rule by the Nazis and Soviets—and how tens of thousands are defying the odds by reversing their assimilation. Buenos Aires is the story of 250,000 Jews who arrived in the early 1900s from Russia, Poland, and the Ottoman Empire, settled in agricultural outposts, and carved a place for themselves in a land that also gave refuge to Nazi henchmen like Adolph Eichmann. Altogether my choices reflect Jewish communities that are growing and ones on the verge of death. There are places like Paris and Boston where everyone knows there are lots of Jews, and ones like Dublin, Düsseldorf, and Atlanta where it is a tightly kept secret. As a group they give a taste of today's diaspora and a flavor of tomorrow's.

For each city I tell the story in part through the experiences of a single family or congregation. Some are religious, some decidedly not. Several had written records of their history; most pieced it together based on stories passed between generations. A couple are famous, the rest are not known outside their community, and one exists in the shadow of its city's old slaughterhouse district. In Boston, the family I explore is my own. That is because it is the story I know best, and even more because my family's roots run deep in Boston's Jewish world, it remains actively involved, and it gives me the confidence that a diaspora existence can be compelling and fulfilling. It is, like most of the other families whose lives I probe, a diaspora success story.

In all seven cities I found evidence of hope alongside reason for despair as Jews negotiate their identities with the secular societies that engulf them. In Paris, the intermarriage rate tops 40 percent, but the Jewish community has never attracted larger crowds to cultural and religious events and never seen stronger bonds between its once-warring Ashkenazic and Sephardic factions. In Atlanta, half the Jews are not affiliated with any Jewish institution—but the other half attends services in such large numbers that existing synagogues are enlarging, new ones are sprouting, and Atlanta is the envy of northern neighbors who a generation ago thought that southern Jewry was an oxymoron.

Faced with such conflicting evidence on the future of Judaism I choose to remain an optimist without, I hope, being a Pollyanna. I believe that promising signs are just that: signs that give reason for real hope, in that they bespeak a vitality that those focusing on the bad news often miss. Appreciating the way young Jews and old are reengaging, for instance, makes it easier to nurture those ties and build on them. The truth is that we have been counseled and cautioned repeatedly about the dreaded threats to the faith—from intermarriage to resurgent anti-Semitism—but the countervailing, contradictory trends do not generate similar headlines or make their way as easily into books.

I see this book as a journey. Each city is a different stop, one that tells the particular tale of that place and, more important, helps answer overriding questions of what the diaspora is all about. What emerges in the end is a scorecard of sorts on the state of world Judaism—along with a measure of the potential for diaspora communities today to sustain their ties with ancestral roots at the same time that they play meaningful roles in their adopted cultures. After returning from the diaspora communities I decided one more trip was essential, to Israel. There, I looked at the changing nature of the diaspora's relationship to the Holy Land and visited with Israeli brothers and cousins, close friends and fellow congregants, of the families I focused on in my seven cities.

*   *   *

The first impression that emerges from those travels is each city's singularity. Jews in Paris not only speak a different language than those in Buenos Aires, they are also occupied with issues that reflect their different geography and economics, history and politics. The former generally are well off and confident; the latter too often are struggling financially and their communal institutions are crumbling. Likewise in Atlanta, Jews speak with a southern drawl and approach their lives with a civility that makes their cousins in Boston wonder whether they really could be Jewish.

Far more striking than the differences, however, is the unity. Jews from Buenos Aires to Dnepropetrovsk have enough customs and rituals in common, along with culture, values, and other traits that matter, for outsiders to see them as part of the same people and for them to define themselves that way. Stop by a synagogue in Dublin or Düsseldorf on a Friday evening or Saturday morning, the way I did, and you will see worshipers donning the same traditional yarmulkes and talliths. They chant prayers in the same age-old Hebraic tongue and pause afterward to break bread, sip wine, and share conversation. They parse the same passages from the Torah, Talmud, and Midrash in search of contemporary applications, and debate the same questions about whether there is a God, whether it is a he or a she, and what that Divine Being requires of mere mortals.

The same energy and vitality also characterize all seven Jewish communities in a way that is eerie and inspiring. Each had some seminal event that sparked a reawakening of spirit, from the arrival of North African refugees in Paris to the bombing of the communal center in Buenos Aires, and each has a passionate leader or leaders along with a community eager to follow. In each, there has been a dramatic reversal of generational roles that sees children speaking Hebrew better than their parents and grandparents, having a clearer grasp of their Jewish heritage, and bringing older relatives back with them to the shul and classroom. There is a sense that the worlds of free trade, global culture, and the Internet, which could make an ancient faith like Judaism seem quaint, have in fact pushed people to reach out for the very sort of spiritual meaning and uncompromised identity offered by Judaism. At the very moment when Jews have more freedom than ever to assimilate in secular society, more of them than ever are reconnecting to their Jewish culture and faith. The first time I observed such signs of renewal I dismissed them as interesting anomalies. But as I saw them repeated in one city after another, I came to believe that they reflect a real and widespread renaissance.

Nowhere is that more visible than in Germany. The Weimar Republic welcomed Jews in a way that promised a Golden Age, just as the Holocaust seemed to spell the end of the diaspora. It is the one land on Earth that Jews vowed never to return to. Yet they are coming back, tens of thousands of them, and Germany's Jewish population is growing faster than that of any other nation, including Israel. Which is, as the leader of Germany's most influential Jewish organization says, "a miracle."

The seven communities are at different stages of evolution in creating a welcoming, nurturing environment for Jews, just as within each community some feel more at home than others. Again, the German case is instructive: most of Düsseldorf's older Jews doubt they can ever again feel like German Jews as opposed to Jews who happen to live in Germany, but their children are more sanguine, as are many who arrived recently from Russia. Jews in Dnepropetrovsk, meanwhile, are at the earliest stages of creating the texture and comfort level that those in their sister city, Boston, have enjoyed for decades. Even in Boston and Atlanta anti-Semitism sometimes surfaces, which makes Jews there question whether they really are as well off as they presume. Yet in those communities and the rest the realization is growing that the challenges they face are so similar that they no longer need to feel alone—and that they can learn from one another rather than having to devise from scratch their own solutions.

That understanding is so logical, so critical, that one is tempted to ask why it has been so slow in coming. History is partly to blame. Diaspora Jews throughout the ages have had a sense that they are in a state of waiting to return to some idealized land where their ancestors flourished. That is the image conjured up by the word "diaspora," which means dispersion, and it is conveyed even more clearly by the often-used label *galut*, which is Hebrew for exile. But the notion that diaspora Jews are residing in some unnatural exile is a distortion of history. The First and Second Temples, and the golden ages they represented, were relatively brief notations on a Jewish time line that is, instead, dominated by diaspora. Abraham, father of the Jews, discovered his God outside Israel. The Torah was given to the Jewish people outside Israel. The most important Talmud, or compilation of Jewish tradition, is the one from Babylon, not the one from Jerusalem. Even during the era of the Second

Temple more Jews lived in the diaspora than in Israel. "Displacement," then, has been the normal state of affairs for Jews for nearly 2,600 years.

Yet when the story of Jews forging new connections in new homelands finds its way into popular accounts, or even scholarly writings, the focus is typically on the exotic and historic rather than on wider patterns and contemporary trends. That makes it difficult to get Jews in a given city to appreciate their own special legacy, not to mention those of other cities that seem a world away. It is not that the stories lack originality and drama. What could be more tension-filled and moving than the Jews of France facing down their accusers when Alfred Dreyfus, a Jewish army captain, was falsely charged with spying for Germany in 1894, or nineteen years later seeing the Jews of Atlanta besieged by enraged mobs after Leo Frank, a Jewish factory manager, was mistakenly convicted for the grisly murder of a teenage girl? Nor do the stories lack relevance. What could have given Atlanta's small and isolated community of Jews more hope in 1913 than the knowledge that fellow Jews in France had confronted an equally chilling onslaught, and that they ultimately triumphed? And what could be more inspiring nowadays to warring factions in the Balkans or Somalia than the Jewish model of a religious and ethnic minority living peaceably in pluralist societies around the globe, promoting universalistic values even as it clings to its ancient culture?

Numbers tell part of the story of today's Jewish diaspora, and many of them are sobering. Most of the world's 13.2 million Jews now live in Israel (37 percent) and the United States (43 percent), with the rest of the world accounting for just 20 percent. In 1936 there were fifty-six countries with more than 5,000 Jews, by the year 2000 there were just thirty-six, and demographers warn that the trend is toward further concentration in Israel and a handful of large cities in America and Western Europe, with outlying areas continuing to lose the critical mass needed to sustain a Jewish community. But those experts never predicted the rekindling of Judaism in the former Soviet bloc, or faraway Australia, and diaspora history is filled with tumultuous shifts in Jewish geography. Worldwide there are 20 percent fewer Jews than there were on the eve of the Holocaust, but there are three times as many as there were in 1850. American Jewry, meanwhile, was rightfully rocked in 1990 by a nationwide survey that showed that, after years of creeping up, the rate of Jews marrying non-Jews topped 50 percent. Yet that survey included people who had a Jewish parent but were not brought up primarily Jewish, or no longer consider themselves Jewish; the intermarriage rate among the narrower group of those who define themselves as Jews was almost 10 percent lower. A look behind the numbers also found that some non-Jewish partners are formally converting while many more embrace Judaism when the Jewish community reaches out to them.

Where does that leave us? The overall number of Jews probably will continue to decline, while many of those at the periphery will continue drifting away to atheism, Buddhism, or nothing at all. But there are just as many signs of strength. Never in the history of the diaspora have there been more opportunities for Jews to connect to their Judaism educationally, culturally, and religiously. Enough are making those connections voluntarily and enthusiastically that communal leaders I met in Paris, Atlanta, and New York offered a nearly identical forecast: in the future there will be "fewer Jews but better Jews."

The deftness of that predication came home to me on a recent Saturday afternoon when I was walking through Harvard Square with a non-Jewish friend. A Jewish family walked by, presumably heading to shul—the father wearing a black hat, the mother with a *shaytl*, or wig, the young boys sprouting sidelocks, and their sister wearing a skirt that reached to her ankles. Twenty years ago, or even ten, I would have talked wistfully about how their clothing and lifestyle were vestiges of a quickly vanishing feature of my people and my immediate family. Today, I told my friend, the Orthodox are growing faster than any other segment of the Jewish population and are a measure of the future as well as the past. The comeback in learning and experiencing is not limited to those in black hats, but has spread to many in the Conservative movement, the Reform, and even to a marginally observant Jew like me.

At the same time that Jews are learning more about their own faith, Americans are learning more about Judaism and warming to it in a way that should uplift the whole of the diaspora. That was particularly apparent when, in the summer of 2000, the Democrats nominated for vice president Senator Joseph Lieberman, an Orthodox Jew. Lieberman energized his running mate, Al Gore, as well as the Democratic Party, charmed the hard-boiled press corps, and proved nearly as enchanting to Southern Baptists and United Methodists as he did to Jews. That is no more extraordinary, however, than Dublin, Cork, and Belfast all at various times having Jewish lords mayor, or France twice elevating a Jew to the post of prime minister.

The story of the diaspora, seen in this context, is a story of triumph. It is a story of Jews surviving in mountains and deserts, when they were in the minority and the majority. It is a story, as Simon Rawidowicz said in his essay of the same title in 1948, of "Israel, the Ever-Dying People." Throughout the 2,600-year history of the Jewish diaspora, its enemies have predicted its demise, and Jews themselves often believed the predictions. It happened in the Roman Era and the Spanish one, it happened during the reign of Khmel the Wicked in Ukraine, and it seems to be happening again now. Each time, Jews have survived and thrived thanks to persistence and an understanding that it is within their power to reverse the prophecies of apocalypse.

It is that uncanny capacity to prevail that makes the Jewish diaspora such a magical experience for historians who these days are consumed with the general topic of diaspora studies. The way Jews have clung to their identity over millennia of separation helps us understand why Americans who have never been to Ireland, or Poles who have to look back to great-grandparents they never knew to find a link to Poland, continue to call themselves Irish- or Polish-Americans and to feel connected to their "homeland." The impact made by a tiny religion—Jews account for about 1 in every 450 people on the planet—gives hope to the Ibos in Nigeria, the East Timorese in Indonesia, and other long-suffering minorities. But there is one thing especially that differentiates the Jewish diaspora from all the others: it is the only one that has been entrusted, for most of its long history, with the very survival of its people. That is what makes the Jewish success story so compelling to a leader like the Dalai Lama of Tibet as he desperately tries to hold his people together and preserve their sacred customs during what is likely to be an extended period of oppression, dispersion, and exile.

The stories of those triumphs, and of connections among Jews separated by geography and nationality, form the centerpiece of this book. They are stories that, like those of the Bible, are grounded in the past—but they are not mired there, as the recent metamorphoses in Germany and the former Soviet Union demonstrate. They make clear that Jews have built permanent places for themselves in their adopted lands—they transformed havens into homes—at the same time that they have maintained ties to their age-old religion and culture.

How, then, should this newly confident diaspora relate to the State of Israel? The founding of Israel half a century ago seemed to answer what Jews of the diaspora were longing for. Now, at last, they had a place of their own to go, a way to end their physical isolation and realize the promise of celebrating a Seder in Jerusalem. That is a potent image, and for more than fifty years its promise and seduction have held the collective Jewish subconscious in a powerful grip. But like many metaphors this one simply does not fit the real-life aspirations and situations of most diaspora Jews today. It is wonderful to know there is, finally, a homeland that would welcome us. Yet most of us have finally built secure lives in our adopted lands and have no interest in adjusting to the strange climate and society of Israel. Indeed the busiest traffic today between Israel and the biggest diaspora country, America, could be called aliyah in reverse, with four times as many Israelis living in America as U.S. Jews living in Israel.

This book will outline the basis for a new, more nuanced relationship between Israel and the diaspora. It is a relationship that is already taking shape, as I saw during my latest visit to Israel, although it is only beginning to be discussed by those on either end, for fear of upsetting a tender balance and reigniting old antagonisms. It is a new encounter of equals, to replace the old one where Israel was seen as the center of the Jewish solar system with diaspora communities orbiting as distant planets. It is a sense that, as Israel becomes more secure and self-sufficient, and the diaspora does too, both will realize they are on parallel quests to promote pluralism and continuity. It is an acknowledgment, finally, that the Jewish diaspora is as critical to the survival of Israel as Israel is to the survival of the Jewish people.

Chapter 1

DÜSSELDORF:

In the Land of the Murderers

Four men are standing on the street corner. They are archetypes of Aryan perfection: the shortest of them is a strapping six feet, and all have sandy hair so brilliant it seems to reflect the fall sunlight. They are trying hard not to appear the federal policemen that they are. Their elbows rest close to their sides to shield the bulge of guns, their hair is pulled forward to conceal the tiny wires running from their ears. They train their sights on one another, avoiding eye contact with passersby, yet their senses are keenly tuned to the squat white brick building behind them.

At last, a middle-aged man emerges. Slightly stooped and graying, he is as obviously Semitic as they are Nordic. His nose is prominent and slanted, his lips full, his blue-gray eyes at once thoughtful and sad.

In an earlier era, the four men in green sweaters and brown pants would not have hesitated to drag the Jew away to certain imprisonment, probable death. That is precisely what plainclothes policemen like these did half a century before to this man's eleven-year-old sister. This time, however, they greet him with an embrace and a joke, helping him into the backseat of one of two idling Mercedeses. Paul Spiegel, top man in the Jewish community of Düsseldorf and vice president of the Central Council of Jews in Germany, is their ward. He is their VIP visitor.

The federal police are there—in bulletproof cars, with holes drilled in the doors so they can shoot out without being shot at—to see that Spiegel gets safely from Düsseldorf to nearby Cologne. He will be the star attraction in a panel entitled "Goethe and the Jews: The Jews and Goethe." They will scour the audience much the way U.S. Secret Service agents stand watch during a presidential address. It is not that the government expects trouble; that is rare these days. But it is making a statement—of respect for Spiegel and his offices, of brotherhood with the Jews who live there, and, most of all, of how much Germany has changed, in case the world is not fully convinced. As if to reinforce that goodwill, the bodyguards make an unscheduled stop on the way back to Düsseldorf at the hospital where Spiegel's wife is nursing a broken leg, waiting in the rain until midnight while he pays a visit.

It is almost impossible to believe. Sixty years ago, on these same streets, Jews were compelled to wear star-shaped badges of shame and were slaughtered by the thousands. It was a campaign of terror unlike any other, one that remains the standard against which all human atrocities are measured. It threatened to exterminate not only the Jews of Germany, but of all of Europe and beyond. Now, as one century blends into another, Jews in Germany are displayed as trophies in the very halls where Hitler inaugurated his Third Reich.

Spiegel's royal treatment is part of the fervent embrace in which Jews are held today in the Federal Republic of Germany. Germany has the fastest-growing Jewish community in the world, with the deluge of Russian Jews during the 1990s swelling its numbers from 27,000 to more than 100,000. While they make up barely .1 percent of the German population, Jews are consulted by the media on everything from politics to the arts, with nearly 200 people turning out to hear Spiegel and others parse the poetry and plays of the revered Johann Wolfgang von Goethe for signs of anti-Semitism. Jewish communities get government funds to rebuild synagogues and schools. Jewish émigrés from the former Soviet Union are given citizenship along with benefits substantially more generous than they would receive in Israel or America. The rare desecration of a Jewish cemetery or synagogue is treated like a crime against the state. Even non-Jews are naming their children Sarah and Jacob, and they are unearthing Jewish grandmothers who, not so long ago, would have ensured them a spot on a deportation train. Being Jewish is, quite simply, high fashion in today's *Deutschland*.

That swelling in size and status of the German Jewish community raises questions that resonate with Jews everywhere—about whether Germany can overcome its Nazi past and return to the prewar glory days, when Jews like Albert Einstein, Martin Buber, and Karl Marx were defining figures in science, the arts, and politics. And whether, after the Holocaust, it is safe for Jews there or anywhere to feel as secure, as much like they belong, as German Jews did at the dawn of the last century.

But recent developments in Germany also raise a profound hope—that if Judaism can make a comeback there, in the land of the murderers, it can happen anywhere.

Spiegel witnessed firsthand the horrors of being a Jew in Germany, and the way that identity is now being renewed and refurbished. When he was a toddler, his mother evacuated him and his sister from their tiny town near Düsseldorf to what seemed like a safe haven in Brussels. Mrs. Spiegel had carefully instructed Rosa, who was eleven, that if a man wearing a uniform asked her if she was Jewish, she should deny it. But no one had counted on the girl's Nazi interrogators wearing street clothes and so, when they stopped her, Rosa told the truth. That affirmation of her faith, Spiegel recalls, "was the last word anyone ever heard from her."

There was no time for Ruth Spiegel to mourn her daughter. She whisked Paul away again, this time to the countryside and the care of a Catholic family that raised him as its own for three and a half years. Anticipating an eventual end to the Nazi nightmare, Ruth had once more rehearsed with her child what to tell those in charge, only this time the message was in English and it was the truth. "Tell the British or American soldiers," she said, "that you are a German Jew." He did, and it worked, drawing gifts and kisses from a U.S. G.I. But Paul did not feel at all German. "Everyone during the war told me the Germans are big,

big people who are killing us," he remembers. And his mother, with whom he was quickly reunited, already had resolved to "take me to America. She had decided that if my father or sister were alive they would never go back to Germany."

His father was alive, barely. He had spent five years behind barbed wire in Auschwitz, Buchenwald, and Dachau, and had dropped from 220 pounds to 88. If Paul, who was seven, had difficulty understanding how the Nazis could have snatched his sister, why they brutalized his father and murdered his uncle and cousin, then he was incredulous when his father insisted the family return to its German roots. "I'm sure I wouldn't have come back to Germany. I always discussed with my father how could he come back, I couldn't believe it," he says, looking back from the comfort of his plush living room in the center of Düsseldorf. "After the war my father said to me, 'Listen, I tell you one time what has happened, what I was going through, but not again. I don't want to be in the past. I want to be in the future.' "

Today, Spiegel sounds like his father as he explains his own choice to remain in Germany, to build a thriving talent agency, create a life for his wife and two daughters, and help rekindle Jewish life there. It was not a decision that came easily or quickly. Sixty years are hardly time enough to forget such horrors, or to stop hating the country that transformed his childhood into a nightmare that never will go away. But Germany, he insists, has changed. And so has he.

"If I every day say, 'I hate the Germans,' I couldn't stay here. I trust most of the German people, the generation after the war. Now I am feeling like a German with the Jewish religion," says Spiegel, who at the end of 1999 was elevated from vice president to president of Germany's most influential Jewish organization. "I'm not feeling that I'm here on a part-time basis. Until ten to fifteen years ago the Jews in Germany who had lived here since 1945 said, 'We are here with packed suitcases.' These suitcases have been unpacked in the meantime.

"Compare that with what happened in Spain during the Inquisition, when they sent all the Jews out. For five hundred years no Jews came back to Spain, not one," he adds. "Here in Germany we had the biggest murdering of a people in history, more than six million Jews killed, and already one or two months after the Holocaust they started again to rebuild this Jewish community. Now we have the fastest-growing Jewish community in the world.

"This is one of the miracles of the century."

*   *   *

To understand that miracle it is necessary to step back into German history, to the time just before the rebuilding began. It also helps to zero in on a single community. Düsseldorf, Spiegel's home and the first big city in Germany to surpass its pre-Holocaust Jewish population, is a compelling place to launch this tour of the Jewish diaspora.

From the tree-shaded promenade along the banks of the Rhine to the medieval tower visible in the distance, it is easy to imagine why Napoleon dubbed the former fishing village "Little Paris." That is how it must have seemed to Jews living there in the early 1930s and sharing in the industrial boom. The official census back then counted 5,000 Jews in Düsseldorf and 500,000 in Germany, or 1 percent of the local and national populations. Add in nearly 500,000 Germans born to marriages between Jews and non-Jews, or with other ties through blood or marriage, and Jews constituted almost as substantial a minority in prewar Germany as they do today in America. And as in America, numbers only begin to reflect their contributions: a Jew drafted the Weimar Republic's constitution, another was foreign minister, and eleven of the thirty-eight Germans awarded the Nobel Prize before 1933 were Jewish. Jews also were overrepresented in influential cities like Düsseldorf, which gave birth to lyrical poet Heinrich Heine, gave an orchestra to classical conductor Felix Mendelssohn, and gave a pulpit to world-famous theologian Rabbi Leo Baeck. Religious ties may have been fraying, but Jewish youth were enlisting in causes from socialism to Zionism while their parents were reaffirming ethnic and cultural connections. The Weimar era truly was a Golden Age for Jews in Düsseldorf and all of Germany—one where a palpable sense of potential, of moving into the mainstream, drowned out warnings by skeptics that age-old anti-Semitism had not really gone away.

World War II made the skeptics into sages. Hundreds of thousands of Germany's 1 million Jews fled in the mid-1930s; most of the rest were deported, with 180,000 choked to death in the gas chambers, starved in slave-labor camps, or shot at the edge of burial pits they had been forced to dig. The situation was equally bleak in Düsseldorf. On November 9, 1938—the infamous *Kristallnacht*, or night of broken glass—Nazi henchmen fire-bombed Düsseldorf's main synagogue on Kasernenstrasse, destroyed five smaller prayer houses, and systematically ransacked Jewish homes, killing seven and wounding seventy. One local religious leader, finally acknowledging that the threat was real, ordered that his congregation's Torah scrolls be buried in the Jewish cemetery. Mass deportations began in 1941, when Rabbi Siegfried Klein, his wife, Lili, and 1,009 others were shipped out to Łódź in Poland. Dr. Siegried Falk, president of the Jewish community, was due to be deported on December 11 but he and his wife, Edith, killed themselves before the trains departed. Altogether, 2,500 Düsseldorf Jews managed to escape; the 2,500 who did not perished.

At war's end 200,000 Jewish Holocaust survivors from outside Germany found themselves on German soil. The Allied armies of occupation labeled them Displaced Persons (DPs), a sterile-sounding reference to the fact that they had been scattered from their homelands and were being housed in camps set up by U.S., British, French, and Soviet troops. They called themselves *Sherit Hapletah*, a biblical name meaning "remnant of the saved." Many had been prisoners in extermination camps in Poland who, as Hitler's forces fled west in the last days of the war, were forced to join them, then were deposited in Dachau, Bergen-Belsen, and other camps in the German heartland. Still more were survivors who had tried to return to their homes in Poland, Lithuania, and elsewhere in Eastern Europe, but were greeted by an anti-Semitism so virulent they had to flee again, this time to the U.S. and British occupation zones in southern Germany. Then there were those who had spent the war in German prisons, hidden in forests in Eastern Europe, or otherwise survived long enough to be liberated by the Allies.

Whatever their reasons for being there, the result was wrenchingly ironic: the only country where those who had survived the death machine could find safe haven was the home of the executioners. Suddenly Bavaria and the rest of southern Germany, where Hitler had hatched his blueprint for making Europe *judenrein*—free of Jews—had more Jews than ever.

Most concentration camp survivors were depressed by the prospect of being in Germany, in another enclosed camp, and they resented having to live side by side with Nazi collaborators from Ukraine, the Baltic states, and other formerly occupied lands. They had been told the camps would be a short stop-off on the way to Israel or America, but they had to wait until 1948 for Britain to sanction the Jewish state and even longer for countries like the United States and Argentina to open their borders. By 1950, however, nearly all the camps had been closed and more than 90 percent of their occupants had abandoned Germany. The rest were too old, too ill, too poor, or simply too tired of moving to contemplate moving again. So they stayed, this eclectic band of 15,000, and they became two-thirds of the founding fathers of Germany's post-Holocaust Jewish community.

The other third had more reason to feel bound to Germany, since they were born there, but they also had more reason to loathe it, having been betrayed by the nation to which they had pledged their allegiance. These Jews survived the war in Germany itself, evading the most efficient extermination apparatus the world had ever witnessed. Most were sheltered by a non-Jewish spouse, relative, or friend; others managed to secure special status or bribed their way out of the noose. While 7,500 or so of the survivors understandably left as quickly as they could for America or Israel, another 7,500 chose to reclaim what they could of their lives before the Nazis.

How could these Jews remain in the land of their tormenters? The ones from Germany often had non-Jewish wives or husbands and were convinced that they, together with the rest of the "righteous few" who had risked their lives to defy the Nazis, would restore the more tolerant prewar society. The DPs, meanwhile, were so frail and disoriented that they could not conceive where else to go. Whatever the necessity, the decision to make their home in Germany still defines their lives—and bedevils them—more than half a century later.

No one had more reasons to stay away than Helen Israel. When the Nazis stormed through Poland they slaughtered her aunts and uncles, her brother and sister, and her parents. Rather than escaping to Palestine the way many Polish Jews were doing, her father, a deeply religious man, had insisted that true believers should wait where they were for the Messiah. Helen had managed to persuade her husband to flee to the Russian zone in eastern Poland, but he could not bear being separated from his pregnant wife. When the Germans pushed out the Russians he remained in Poland, and was last seen just before German troops raided his home. Then the Nazis took an even more precious possession, her infant son, Lech. Helen was shipped to a work camp and forced to leave the baby behind with her parents, only to hear later that he had perished in Auschwitz at age three and a half. Today, all the eighty-one-year-old Israel has to remember Lech by is a pair of fading photographs, one taken at eleven months, the other not quite a year later. "At least I can see the pictures every day," she says as she takes down from the mantel the snapshots of the toddler with brilliant blond hair. Tears well up as she recalls how proud she was to give the baby his Hebrew name, Shlomo-Arie. And she still insists that, if she could find her son's murderers, "I would kill them right away."

After she was liberated from the last of her nine work and prison camps, Helen went to work for the Red Cross in Holland. Those years seem now like one long stupor, broken only by her meeting and marrying another concentration camp survivor, Kurt Israel, and having another son, Robert Viktor. Four years later, Kurt's clothing shop began to falter and he decided to move his family back to his hometown of Düsseldorf. Helen detested Germany but loved Kurt so she did not resist, although she made him promise they eventually would go back to Holland.

"Day and night I was crying," she recalls. "It was terrible for me. Terrible. Terrible. For two years I held my flat in Amsterdam while I lived in Düsseldorf. I paid rent in Amsterdam and went there sometimes with my child. Then I saw it made no sense, and from two years in Düsseldorf it became four, and six, and now forty-five years."

She tried to leave once, in 1967, two years after her husband died. Robert Viktor enrolled in college in Amsterdam and she joined him there. But she had trouble feeling at home, having been away for a dozen years, and when her son decided a year later to transfer to the Hebrew University of Jerusalem, Helen decided it would be unfair to both of them to follow him a second time. "I said, 'Okay, you go, but I will go back to Düsseldorf.' I said, 'I have there my friends, my interests, my Yiddish interests.' There's an old saying in Yiddish that you can't plant an old tree in another place."

Her work with the Jewish community helped. She served for a record-setting thirty years as chapter president of the Women's International Zionist Organization, and for thirty-three years she helped restore and run the Jewish community of Düsseldorf, all of which, she says, "helped me to stay in Germany. I was looking for something that would make it lighter to live in Germany."

But she could not erase the nagging sense that she did not belong there, that no Jew did after what had happened. It started with the anguish anyone feels who has lost a cherished parent, sibling, or, worse still, a child. For Helen Israel and other Holocaust survivors in Germany that was just the beginning. What they suffered was so terrible, they never will get over it. They are haunted by knowing the ones they loved died alone and in agony. They are consumed by not being able to identify the murderers or, more precisely, knowing that an entire country was in some sense to blame. They are tormented by having to live shoulder to shoulder with those they suspect were the executioners, wondering whether it is the elderly person they pass on the street, the shopper standing beside them in the market, their neighbor next door.

In the early 1970s the justice minister of the state of North Rhine Westphalia, a Jew named Joseph Neuberger, nominated Helen for the German Cross to honor her work with the Jewish community. "I said, 'Thank you, Joseph, but not for me. I would never take a German medal. How can I have together a concentration camp and a German medal? What do you think of me?' " A decade later a friend proposed it again, but "I said to her, 'You don't know that I have said never. This is the same medal that Hitler had for his heroes, only this time there is no swastika, now there is an eagle there. I have no split existence. It is the same now as it was for me as a child in Poland. I never felt Polish. I was a Jew in Poland.' "

Turning down the medal let her give voice to the frustration and resentment she generally kept bottled up. Robert Viktor knew no such constraints. He never wanted to be in Germany and could not understand why his parents did. He told them that from the time he could talk, making his mother proud while at the same time deepening her shame. "When he was eleven my son said, 'You and Dad are characterless that you live in Germany,' " Helen remembers. "He said, 'You must send me away. If you don't do it voluntarily I will make you.' When he was twelve he said we must send him to a school abroad, an international boarding school in Amsterdam. He stayed there until his graduation six years later."

Germany had robbed her of a second son. Robert Viktor, now a fifty-year-old bank consultant in Holland, had forsaken his parents out of hatred for their country. "He comes to visit me now," Helen says as she sits in the front room of her apartment down the street from the Düsseldorf synagogue. "But he can't forgive me that I live in Germany."

For his part, Robert Viktor says that he very much loves his mother, and always has. But he has not changed his mind about Germany: "I am still of the opinion that it is absolutely absurd for Jews to be living in Germany. It's absurd because, in historical terms, what happened during the *Shoah* was a very few years ago. Establishing ourselves again in Germany, as Jewish communities, is to start the process of forgiving. As I said once to a very highly placed German, 'Let's try again in a few hundred years, not now.' The boycott of Spain after the Inquisition lasted five or six hundred years, I don't see how we are entitled already to lift such a boycott of Germany. That's giving Germany the chance to act as though we were almost through it, as though it were almost forgiven if not forgotten. I'm not preaching that we should start a war against Germany. I'm just saying we should behave much more honorably in this context."

Paul Spiegel was equally unforgiving of his parents' decision to return to Germany, at least at first. But the more he heard of his father's story, the more he understood. When the gates at Dachau opened, Hugo Spiegel headed for the only place he knew, his hometown of Warendorf, walking there in his prison clothes. On the way he met a non-Jew he knew from the town who invited him home. "That man said to my father, 'Before we start to eat we will go to the cellar,' " Paul recalls. "There was a small curtain. The man opened another door on the floor and went down. He came back with *mahzorim*, with prayer books, that he had saved from the burned synagogue in their small town. He said to my father, 'Now it's up to you.' He was a neighbor of the old synagogue. He had ten books and the Torah. With these books and the Torah my father founded the Jewish community in Warendorf.

"If my father had thought before whether it was right or not to go back to Germany, that was the last time."

That is not quite the end of the story. Even Hugo Spiegel, who felt himself as German as he was Jewish, hated Germans, or at least some of them. He had returned to his old job of buying and selling cows and horses. While his old customers greeted him warmly, saying it was "fantastic" to see him back, he made it his point to find out how each had treated Jews during the reign of terror. "One time," Paul remembers, "another cow agent said, 'Look, the Jew is back here.' My father gave him the back of his stick, he wanted to kill him. It was only the English military police who kept my father from doing it."

In 1958 Paul moved from Warendorf to Düsseldorf, in search of more Jews. What he found was a Jewish community of just under 1,000 in the city of half a million. Allied bombers had been drawn to Düsseldorf by its control over the vital Ruhr region and its concentration of heavy industry, most of which they turned to rubble. But by the time Spiegel arrived the city was giving rise to a collection of theaters, museums, and performance halls, and construction was being completed on a stately synagogue, the first permanent house of Jewish worship since the war and a sure sign that Jewish life was being revived. As much as any place in Germany, Düsseldorf epitomized the postwar comeback, building a powerful manufacturing base in steel, coal, and cars, serving as the nation's center of fashion, and offering economic and political opportunities to natives and refugees alike.

Jewish refugees continued to stream in, drawn by a government that wanted to put things right after the Nazi wrongs, by a scarcity of other options, and by the takeover of Eastern Europe by communist regimes, most of which were hostile to Jews. By 1959, when the new synagogue was finished, Jews had settled in Düsseldorf from Czechoslovakia and Hungary, Argentina, Poland, Israel, and, most of all, Romania. Some chose Germany because it promised a more comfortable life than Israel, the other country willing to take them. Others, having come from Europe, felt a European neighbor like Germany offered more familiarity and more opportunity to visit friends and relatives left behind. No matter that they were going to a land with a long history of hating Jews.

In the early postwar days it was tensions within their community, rather than with Gentiles living around them, that occupied most Jews. Those with German roots abhorred the Nazis but embraced their native language and culture. The Displaced Persons and others from Eastern Europe, by contrast, spoke Yiddish, felt they were living in a foreign land, and had their sense of alienation reinforced by organizations like the World Jewish Congress, which urged all Jews to get out of Germany.

The German Jews typically came from an assimilated world and had never been religious or worried about marrying outside the faith, whereas the East Europeans were steeped in Judaism, as a faith whose practices they scrupulously observed and a way of life that defined them more than the nation they happened to live in. To the Germans, the DPs were unwashed outsiders who threatened their acceptance by the wider society. The East Europeans saw their German coreligionists as pseudo-Jews who had forsaken tradition and made unseemly accommodations with the unrepentant Germans.

Over time the two camps learned to live together in Düsseldorf and elsewhere, much the way warring Jewish refugees have across the diaspora. They also forged a partnership with successive German governments and the wider society. Some felt such patching up of differences amounted to papering over critical distinctions in and outside the community. But others wondered why, having lived through the Holocaust, they should feel any guiltier than Jews who were forging similar alliances in England and America, two countries that had ignored compelling evidence of the ongoing slaughter.

Accommodation was partly a natural response by Germany's Jewish leaders to what was happening around them. The Allies had withdrawn as an occupying force and now regarded Germany as a critical collaborator in the Cold War against the Soviet bloc, and international Jewish organizations had withdrawn once the DP camps were shut. Germany's Jews suddenly were left to fend for themselves. At the same time German leaders from Conrad Adenauer to Helmut Kohl were savvy enough to realize they could score points with their Western allies by doing favors for their tiny community of Jews, from helping rebuild synagogues to offering modest restitution to Holocaust victims, and Jewish leaders were savvy enough to accept. The result: the community rebuilt synagogues, reopened Jewish cemeteries, and resumed circumcisions and other traditional practices, although most Jews remained nonreligious. Jewish leaders spoke out on safe subjects, condemning international terrorism and backing the State of Israel, but they avoided public criticism of the German state. And the community grew with the arrival of East European Jews who had found it difficult to adapt to conditions in Israel, the United States, and South America, along with others from Iran and the Soviet Union. Still, as late as 1989 there were fewer than 30,000 Jews in all of Germany and about 1,500 in Düsseldorf, only slightly more than in 1950.

Most of the rest of the world, even the Jewish world, did not know there were any Jews left in Germany. Those who did know were unrestrained in their condemnation and unapologetic about making pariahs out of the Jews who chose to settle there. "My mother's family didn't call for ten years. My family didn't want to speak to us," recalls Dora Tamler, an Israeli who came to Düsseldorf in 1967 with her Romanian-born husband. "Finally my aunt, who had strong ties to Germany, decided to visit. She was our guest and saw that it's not that bad. So she brought the good news to the family in Israel and ever since they've been talking to us."

What worried the Tamlers even more than the reaction of Jews to Germany was the reaction of Germans to Jews like them. When they first arrived they were open about telling people they were from Israel, and Jewish. "The reaction was either too positive, with people saying they had Jewish friends and had saved hundreds of Jews during the war, or they made derogatory comments," says Dora's husband, Alexander, one in a line of successful dentists from Romania, and before that from Austria. "No matter what happened there always were feelings of uneasiness between us and our acquaintances."

Their solution was to stop telling anyone where they were from or what religion they were—not their neighbors, or his patients, or even his dental assistant of twenty years. And they instructed their only child to do the same. They all simply said they were from Romania. "They were explicit, twice a day, about telling me not to tell anybody that we were Jewish," recalls Ronald Tamler, now twenty-four and a recent graduate of medical school. "In reality, even though we were thinking that nobody knew, we found out in mysterious ways that most people did know, especially our neighbors. We live in a very conservative, well-maintained area. We have a tennis club on our street and my parents wanted to get me in it, but it wouldn't have me, and my parents found out why. It was because we were Jews. My parents went directly to our neighbors across the street. They made a scandal and I was accepted, but I didn't want to be in that club anymore.

"In retrospect my parents were overly sensitive, but it was the way that most Jews behaved then. I was no exception, my parents were no exceptions. Nowadays, everyone is a hero. They say, 'I was walking around with a *kippah* ten years ago.' But of course it's not true."

A series of unrelated events encouraged Jews across Germany to become more assertive about their religion and their rights. There was the Six-Day War in 1967, when the Jewish state outfoxed and outfought vastly larger Arab armies, in the process inspiring Jews across the diaspora. There were a series of anti-Zionist and anti-Semitic incidents in the 1970s, from the murder of Israeli Olympic athletes by Palestinian terrorists in Munich to the increasingly vituperative attacks against Israel by German leftists. There were perceived slights during the 1980s, including Chancellor Kohl's invitation to President Ronald Reagan to honor the war dead at a military cemetery in Bitburg, even though they included SS officers, and bids by historians to cut off discussion of the Holocaust. And there was the Gulf War in 1991, when Germans demonstrated against alleged American and Israeli imperialism and Jews there felt compelled to come to America's and Israel's defense. They spoke out again, a year later, when Turks and other "foreigners" came under attack and Jewish graves were desecrated. Even the fall of communism generated a reaction. Many young, idealistic Jews who in an earlier era would have been attracted to socialist ideals now turned to religion for identity and meaning, the fact that their parents neither knew nor cared much about Judaism making it even more attractive.

The same sort of confidence-building was under way in Düsseldorf during the 1970s and '80s. Jewish life centered on the grand marble synagogue whose large semicircular front steps led to ponderous metal doors that were forever bolted. The image was meant to be imposing to outsiders, to convey a grandeur as well as an impenetrability, but behind the barriers were warmth and welcome. The rabbi and other Torah readers led services from a pulpit that seemed unusually close to worshipers. The community was like a little village, an intimate gathering place with a Maccabee sports club for children to hone their athletic skills, a religious school to learn the basics of the faith, and regular excursions across the Belgian border to Antwerp where the few who kept kosher loaded up on ritually prepared chicken, beef, and other foods. Intimacy, however, had its price: finding the ten men needed at daily prayer services for a minyan, or quorum, was difficult enough that the community had to offer bribes that sometimes required cash, although a warm meal in the morning generally was enough.

While their numbers were not growing, Düsseldorf Jews' sense of themselves was, which made it easier for the Tamlers to acknowledge their Judaism and begin to feel at home. At the same time it was becoming more problematic for them to stick with their story about being Romanian. "After the downfall of communism and the opening of the Wall, many Romanians who came here were burglars and gypsies," says Alexander. "I started telling people I am Jewish and I got amazing responses. Friends think better of me now that I'm Jewish versus when I was Romanian."

What is their actual identity? As with all Jews in Germany, the answer is never simple. "An American Jew would die for his country. Same for an English Jew and a French Jew," says Alexander. "But not a German Jew. My uncles died for Germany in the First World War and were very proud to be Austrians and Germans, but not anymore. By living here for such a long time I am a German culturally. I'm used to the fact that people here do not cross the street on red, that people are on time, and when I visit a foreign country, I feel pretty German. It used to be my dream to return to Israel but I imagined an Israel with German TV, German newspapers, German punctuality, and German culture. Everybody is trying to find a different excuse for why he can be here as a Jew, how to legitimize himself. Mine is that we have a good life here. I've seen war and poverty in my life, and it's a good life here."

His wife offers a slightly different slant, saying, "He's gotten used to the German lifestyle. He's grown fat here."

Tamler is not the only one. Excluding the Russians, Jews in Germany are better educated than non-Jews, more entrenched in the white-collar work world, and richer. Forty percent of Jews were earning more than $3,000 a month as of 1990, compared to just 12 percent of all Germans. Tamler is also right that his generation of older arrivals typically feels the need to rationalize being a Jew in Germany, to themselves as well as others—and their answers often are colored by contradictions.

"It was easier to make a new start here, easier than anywhere in the world," says Adrian Flohr, a gynecologist who came to Düsseldorf from Romania with his parents in 1969, when he was eighteen. "After three months we had citizenship. The language was not a problem. My father got a job and people helped us." As he grew older and had a family of his own, Flohr got more involved in Düsseldorf's Jewish community, serving as its president and later heading the city's chapter of the United Jewish Appeal. Yet as the child of Holocaust survivors, he never felt completely comfortable. "I don't feel as if I am living in Germany. I am living on the Sohnstrasse in Düsseldorf. I'm not living here with eighty million Germans. I have a very big practice and I have friends. It's very easy for me. But if tomorrow I get the big lotto I would like to go to Israel or the United States. One of the most important things, of course, is the money. Life is easier here. If money were not so important I can imagine I would be in Israel or the United States."

While he says the money is all that kept him, the truth is more complicated. He had the money, professional credentials, and mastery of English to have gone anytime he wanted. There would have been adjustments, but fewer than his parents faced moving to Germany. Hearing him struggle over several hours to sort out his feelings about his adopted homeland, it becomes clear that he is, by most definitions, decidedly German. Germany is where he has lived for thirty of his forty-eight years, and where he owns an elegant home with a BMW-735 parked out front. It is where he runs his busy medical practice, fought for and achieved unprecedented acceptance for himself and other Jews, chose to raise his two children, and, even if he wins that lottery, it is where he is likely to retire. Yet he senses, the way Tamler did, that there is something wrong with how comfortable he has become. He thinks that he should feel guilty, even though he has built a good life not only for his wife and children but for his parents, who live nearby in an apartment he purchased for them. He deals with the conflicts by refusing to acknowledge, to himself or anyone, his unmistakable identity as a German.

His wife is the same way. Jaffa Flohr was born in Israel but has spent her adult life in Germany. Her parents brought her to Düsseldorf thirty-five years ago, her father having survived Auschwitz and her mother Theresienstadt. "My father came here to Germany to meet an old friend, and his friend said, 'Stay here. Take the money from the government, from the Germans.' So we came. My parents are still here. They say that their luggage is always packed, but they're still living here. For the Germans we say we are German, but I don't feel like a German. Everyone

Jewish who you talk to will tell you, if he tells the truth, that he's not a German. It's not nice to say it but I think they are not like us, they're different. I grew up with Germans. Our best friends are German. But they don't feel like us."

Although it is all right for them to question their decision to stay, the Flohrs resent others questioning it. "We don't allow the Germans to tell us that we are not German," says Adrian. Jaffa recalls how, in 1991, her twelve-year-old son Yoel and four other Jewish children from Germany went to a summer camp with Jews from France. "One day some French kids came to them and made the Nazi '*heil* Hitler' and told them, 'What are you doing here, you Nazis?' I called the camp leaders and told them what happened, that we could not imagine that Jewish children would do these things to other Jewish children all the way from Germany. We know that all people don't like it that Jews are living in Germany, but that it goes to this level really is a shock."

Such attempts to work out an identity, and work through their guilt, have produced a schizophrenic existence for many Jews of Adrian Flohr and Alexander Tamler's generation. They resent Germans treating them like foreigners, assuming that their true allegiance is to Israel and wondering when they will be going back. Yet they admit that, just in case they *do* have to leave again suddenly, they have raised their children with as international and cosmopolitan an upbringing as possible, teaching them different languages, vacationing overseas, and exposing them to other cultures—which, to Germans, merely confirms the image of Jews as outsiders. These Jews deal with their feeling of being apart by looking for more intimate settings where they can fit in. For doctors it might be medical societies, for professors the university, and for many others it has been the Jewish community. They turn to other Jews for kinship and brotherhood, for religious, cultural, and spiritual identity in a land that, even though it is where they have lived most of their lives, still does not feel entirely comfortable.

The next generation is likely to be different. These young people were born in Germany and have studied there. They know of the Holocaust only through stories passed down from their grandparents, which is the way it is for their non-Jewish friends. They grew up hearing their parents question the wisdom of living in Germany, and they internalized some of those doubts, but they also grew up as full-fledged participants in

German society. They have German friends. They are German citizens. And their way of looking at the world is more German than their parents' at the same time that it is more Jewish.

"I have no problem with Germany," says Michael Bleiberg, a twenty-seven-year-old banker who is part of the young leadership of the Düsseldorf Jewish community. Like many in his generation he understands the doubts of those who came before but does not share their ambivalence or rootlessness. Germany, he explains, "offered me almost everything. I have a good job, and Jewish life is growing year to year. It's not a problem being a Jew here. There is no reason to leave this country."

Yoel Flohr, now twenty, is less certain. "I am German," he says, "but I don't feel really like a German. If someone asks me, I am a Jew." Then he wavers in a way his father and mother will not let themselves: "Until now I said every time that I would go to live in Israel. But now I'm starting to study, starting to go a little bit deeper into life, and I'm not sure actually. I can't tell you. Maybe I will stay here. I feel it's something like our job, to show them that we are here, that fifty years after the Holocaust we can live here. Some Jews have to live here to show that Hitler doesn't get what he wants."

*   *   *

Questions about whether these children and grandchildren of the post–World War II generation would stay—and whether they could blend their German and Jewish identities in ways that had eluded their forebears—seemed academic as recently as 1990. Whatever they did, Germany's Jewish population would continue aging, its numbers would wane, and it seemed certain that there would not be much of a Jewish community left in the newly unified German state by the time Yoel and Michael came of age.

Then came the Russians. The influx of immigrants from the old Soviet Union began as the 1980s were ending, and it swelled the size of the Jewish community nationwide—from 27,000 in 1989 to 54,000 in 1996, 68,000 in 1998, and 87,000 by the end of 2000. And those are just the ones officially registered with the Central Council of Jews. Another 20,000 to 30,000 are not registered, and 30,000 more Jewish émigrés from Russia and Ukraine are expected over the next few years.

The surge was even more dramatic in Düsseldorf. Just 35 Russians arrived in 1990, but 456 came the following year. By 1999 the annual number of new immigrants was up to 755. Düsseldorf and surrounding communities in the state of North Rhine Westphalia welcomed Jews more warmly than anywhere in the Federal Republic of Germany, in part because of the region's history of tolerance and because its political leaders were determined to reach out. The result was that in 1999, Düsseldorf became the first major city in Germany to exceed its pre-Holocaust population of Jews, with 5,900 compared to the prewar high of 5,150 in 1925.

Jewish institutions have mushroomed in a bid to accommodate all the new Jews. New synagogues went up from Recklinghausen in the west to Offenbach in the south, with the one in Kassel being expanded. New rabbis, cantors, and teachers were recruited from around the globe. Enrollment in Jewish elementary and high schools was way up. So was attendance in Jewish history and culture programs at universities and at more informal continuing-education programs. Most impressive of all, Germany now has seventy-eight cities and towns with a critical mass of Jews.

In Düsseldorf, there is a Jewish elementary school for the first time since 1942. The kindergarten, youth center, religious school, and retirees' society all have expanded, and Russian-speaking clubs were founded around topics such as literature and science. The large marble synagogue, which was always grand but was typically deserted, finally has enough congregants to fill it. Children stream in and out of the sanctuary from a playground in the abutting courtyard. The religious school, on the other side of the playground, is bursting with 300 students, and construction is about to begin on a new set of buildings for youth programs. Another attached structure is home to the community's welfare agencies. The complex is open every day, and it is almost always filled with a stew of newly arrived immigrants seeking advice on launching their new lives, grandparents there to sing with the choir or listen to a lecture, toddlers looking for a playground and playmates. Unlike synagogues in much of the diaspora that are used mainly on Shabbat, that one is a center of community life.

To Jews already in Germany, the Russians' coming has meant a top-to-bottom transformation of the community they grew up in—often stretching its finances to the point of bankruptcy, disrupting the status quo, and harking back to the tensions and soul-searching they had experienced fifty years before, when German-born and East European Jews were struggling to get along. But it also has meant that their Jewish world, which just a decade ago seemed to be dying, today is being reborn.

To world Jewry, the message was even clearer: it could no longer wish away a community that was growing so fast and yielding such life.

While everyone calls them Russians, the immigrants who began arriving in 1989 came not only from Russia, but also from Ukraine, Latvia, Georgia, and other remnants of the old Soviet empire. Those refugees today make up the majority in 90 percent of the cities and towns across Germany with recognizable Jewish communities. In Düsseldorf, they account for more than 80 percent of the 6,480 Jews living there as of the end of 2000 and their share is growing. Only about 40 percent are affiliated with the synagogue and other Jewish institutions, most came speaking no German and still cannot find the words they want or an accent Germans can comprehend, and nearly all arrived with empty pockets.

That poverty is the key to why most came. That is not to say they were not tormented back home for being Jewish, sometimes even terrorized, and that they did not face political persecution. Most were, and did. Some say they had KILL THE JEWS written on the doors of their apartments, and heard that lists of prominent Jews were being prepared for arrest or worse. But most Jews who really embraced their religion, or felt imperiled by their political circumstances, left shortly after the Soviet empire crumbled in 1989. The German tidal wave, by contrast, did not begin until 1994. And most religious and political refugees went to Israel or America, where they could easily find yeshivas to study in and food that was kosher, political systems that were open and countries where their being Jewish, if it mattered at all, was an asset.

The ones who came to Germany were primarily refugees from an economy gone haywire and a social safety net that was leaking badly. They had impressive professional credentials—as doctors, lawyers, and engineers—with an equally solid grounding in literature, music, and world affairs. But that education had raised their expectations in a land where there was no opportunity for satisfaction. Many stuck it out for years after communism collapsed, hoping the promised economic and political reforms would be realized and the state would honor its commitments to the old and infirm, which were cornerstones of the Soviet system. When neither happened, they felt they had to go.

The question of where was an easier one. Everyone knew the stories of how hard life was in Israel, and how the Israeli media were stereotyping Russian émigrés as freeloaders, mobsters, or some other variation of second-class citizen. They knew that America, as of 1989, had closed its doors to Russians unless they had close relatives willing to serve as sponsors or were lucky enough to qualify under strict new quotas. They realized that it was even more difficult to get into France, the Netherlands, and other countries in Western Europe, none of which gave priority to Jews and all of which were inundated with émigrés from the former Soviet Union.

Their only real option was Germany, a country that a mere sixty years ago had killed 6 million of their coreligionists and 10 million of their countrymen, that had starved their grandparents during the siege of Leningrad or hunted them down with squads of Sonderkommandos expert in executing Jews, and that today is the only Western nation willing to embrace Russian Jews. It was, of course, an impossible choice.

Ervin Nagy grew up loathing Germans. The Nazis had murdered his grandparents, along with his aunt and cousin. It happened not during the waging of war, which might have been forgivable, but after they had won the battle and could get down to the business of liquidating Jews. Nagy was just fifteen then, but he still can see the German prisoners being paraded around the ring of Moscow. He can still taste the hatred he felt then.

Today Nagy lives in Düsseldorf, among the hated Germans. Sitting at the dining room table in his subsidized apartment, his thinning white hair brushed back and his blue jeans and suspenders reflecting the reality that his life there offers more leisure than work, he explains why he and his family left Russia even though he had a good job as an industrial engineer and his wife and daughter were neurologists. And why they chose Germany. "One reason was that we are a people who belong to a European culture," he says. "We have also family matters, we didn't want to be that far away from Russia. And just before we applied to immigrate to the United States we were told that George Bush had closed the border for Russian Jews and it would be almost impossible. Then we decided to come to Germany."

Nagy came because there was nowhere else to go. That was difficult, but life in the Soviet Union had prepared him for worse. Joseph Stalin and his henchmen had killed Nagy's father, who had been a correspondent in Japan for the Soviet newspaper *Tass*. They may have suspected he was a spy, or that he was not faithful enough to Stalin. No one ever said. The only thing that was made clear was that he was an enemy of the state, and by extension his wife and children were, too. If ideology was the reason for persecuting the Nagys in the 1930s and '40s, religion took over in the 1950s. "They never let us forget that we were Jews," he recalls. "On our Russian passport a nationality was stamped, which was Jewish. Persecution was what Russian Jews had in common."

So while most Jews could not conceive of voluntarily moving to a country with Germany's history of anti-Semitism, to Russians like Nagy it seemed no worse than what they were used to. And so far it has proved dramatically better. He does often wonder what Germans who are his age were doing during the Holocaust, something he says is automatic. "But when I lived in the Soviet Union I could suspect that every Russian I met was the person who killed my father," he explains. "The Holocaust is a horrible thing, with six million people killed because of their religious background. But what would you say to the question of why there were twenty million Soviet citizens killed just because of their ideological differences with the state?" Being in Germany also gives Nagy the same ironic satisfaction it gave Jewish refugees of an earlier era: "The fact that I now live in Germany, as a Jew, is a contradiction of the ideas of Hitler. It's just the understanding that what Hitler wanted to achieve with the Jews he didn't achieve."

That Nazi past, a past spent trying to cleanse its soil and soul of anything remotely Jewish, is why Germany has opened its doors to Jewish émigrés when its neighbors and allies are slamming theirs shut. It is doing penance. If the world happens to notice, and pay homage to how much Germany has changed, all the better. "Germany is the only country in Western Europe to accept this Russian Jewish immigration," says Michael Szentei-Heise, the chief administrator in Düsseldorf's Jewish community. "A year and a half ago we had an international meeting on

Jewish immigration with representatives of the French, British, Dutch, and others. France proudly said, 'We are accepting Russian Jews at the rate of fifty per year.' Well, in Düsseldorf we accept them at the rate of fifty per week."

While that acceptance has met with little resistance within Germany, it has aroused the ire of Israelis. In the early 1990s senior Israeli officials told then-chancellor Kohl to stop taking in Russian Jews who belong in Israel—and most decidedly do not belong in a state with Germany's record of anti-Semitism. "I met several times, during visits to Jerusalem, with high-ranking political groups who said, 'Why do you let Jews from Russia immigrate to Germany? We need them in Israel,'" recalls Burkhard Hirsch, the former vice president of the German Bundestag. "Our answer was, 'What is our right to tell them where they have to live?'" Spiegel, the German Jewish leader, remembers offering Kohl comparable advice: "I said, 'If you decide today no Jews can come to Germany, what will be the reaction of the world?' He said, 'You are right.'" Spiegel and his colleagues also recognized how badly Germany's aging and shrinking Jewish communities needed new blood, and they knew that the only Jews who would be willing to venture to Germany were those, like the Russians, who had to leave their birthplace and had so few options where to go.

Germany not only let them in, it let them in with most of the generous benefits it gives its own citizens and immigrants with Germanic roots.

For Eugene Mann, that has meant medical schools that were top-notch and free, along with a work permit that lets him earn money to support himself. He left Russia for Israel in 1992, which was an easy decision: "The terms of living in Russia were not good, not the financial ones, not spiritual ones, not human rights, not anything." It was harder, three years later, to leave Israel for Germany. He liked the freedom Israel gave him to practice his religion and he liked the country, but he was not accepted to medical school there and was not happy about the way Israelis treat Russians. "There are a lot of prejudices," explains Mann, who is twenty-six and works part-time translating Russian to German, German to English, and English to Russian. "Israelis say that Russian immigrants come with false papers, that the majority are not Jewish, that they've brought persecution to Israel. That is sometimes right but is quite exaggerated." In Germany, he adds, "my life is very comfortable. I am very well accepted in this society. Germany has the best conditions in the world for students."

Mann's parents and grandmother have even better deals in Germany, starting with housing. The government gives new arrivals like his parents $279 a month for rent if they live alone and $559 for a family of four—enough, in Düsseldorf, for a comfortable place in a good neighborhood. Handicapped people like his grandmother get $363 a month for a single apartment or $727 if they share with three others. And there is more: vouchers that give them access to less expensive apartments, fees for rental agents to help find a place, up to $70 a month for heating, and full funding for furniture if it is used and partial payment if it is new. A refrigerator also is considered essential, as are a washing machine and a used black-and-white TV, so the state pays.

There is even an allowance of sorts. A single adult gets $324 a month, the second adult brings in another $259, and each child up to seven means an extra $162. Men get $148, twice a year, for clothes. Women, who presumably cost more to dress, receive $189. Pregnant women are eligible for a 20 percent premium in living expenses, a one-time clothing allowance of $222, and $136 for a stroller.

The state helps young Jewish boys become men by contributing to the costs of a bar mitzvah, and it lets old people die with dignity by paying for the funeral. Émigrés' medical bills are fully covered, along with part of dental costs, and the government will pay up to $2,367 a month for a nursing home. Transportation to the doctor is free. Mann's grandmother, who broke a bone in her pelvis, also gets money for a device that lifts her into the bathtub and for a wheelchair. She can ride the trolleys, buses, and subways for free, and twice a month the state pays for a taxi to the movies or anywhere else she wants to go. Money is available for a caretaker to help her bathe—up to $769 a month if someone is sick enough. Anyone sixty and under is supposed to be looking for work, and the government will pay for six months of language instruction to make them more attractive to employers. Those over sixty do not get that language training, but they also do not have to look for work.

What really distinguishes that welfare system from the one in the United States, however, is the fact that in America most recipients are kicked off the rolls after two consecutive years, or five years over a lifetime. In Germany they can keep collecting as long as they need it, which can be forever.

Word of that generosity quickly made its way back to Moscow and Kiev. "I don't think persecution is the main reason people come to Germany," says Vera Steyvers, who heads the Social Welfare Department of the Jewish community and works mainly with Russian émigrés. "The main reason is because of the benefits they get here. It's more or less the only country where they can come that is not so hard with the regulations." That is also a major reason why the population of Russian émigrés in Düsseldorf is skewed toward the old and the ill. Steyvers estimates that a third of those who have come over the last decade are sixty or older, and "every second one of them, at least, is sick. Among those who come from Ukraine, even the younger people are sicker, on average, compared to Germans of their age group." The logic, immigrants say, is simple: pensions are so low in the former Soviet Union that the old are forced to peddle cigarettes and candy or take other desperate measures to stay alive, the sick are denied care and support, and most who can leave do, with Germany now their destination of choice.

Since being Jewish is the easiest way to get in, lots of Russians who under the old Soviet regime denied any ties to the repressed religion suddenly are reciting the Shema and proclaiming their piety. "At the very beginning we were very naive, our means and capabilities to find fake documents were very low," says Szentei-Heise, who oversees day-to-day operations of Düsseldorf's Jewish community. "Today it's me who personally checks all documents, and if I'm on holiday people are told they'll be checked later, when I am back. I'd say I'm able to discover most fakes. If I'm not able to discover those documents, they're so well made that it would cost twenty to thirty thousand dollars. This amount of money only a very few can afford."

Fakery is tougher to uncover once the Russians have settled in, at which point those who are young and healthy are supposed to think about finding a job. But why look too hard when the government is willing to pay so much for you not to work? "Most of the time people from forty-five years on depend for the rest of their life on social welfare," says Steyvers. A 1999 nationwide survey by the University of Potsdam bears her out: nearly 70 percent of Russian Jews of working age are unemployed, and those who are working on average took five years or more to land the job. That is partly because Germany has had such high unemployment since reunification of the East and West, and because it requires Russian doctors, engineers, and other professionals to be retrained before they are allowed to work. Language also is a barrier, the Potsdam authors found, with only 10 to 15 percent of those surveyed fluent in German.

Jan Katschko is one of the success stories. He left Moscow for Germany in 1991, with the first wave of refugees, having chosen it over Israel and America. Getting out was not easy. Katschko worked in radio physics, which in the eyes of the Russians made him a security risk. Life after he arrived was also difficult, with Katschko, his wife, and their thirteen-year-old daughter living in a tiny bungalow and sleeping in bunk beds. He could not find work in physics so he took what he could until, in 1995, he opened a travel agency in Düsseldorf that caters to the Russian-speaking community.

Like most Russian Jewish refugees, Katschko is of two minds about Germany. He is grateful for the economic opportunities and, even more, for the way German doctors cured his daughter, who had been paralyzed by a car accident a year before they left Russia. "I am sincerely thankful to this country that gave me all the civilities to live, work, develop my family, and save my child," he says. "My parents live here as well. They receive a social charge and will receive it forever. Soon I will receive German citizenship." But he has reservations: "I don't feel German and I will surely never feel German. I feel as a person living in Europe, who was born and lived a big part of his life in Moscow. I'm quite a flexible person, and if tomorrow I find myself living in the United States or Israel, I will feel like a Muscovite living there. I'm not going to feel like a German when three of my five uncles didn't come back from the front and the war."

Starting off with expectations that low might seem like an ominous way to begin life in a new land. But things have worked out much better than most of the new arrivals expected. The Russians came from a country where the government was the enemy, and found that in Germany it is their benefactor. They came from a place where non-Jewish neighbors might be informants and rarely were friends, and found that their German neighbors are at worst indifferent and oftentimes are openly welcoming. They came mainly to escape the bleak economic and political realities of post-Soviet society—then they got generous social benefits, became citizens, and, like Helen Israel, Adrian Flohr, and others who came before, they settled in. They came expecting nothing, which is what they had gotten in Russia, and slowly realized they were building new and better lives.

In the process of adjusting to their new surroundings the Russians tried to re-create what was familiar to them. They settled in a neighborhood of Düsseldorf that officially is known as Reisholz, but that they renamed Russeholz. The big brick buildings had the same feel as the complexes they lived in in Russia, only with more color and more creature comforts. There were Russian-language newspapers and TV stations, Soviet-style stores, and other amenities that made them feel at home and were a function of the fact that along with its Russian Jews, Germany has admitted more than 1 million ethnic Germans from the former Soviet Union.

While Russeholz looked like their old neighborhoods in Russia, there was one telling difference: in Germany they could, for the first time, openly and safely be Jews—which took getting used to. The world where they had been reared was brimming with prohibitions and embargoes. Jews in the Soviet Union could not join in Passover's celebration of freedom or Yom Kippur's reflection and redemption. They were not allowed to learn Hebrew or Yiddish, and if they did they were afraid to speak them in public. They were kept from arguing about the Torah and Midrash and honoring their children's coming of age with bar and bat mitzvahs. Jewish sports clubs were banned, along with Zionist collectives and other organizations based on culture or religion. Yet even as they were denied the fruits of their faith, they could not escape the scarlet stamp that branded them as Jews on their passport, in the workplace, and in everything else they did in their socialist society.

In Germany, by contrast, they can define their Judaism any way they choose. For Katschko, that means identifying himself more with the Jewish people than the Jewish faith. He attends synagogue, but only on Yom Kippur and Rosh Hashanah, and while his twenty-one-year-old daughter keeps kosher, he and his wife do not. Yet his Jewishness still defines how he thinks about himself and who he chooses as friends. "My family in Russia was Yiddish speaking. My grandparents came from a small shtetl in Ukraine," he says. "From the beginning of my coming here I felt like a Jew, and I will always feel like a Jew."

It was the same for other Russian refugees. "The big majority of Soviet new arrivals have almost no connection to religion," says Ervin Nagy, the engineer who came in 1994 and is now a fixture at the Düsseldorf synagogue. "But it is a very important point that we Russian Jews do have a sort of Jewish mentality that was developed in us because of the repressions of the Soviets. Our Jewish mentality, which was in this way always supported by persecution, has not so much in common with classical Judaism in a religious sense. It's more an ethnic and national thing."

That interpretation of Judaism generated a strange reaction in Germany. The wider population of Germans seemed willing to let the Russians identify as Jews or anything else they wanted to be, but the existing Jewish community has been less welcoming. The resentment of new arrivals by older ones is a pattern familiar in Jewish communities from Paris to Atlanta. But this time, in Germany, there is even more at stake. The Russians, Poles, and Ukrainians who came to America generations ago seemed too Jewish to their assimilated coreligionists, too steeped in Orthodoxy and ceremony. The Russians arriving now in Germany, by contrast, do not seem Jewish enough. New arrivals to America were famously hardworking and entrepreneurial, in part because there were no social programs to fall back on. Russians in Düsseldorf start out on welfare and often stay there, in part because they are too old and sick to work even if they could master the language and find a job. The biggest difference, however, is the numbers. New arrivals to America came in successive waves, rarely threatening to take over communities long run by Jews who had come before. In Germany they have come seemingly all at once, to big cities like Frankfurt and Berlin and small ones like Erfurt in the east and Recklinghausen in the west, numerically and psychologically overwhelming those who came before.

The older arrivals have responded by compiling a list of gripes, starting with money. Jews, like Catholics and Protestants, are supposed to tell the government their religion and pay a 9 percent surcharge on their income tax to support their religious community. But some Russians do not register, and most who do are not earning anything so they cannot pay taxes. All of which helps explain why, at a time when the flood of

Russians requires the synagogue and other Jewish institutions to expand and swells the Düsseldorf community's budget to more than $4 million a year, it collects less than $700,000 in taxes. For the rest it turns to the government, to a few wealthy donors, and to the time-honored technique of deficit spending.

The catalog of complaints goes on from there. The Russians are too willing to accept handouts and dabble in the black market. They are rude to city and state welfare workers, giving the Jewish community a bad name. They wear loud clothing made of cheap man-made fibers, do not wash enough or groom their hair, and do not try to master the German language or learn German comportment. Worst of all, half of them are not really Jewish, only pretending to be so that Germany will let them in, while the rest neither know what it means to be a Jew nor care about Israel. There is a grain of truth to all the charges, although none are generalizable and most are explainable. What matters is the perception on the part of older arrivals that the Russians are another race and not really part of their religion.

"There is a big problem, believe me," says Helen Israel, who came to Germany forty-five years ago. "Yesterday afternoon I was with a Russian group, survivors of the Holocaust, and there were two ladies who had birthdays. I had sandwiches and cookies. They took the rolls with butter and honey and put them on a plate with sausages. I said, 'Ladies, you can't do that. You're in the Jewish community center. At home I also am not kosher, but here you must make kosher.'" Jaffa Flohr's concerns are more generalized and deep-seated: "It's not our community anymore. It grows different. The people who came here from Russia don't have the same mentality, they have another mentality. What I am very angry about is that they don't care about Israel and we care very much about Israel. They only want to have a good life. Every one of us is a stranger with them. I think most of them are not Jews and they are not interested in Judaism."

Ronald Tamler, the young doctor, is better acquainted with the Russians as friends and colleagues and he is less vested in the community's hidebound ways. Tamler is also more realistic about where Düsseldorf's Jewish community would be without them. "The community would have died if the Russian Jews hadn't come and saved us," he says, echoing the findings of demographers. "Everybody was old and people who were not old were trying to leave. Don't believe anyone who is telling you the Russian Jews are killing us."

*   *   *

The schisms between Jews who came years ago and the recently arrived Russians, and between Jews and non-Jews, are real and painful. But they are just half the story. What matters even more to the future of the Jewish community in Düsseldorf, and Germany, are the bridges that are being built.

Consider the way the Russians are learning to be Jews through the Club of Jewish Tradition. They sing songs like *Hava Nagila* and *Hatik-vah*, following along with Russian transliteration since they cannot read Hebrew and sounding more like Cossacks than cantors. They learn about Rosh Hashanah, Passover, and other holidays, from what to wear to what to eat. They rehearse a Shabbat dinner, sitting behind long tables covered with challah and fruit, lighting candles and chanting the *Motzi* over bread and the Kiddush over wine. More than 1,000 refugees have gotten involved, coming to know things they would have picked up as children if the Soviets had let Jewish children attend Sunday school or Hebrew school, and expanding on the random bits of tradition passed down by their *bobbeh*s and *zeydeh*s.

Other Russian Jews are learning on their own. They read Jewish books, study Jewish history, watch Jewish movies. In Russia the only Jewish culture available was the Yiddish writings of Ukrainian-born humorist Sholom Aleichem, whose work inspired the Broadway play *Fiddler on the Roof.* In Germany they can get anything they want, and what they want increasingly includes attending synagogue for daily min-yans, Sabbath services, and special celebrations. To make things easier, the community now offers prayer books with Russian and Hebrew text as well as German and Hebrew.

To serious scholars, the new refugees' rudimentary knowledge is frustrating, especially since most older arrivals also are relative neophytes when it comes to Jewish laws and texts. "Naturally it's very difficult," says Michael Jedwabny, the twenty-three-year-old assistant rabbi who is from Moscow, came to Düsseldorf by way of Israel, and is part of the Litvak sect of the ultra-Orthodox. On the one hand, he explains, the community is run by the Orthodox and adheres to halakhah, or Jewish law, for everything from burying the dead to ensuring the kitchen is kosher and bar mitzvahs are performed properly. But it is not a brand of Orthodoxy most traditionalists around the world would recognize or sanction, with everyone, regardless of how observant they are, welcome to join in. For him, Jedwabny says, that means that "I don't have a partner to learn the Gemara and the rest of the Talmud with every day. And every time, if I meet somebody who will learn it, I have to teach them from the beginning. I have to begin from the beginning, to adjust myself to their level. Thank God I have my books and I can study myself. I also have friends in Israel and I can fax to them if we have a discussion in writing. I send faxes all the time.

"For the whole amount of Russian people here I could not influence so much, but for certain people it works well," adds the young Torah reader, who walks the street with a black yarmulke topped by a wide-brimmed black hat, a brown beard, sideburns that are thick around the ears in the Orthodox style, and the frilly white tzitzis of his undergarment showing. "There are people who I reached and who I succeeded in turning back to Judaism, to do *brit milah,* to learn Torah."

Where Jedwabny sees himself reaching down to lift up his fellow Russian refugees, his boss, Rabbi Michael Goldberger, considers it reaching out. And he relishes it. It is partly that he has no choice. His is the only synagogue in Düsseldorf. He is its only full-fledged rabbi. His community ranges from Jews who can daven on their own and are as versed as he is in the Mishnah, Talmud, and other holy books, to those who are not sure how to put on a prayer shawl and would have no idea what to do with tefillin, the tiny leather cases filled with scriptures that an observant Jewish male binds to his forehead and arms during morning prayers.

That is precisely the sort of broad-based outreach that the thirty-eight-year-old Orthodox rabbi was trained for when he studied in Boulder, Colorado, with Rabbi Zalman Schachter-Shalomi, father of the Jewish Renewal movement. "Orthodox people all the time say, 'We have Judaism today because we did everything exactly as Jews did it two thousand years ago,' and they are right," explains Goldberger. "The Reform say, 'Judaism exists today because we were ready to assimilate and change, we were pragmatic and did what was necessary,' and they are right, too. Our answer is a pluralistic Judaism that accepts most everything, that accepts every serious expression of Judaism. In France, England, and even in America, we have these denominations where the Orthodox rabbi doesn't speak with the Reform rabbi. The only country where this new structure of pluralistic Judaism could grow is Germany, because we have here Orthodox, Reform, and everything under one roof. If we succeed not to split these congregations, to have one congregation and maybe several synagogues under one umbrella, then the whole world will realize this form of congregation can function."

It does function, at least for now, in Düsseldorf and scores of other German cities. It captures under one umbrella, or one synagogue roof, not only the various denominations of Jews, but also old arrivals and as many new ones as it can. For most of the last fifty years there was a single synagogue because there were too few Jews to support more. Since the Russians came, there have been enough in many places to fill a second or third, but with the exception of Berlin, Munich, and Frankfurt, there is still just one synagogue. In some cases that is because the Russians are so poor that communities cannot afford more, because the synagogue is filled only on the High Holidays, and because Orthodox leaders have resisted sharing funds and legitimacy with those trying to launch Liberal or Conservative congregations. But there is also a sense, among Goldberger and others, that Germany is forging a paradigm for a pluralistic Judaism that could be a model for the diaspora, uniting denominations and nationalities.

Russian Jews are like the Four Sons in the Passover Haggadah, Goldberger says as he removes his wire-rimmed glasses and rubs his tired eyes. The wise son was born four generations ago, when there still were Jews there free to practice the religion. "Then we had the wicked children who made revolution in Russia, saying, 'We don't want religion, we are communists,' " the rabbi continues. "The ignorant son of the third generation didn't know a lot about Judaism; the only thing he knew was that his grandfather was Jewish. These are the ones we have today who are forty or fifty years old and still can remember their Jewish grandma; they knew she used to make gefilte fish. The last generation is their children, who don't even know what to ask because they can't remember their great-grandparents."

Goldberger is imposing, standing six feet three inches, with a brown beard and a scholar's air, and his mission is no less monumental. He intends to send a lifeline to those last sons made famous through the Passover fable, the simple one and the one so ill-informed he does not even know what question to ask. In Düsseldorf's case they are Russians, but throughout the diaspora they assume different shapes, from the boy in Boston who calls himself Jewish yet cannot explain what that means, to the daughter of Moroccan Jews in Paris who insists she is neither Sephardic nor Hebraic. Comparable exercises in Jewish learning are being tried in Boston, Paris, and elsewhere. But the experiment under way in the Federal Republic of Germany—involving refugees from Russia, the world's largest community of unschooled Jews, now living in Germany, with its unrivaled history of hostility toward Jews—seems particularly poignant and especially relevant to the Haggadah story.

The Düsseldorf rabbi puts it more simply: "If we treat them friendly and wisely and everything that I learned from the Torah then they will realize, 'Oh, the synagogue is a good place to be.' They'll see that there is a Jewish atmosphere, a Jewish way of creating friendships with other people." Even as he teaches the Russians about rituals, rules, and the written words, Goldberger is acutely aware that "they also can teach me about Judaism. We are going into it together. You know how great it is to learn Torah with people who never learned Torah and don't know Torah and don't know *Rashi?* They are brilliant, they have brilliant ideas."

Learning what it means to be Jewish benefits the Russians in several measurable ways. After years of being repressed for their religion without really understanding it, they are finally seeing Jewishness as a cause for celebration. As important, learning Hebrew, studying Torah, and going to synagogue all offer links to older arrivals in Düsseldorf and other German cities.

The new bonds that have formed are on full view on Simchas Torah, the holiday commemorating completion of the yearlong reading of the Torah. Mothers and daughters in the balcony rain down a shower of candies on the men and boys below as they march around the shul, then around again, Torahs cradled in their arms, celebrating the work accomplished and the joy of starting over. The cantor, dressed in a Mickey Mouse tie from Disney World, reaches a high note and beckons congregants to join in. An assistant rabbi wearing a black hat and thick *payess* prays next to another assistant wearing conventional clothes and close-cropped hair. As they sing and dance, worship and reflect, it's difficult to discern which Jew is from Moscow and which from Romania, who has been in Düsseldorf thirty years and who arrived three weeks before.

The blurring of divisions is even more striking in conversations with the community's established leadership, men like Esra Cohn. His German roots go back to the 1700s. He was born in Israel, came to Düsseldorf in the 1950s, and, as head of the three-member board that runs the Jewish community, is one of the oldest of the old guard. Yet it is the Russians, Cohn says, who matter most today: "I'm not sure that all of us understand how important and how good it was for us, and Jews in Germany, that the Russians came. We live again since the Russians are here.

"People are afraid that the Russians will take over our Jewish communities. They *will* change the communities completely, and they *will* take over certainly. We are getting older and there are no more young people from the beginners. All the young Jews will be from the Russian people one day and it won't take very long," says Cohn. But that can be a good thing, he insists, if older arrivals like him remember that they were once refugees, with accents that identified them as outsiders and job training that the Germans found deficient. "Most of the people who came with me didn't study, they just began to work," recalls Cohn. "They were maybe not the best Jews we had. Not many intellectual people came back to Germany, more the average people came. The Jewish people were very high intellectual people before the war, many of them, and suddenly we didn't have it." The Russians, by contrast, bring with them "culture, music, theater, and other things. They are much more interested in these things than the Jews who have come before."

For the young, lust and love often are the best barometers of how life is going, and by those measures the Russians already have transformed Düsseldorf Jewry. "When I was seventeen," recalls Ronald Tamler, who was born in Germany in 1975, "I could choose whether I wanted to go out with the fat Jewish girl, the ugly Jewish girl, or the arrogant Jewish girl. I could choose between those three in my age group. Fortunately that has changed since the Russians came. That has changed because our community has changed. Now we have more choices." Such a metamorphosis may seem insubstantial or even irreverent. But Jewish parents intent on their child marrying within the faith, or any child determined to do so, understand that adding a major pool of eligible singles substantially increases the odds that the Jewish community will survive and thrive.

A different but equally critical sort of reaching out is happening with converts to Judaism, and potential converts. That is not surprising since one in every three Jews in Germany is married to a non-Jew, with an even higher rate among newer arrivals. Rabbi Goldberger's ties to Orthodoxy sometimes constrain him from embracing converts as warmly as he would like, but he feels even more strongly about his ties to pluralism and the Jewish Renewal movement. "We have to make it possible for these people who want to convert to learn, to study, to experience Judaism, and to convert," he says. "We have classes, we teach them. We had last year the first class who finished conversions, seven people and they converted. Now is the second formal course. It has to be clear for these non-Jewish partners that they could be welcomed if they decide to. Of course they have to learn, but it has to be clear that they can succeed."

One way of making that clear was when the rabbi took his first class of converts to Boulder to introduce them to the Jewish Renewal movement and show them off. Another is the key posts converts hold in the Düsseldorf community—from one of the assistant rabbis, to Rabbi Goldberger's secretary, to the chief of religious instruction at the Jewish school, with the latter now leading conversion classes.

While most of those interested in converting have a spouse who is Jewish, or another relative, Bettina Schneider was entirely new to the faith and there was no apparent reason why she should care—which makes her explanation of her conversion even more interesting. A slim, studious, twenty-eight-year-old with curly chocolate-colored hair and wire-rimmed glasses, Schneider grew up in a leftist family where her parents were nonpracticing Protestants. Her only connection with Judaism was through the husband of a great-aunt, who was deported more than forty years before Bettina was born and later died at the Theresienstadt concentration camp.

"I was just kind of intrigued," she recalls, "and later, when I was eighteen, I thought I wanted to go to Israel and see what has become of the people who survived the Holocaust." She made the trip, spending six weeks on a kibbutz near Haifa, "and I was just intrigued by the fact that people seemed to be so energetic and turbulent and wild on the outside, but so calm inside. People my age were so much more grown-up than I was. I liked the country, I liked the kibbutz, I liked the people I met." That trip led to two more, as well as to Hebrew lessons back in Düsseldorf, contacts with young Jews across Germany and, finally, to a decision to convert, a process that lasted fifteen months and was finalized early in 1999. The adjustments continue, as she is beginning to keep kosher and has moved closer to the synagogue so she can walk to services. She recently became involved with a non-Jewish man who was "the sweetest guy I ever met," but she "ended up dumping him because he wasn't Jewish. I knew problems would develop."

Her initial attraction to Judaism, Bettina explains, "was because of my interest in history, in the Holocaust. It is part of the German mentality. We grew up even as small children knowing what happened, being aware of our responsibilities, of the things that had happened, and avoiding something like that happening again. The first thought of going to Israel occurred to me because I was German. But everything that happened afterward had nothing to do with being German. Being German made it harder. In Germany, converts are seen with more prejudice, from the Jewish side as well. Jews think, 'Why should Germans convert? Do they feel remorse and want to make up for something?' And from the German side people were asking, 'Why the hell would you want to do that?' Nobody really understood.

"What I feel today is that I was just born wrong. Not being born a Jew was a mistake and I had to correct the mistake."

Few Germans go so far as to say it was a mistake that they are not Jewish, but most admit their country has made monumental mistakes in its treatment of Jews, not just during the Holocaust but before and since. Much as Russian and Eastern European Jews are trying to make peace with one another, many Jews and non-Jews are, too.

Moving beyond Germany's long-simmering anti-Semitism first requires facing up to it, in its past and present incarnations, in Düsseldorf as well as the nation. Intolerance toward Jews is now an acknowledged part of the city's history, one that began 500 years before the

Holocaust. Jews were expelled in 1438 and kept out for more than 100 years. Later, hatred occasionally erupted into violence of the sort seen in 1843 when the killing of a young boy brought rioters into the streets charging Jews with ritual murder. It was not until 1872 that Jews got full citizenship and civil rights, and even then there were exceptions.

Jews remain targets, the way they do across the diaspora and in Israel, although today's attacks almost always are against property rather than people. A synagogue is defiled in Munich, and another in Lübeck is firebombed twice in two years. The marble grave of a Jewish leader is blown up in Berlin while ten headstones are toppled in a Jewish cemetery in Guben. As the number of Jews in Germany has grown, the number of anti-Semitic incidents has climbed—from just over 300 a year in the early 1990s to 817 in 1999. But now such acts are taken seriously, with news organizations trumpeting them and German authorities investigating quickly and thoroughly. It is against the law to disparage anyone because of their race or religion. Far from inciting the public against Jews, today's incidents of intolerance are condemned by all but a marginal movement of skinheads and other, mainly young fanatics.

That does not mean a century of anti-Semitic animus has suddenly evaporated. You still can hear it in the *stammtisch* sessions where ordinary Germans gather at a pub to drink freely and pour out their uncensored feelings, making clear that it is not just Turks they resent as drains on the welfare state, but also Russian Jews. Sometimes it spills into public view, such as when Düsseldorf's largest newspaper wrote an article calling Ignatz Bubis, the recently deceased chairman of the Central Council of Jews, a "rich, clever Jew"—then refused to apologize when community leaders complained about the inflammatory stereotyping. Nearly every Düsseldorf Jew has a personal tale of anti-Semitism— from the high school student whose classmate drew a swastika on the back of her jacket with chalk, to Assistant Rabbi Jedwabny hearing someone whisper "fucking Jew" as he walked down the street in Orthodox garb. At the synagogue each piece of mail is checked for explosives with a metal detector that looks like an oversized magnifying glass, a green-and-white police car patrols out front during Friday night services, red-and-white cement poles encircle the building to keep car bombs from ramming it, and security officers check everyone who comes in the one public entrance.

To many, such precautions seemed extreme—until a World War II–era hand grenade exploded near the entrance to a Düsseldorf train station in July 2000, wounding ten, all of them immigrants from the former Soviet Union and six of them Jewish. Two of the injuries were severe, and a pregnant woman lost her unborn baby. While the motive remained unclear, it is almost certain that the attack was directed against Jews or immigrants, or both. The victims, who walked as a group from the station to a German-language class and back at the same times every week, made an easy target for hate groups. "In the community we already are very vigilant, so there is no need to exaggerate or get in a panic after this bombing," says Szentei-Heise, the community's chief administrator. "Of course we do open our eyes a little bit more, and are more aware of anything happening around us."

Even more eye-opening were the three Molotov cocktails lobbed at the Düsseldorf synagogue just three months after the attack at the train station. Although no one was injured and damage was minimal, the timing of the firebombing was especially disturbing: during the Jewish holy week that runs from Rosh Hashana to Yom Kippur, and on the eve of celebrations marking ten years of German unity. It also came during a period of heightened tensions between Israelis and Palestinians; one of the accused bombers was Palestinian and the other was a native of Morocco.

Almost as troubling is the recent backlash against efforts to remind Germans of wartime atrocities, and to make German firms pay billions of dollars in restitution. Martin Walser, a respected author, raised the specter of resentment at a ceremony in 1998 when he said Germans were being overexposed to the Holocaust and warned that the horrors of Auschwitz were being misused as a "moral club." Bubis, the German-Jewish leader, shot back that Walser was guilty of "spiritual arson." A national survey several years before had found that 22 percent of Germans preferred not to have Jews as neighbors, a third said Jews had too much influence on world events, and 40 percent felt Jews were exploiting the Holocaust.

A similar feeling—that Jews are nagging, that they are pushing for too much money and asking a new generation to unfairly bear the guilt for actions of an earlier generation—has been echoed by other intellectual and political leaders, the more so since the reunification of East and

West Germany created hard economic times. "My son, who was born in 1970 and has been twice to Israel, discusses with me Germany's pledge of thirty billion dollars in compensation for forced labor. He says that's incredible and asks, 'Why do I have to pay for that? I was not even a child at those times. I didn't exist,' " recounts Burkhard Hirsch, the widely esteemed former vice president of the Bundestag who, while not a Jew, has long backed Jewish causes. "That is normal, it is not anti-Jewish, not anti-Semitic. It's a question of younger people saying that that war was fifty years ago. It was incredible what happened, and they ask what we did during those times, what our fathers did. But they also ask why have they to pay for it.

"My answer," adds the white-haired Hirsch, "is that I believe there will be a time when we come to see these matters without emotion, as a historical fact. But how long it takes cannot be decided by those who did it, or their descendants. It must be decided by those who suffered and their descendants."

Spiegel, however, takes issue with the argument that Germans are weary of the Holocaust. "I hear that a lot, that enough is enough, that people don't want to hear any more," the Jewish leader and Holocaust survivor says. "The opposite is true. Now I have the most invitations ever to give lectures about the Holocaust and what is the Jewish community. They come from schools, from organizations. If I didn't have a job I could go every day to a school, and the next week to organizations of four hundred men, to talk about my history, how I survived. They are so quiet and interested. Teachers present this to young people who want to know what was the reason, what was the history. They want to hear from people who are survivors what it was like, not just to be shown pictures and books."

He is not the only one getting such invitations. "I could give speeches every night before different classes, Christian classes. I'm invited so much I can't do anything. They're really interested in Judaism," says Rabbi Goldberger.

German society, and especially its political elite, know they are being judged by how they treat their Jews, which is one reason they made it a crime to print anti-Semitic literature or deny that the Holocaust happened. Jewish youth are excused from military service if a parent or grandparent was a victim of the Nazis or if serving would make it difficult to practice their religion. And Germans have done more to open their borders to Jewish immigrants than the French, British, or anyone else in Europe or North America. Neofacist parties do exist in Germany, and they rail against what they see as Germany's overly liberal immigration laws, but those parties attract a fraction of the vote that their counterparts do in Austria and France, and their leaders go to great lengths to proclaim they are not anti-Jewish. "One can say to me that I'm blind, but I don't see any anti-Semitism nowadays in Germany," says Juergen Krueger, a thirty-four-year-old member of the far-right Republican Party who was recently elected, for the second time, to Düsseldorf's city council.

Germany has even modified the meaning of words in a bid to be sensitive to its Nazi past, recasting *Kristallnacht* as *Pogromnacht*, for instance, to make clear that Jewish lives were smashed along with property the night in 1938 that the Brownshirts went on a rampage. A political correctness has taken hold among the politically involved that makes it difficult to question the admission of Russian Jews and awarding of benefits to them or other matters that, with other immigrant groups, are part of normal discourse.

The notion that anti-Semitism is on the wane is shared by nearly all Düsseldorf Jews, but there is less consensus about what to make of the new trend of philo-Semitism, or fascination with things Jewish. The evidence is everywhere. Germany now has more Jewish studies programs than any nation outside Israel and America, and 80 percent of the students are not Jewish. Non-Jews also account for a quarter of those attending Hebrew classes in Düsseldorf, and they flocked to the synagogue until it limited their participation several years ago. The German media followed the election of Bubis's successor with the kind of intensity normally reserved for a presidential campaign, and Jewish leaders are solicited for their opinions on everything from the race for mayor of Düsseldorf to the Kosovo crisis. Ask average Germans how many Jews there are in Germany and they will guess anywhere from 500,000 to 10 million, based on all they hear about Jews in the media, even though most admit they never met a Jew and the true total is slightly over 100,000.

That curiosity about things Jewish is natural, and probably healthy, given the country's history of accepting myths and rumors about Jews and Judaism. But philo-Semitism makes some Düsseldorf Jews almost as uncomfortable as anti-Semitism. "It's fashionable now to be Jewish in Germany," says Daniel Padan, a twenty-seven-year-old who just graduated from medical school. But he worries that such fashion carries a price: "Here you're like a piece of a human museum. You're a mixture of a rabbi, a stranger, an alien, and something weird. You're like a rabbi because they think if you're Jewish you have to know everything about Judaism. You're like an alien, you're something strange, because they can't really touch you, you have your own religion. Maybe it's all part of an excuse. They say, 'I have children with Jewish names. I made something for the Jews. I don't have problems with Jews.' "

*   *   *

What Daniel Padan and other Düsseldorf Jews want is something that their coreligionists in much of the world take for granted: normalcy.

Normalcy is easier to define through its absence than its presence, and there has not been enough of it in Germany since Jews began coming back after the Holocaust. Being normal would mean that, when they walk by an elderly person, Jews no longer would calculate how old he or she was during the Nazi era and wonder whether they were, as American author Daniel Goldhagen dubbed them, one of "Hitler's willing executioners." It would mean that a Jew with a *kippah,* or even a black hat and sidelocks, could walk the streets without people snickering. Normalcy would let Jews and Germans remember the death of the 6 million during the Nazi reign of terror, passing on its lessons and compensating its victims, but not be immobilized by it. Most of all, being normal would mean that being Jewish and being German no longer would be seen by so many, on both sides, as mutually exclusive. It would let Jews feel they could be both without denying their past, and it would let Germans understand that the hyphenated identity of German-Jewish can affirm a national identity rather than signal questionable loyalties. It would allow young German Jews and old ones, recent arrivals and ones who came a generation ago, finally and forever to feel at home.

On a day-to-day basis Padan treats Germany as if it is his home. He was born in Israel, moved to Germany when he was five, and today is one of the most politically active young Jews in Düsseldorf. He studied there, his girlfriend is there, and the opportunities for advancement seem endless for a doctor like him. His sister and mother live in Düsseldorf, and he insists that "we're not sitting on packed suitcases." Still, there is an ambivalence, a feeling that "we are just here part-time, that even if I stay my whole life, in the bottom of my heart this will not be the place where I die.

"When my father died six years ago we had a discussion whether to bury him in Germany or Israel. We asked the rabbi about burial and he said we could transfer the body, even after several years, from one place to another. That was really important as we decided whether or not to bury him in Israel. Because we are living here, and my mom is here, we buried him first here. But if we decide to leave, if my mom leaves Germany, she would not leave without him."

Maybe Padan is right to hedge his bets. The Holocaust had such a traumatic effect on Germany that it is difficult for outsiders to understand. Jews living in Germany, and many non-Jews, too, are haunted by the 6 million who perished and are gripped by a shock that makes normal life nearly impossible. It has, after all, only been sixty years. Maybe things never can be really normal for them.

Or can they? Jeannette Barth, who lost her father and other close relatives to the Holocaust, cannot accept that such pathos has to continue to define her life or that of other Jews. She will not let herself bask in or be brought down by the anguish. "I try to live a normal life," explains the eighty-one-year-old who escaped Germany three weeks before war broke out and returned in 1948. She had to flee again two years later, this time from impending imprisonment by the communists in East Berlin, and came with her husband to Düsseldorf. "I want to leave behind me what happened in Germany in 1939. You can't always live behind you because you get depressed if you do."

Barth says she does not feel alienated being Jewish in Germany, and does not worry about assimilating. What she worries about more is living in a separate society of Jews, which is one reason she limits her participation in the Düsseldorf synagogue to attending High Holiday services and occasional meetings. "I don't get more involved with the Jewish community because I don't want to be put into a box, to live Orthodox and eat kosher and goodness knows what else," she explains. "We can be Germans and Jews, of course."

The city of Düsseldorf hopes that is true, and has been working for years to make it so. It is helping build a new Jewish community by welcoming and subsidizing Russian refugees, doing more of both than any German city its size. It also is acknowledging its Nazi past and trying, in modest but meaningful ways, to make amends. In 1981 it started bringing back Düsseldorf natives who survived the Nazis and now live in America, Israel, and other parts of the world. Forty or so came a year, with the city paying their bills, taking them to the site of the old synagogue and their families' former homes, and piecing together as much of their past as was preserved in records of the Jewish community or the city.

Düsseldorf has also set up a museum that memorializes its Holocaust past, in an unusual and expensive way. "I'm visiting survivors from here and interviewing them in the places where they live. I've done one hundred and thirty so far in America, England, and Israel. I'm doing it for them. It's very important for them that somebody is asking them for their history, their story, their experiences," explains Angela Genger, a historian who runs the memorial institute. "Some don't want to talk about their experiences. They say, 'You didn't ask us for forty or fifty years and now you are coming to ask.' They are so hurt and traumatized. Two years ago I had somebody here who had never talked about his experience. His sister told him to come and see us. He said, 'I don't remember anything.' Then he talked to us for two to three hours about what happened to him as a young boy, how he was terrorized and sent to Auschwitz. He talked about it in German, in perfect German, and he hadn't spoken German for fifty years.

"The other thing, of course, is that we come to know a lot about our story, the story of what happened to Düsseldorf. In the last twenty years at least a minority of the Germans have taken responsibility for what happened, not because they felt guilty personally, but because they felt it is part of their history."

Still, many Jews remain skeptical about the motives of individual Germans and the society as a whole, worrying that the outreach is more to assuage their guilt than understand the suffering of Jews, then and now. "I am not here because the Germans want to become a normal country, I am not here to help them," says Adrian Flohr, the gynecologist. "I am here because I want to be here. Of course my being here makes it easier for them to say they are a normal country."

Rabbi Goldberger started out an even more entrenched skeptic. He grew up in Basel, Switzerland, just five minutes from the German border, "but it was very clear to me that I would never step into Germany. My mother is a survivor of the Holocaust and while we never spoke about this, it was clear. You didn't drive German cars, you didn't use anything German, and you didn't come to Germany. For us it was clear that all the Germans were Nazis." He did come, however, in 1988, with his pregnant wife, to run the Jewish youth center. And over time he came to differentiate the kinds of Germans. "I told my mother, 'You are right, there are very bad Germans, but there are good ones as well.' And she remembered that in Auschwitz, she survived once because a German soldier gave her his potato skins.

"I'm finished to hate this country. I've learned not to hate people but to hate what they do. The only reason for me not to feel really comfortable in Germany is the lack of Jewish education on a high level, which I used to have in Switzerland. It won't be here in time for my children because it takes a long time to develop. Sometimes in the evening when I'm alone, I think it would have been nice for my oldest, who is eleven, to have friends who eat kosher like him, who keep Shabbat like him. All the time he's invited to bar mitzvahs on Friday evenings and he can't go. This is the reason why I don't feel comfortable. If there would be this religious infrastructure here, and religious people in Düsseldorf, then it would be perfect."

The lack of that religious support system—and the effect it was having on his children—ultimately convinced the rabbi to resign his pulpit and return to Switzerland. He stayed on through the end of 2000 to give the community more time to find a successor and says he deeply regretted having to go. He takes hope, however, from the fact that most of his congregants seem determined to persevere.

The sense that things are improving for Jews in Düsseldorf, and Germany, is apparent among the twenty- to thirty-year-old leaders of Kesher, the city's Jewish youth group. They say they feel considerably more Jewish than their parents, from their facility with Hebrew to their understanding of Jewish history to their deep involvement in Jewish communal affairs. Being comfortable with their cultural and religious identities is likely to make them more comfortable in whatever country they find themselves, even Germany.

"Yeah, I will stay, yeah. I can't say it a hundred percent because I don't know what's going on in the next years, but the plan is to be here," says Judith Jacobius, thirty-three, a Kesher director who was born in Germany to parents who also were born there, immigrated as children to Latin America, then returned. Marcus Thill, a thirty-year-old Talmud scholar who works as a consultant for McKenzie & Co., was born in Germany, spent two years as a fellow at the Hebrew University of Jerusalem, but "I couldn't stand living in Israel any longer. The reason why I came back is that I feel much too Western European to live anywhere else." And Daniel Padan, the young doctor who was born in Israel and moved to Germany when he was five, says, "I've built up a life here, my whole family built up lives here, of course I feel comfortable here."

As for the next generation, the one now in their teens and younger, visits to public schools and Jewish ones suggest that these youth understand their history but do not feel constrained by it. "We talk about the Holocaust in school. We have to talk about it because our ancestors are responsible for it," says Melike Karamustafa, a seventeen-year-old at the Humbold Gymnasium who is not Jewish. Maxim, a fourteen-year-old student at the Jewish community's religious school, says it is "easier to be Jewish here than in Russia. There people hate Jews and don't understand them, but in Germany you can be Jewish and no one forbids it."

The Jewish community that children like Maxim inherit is almost certain to be bigger, more vital, and more self-confident than the one their parents inhabited, especially if they came before 1990. While many want to try living in America or another part of Europe, most feel part of German society and feel accepted by their non-Jewish contemporaries. At the same time that they are more German than their parents, they are also more Jewish—and less troubled by seeing themselves as both at once. Their parents and grandparents were generations in transition, who tried but were never fully able to recover from the horrors of the Holocaust. These children and grandchildren say they have arrived. They understand their parents' anxieties but most have decided that Germany is as good a place as any for a Jew to live.

Paul Spiegel is from the generation of Holocaust survivors who never could feel entirely at home in Germany even though they lived there nearly all their lives. He says he understands the lingering fears and resentments, but he agrees with his children's generation that it is time to think of Germany as a home rather than just a haven. And he is "sure" that sometime soon, as the Russians settle in and younger Jews assume control of the community, the organization he runs will signal the rising comfort level by changing its name from the Central Council of Jews in Germany to the Central Council of German Jews.

Chapter 2

DNEPROPETROVSK:

Lifting the Iron Curtain

There were not supposed to be any Jews left in Dnepropetrovsk.

Not after Bohdan Khmelnytsky rallied the Cossacks 350 years ago to rise up against Poland and, along the way, to massacre the Jews. Ukrainians still celebrate him as a liberator and folk hero, displaying his statue in public squares and his picture on vodka bottles. Russians toast him for reuniting Ukraine with Mother Russia. But what Jews in that part of the world remember is stories of how "Khmel the Wicked" burned, beheaded, or strangled their ancestors. How he slaughtered Jewish infants in their mothers' laps, ripped open pregnant Jewish women's bellies and chopped off their hands, and cleaved Jewish men with butcher knives, denouncing them as the footmen of Polish nobility. And how he burned the synagogues, salvaging only the holy Torahs, which his soldiers used to pave the streets.

Adolf Hitler had more advanced appliances of extermination. In October 1941, during the harvest festival of Sukkoth, Nazis troops and Ukrainian police marched 11,000 Jews to a ravine on what is now the campus of the State University of Dnepropetrovsk, then mowed them down with machine guns. The *Aktion* took nearly two days. A band played throughout to muffle the screams and the rat-a-tat of the rapid guns. Board members of the Jewish community were dispatched in a separate action in the yard of the Jewish school, their blood staining the fringed prayer shawls draped over their heads and shoulders. Jewish patients in the Eigren Quarter hospital were herded outdoors during winter, made to strip, ordered to crawl on all fours to the courtyard, then were shot at the edge of a ditch and tossed in. All told, 20,000 Jews were executed in Dnepropetrovsk during the war.

The Soviets were subtler. Jews were identified as Jews on their passports, which was supposed to signal that the communists accepted their religion and culture. In fact, the stamp set them apart and limited their chance for professional or personal advancement. The KGB drove home the message that Jews were worthy of special treatment by shuttering forty-two of the forty-three synagogues in Dnepropetrovsk, an isolated city southeast of Kiev. No effort was made to track down the anti-Semitic hooligans who broke into the remaining shul during High Holiday services in 1963. There was no kosher food, no bar mitzvahs, no circumcisions. Jewish children had no clue who tried to build the Tower of Babel or why, or what was in the Garden of Eden. Seders were held, secretly, without Haggadoth to tell participants how to proceed or matzo to remind them what Passover was about.

Then there were the Israelis, and to a lesser extent the Americans and Germans. By opening their doors to immigrants they unwittingly completed the displacement begun by the Cossacks, Nazis, and Soviets. The opportunity to leave Dnepropetrovsk was a godsend to the nearly 30,000 who took it, and they helped revive Jewish life in places like Düsseldorf by moving there. But it all added up to a final sentence of death for the Jewish community they left behind. Or so it seemed.

There are still Jews in Dnepropetrovsk. Thousands of them. Some wear yarmulkes, attend synagogue regularly, and proudly and publicly display their Jewishness. Others blend in with their Slavic surroundings, struggling to find a place in the confusing post-Soviet society yet taking quiet joy in slowly getting to know what it means to be a Jew.

What they all have in common is a resilience that stands out even in the history of the ever-resilient Jewish people. They simply would not accept the accepted wisdom that Jews could not survive in the former Soviet Union, and in the process they set a bolder expectation. Exhibiting a determination that would have made Job look like a goldbrick and the Maccabees like mere mortals, the Jews of Dnepropetrovsk reconstructed their synagogue and built Jewish schools. They reminded old and young of age-old customs and rituals that had slowly eroded during seventy long years of socialist secularism. They reclaimed their Jewishness not all at once, but in a series of small steps throughout the 1990s. Along the way the Jews in the curious city that few in the West had even heard of mourned their coreligionists who immigrated to Israel, but were not crippled by the departures. For each who left another two surfaced from what seemed like nowhere, reasserting their roots and reestablishing that their Jewish community is here to stay.

Today, the skeptics say there are 10,000 Jews in the city of 1.3 million. The optimists say 75,000. Whoever is right, Dnepropetrovsk offers a model of survival and revival that is being studied by Jews from Warsaw to Moscow. It captivates those who wonder why Jews remain Jews despite the obstacles, for nowhere were there more obstacles than there. Its successful collaboration with Jews from Boston, New York, and Tel Aviv makes clear that the wider Jewish community can still make a difference in the old Soviet bloc a dozen years after the tumbling of the Berlin Wall. And Dnepropetrovsk's determination to keep growing and building suggests that, in the twenty-first century, it is struggling diaspora communities like that one, at least as much as the comparatively comfortable State of Israel, that will capture the imagination of world Jewry.

"I was tempted to go to Israel. My son has lived there three years already," explains Alexandr Abramovitch Fridkis, a fifty-year-old surgeon and lay leader in Dnepropetrovsk who regularly prayed at the synagogue during Soviet times, when only the very old dared to come. "But I thought it was necessary to be here. I couldn't just leave. Those who go are not a problem because, no matter how it seems, all of us never will leave.

"We have a joke here: when the last Jew leaves this city, two thousand Jews will see him off."

*   *   *

The story of Dnepropetrovsk's extraordinary comeback in many respects distills down to the story of its extraordinary rabbi, Shmuel Kaminezki.

When he arrived from Brooklyn in 1990 people did not ask who he was, but what. With good reason. Rabbi Shmuel, as he is known across the city, stands just five feet five. His bushy black beard and doughy frame fill out the image of a teddy bear and make him stand out in a land where men generally stand tall, with faces close if not clean shaven. Then there are his sidelocks, the wide-brimmed black hat and black coat he wears even in suffocating summer heat, a white T-shirt that shows through his white dress shirt, and the white tassels of his tzitzis that hang from his waist and remind observant Jews like him to heed all the Torah's commandments. Ukrainians thought they knew what Jews looked like, but only the very old could remember back far enough to recall one like this.

The smog-filled city of sprawl in the middle of vast nothingness looked at least as foreign to the unorthodox Hasidic rabbi as he did to it. He grew up in the intellectually thirsty world of the Israeli yeshiva, then lived in Brooklyn's bustling neighborhood of Crown Heights, where nearly everyone groomed and dressed like him. His father, a bookkeeper, was from Byelorussia, his mother from Moscow; both had escaped after World War II and happily settled in Israel. Shmuel moved to New York on his own at fifteen and studied at Morristown Rabbinical College with other young men from the insular but influential Lubavitch branch of Hasidism. But Shmuel knew he never wanted to be a practicing rabbi and certainly never conceived of coming to Ukraine. "I liked learning and being a religious Jew but I didn't want it to be my job," he says. "All my mother's brothers were very successful businessmen and I wanted to be a businessman. I always wanted to be rich and live a good life. I didn't have a dream to be a big rabbi."

Whatever dreams he had for himself, the Lubavitcher Rebbe had something else in mind. The late Rabbi Menachem Mendel Schneerson, seventh in a line of grand rabbis tracing back to the eighteenth century, was a famously convincing man—enough so that he had successfully planted a series of Chabad Houses from Kathmandu to Bangkok to bring wayward Jews back into the fold and into Orthodoxy, and that many of his 200,000 followers were certain he was the Messiah. Schneerson also had an understandable interest in Dnepropetrovsk since his grandfather and father had served there as chief rabbi, and he lived there from age seven to twenty-two. His father was arrested, tortured, and exiled by the Soviets to Kazakhstan, where he died in 1944, while his grandfather was murdered by the Nazis. Tradition called for Menachem

Mendel, as the oldest of his father's three sons, to take up the succession as the city's chief rabbi, but he was ninety and ailing by the time the Soviet Empire opened up, and he had an expansive religious empire to oversee and rarely ventured outside his base in Crown Heights. So he turned to the diminutive twenty-five-year-old with the sparkling eyes and cutting wit. Whatever his plans had been, Shmuel could not resist when the Lubavitcher Rebbe asked him to pick up the proud pulpit in Dnepropetrovsk.

The Dnepropetrovsk that awaited Shmuel was a decidedly different one than the thriving center of Jewish population and culture that the Rebbe's ancestors had presided over. The city was always a fulcrum of commerce, given its location on the banks of the Dnepr River in the middle of a region rich in iron ore, coal, and manganese. It had more trees and wider roads than most cities in that part of the world, but also more rackety railroads and polluting factories. The Soviets added their own flourishes, making it a monument not only to architectural drabness but to political power and military might. It was the birthplace of socialist strongman Leonid Brezhnev and enough of his Kremlin comrades for the group to be dubbed the "Dnepropetrovsk Mafia," and the current Ukrainian president hails from there. It also was home, during the Soviet era, to the world's largest spacecraft factory and it supplied the nation with SS-20 ballistic missiles and booster rockets—which made it off limits to Westerners, and even more difficult than in cities like Moscow and Kiev for world Jewry to monitor the treatment of Soviet Jews.

Shmuel arrived just as the city was opening to the outside world for the first time since the 1950s. The young rabbi and his wife were met at the train by a local youth who was studying Torah and came bearing flowers. What they found when they disembarked made them consider turning back for New York: the only one of forty-three synagogues still open was a makeshift structure off a narrow courtyard. It was in shambles and was used only on the Sabbath. The aged worshipers knew little Hebrew and even less of the holy books, fought among themselves, and were as impoverished as the surrounding community and country. Shmuel had been promised a city brimming with Jews. What he found was barely enough for a minyan.

"I cried the first day I came. I went to the shul and on the way home I said to my husband, 'What the hell are we doing here? It's not for me,' " Chany, the rabbi's wife and full partner in the adventure, recalls a decade later from her kitchen as she supervises her husband's frenzied preparation of a Yemenite fried dough called *malawach*. "I had no friends, no people to talk to. I couldn't call home because I didn't know the language and when I finally got an operator she said I'd have to arrange the call for three days later. The hotel was a horrible place. We had fifteen boxes in a tiny room and I had to cook in there. We moved the television set and put in a burner. We had nothing to eat the first month because I didn't know who to talk to and what to buy that would be kosher."

Some things they learned to do without, for others they found substitutes. But there was no replacement for milk, especially after they had their first child. So they improvised, buying a cow for $50. A young yeshiva student milked it five days a week, bringing his kosher yield to Chany and the baby, while the non-Jewish owner of the farm where the cow was kept had rights to the udder the other two days.

It was more difficult making do when it came to rebuilding the Jewish community. "We were told there would be many, many, many Jews," Shmuel says, looking back. "We didn't see where all the Jews were that they were talking about. We didn't see any. People were still afraid to say that they were Jewish, they didn't want to come to the synagogue. They were used to the idea that to be a Jew was a problem, to be a Jew was like being an invalid. Until 1989 it was against the law to be a Jew. It wasn't so long ago that people were suffering just because they were Jewish. They weren't let into the university or college. Suddenly times had changed and you were allowed to practice your religion." But the rabbi saw a silver lining in the dark history: "Whatever is not allowed you want even more. There's an expression, '*Ta'im k'mo chet*,' 'It's delicious like a sin.' "

Before anyone could indulge in such a religious feast, the community needed certain foundations, which is where Shmuel began his rebuilding. He assembled what able-bodied Jews he could find to renovate the synagogue, which from the outside looked like someone's long-neglected home and inside had little other than an ark and tattered books marking it as a house of worship. He opened a yeshiva, or religious academy, which in the *Chabad* tradition was the place from which a new generation of learned Jews would be spawned. Because those who came to pray and study often were doing so on empty stomachs, Chany launched a soup kitchen next door to the shul.

"The idea was to show people what's nice about being a Jew, what's positive about it," says Shmuel, who was officially named chief rabbi of the whole oblast, or state, almost as soon as he arrived. He was the first to hold the title in fifty-two years, and it had a magisterial ring. But he was the only real rabbi around and he spent morning to night in the synagogue telling anyone who would listen what a tallith is, how to put on tefillin, and other basics of behaving like a traditional Jew. His students ranged from a former propagandist for the Soviets to old men who for seventy years had refused to touch meat because they could not find any that was kosher. "I organized Shabbat meals for families," he says. "I'd invite them to my hotel room, where I was living for three months with big cockroaches."

Shortly after they arrived the rabbi and *rebbitzen* had a minor breakthrough. They planned a reception at their hotel on a Friday evening and expected the normal handful of Jews to attend. "It was the most amazing thing, there were five hundred Jews sitting in the café at Hotel Dnepropetrovsk when we got there," recalls Chany, "I was on a different planet. I was pregnant, I was nauseated, and I was nervous. I brought down two big silver candlesticks and lit candles, my husband made a Kiddush, and the place was in tears. Those people hadn't seen anything like this for seventy years. The place was just bawling."

Next on the agenda was a Jewish day school, which required the approval of the mayor. Shmuel asked and Mayor Valery Pustovoitenko refused, insisting that no one wanted such a school and no one would attend. So Shmuel asked again. And again. "I didn't do anything to offend him, I was just a nudnick. I just knew we had to have a Jewish day school," he says. And it worked, sort of. He got permission for the school, but not for a building to house it. The school operated out of the same building as a non-Jewish school, a situation he likened to "two couples in one bedroom. Couples that don't really like each other." Shmuel did not give up. He had his eye on a large building he felt would be ideal, and resolved to do whatever it took to win the approval of Pustovoitenko, who went on to become prime minister. What it took was traveling with the mayor to Israel in 1991, showing him the sights, introducing him to Jewish religion and culture, and indulging his appetite for vodka. It also took using Shmuel's connections in America to get the U.S. government to donate 3,500 tons of butter to Dnepropetrovsk, a gift that voters credited to the mayor, the mayor credited to Shmuel, and actually came courtesy of Shmuel's old classmate, Rabbi Eliezer Avtzon of Brooklyn. The result, Shmuel says, was that "the mayor became a major friend of ours and we now have the largest Jewish day school in Eastern Europe."

The approach was the same for other things Shmuel went after. College-age kids in Dnepropetrovsk simply had to have a school, their own school, where they could train to be teachers in Jewish academies. Children could not get by without a summer camp, women required a ritual bath known as a *mikvah*, and old people needed a choir that could belt out tunes in Hebrew, Yiddish, and Russian. The community as a whole, meanwhile, could not be whole unless it began to plan for a grand synagogue that could seat a thousand. No matter that few if any other cities in the former Soviet Union had such a facility back then, or that there was no demand for it or money. He would find a way and once it happened, people would see that the need had always been there.

That kind of chutzpah might be at home in Brooklyn or Brookline, but it was decidedly uncommon in Ukraine. It was not just that everything was harder to come by there, from financing to building materials. It was that, after nearly a century of Stalinist purges and communist control, the can-do attitude Shmuel counted on had been supplanted by one of it-won't-work.

The attitude of despair was well founded. All across the city were reminders of the dysfunction of communal factories and the inefficiencies of collective agriculture that had toppled the seemingly unshakable Soviet empire. Rusting cranes hovered over the rusting skeleton of a hotel whose construction was launched thirty years ago, but will never be completed. A bridge begun from opposing banks of the Dnepr River was stopped because money ran out before the sides could be linked, and one segment had sunk so deep it was difficult to imagine a connection being forged. Russian-made toilets sometimes flushed and always sounded like a passing train, pulse phones required waiting for the switches to catch up to the dialing, and shower water typically flowed from a tube attached to the sink, with "cold" often the only option. The upshot was practical hurdles for everything the young rabbi hoped to accomplish there, along with a mind-set that wondered, "Why bother trying?"

Shmuel fought back with a simple motto: whatever it takes. Sometimes he borrowed, as when he went to Morristown and Montreal and convinced ten rabbis-in-training to come to Dnepropetrovsk for a year, where they spent half a day studying and half helping the community. Sometimes he seduced, such as when he got the New York–based Joint Distribution Committee, the Jewish Community Relations Council of Boston, and other benefactors from London to Miami to commit millions of dollars to programs for the sick, the poor, and the young in a city they barely knew, in a region most of the world had given up on. Sometimes he brokered, as when he secured medical treatment for a local Mafia chieftain in return for a hands off policy toward Jews. Best of all he led by example, such as when he went without a salary in the early years and, after money promised from America did not arrive to support a community project, he and Chany kicked in $60,000 of their wedding gifts and personal savings. Or when he had so little money he relied on handouts from his mother in Brooklyn to support his wife and family.

The tactics differed, but his strategy in each case was the same. The only way to overcome a defeatism built up over a lifetime was to show people rather than just tell them that things could improve. Instinctively grasping what others needed, he found ways of matching their needs to his with an ease that would make him the envy of any backslapping business baron or union boss. The fact that his "needs" were altruistic, from building a school to enlarging a shul, let him speak with conviction when he assured his patrons that they were doing the Lord's work. The fact that he was a rabbi let him choose settings that were calculably disarming, from a Shabbat dinner in his backyard with his charming children seated around a table teeming with kosher delicacies, to his office above the sanctuary where the sound of aging ex-socialists singing in Hebrew and Yiddish seeped through the walls. What he offered was straightforward but highly prized: a savvy sense of how to get around red tape there and in America along with an ability to talk to anyone, in part because no one would be threatened by a roly-poly rabbi who could speak in the vernacular. He was a doer and a deal maker. A fixer. All of which was in the best tradition of a Chabad movement that, despite its focus on the philosophic, was famous for borrowing from the secular world any techniques that would draw Jews back to Orthodoxy. The Lubavitch used toll-free telephone numbers and satellite television hookups, converted campers into rolling recruiting stations, and set up a fax network to respond to Talmudic inquiries.

"The rabbi is the one who made the connection between us and our Russian partners," explains Uri Laber, an American and head of Dnepropetrovsk's Optima conglomerate, which runs telecommunications, petroleum, and real estate businesses. "I didn't know who was honest and who wasn't, who we could work with, all the problems you run into in this part of the world. Without him saying that 'this is an honest person' we wouldn't have known. Anyone can introduce you to another person; the point here is the reliability. He knows what's up, basically." And it was not just advice that Shmuel gave the Orthodox businessman when he first arrived: "The rabbi took us into his house. He had cans of kosher tuna, macaroni. He would divvy up whatever little chicken he had, half of a half came on our plate. There was no kosher food at that time."

The rabbi was not dispensing advice and food solely because he expected something in return. That would have violated his *Yiddishkeyt* ideals of charity and generosity. But it was those very ideals that drove him to launch expensive programs for the Jewish community and if those he helped chose to give something back, well, he would not refuse. "It's the whole concept of wealthy Jews helping the community," says Laber, who, as his business prospered, became a major donor to Jewish causes. "You can't have a shul where the tiles are coming off. The rabbi said, 'Let's build something nice. There should be air conditioning, you should want to daven there.'"

It was not just the rich and important whom he doted on, although they did get special attention, and even with them there were limits. "I'll never forget when a big sponsor called him. The rabbi was busy and the sponsor was upset, he wasn't very polite," says Vyacheslav Brez, twenty-five, who at the time was Shmuel's personal assistant and now is his federation director. "Even though he needed this person, who was donating money that the community depended on, the rabbi told him, 'For me you are just like an old woman who is getting ten dollars a month.' I was in the next room and I began to admire him. To tell you the truth, I fell in love."

Barbara Gaffin fell in love the first time she met Shmuel, and the relationship continues to blossom during the two trips she makes each year from Boston. "Shmuel is the spark," explains Gaffin, who runs a sister city program linking the Jewish communities of Boston and Dnepropetrovsk on initiatives ranging from maternal care to assistance for the handicapped. "I could have this same project somewhere like St. Petersburg and it would be an exciting project, it would be really great. But would it catch on like wildfire without Shmuel Kaminezki? Probably not. And it definitely would not be as much fun. People love coming and sitting with Shmuel and Chany on Shabbat."

Everyone has their own Shmuel story. Yossi Drizin remembers how naive he was when his father dispatched him to Dnepropetrovsk from Brooklyn's Borough Park to set up a factory manufacturing yarmulkes and other religious articles. His cousin Shmuel got him going. "He's very, very connected. His word is very, very powerful," says Drizin. Sometimes those connections helped find willing workers, other times they kept at bay the omnipresent and omnipotent underworld. "I never saw a person frown at me while I was here," explains the bearded Drizin as he taps his skullcap and fingers his *payess*. "Everyone trusts me. Why? This guy who works with me tells everyone that I'm Rebbe Shmuel's cousin." Drizin loves just watching his cousin: "Whenever he comes out at the end of the day he asks me if I have five or ten *hryvnas* for a taxi. He starts out the day with his pockets full of coins and slowly empties them. All day he has people coming into his office who he gives money to." But the young Hasid says that even as Shmuel amasses amazing influence, he never forgets what it is for: "Of course he enjoys his achievements, but the main idea is that it's not his personal achievement. This place is the most successful in the world in terms of a whole community growing together in Judaism."

That may be an exaggeration, but not by much. Consider the Jewish institutions that Shmuel has helped plant. There is the first Jewish old-age home in the former Soviet Union and the first program for Jewish youth in trouble, whether that trouble is physical or mental, with parents who cannot cope or no parents at all. There is the first weekly all-Jewish TV program, which reaches tens of thousands of viewers who cannot make it to synagogue or prefer getting their religion and culture from the comfort of home. There is a boys' choir that has performed at Manhattan's Metropolitan Opera House, a Jewish game show team that won repeated trophies, and a factory that raises and kills chickens according to the laws of kashruth. There also is a program that trains "mini-rabbis" to cater to the religious needs of communities in the countryside. Initiatives like those are staples in thriving Jewish communities like Paris and Buenos Aires, but tell anyone about them in this part of the world and they will tell you, "Ah, it must be Shmuel."

Federations are something else much of the Jewish world takes for granted. Relying on finely tuned fund-raising machines, they reach out each year to congregants, ensuring sufficient donations to pay for programs such as Shmuel set up. In the former Soviet Union no one knew from federations. In his early days the rabbi made the rounds drumming up support, and wealthy congregants like Laber contributed when and how much they wanted. The payoff was that the community could plan ahead, knowing day to day whether it had enough money to sustain schools and orphanages, food pantries, and bread-and-milk runs. Today, Dnepropetrovsk has its own Philanthropic Fund, one that Shmuel modeled after the Combined Jewish Philanthropies of Greater Boston and that is a model for Eastern Europe. A board of forty-five local leaders and a presidium of nine oversee the fund, while forty successful businessmen contribute a minimum of $500 a month for community projects. Altogether the Jewish community raises nearly $4 million a year from local and international sources—a record in the region and enough for it not only to pay its bills on time but to provide Shmuel with a salary, which again is a novelty.

His fellow religious leaders were impressed enough with his accomplishments that they elected Shmuel as the first chairman of the board of Ukrainian rabbis, a post that involves representing the rabbis in dealings with the government, church leaders, and the State of Israel. "Rabbi Kaminezki was the most successful rabbi in setting up an organized community," says Yaakov D. Bleich, who holds the appointive positions of chief rabbi of Kiev and chief rabbi of Ukraine. "He succeeded in creating a modern Jewish community in an old historical city. . . . That is quite unique here in a city that's not a capital, that's more suburbia or small town."

Dnepropetrovsk is unique in another way, too. It has as diverse an array of Jewish institutions as any city in the former Soviet Union, if not the diaspora, but it does not reflect the diaspora's diversity of approaches to experiencing Jewish faith and culture, or even the more limited freedom of choice of other ex-Soviet cities. Only one branch of Judaism operates in Dnepropetrovsk: the Orthodox. Only one offshoot of Orthodoxy is authorized: the mystical movement of Hasidism. Only one Hasidic group has a voice: the Lubavitch.

The canon of Kaminezki is simple: the rabbi sets the rules. Others have tried to come in, from the Reform to Hasidics like the Karliner-Stoliners who dominate in Kiev. But they all have stories about how Shmuel's friends in powerful places quashed their bids for a building or a foothold, presumably at Shmuel's bidding. In other cases Shmuel himself discouraged them from coming, insisting it would distract Jews in Dnepropetrovsk from their vital community-building. It happened when Project Kesher tried in 1998 to launch the same sort of program training Jewish women for leadership that it operates in seventy communities across the former Soviet Union; in Dnepropetrovsk, for the first time, it was told it was not welcome. It happened again with attempts to open Reform congregations. "I had a conversation with Kaminezki in April 1999. He said he had an arrangement that no other Jewish groups would function in Dnepropetrovsk. He said, 'You can set up Reform congregations elsewhere but I ask you not to set up communities here out of respect for the spirit of the Lubavitcher Rebbe,' " recalls Rabbi David Wilfond of Massachusetts, who spent two years in Ukraine working for the World Union for Progressive Judaism and running a college that trains Reform "para-rabbis" to reach out to small communities much the way Shmuel's "mini-rabbis" do.

The result, Shmuel's critics say, is that Dnepropetrovsk has its own Jewish czar—a benevolent dictator—as ill-fitting as the titles might seem for this jovial, rotund rabbi from Brooklyn. They all admire the work Shmuel is doing, are charmed by his charisma, and acknowledge that he and Chany were pioneers during a period when few others would venture there. They also admit that lots of rabbis around the world, especially ones in the Lubavitch movement, like to be the only show in their town, although few have succeeded to the extent Shmuel has. While that may have made sense at the beginning, many insist the Jewish community of Dnepropetrovsk now is mature and secure enough that it should be run more democratically and more pluralistically.

"In no other city does a single rabbi exert as much control as Rabbi Kaminezki does in Dnepropetrovsk," says Betsy Gidwitz, an independent consultant who has been traveling to, writing about, and helping support Jewish communities in that part of the world for thirty years. She respects the way that "Shmuel sees a need, he finds sponsorship, he finds a way of doing things," and she concedes that "Dnepropetrovsk is a Jewish role model because of Kaminezki." But she also says that "the major reason Shmuel has no competition is that he won't permit competitors to set up shop in the city. His original public rationale was that Ukrainian and Russian Jews are so far away from Judaism that they lack the experience to tell one philosophy from another, to distinguish one from another, and therefore they would very easily become confused. I consider this a very patronizing point of view.

"More recently, Shmuel has dropped that line of explanation, perhaps because he realizes that others consider it patronizing. In the last year or so, he has explained his exclusionary view by saying that Dnepropetrovsk must be reserved for *Chabad* out of respect for the great importance of the city in *Chabad* history. Furthermore, he fears that competition and squabbling between different groups might undermine the united front he is able to present to local authorities on behalf of the Jewish community. Whatever explanation he offers, he imposes unity."

Judy Patkin has worked even more closely with Shmuel and his community in her role as executive director of the Massachusetts-based Action for Post-Soviet Jewry. She went back and forth regularly through the 1990s and thinks Shmuel "has done a marvelous job. But he won't brook any other form of Judaism coming into his city. He's squelched several attempts. He was very flexible at the beginning, but is less so as time goes on." Patkin believes Shmuel's ultimate objective is to make

Dnepropetrovsk a stronghold for the Lubavitch and to spread the move-ment across the region, which is what many movements in Judaism and other faiths aspire to. Yet she worries that his approach will alienate rather than attract Jews: "It is much too strict for these people, most of whom don't know from keeping kosher and are not about to buy in to all that. They are, however, hungry for a spiritual sense and a sense of the heritage they have lost."

Shmuel accepts his critics' concerns but not their conclusions. Where they see diversity, he sees disabling divisions. While they yearn for democracy, he longs for unity and clarity. When they propound goals like pluralism, he replies that those may be appropriate aspirations for America but not for Ukraine. At least not yet.

"We never actually said 'no' to anybody or kicked anybody out. I never would offend anybody, I would never think of doing anything undemocratic," says Shmuel. "This really is about politics here. There is a political war between the Orthodox and Reform in Israel and America. We don't want it here now. This will interrupt our work.

"I can tell you that I don't force on anybody the Orthodox way of life. Our JCC, where I am chairman of the board, has all kinds of activ-ities with no limits on the Orthodox way of life. They are having Shabbat with men and women, mixed dancing. We already have Jews who want to have liberal ways of being Jews but we don't have the label for them that 'you are Reform, you are Orthodox, you are Conservative.' We are not ready for that." His whole philosophy, Shmuel says, is building a Jewish community through a series of baby steps. "What do you do if you have a Jewish grandfather who comes to you with tears in his eyes and says, 'I have made a mistake and married a non-Jewish woman. My children should be Jewish and my grandchildren should be Jewish'?" the Hasidic rabbi asks out loud. He answers himself in a way that would make many of his Orthodox brethren wince: "We are not ready to give him up. We have to help him come back. If he comes to you and wants to be Jewish we have an obligation to help because in those times when he intermarried, times were very, very difficult.

"Sometimes we are tempted to look at the books, but we have to look at life. Every Jew for us that is left today, after everything they went through, is very precious. I was the first one who started taking children from non-Jewish mothers to my Jewish day school, and I got very serious criticism from outsiders who said, 'You and your goyim.' I'd explain that nobody forces me to take these kids. I want to help them. The Rebbe wanted it this way, also. The Lubavitcher Rebbe said that for Jews in the Soviet Union, it is not their fault that they are not Jews. If you become the rabbi of the community you have to feel how their situation is."

Shmuel has been taking that pulse ever since he came. His diagnosis: "This is not a Chabad House like in Boston. We don't expect Jews to become Lubavitch. Everything I do has the spice of Lubavitch in a positive way, but it's not like Paris or Boston. We are the Jewish community of Dnepropetrovsk, and I happen to be a Lubavitch."

The rabbi is right—and so are his critics. His recipe for resuscitating Jewish life in Dnepropetrovsk often starts with small things, from keeping kosher to visiting a *mikvah* or observing Shabbat. It is the same formula that Rabbi Michael Goldberger used in Düsseldorf. The first simple gestures establish a critical connection that lets a Jew know he is Jewish. "Each person," Shmuel says, "has to decide for himself if he wants to walk fast back to his heritage or wants to walk slow." But while he is patient about how they get there, Shmuel has in mind a definition of "heritage" that is the one his critics fear most. He is not leading Jews back just anywhere, but to Hasidism and, more particularly, to a Lubavitch lifestyle that will be a monument to the memory of the revered Rebbe Schneerson.

The seventh grand rebbe not only provided a vision for Shmuel and Chany, he left them a blueprint for how to realize it. Schneerson led the Lubavitch movement for forty-four years and succeeded in transforming an insular Hasidic sect from near-ruin at the end of the Holocaust to a highly influential movement that today takes in $100 million in annual contributions, claims to be the world's largest distributor of Jewish books, and has devoted itself to battling back against the assimilation that the rebbe called a "spiritual holocaust." The Sorbonne-educated Schneerson also had vivid memories of how the Dnepropetrovsk of his youth was the center of Jewish life in Ukraine. He said reaching children was the key to reaching parents and grandparents there, so Shmuel made building schools his primary priority. All Lubavitch rabbis around the world adore the rebbe, and adorn their walls with his picture in full white beard and piercing blue eyes. Shmuel, however, was the only one dispatched to the rebbe's hometown, and his mission caught the rebbe's imagination in a special way, even—and perhaps especially—as he was dying. "When people used to come to see the rebbe he'd ask, 'How's Kaminezki?' And he used words like 'he should long live in his kingdom.' When the rebbe got reports on how this Schneerson community is developing he used expressions he had never used in his history like 'that news is like cold water on a tired soul,' " says Shmuel.

But the rebbe complicated his protégé's mission in one critical area, insisting that as important as Dnepropetrovsk was, Israel came first. "The rebbe told me that all young people should go to Israel," says Shmuel. "When you have a Jew in Israel there's a better chance he will not intermarry. If I get a Jew closer to *Yiddishkeyt* and he finds out what Shabbat is all about, what kosher is all about, it's much harder for him to keep those things in this city than in Israel. For me, Dnepropetrovsk and Israel are one thing. I'm part of Israel and my job is to bring them to Israel." Which is why, although he has kept out the Reform movement and even other Orthodox, Shmuel put out the welcome mat for the Jewish Agency for Israel, the Israel Culture Center, and other apostles for Zionism.

That does not run counter to his mission of reviving Jewish life in Dnepropetrovsk, its rabbi maintains: "There are enough Jews here to have a community here and send them to Israel. Every week I have people who find out they are Jewish." Perhaps. But 25,000 already have gone, to Israel as well as Germany and America, and they include what Shmuel acknowledges are his city's "best and brightest." At some point he will have to choose between being an agent for the Jewish state and an architect of the Jewish communities of Dnepropetrovsk and Ukraine. The choice seems obvious: Israel can get by fine without his help, and might even be better off without having to worry about absorbing still more Jews from the former Soviet Union. But Ukraine needs every Jewish soul it can muster.

Just how many Jewish souls reside there is hotly contested, especially by leaders who visit from America and Israel, where adding up numbers is an obsession. The controversy stems partly from the difficulty of defining who is a Jew. Is it someone who watches a Jewish television program each week and buys matzo at Passover, or does it require regular attendance at synagogue? Is a Jew one whose mother was Jewish, as required by Jewish law, or is it enough that any of four grandparents were Jewish, as specified in Israel's Law of Return? Sergio DellaPergola, a demographer at the Hebrew University of Jerusalem widely considered to be the world's most reliable counter of Jews, says he includes only those who declare themselves to be Jewish. He concludes that, as of the year 2000, there were just 100,000 Jews left in Ukraine, which would make it the eighth largest Jewish community in the world. And he says there are only 10,000 Jews left in Dnepropetrovsk. Yet he concedes that "while there is good data for Russia, that is not true for Ukraine."

Bleich, Ukraine's chief rabbi, comes up with a decidedly more upbeat assessment. Adding in all those who are just beginning to acknowledge their Judaism, he says there are nearly 600,000 Jews nationwide, or enough to rank it third in the world, trailing only Israel and the United States.

Shmuel, the undisputed pied piper of Ukrainian Jewry, has his own ways of counting. He starts with the 10,000 people who he says line up on Yom Kippur to get a holy man to say a prayer for their loved ones and the 2,500 who packed in and around the old shul to hear the sweet shrill sound of the shofar. Then he considers the 7,000 who sit or stand in a rented hall to hear concerts by Israeli musicians, the 1,000 elderly Jews who get food delivered to their homes, and the 1,500 who are fed at one of several soup kitchens. There have been 300 Jewish weddings since he arrived, along with thousands of bar and bat mitzvahs, conversions are up to twenty a year, and 1,200 students are being educated in Jewish nursery, elementary, secondary, and college programs. The best barometer, Shmuel adds, may be the 35,000 households who order matzo for Passover, accounting for a total of twenty-seven tons a year of the unleavened bread.

So how many Jews does he think there are in his city? The official count shows 30,000, Shmuel says, with at least 20,000 more who are not on anyone's rolls. Using the loosest definition of all, which is the one Israel uses, there may be as many as 100,000.

Like her husband, Chany Kaminezki is happy to see Jews from Dnepropetrovsk immigrate to Israel if that is what they want. She is also frustrated. "It's upsetting," she confesses. "I've made friends. We've been close to families and are able to talk to them. They've been at all the holidays and were coming back to Judaism. Then they run away. It feels like you're constantly, constantly going to the train station and saying good-bye. They're just as upset as we are, leaving the place where their parents and grandparents are, and they know they may never come back."

Each time she and Shmuel leave for America she assures her friends in Dnepropetrovsk that they will be back, yet "they don't believe me. I don't see myself dying here. But if you say, 'Are we leaving tomorrow?' no, we are not. For me it's hard to leave such a place. We have done so much. We have given, we have gotten. It would be awkward to leave."

*   *   *

Dnepropetrovsk stirs the same mixed reactions in Jews who have lived there all their lives. To some, its tortured history is all the reason they need to escape. Others, often in the same household, say that after all they have endured it would be sad to abandon their birthplace just as they taste their first freedom. Whether they see it as limiting or liberating, all agree that for them history has been a defining experience.

The earliest historic reference point for most Jews of Dnepropetrovsk is the Cossacks' insurrection against their Polish overlords in the mid-1600s and, more especially, the rule of Bohdan Khmelnytsky, chief of the Cossacks. Contemporary Ukrainian historians say that Jews were a secondary target of the revolt, attacked mainly because they were estate managers or tax collectors for the Poles and were easier to get at than the Polish masters. Khmelnytsky, they add, is rightfully considered the father of the modern Ukrainian state. While as many as 10,000 Jews were killed along the way, including some in the region that later became Dnepropetrovsk, these mainly non-Jewish scholars insist that it was not the hundreds of thousands claimed by Jewish chroniclers back then. Even worse, they add, is for Jews today to equate Khmelnytsky with Hitler, given that the former lacked the latter's intent to destroy the Jewish people and his massacres were on a significantly smaller scale.

The Jews of Dnepropetrovsk offer a decidedly different version of the 300-year-old events, insisting it was indeed the bloodiest chapter in Jewish history until the Nazis. It was not just the death toll, which they put at 100,000, but the cruelty with which the killings were carried out.

Records left by Jews back then tell of Cossacks cutting open pregnant women, replacing their fetuses with live cats, then sewing them up again. The soldiers trampled as many as 700 Jewish villages, burning the sacred texts that were the key to the community's continuity. Three centuries later those wounds might have healed, Jews there add, if Ukrainians would acknowledge the horrors the way that Germans now accept responsibility for Hitler.

Tragedy has been revisited on the Jews of Dnepropetrovsk repeatedly since the Khmelnytsky era. In the mid-1800s Russian emperor Nicholas I issued the decree of "cantonistim," which forced Jewish boys twelve and older to join the Russian army for twenty-five years and, once there, compelled them to convert to Christianity. There were pogroms in 1881, 1883, and 1905, with the last leading to sixty-seven deaths, a hundred injuries, and the looting of hundreds of Jewish-owned businesses. The worst massacres of all were in 1919, with more than 50,000 Jews killed across Ukraine, although Dnepropetrovsk was spared the level of atrocities experienced in other regions.

Documenting the violence is easier than explaining it. Most pogroms against Ukrainian Jews during the waning years of the nineteenth century and the early years of the twentieth were sparked by unhappy urban workers who had lost their jobs and were far from their families. Many of them were ethnic Russians, a group that in the cities vastly outnumbered ethnic Ukrainians. Men who had witnessed the horrors of World War I thought nothing of taking human lives and everything about taking loot and land. And during the Civil War years of 1918 to 1920 the entire landscape was drenched with blood as Bolsheviks killed landowners and the urban elite, anticommunist White Russians slaughtered leftist peasants and industrial workers, and roving bands of various stripes targeted Poles, Germans, and Mennonites. Festering socioeconomic conflict, imported and indigenous anti-Semitism, and fundamental religious differences put Jews in the eye of the maelstrom and made them a tempting target for any passing thug.

The Soviets took control of Dnepropetrovsk in 1917, and at the beginning the Jews thrived. They published newspapers, launched political parties, and took jobs in government. But by 1918 the general economic woes of the country had spread to the Dnepropetrovsk region and things began to go bad for its Jews. First the Imperial German army occupied the city, then the White Russians, and finally the Bolsheviks came back, this time with no pretense of accommodating Jews, who by 1920 numbered 73,000. Most shuls and Jewish schools were shuttered, observant Jews were harassed and imprisoned, and Jewish businesses were nationalized along with non-Jewish ones. Some of the dirty work was done by the *Yevsektsii*, or Jewish communists. In 1926 the city changed its name from Yekaterinoslav, which had memorialized the now-out-of-favor Catherine the Great, to Dnepropetrovsk, in honor of the Dnepr River that flows through it and Grigory Petrovsky, then head of the Supreme Soviet of Ukraine. By then the Jewish population was down to 62,000, the city's biggest synagogue had been converted to a craftsman's club, and the government had confiscated the gilded crowns of Torahs and any other communal valuables they could lay their hands on. Two years later an official order was issued forbidding Jews to attend any shul, but by then only one was open and most Jews had already been intimidated into submission.

At the start of World War II Jews flocked back to the city from nearby villages in search of safety, driving the Jewish population up to about 100,000, or a fifth of Dnepropetrovsk's total. The front lines seemed a long way away at first, and many Jews remembered that the Germans who took over the city briefly during the First World War were not that bad. But as the battle grew closer, others gave more weight to rumors about Nazi atrocities. About 75,000 fled, many to central Asia or Russia's Ural Mountains. The Nazis invaded in the summer of 1941 and, during two years of occupation, they or their Ukrainian henchmen murdered nearly all the Jews who were left.

Looking back over the full 300 years from Khmel through the pogroms and the Holocaust, two things are clear about the treatment of Jews in Dnepropetrovsk and across the country. Ukraine's record of carnage, in terms of its magnitude and its persistence, was the worst of any nation on earth, with the possible exception of Germany. Yet unlike the Nazis and other butchers, Ukrainians seldom demonized the Jews based on their religion or race. Rather, as historian and author Henry Abramson notes, "the Ukrainian hatred is based on a long-standing feud and struggle for existence." In Khmel's case, it was a tragic side effect of anti-Polish and anti-Catholic sentiments. The later pogroms and collaboration with the Nazis grew in large part out of a perception that Jews were allied with the detested Bolsheviks. Such socioeconomic interpretations do not excuse the unprecedented brutality, but they do help explain it—and they may offer hope of reducing Ukrainian-Jewish tensions in the post-Soviet era.

After World War II Jews gradually returned to Dnepropetrovsk, with a 1959 census finding 13,256 and a 1970 count putting the figure at 25,000. Given their rueful history, one might have expected that anyone who could would leave as soon as the opportunity arose with the fall of the Soviet Union in 1989. Or, better still, would simply give up on being Jewish, since all it seemed to bring were pain and persecution. Some did leave, while others cut ties to the faith. A growing number, however, were defiant. The more others said they could not be Jews, the more they insisted they could be and would, much as other Jews had throughout the ages.

"I came here to the synagogue during the whole Soviet era, when the KGB kept watch," says Alexandr Abramovitch Fridkis, the fifty-year-old surgeon and lay leader. He started coming at age thirteen, and almost always was the only young person there. He and a handful of old men prayed in the main shul during warm weather, and when it got cold they headed up to the balcony, where there was a small stove. In 1986, when perestroika eased restrictions, they were able to order Passover matzo from Moscow, then resell it to pay for electricity, water, and a lady to clean the synagogue. But even with the easing he still had to dream up ways to sneak past KGB agents. That generally meant accompanying an elderly worshiper, arguing that the old man could not make it up the steep entrance without him. "I remember one time, twenty-five years ago," Fridkis says, "and it was Pesach. There was a military captain and a lieutenant. They asked, 'What did you forget here? Go to a discotheque. Go to a movie.' "

Vyacheslav Brez, the federation leader, who is half Fridkis's age, has his own memories of youthful defiance: "I was seven, and we were sitting in the kitchen in our apartment on the second floor. We had neighbors on the first floor and the mother was Jewish. She had paid somebody to change the nationality in her two children's passports so it wouldn't say they were Jewish. They baptized the children, they wore crosses, and of course they didn't tell anybody they were Jewish. I remember telling my parents that I will never do that. Even if they will kill me, will beat me, I want to stay Jewish."

Like most Jews then, Brez had no idea what it meant to be Jewish. He had never been to synagogue or met a rabbi, never seen a Jewish text or been schooled in his Jewish roots. The one holiday he and his family celebrated was Passover, but they had a strange sort of Seder. "We didn't know about the Haggadah and didn't know about slavery in Egypt," he recalls. "We thought it was a Jewish version of Christian Easter. They are spelled nearly the same in Russian. We had chicken soup and special farfelach and kreplach. We had kishke and gefilte fish. We of course invited only Jewish people to this party. We discussed politics, how hard it was to be Jews here and how much better it probably was in America. I used this opportunity to ask my grandparents how to say things in Yiddish, and they told me mainly Jewish insults and jokes."

What Brez did know was that being Jewish meant being taunted. Or beaten. "Once in my yard a guy threatened me with a knife because I was Jewish; he almost killed me. Another time I answered a question in class and the teacher gave me a very bad mark. I wanted to prove why that was not just and fair and asked her what she did not like in my answer. She told me, in front of all my classmates, that it was my long nose," he says. "During Soviet times they gave all children application forms to fill out saying where you were born, your name and address, the occupation of your parents, and your nationality, which for me was Jewish. I felt as if I were an animal in a cage and there was a big temptation to hide it. But everyone knew who I was and I was proud. This was the most difficult moment each year."

Every Jew in Dnepropetrovsk has similar stories of humiliation and ostracism, of being denied entrance to the university, refused promotion at work, or barred from high-level jobs in the Communist Party. All of which seems an odd way to treat Jews if, as the Soviets insisted, they wanted to welcome them as comrades. Yet it is no stranger than stamping their passports "Jewish" and saying that was their nationality, at the same time they were bent on the "systematic destruction of Zionist and bourgeois institutions." Or in expecting that a socialist ideology would be enough for people to give up age-old identities, be they spiritual or cultural. If there ever was a chance that Judaism would simply wither away in the Soviet Union, the clumsy Soviet strategy to make it happen ensured it would not.

The fall of socialism in 1989 created new openings. Suddenly legal bans on religious and ethnic affiliations were gone. So, too, were the political principles that, however lumbering, had provided stability and purpose. With the economy in ruins and communism discredited there was a free-for-all competition for people's allegiance. Capitalists, former communists, and various would-be reformers offered manifestos for a new economic order. Nationalists sought to fill the void with an often-militant new nationalism. Pentecostals and other evangelical Christians provided their own outlets for passion and promises of empowerment. More quietly, a growing number of Jews began turning back to Judaism.

"Thirty years ago my parents decided it would be useful for me if the nationality on my passport said I was not a Jew. They paid a bribe to get it done," says Vadim Mnushkin, forty-seven, a highly successful attorney and developer who began his embrace of Judaism five years ago. As he tells his story he begins to cry. "My parents changed my nationality but they did not change it inside me. They changed it only in my passport. My guess now is that maybe they knew that I was a Jew and I will be a Jew.

"To be a Jew is the main aim of my life," he explains from behind a large desk in his plush office overlooking the synagogue, a statue of a rooftop fiddler on prominent display. But where Christian converts typically take the plunge all at once, Mnushkin, as is the custom in Judaism, is doing it by inches. First he switched from a hand razor to an electric one because straight-edged razors are biblically forbidden. Then he got what he calls the "sharp cut," a circumcision normally done eight days after birth. He took on the Hebrew name Yosef, began saying prayers just after waking and at sundown, washed his hands ritualistically three times a day from a special pitcher, and joined Shmuel's shul along with a Hasidic one in Milwaukee, where he spends part of each year. He went on the board of the Dnepropetrovsk synagogue and became one of its biggest contributors, making monthly donations and giving ad hoc gifts whenever he learned of someone with a special need. He studied Hebrew two to four hours a day—the aleph-bet chart of Hebrew letters is on the wall in his office—and read an hour a day from a Russian-language Torah. "Reading has always been my best love, but for a few years now I have used the word 'book' only for the Torah," he explains. "The other things I read are literature, and there's a difference. Every word in the Torah has a tremendous meaning."

Mnushkin hopes some day to learn to put on tefillin, tzitzis, and other garments worn by the observant, yet he feels it is essential not to move too quickly with that or any aspect of Jewish expression. "I don't do these things now because I think that I am not ready yet," he says. "I'm afraid. I take it step by step. I don't want to seem more Jewish than I am really at this point."

Brez also reconnected with Judaism slowly and by way of an unorthodox channel. In 1992, when the country was undergoing profound changes, he got to know a Jews-for-Jesus missionary. Brez wanted to learn English and the missionary was one of the few who spoke it, so he followed the missionary to the synagogue and listened as the Christian tried to convince elderly Jews that Jesus was their messiah. Shmuel witnessed the encounter and, as he had done with so many others, asked Brez home for a Shabbat dinner. "I saw the Saturday candles, I saw the way they celebrate this day, and immediately I fell in love with this way of life," Brez recalls. "I saw how full of different things real Judaism is, how much I didn't know, and of course I started to ask questions on basic topics. 'Who is Abraham? How did we do that in Egypt? How are Jews living now in America?' "

It is easy to understand his curiosity. His entire life he had identified as a Jew, without knowing what that meant. He had been made to suffer for the identity, but had no sense that the religion or culture could offer anything positive. Now he began attending classes three times a week with the American scholars Shmuel had enticed over to help launch a yeshiva. "I can't express the feeling I had when I came to the synagogue," Brez says. "I saw this wall, I saw the ark, something inside me was turning upside down. There was a magical source that was pulling me here. It was partly religious, partly cultural, partly curiosity. Most of all it was a desire to be surrounded by Jews, not to be the only one the way I was in school, to be with people who understood you and with whom you had something in common. I suffered a lot before and I knew there was nothing to be afraid of here. For the first time in my life I started to have real friends."

Although his connection to Judaism as a people came relatively quickly, it took longer to feel a religious tie. He had grown up in the Soviet era, when communism was the deity and Darwinian evolution was the only explanation offered for the ways of the world. "I didn't believe in God. I didn't believe in full faith. It was nonsense for me, I was a materialist," he remembers. "One day I met a Hasidic guy from Australia. We spoke about everything, we spoke about the nature of God, about life, about people here. Step-by-step I changed my whole view about this topic. I saw that it's very unlikely that the Jewish nation could have survived such a terrible persecution without a higher force taking care of it."

He began attending synagogue more regularly and eventually stopped working on the Sabbath. Then, like so many renewed Jews across the former Soviet Union, he had to decide whether the best and perhaps the only place to live as a Jew was Israel. Many went, but he resisted, feeling that Dnepropetrovsk was the best place to continue his search. "When you're in Israel," he explains, "if you don't know how to pray properly people are laughing at you. Here people are not trying to show you they are a big rabbi, a bigger sage. No one is pushing you, telling you what time to wake up, what prayer to practice. Right away someone comes to you and asks how to help."

That someone typically is Shmuel. While he encourages those who want to leave, he nurtures those who stay. He helps them learn the Torah and rituals, find a job, and make sense of the horrors Ukrainian Jews have suffered. He insists he is not doing anything special, but the evidence suggests otherwise. It is his support and sustenance that encouraged Jews like Mnushkin and Brez to remain in Dnepropetrovsk when they could have fled, and to embrace Judaism when it would have been easier to keep their distance. "The rabbi asked me if I wanted to be his assistant," Brez remembers. "I was studying economics. I thought, 'What does he want from me?' It was such a big honor. I didn't even know what I should have to do. He picked me out of a big group and I agreed. It was like a miracle."

Alexander Dolnik also believes in Shmuel and his ability to work wonders, calling him the "epicenter" of the revival process. Yet Dolnik, who is probably Dnepropetrovsk's most prominent architect, thinks his city's history is an equally important factor in its Jewish renaissance. Not just the history of repression, but the lesser-known periods when the religion and culture flourished.

The Jewish presence in east central Ukraine goes back more than 2,000 years, to a time when Jewish merchants passed through what was then a common trade route. Over the next millennium Jews settled in, fleeing from or learning to live with Greek rulers, then Turkish and Armenian ones. From the seventh to the fifteenth centuries they lived in towns and cities in the region, mixing at will with non-Jews. They were not granted special privileges but generally were not singled out for persecution. What mattered most was that they were allowed to run their lives according to the laws of their Torah.

In later years the persecution grew—but so did the Jewish cultural and religious presence in the region. Consider what happened in the wake of the Khmelnytsky massacres in the mid 1600s. That brutality, and the savage Russian-Swedish war that followed, helped produce Shabbateanism, the largest messianic movement in Jewish history. A century later war and persecution were the backdrops against which Rabbi Israel ben Eliezer, better known as the Ba'al Shem Tov, founded the mystical movement of Hasidism. The cycle continued to repeat itself from the 1880s through the early 1900s, as violent pogroms encouraged Jews to launch Zionist and socialist organizations, and to revive literary as well as religious traditions. The most disconcerting instance of brutality existing side by side with civility came in 1919. Troops of the new Ukrainian government participated in the deadliest anti-Jewish pogroms in Europe in nearly 300 years at the very time that that government was extending unprecedented liberties to Jews.

The contrast is striking: Ukraine was one of the most dangerous settings ever for Jews, and one of the most fertile. It was home to Khmel the Wicked and to a rich Yiddish culture. It produced many of Judaism's most horrific memories, along with the romantic images from the shtetl that Ukrainian native Sholom Aleichem set to stories of unlucky marriage brokers, enchanted tailors, and a fiddler who danced along the rooftops. The notion that violent actions beget creative social reactions is not new to Ukraine or to Jews. Faced with persecution it is only natural that people look to leaders who promise to free them, physically or spiritually, with real or imagined solutions. But the way the unthinkable and the hopeful coexisted there over so many hundreds of years suggests the paradoxical position that the country occupies in Jewish narrative.

Nowhere does that paradox stand in starker relief than in Dnepropetrovsk. Jews have played an important role in the city ever since the Russian statesman Grigory A. Potemkin founded it in 1787. They were among its earliest settlers and its earliest contractors, merchants, and government officials. The decision to set down roots there was not entirely accidental. In 1794 Dnepropetrovsk was included in Catherine the Great's Pale of Settlement, which meant it was one of a limited number of communities where Jews were allowed to live. They brought with them shuls and *mikvah*s, a Jewish cemetery, hospital, nursing home, and even Jewish agricultural colonies. Jews continued to move to Dnepropetrovsk from across Russia during the second half of the nineteenth century, and by 1897 their numbers had swelled to 41,000, or more than a third of the total population. Even during the Soviet era Jews held influence, with a disproportionate number serving as scientists and authors, engineers, architects, doctors, and other professionals critical to the operation of the city.

All of which meant that Jewish life flourished there in the past, and Jews flocked there. It also helps explain why, despite all that was lost at the hands of the Nazis and Soviets, more and more residents of Dnepropetrovsk today are enthusiastically reclaiming their long-forgotten Jewish ancestry. "I see this city as a sui generis Babylon," says Dolnik, whose family has been there since the city's founding. "This is a special city. It is neither Ukrainian nor Russian. And this special tradition, no matter how strange it may sound, is still existing today. There are unusual things that happen here today. We haven't lived through a renaissance yet, but we are at the gateway to the renaissance."

*   *   *

Dnepropetrovsk did not get to that gateway alone. It had Jewish partners from across the diaspora, the same way pioneers in Israel and refuseniks in Russia did. But the quiet way the partnership in Dnepropetrovsk evolved, with a targeted marshaling of limited resources and the involvement of grassroots groups on both ends, offers a prototype for cross-diaspora unions at least as compelling as the earlier models.

Consider the role of Boston Jewry. In the early 1990s Jewish communities across America were forging links with their Soviet counterparts to lend a hand and follow up on the decades-long drive to free Russian Jews. The National Conference on Soviet Jewry suggested a Boston-Dnepropetrovsk matchup. It was partly that Shmuel and Chany were making progress and needed help. And the two cities just seemed to fit, both being midsized, with a medical academy, on a major river. Most "sister city" arrangements involve mostly ceremony, and quickly peter out, but this one between Jewish communities generated a kinship and mutual satisfaction that make it a model in the region and have both sides looking for ways to extend the relationship. Shmuel is almost as well-known today in Boston Jewish circles as he is in Ukraine, while Jewish leaders from Boston enjoy equivalent celebrity in Dnepropetrovsk.

The sharing began in a modest way, with Boston shipping more than forty boxes of art supplies, toys, boots, winter clothing, and cosmetics, along with a hundred handwritten Hanukkah cards from Boston kids. Dnepropetrovsk shipped back sketchings and other artwork that went up at the Boston Public Library. Medicine and food were next. Boston sent a forty-foot container filled with $80,000 in canned goods and other foodstuffs, along with diapers, baby formula, syringes, and medicines. Assembling supplies like those sounds straightforward, but nothing involving the two cities was simple in those days. Community leaders from Boston came over to investigate the need. Bob Gordon, head of the Store 24 food chain, tapped his suppliers for donations and offered his warehouse for storage. Organizers in Boston patiently and endlessly explained to their patrons where Dnepropetrovsk is and why they should care.

As the message began to sink in, new exchanges ensued. Children in Dnepropetrovsk's Jewish day school get 1,200 hot meals partly paid for by contributions from parents in Boston and its suburbs. Boston sends its children over, seventy-five in five years, for winter camps that let young people from the two cities forge friendships and probe the vastly different worlds they grew up in. Elderly Jews in Boston embroider challah covers and homemade quilts for their counterparts in Dnepropetrovsk. Teachers help teachers with schemes for getting parents involved

in learning, community workers suggest ways to get children with cere-
bral palsy and other special needs into the classroom, and program
administrators from Boston show their Ukrainian colleagues how to
make their programs run better. Even the white-haired, potbellied deputy mayor of Dnepropetrovsk has traveled to Boston to meet his coun-
terpart and be feted by the Jewish community. There is barely a program
in the Jewish community of Dnepropetrovsk, from the college for teachers to food pantries for the poor, where Boston Jews did not help out
with money or supplies, advice or administrative support.

All the exchanges yield results, but they are easiest to measure in
medicine. Health care was a priority in the Soviet Union, with treatments
and drugs available to anyone who needed them, although they were not
always of the best quality. These days some hospitals require patients to
bring their own linen and food, and nearly all are short-staffed and have
too little of the equipment and supplies that are considered staples in
the West. Getting to the hospital also poses a challenge, with patients
having to wait up to three hours for ambulances. People understandably
worry that radiation has spread to Dnepropetrovsk from the Chernobyl
reactor, which is 300 miles away, but they should be even more concerned about the deadly sulfur, nitrogen, and carbon contaminants that
they can see, taste, and measure in their air and water. The bottom line
is that residents of Dnepropetrovsk are exceedingly anxious about their
health, which made them exceedingly grateful when Boston doctors in
1997 opened a women's health center in a wing of a local gynecological
hospital.

In its first two years the clinic saw 9,686 patients, most of whom had
the kinds of complaints Western doctors saw half a century ago and
have largely eliminated with modern treatment. There was infertility
caused by having as many as a dozen abortions, which was the only
choice for many of those women since contraceptives are difficult to get
and out of their price range. There was cervical cancer, which has
reached epidemic proportions because doctors do not do the simple,
low-cost pap smear that is the standard in the developed world. And
there were far too many cases of gynecological infection, babies being
born with brain disease because their mothers took a dangerous drug to
speed up labor, and doctors misreading redness in the cervix as a sure
sign of cancer and amputating the entire cervix.

The clinic administered 10,353 pap smears and distributed 7,800 months' worth of contraceptives from the time it opened in 1997 through mid-1999. It began training doctors from across Ukraine, reaching as many as 600 a year. It also started getting dramatic, measurable outcomes: the abortion rate for the district fell from 63.2 per thousand women in 1996 to 8 per thousand in 1999. Its tests picked up 280 cases of gonorrhea or chlamydia, along with 245 positive pap smears, which let doctors offer proven therapies. The total annual cost for the program was $50,000, which worked out to just $5 per visit.

Boston pays for the training, equipment, and supplies, while the city of Dnepropetrovsk picks up salaries and overhead. In the spirit of that collaboration it is not just Ukrainian doctors who have gotten a boost from the program, but also the twenty or so from Boston who have been visiting for a week or two at a time since 1997. "For many of them, who haven't traveled much in the past, this is an eye-opening experience," says Dr. Benjamin Sachs, head of obstetrics and gynecology at Beth Israel Deaconess Medical Center in Boston and founder of the medical exchange with Dnepropetrovsk. Sachs, who comes twice a year lugging duffel bags filled with medical supplies, says the U.S. doctors who accompany him are "reminded why they went to medical school at a time when, on a daily basis in America, it's hard to be a physician. Sometimes you have to send people five thousand miles away for them to understand."

The same thing happened with the clinic set up at a children's hospital in Dnepropetrovsk and affiliated with the pediatrics programs at Mount Auburn and Cambridge hospitals just outside Boston. It was not high-tech medicine, but things like a 10-cent dipstick and $1 culture slide to detect urinary tract infections that, gone undetected, could eat away at the kidney. Or basic equipment to unmask middle ear infections and anemia. Or something as simple as a vaccine for diphtheria. The Boston doctors are encouraging local and national health officials in Ukraine to expand those life-saving initiatives across the country. While other programs that the Boston community sponsors are exclusively for Jews, the medical ones are open to anyone who needs them.

The Boston sister-city effort has had a cascade of effects on Ukraine that go beyond its particulars. It encouraged wealthy Jews in Dnepropetrovsk, which has scores of them, to set up a federation like Boston's and give generously. It offered clear proof that the Jews of Dnepropetrovsk have powerful friends from abroad—including ones from the prestigious Harvard Medical School—which has given them added clout in dealing with the non-Jewish world. It also told Shmuel that what he is doing matters to the outside world, which has encouraged him to keep tapping his newfound friends for bigger and better programs.

"Suddenly the idea that my wife and I had American friends who were coming down made a big difference in our lives," says the Dnepropetrovsk rabbi. "It's the ideal model for a relationship between two communities in the diaspora. The idea that people from over the ocean care, and come, is unbelievable for people here."

It is exceptional for people in Boston, too. "It is reawakening in them a sense of identity that they have taken for granted," says Barbara Gaffin of the Jewish Community Relations Council of Greater Boston, which launched the sister-cities partnership with help from the Combined Jewish Philanthropies, the Boston-area federation that provides $225,000 a year in funding for Dnepropetrovsk projects. "It's like watching the world from a child's eyes. Seeing people discover their Judaism instills an excitement in us. We didn't have to discover our Judaism, we've been fortunate to have always had it. Jews in America are spoiled." Gaffin, who was deeply involved with the refuseniks, says that was mainly a case of working against something, of pulling down barriers to Jewish emigration and battling anti-Semitism. Watching a community rebuild its Jewish life, she adds as she sits in Shmuel's office, is much more uplifting. "To come here and witness this, to feel you are part of a renaissance and a new historic era for the Jewish people, it's a fulfilling moment."

A litany of other individuals and organizations from overseas has been in Dnepropetrovsk and helped out. The Chabad movement brought everything from Bibles and butter to programs to care for orphans. Financiers from Zurich to Paris and Chicago kicked in, because they care and because it is difficult to say no to Shmuel. The Joint Distribution Committee, the New York–based philanthropy, is a huge part of the revival there, as it is across the diaspora, feeding several thousand Jews every day, subsidizing education programs, and picking up part of the tab for the mini-rabbi initiative. The JDC also pays for Dnepropetrovsk's summer and winter camps, along with its Jewish community center, prayer books, Seders, and programs that support poets, writers, and other Jewish scholars.

All that attention says something not only about the city in the middle of Ukraine, but about the wider relationship between rich and poor communities across the diaspora. "Dnepropetrovsk may prefigure a sense that, in the twenty-first century, it's the diaspora that really needs to be the focus of Jewish attention. America's role may become far more significant in sustaining diaspora Jewish communities," says Jonathan Sarna, a historian and diaspora scholar at Brandeis University. "The older agenda of building up a young Jewish state is ridiculous in the current situation. Israel still will be a focus of attention, but it has developed into a high-tech country and a majority of world Jews soon will be living in Israel."

Israel has already gotten the message and it, too, is helping out. Levi Levayev, a developer whom Shmuel calls "the richest man in Israel," gives as much as $500,000 a year to Dnepropetrovsk's Jewish community. He set up the Beit Chana school that trains Russian-speaking Jewish women to teach in Jewish preschools and elementary schools, and the Israeli Ministry of Education now helps support it. Israel also provides five teachers for Dnepropetrovsk's Jewish day school and runs an Israeli cultural center that teaches anyone who is interested, and especially young people, what Israel is like. The Jewish Agency sponsors a youth club, summer camps, intensive Hebrew classes, and informational programs on Israel. Such programs are designed to help the Jewish community in Dnepropetrovsk—and to convince as much of that community as possible to make aliyah to Israel. At Beit Chana, for instance, graduates are expected to spend several years teaching in the former Soviet Union, then to look for teaching jobs in Israel. At the cultural center, part of the mission is "to advertise Israel for everyone." To make the move even easier, the Israeli contingent in Dnepropetrovsk has organized two charter flights a month to Tel Aviv to complement the twice-a-week commercial flights.

Such aggressive recruitment clearly has worked in the past, but there are signs it is beginning to backfire. "The majority of Israelis who are here have had an attitude. They walk around as though Ukraine and the former Soviet Union are their colonies, and they have come to repatriate their poor brothers," says Rabbi David Wilfond of the World Union for Progressive Judaism. "Most Jews here think the Israelis are very disrespectful and condescending. The Soviet Union was one of the most powerful nations in the world, and its people now are nationally depressed. The great former Soviet Union was broken into fifteen post-Soviet states and little Israel suddenly is dictating to them. There is a lot of resentment."

Aliza Shenhar, the president of Emek Yezreel College in Haifa and Israel's ambassador to Russia from 1994 to 1997, also thinks the Jewish state has a tendency to push too hard in places like Dnepropetrovsk. "This colonistic approach, I don't like it," she says. "It's not our duty to tell them what to do. I wish to see them come to Israel but it's going to be their choice. Our duty, as Jewish people, is to help them. To help them re-create their Jewishness, first and foremost. They have to decide where they're going to live."

Many who had the choice in the early days opted for the United States. When it closed its doors in 1989 they started choosing Germany. That was partly because the social benefits there were more generous than in Israel and the lifestyle was less stressful. Dnepropetrovsk Jews who moved to Düsseldorf say they also were worried that while the Israeli government was pushing hard for them to come, average Israelis think of them as freeloaders and doubt whether they really are Jewish.

Whether or not it likes all the ways it is being reached out to, the Jewish community of Dnepropetrovsk understands the impact and is now doing outreach of its own. With support from an Argentine businessman, Shmuel has launched the Institute for Jewish Leaders. Seventeen young Jewish men from the area are taking a two- to three-year course that will let them perform circumcisions and funerals for Jews in outlying areas that do not have rabbis. The students also provide instruction in how to celebrate Purim, Sukkoth, and Passover, how to put on tefillin and put up mezuzahs, and in general what it means to be a Jew in communities where the Jewish population can be as small as 5 or as large as 3,000.

"We don't prepare rabbis, we prepare 'mini-rabbis,' " explains Elicha Baram, the thirty-four-year-old rabbi from Israel who runs the training program. "These people won't have the diplomas people studying in America and Israel might have, but they'll have more than enough knowledge for those small towns. They will be able to show people there all the things connected with Judaism, starting from birth and, God forbid, ending with death. As we are in the center of this region, we assume the mission of telling those other cities about Jewishness, about our traditions, our history, our language."

* * *

The Beit Baruch Jewish Center was the focal point for the Jewish community of Dnepropetrovsk through the 1990s. It was also a metaphor for how far the community had come and all that remained for it to do. The complex, which housed the synagogue, the rabbi's office, and a communal kitchen, got a major face-lift after the Soviet Union crumbled in 1991. The pine benches in the shul were rebuilt. There was an ark of brown wood with gold trim, and purple velvet brightened the pulpit. There were two air conditioners to battle oppressive summer heat and modern heating so bitter-cold winters no longer would force worshipers to the warmth of a tiny stove in the balcony. Huge kettles of soup were always on in the kitchen, which served the old and poor more than 200 hot meals a day, and the rabbi was almost always holding court in his office. Music wafted through the complex as the seniors' choir practiced for a holiday concert, and old people lined the alleyway on their way to Yiddish Club or Torah study, or just gathered to gossip and maybe offer a quick prayer. None of which would have been imaginable a decade before, when the synagogue was in tatters, without a rabbi or a real congregation.

Yet the Jews there had far more daring dreams than could be realized in the ramshackle Beit Baruch complex. It was a wonderful way station, a place to begin the process of reawakening from a seventy-year-long nightmare of socialist secularism, and it is still used for rabbinical classes and the soup kitchen. But the Jews of Dnepropetrovsk felt that the proper metaphor for their future, for the future of a thriving community of as many as 50,000 Jews, was the majestic Golden Rose Choral Synagogue.

The Golden Rose was the grandest synagogue in Dnepropetrovsk in the days when there were forty-three synagogues there, but it was shuttered with the rest and until 1996 was used as a warehouse by the clothing factory next door. The building is now back in the hands of the

Jewish community, a gift from the government, and it has been dramatically redesigned, a gift from architect Alexander Dolnik. In its new incarnation the house of worship includes a gargantuan dome that captures the enormity of the universe, propped up by twelve mammoth columns corresponding to Israel's twelve tribes. All the building blocks are granite, polished black or rough-cut white, colors that Dolnik chose so as not to distract from the eternal themes of the synagogue itself. Scenes from Israel are interspersed with ones from Egypt, reflecting the passages of the Jewish people. Taken as a whole, the interior looks like an Italian marble chess set, writ large. There is comfortable seating for 500, with 2,000 able to squeeze in for the High Holidays and other special occasions.

The very fact that the community could complete such a magnificent synagogue, with a price tag of $1.5 million and a design that seems better suited to Beverly Hills or Fifth Avenue, is a sign of how far it has come in its vision. Not to mention its fund-raising. Shmuel says he understands concerns that such a glamorous edifice is inappropriate and perhaps even offensive for a city so poor, but he believes the new synagogue will be uplifting for the Jews of Dnepropetrovsk. "I was going to build just a plain room that fit many people," he recounts. "But then came my people, my sponsors, my board of directors. They said to me, 'We live in very nice homes. The cars we drive are very nice. We want our shul to be very nice. It can't be that the shul looks worse than our homes.' Each promised $100,000, $80,000, $50,000.

"On the one hand you can say we should give it to the poor people, we have so many poor people. But these sponsors are also helping the poor. The condition I set is that our sponsors can give to the shul but that shouldn't come instead of money they are obligated to give as members. I am not going to be the one to say to them 'no.' "

The new synagogue is one of several bold projects under way in the Jewish world of Dnepropetrovsk. There is a new four-story Jewish community center with a library and Internet club behind the Golden Rose, a new home for children with special needs, and a new kindergarten for 200 children. A $10 million Jewish medical center is due to be completed soon, as is an old-age home able to house 100 and with a design, as Shmuel says, "like a five-star hotel." Funding for those projects comes, as always, from eclectic sources, including the U.S. Treasury, the

Brooklyn-based Global Jewish Assistance and Relief Network, and wealthy individuals from around the world.

Taken together, the synagogue and other new developments reflect not only the confidence that the community could raise the needed funds, but the assurance that it will continue to grow and prosper. To many, that seems like wishful and wasteful thinking.

Anti-Semitism remains a persistent worry in Dnepropetrovsk, especially for those who have seen for themselves the havoc wreaked by pogroms and the Holocaust. In recent years Ukrainian nationalists have become more outspoken and more anti-Semitic, and vandals painted a swastika on the old synagogue and defaced the gate to Beit Baruch. The president of the community got calls telling him to "get your Jews out of there," and congregants tell of people in the streets urging them to "go back to Israel." Shmuel was accosted once walking home from synagogue by a man yelling taunts about Hitler, which made him so angry that, as Chany recalls, "he smacked the man. He hit him so hard and the man was so big." And Dolnik recently was badly beaten, although his attackers were apparently more interested in his money than his faith.

There is a sense that, while officials pay deference these days to Jews, they are still slow to acknowledge sins of the past. The likeness of Cossack chief Khmelnytsky still adorns vodka bottles, despite the offense that causes Jews. And until recently the only public remembrance of the Nazis' Sukkoth massacre was a Soviet-era plaque that pays tribute not to the 11,000 fallen Jews, but to the more generalized "victims of fascism." The Jewish community protested for years and, in 2000, finally succeeded in constructing its own monument to its murdered forebears.

There are also questions about whether the pace of emigration will slow, whether the most committed Jews will continue to predominate among those who are leaving, and whether hidden Jews will keep emerging to replace them. About whether, as they become more religious, Jews will find it easier than it has been to do serious Torah studies in Dnepropetrovsk and to find kosher foods. And about whether those who are less observant will finally be free to form their own communities of Reform or Conservative Jews. Most chilling of all is the uncertainty over whether the stuttering economy will ever get into gear and, if it fails to, what will happen to Jews' relative wealth and their sense of physical and financial security. Ukrainian Jews already face a depressing death-to-birth rate of 10 to 1, which is a reflection of the facts that their average age is fifty-six, medical care is declining even as infant mortality remains high, and parents who stay do not have sufficient money or confidence in the future to have many children. Meanwhile, upward of 50 percent of Jews there—possibly as high as 80 percent—marry non-Jews. And whereas Jews accounted for 9 percent of the Ukrainian population at the end of the nineteenth century, by the end of the twentieth they made up less than 1 percent.

It is the generation now coming of age that will answer those questions, says Zvi Gitelman, a professor of Judaic Studies at the University of Michigan who has been exploring such issues since the early 1960s. "Today there are around 10,000 young people in the former Soviet Union studying either in a Jewish day school or a supplementary Jewish school," he says. "Much of what happens in the future depends on whether they stay or leave. If they stay, they will be the core of a relatively well-educated, viable Jewish community. If they leave, the Jewish communities are likely to disappear. These young people's decision will depend on quite a few variables, including the situation in Israel and the Middle East. If that is volatile, or there is an economic downturn, emigration will decline. If Russia and Ukraine become more stable and prosperous the likelihood is that emigration will go down, these people will stay, and they will form a cadre of knowledgeable leaders and Jews."

Betsy Gidwitz, who has spent almost as long as Gitelman chronicling Soviet Jewry, is not sanguine: "I think it's all going to end up like Romania. Rabbi Moses Rosen was a towering figure there who for many years worked very diligently to send all Romanian Jews to Israel. When he died there were about fourteen thousand Jews left there. I understand that about twelve thousand remain now, about half of them in Bucharest and the other half scattered in more than forty other cities and towns around the country. The few young who still live there are leaving and within decades it probably will be down to zero. This is what I think will happen in Ukraine and in Russia, although the process will take longer because the base number is much higher. Certainly, current demographic figures give no reason for optimism that a significant Jewish community can be sustained into the long-term future."

For every measure of doubt, however, there is a dose of hope. A pride in what the community has built, a Jewish nationalism of sorts, is at least as much of a defining force in Dnepropetrovsk these days as its long-held pride in the accomplishments of the State of Israel. Jews hold seven of eighty seats on the city council, although only two have last names that clearly mark them as Jewish. Hundreds of children are attending Jewish day schools, and the local chapter of the campus Hillel program has fifty members, most of whom say they plan to stay in Dnepropetrovsk. Shmuel has eighteen rabbis working under him now— teaching, leading religious services across the countryside, or meticulously copying the scriptures that will be inserted into mezuzahs and attached to the doorposts of Jewish homes. It is easier these days to find kosher chicken and beef, and to find Jews who care. It is easier to get a Coke and a telephone that works, and Ukraine continues to be the third-largest recipient of U.S. assistance, trailing only Israel and Egypt.

Ukrainian society also shows signs of growing tolerance. Jewish and non-Jewish scholars are finally beginning to face up to Ukraine's incomparably brutal record of persecuting its Jews—and to put that oppression in the context of wider social upheaval. Leading politicians are making clear that anti-Jewish agitation no longer will be condoned. Anti-Semitism lingers, but it is far less prevalent than in Russia and surveys suggest that most Ukrainians see Jews as deserving members of the post-Soviet world they are trying to build. Among some segments of society, it actually is "in" to be Jewish today in Dnepropetrovsk much the way it is in Düsseldorf.

"Previously being a Jew was a shame mark, today it's prestigious," says Dolnik, the architect. "It's because of the great success of Jews in finance and trade. Many people who had no relation to Jews up until right now are trying to find some relation. It's like the period of the bureaucracies of old where they were trying to find some blue blood."

The same thing is happening in other cities across the old Soviet Union, in big ones like Kiev and Moscow and midsized ones like Kharkov and Odessa. One hundred and fifty libraries of Judaica have sprung up across the former Soviet Union. Ukraine alone now boasts 243 communities with at least some Jews, and a dozen with major Jewish populations. "Not all of them are going to come to Israel," says Aliza Shenhar, Israel's ambassador to Russia in the mid-1990s. "Jews are going to stay. They are going to create their own communities. It's not the father or grandfather who is teaching the children about Judaism, it's the children who join the kindergarten who are teaching their grandparents. That's happening in the diaspora in general, but in Russia it's really remarkable."

What also is remarkable is how Dnepropetrovsk has distinguished itself among all the Jewish success stories in the former Soviet Union. Moscow, Kiev, and other communities have made impressive strides, but they are also plagued by problems, from squabbling within to resistance from outside. If any Jewish population there has a chance to survive and thrive it is Dnepropetrovsk's, with its history of defying the odds, its charismatic rabbi from Brooklyn, and its backing from places like Boston. Mark Shlyak knows the challenges facing Jews there, especially wealthy, successful ones like him. Tanned and carefully coifed, he drives an oversized Mercedes and wears a black polo shirt, tailored blue pants, and black suede shoes that would make him at home in the Hamptons. He also has enough money to build a comfortable life in America or Israel, Germany or Canada, but he plans to stay in Dnepropetrovsk. "The position of the Jews here, and the authority of the Jews, is higher now than anytime before," says Shlyak, who is a member of the synagogue board.

"We can't stop emigration. I like the Jewish state and think the return of Jews to their historical model is a big step and a great step. But the strength and influence of the Jewish people today is mainly explained by the fact that they live across the world and that they are influencing the way other countries believe and live. The task of helping the diaspora, of creating conditions in the diaspora that will let communities like this flower again, is not any less important than Jews immigrating to Israel. We want to make sure that Jews here are not any less happy than Jews in the Holy Land of Israel."

Chapter 3

BOSTON:

Athens and Jerusalem

I am an imposter.

Although the name on the cover of this book reads Larry Tye, my real name is Larry Tikotsky. Or at least Tikotsky is the name my father was born with and that I should have inherited. But it was a name that in Depression-era Boston—a city flooded with immigrants and none too sure how it felt about them—was a problem. Just how much of one became apparent when my father applied to college in 1935. Mauray Joel Tikotsky was editor-in-chief of *The Brown & Gold* at Haverhill High, an A student, and confident enough that he applied just to the school he wanted to attend—Tufts University. Tufts, however, said no. The sticking point was not his academic record or his extracurricular activities. It was his religion. My father was Jewish, and Tufts, like many colleges back then, was worried about being overrun with Jews. So it set limits, and Mauray Tikotsky was rejected. Tufts eventually reversed itself after the principal at Haverhill High, Arlington I. Clow, threatened never to send another student its way. My father enrolled and graduated four years later. But the message had gotten through to my grandmother, a savvy, stubborn lady reared on the Texas frontier: having a manifestly Jewish name like Tikotsky could be a serious liability.

The incident at Tufts might not have weighed so heavily on Minnie Tikotsky if it were the only one. Her last name, however, seemed to lend itself to bigotry. There was the neighborhood bully who insisted on calling her middle son "Isaac" although he knew his name was Raymond. There was the way non-Jewish mothers along Fountain Street let their children play with Mauray, Raymond, and her youngest son, David, but would not invite them in with the other kids for milk and cookies. Most of all there was the fear that carrying around a foreign-sounding surname like Tikotsky might threaten my father's dream of becoming a doctor and his brothers' hopes for getting out of Haverhill, which while it was just an hour outside of Boston seemed to them like a dreadfully small dead-end town.

So in 1936, in a move she rightfully predicted would be read as a declaration of war by her mother-in-law, Minnie convinced her husband, Joseph, that they should legally change the family's name from the burdensome Tikotsky to the benign Tye. Over the years other Tikotskys did the same, knowing some would see them as denying their religion and culture, but also knowing that they cherished their Judaism whatever they were called. Tye was the logical choice because it was what Americans who could not pronounce Tikotsky had always called them. And Tikotsky may not have been the sacred family inheritance that Minnie's mother-in-law made it out to be. My great-grandfather was a Tikotsky but his brother, who moved to Detroit, was named Kosofsky, which might have been the original family name or could have been a takeoff on the tiny town of Kosovo in Poland where they all came from.

That sort of shaping and shaving of proud old Ashkenazic and Sephardic names became so common as to be a rite of passage at many doorways to America. Sometimes it was immigration officials at Ellis Island who did the butchering, writing into the records their imprecise rendering of what the foreign-speaking new arrivals said. Other times it was done in transit, with the ship's crew doing the best it could to prepare arrival lists. Immigrants themselves also often decided to take on a new identity as they entered the New World, casting off their East European appellation for one of the neat, trim American ones they might have heard someone else use. Then there was the shortening that Jews like my grandparents did years after arriving, having seen firsthand how an ethnic identity severely constricted their opportunities in Boston, which despite its progressive reputation could be especially cruel to new-comers. So Rabinovitz became Rabb. Israel became Allen. And Tikotsky became Tye, a monosyllabic, ethnically vanilla name that people who do not know me assume is Chinese, Irish, or mere mongrel.

But if Boston had a history of oppression, it also had a history of Jewish achievement and advancement that rivaled that of any city in America. It was the city that produced or nurtured crusading Jewish jurists like Louis D. Brandeis and Felix Frankfurter, brilliant rabbinic scholars like Joseph B. Soloveitchik, and gifted Jewish artists like Leonard Bernstein and Arthur Fiedler. It gave birth to America's fin-est Jewish-oriented university, Brandeis, and its first Jewish federation, now known as the Combined Jewish Philanthropies. Just as the roiling of social stresses in the wider community at times spilled over into rancor toward Jews, so the Jewish community oftentimes mirrored the best of Boston. It was passionate about academic excellence. It rel-ished pushing old limits and trying new approaches. It believed that ethnic neighborhoods and identities were traits to be preserved rather than purged.

My family shared in those opportunities even more than it had in the injustices. My father graduated from Tufts Medical School and returned to Haverhill to open a dermatology practice and raise a family. He was a leader in promoting social justice in the Jewish and general commu-nities, and drove into Boston once a week for forty-five years to teach at Boston City, the hospital for the poor. At the time of his death in 1995 he may have been the most universally admired man in the Haver-hill area, which is why his obituary was the lead story in the next day's newspaper. Everyone who knew him also knew, despite his nondescript name, that he was a Jew.

My mother's life also has embodied the social forces swirling around Jews of her generation. Dorothy Tye grew up in Portland, Maine, in the 1920s, in a family whose roots traced back through eight generations of scholarly rabbis. Her last name in those days was Rubinoff, a proud Jewish name brought over from Lithuania and kept intact in America. At home, my mother lit Sabbath candles, hosted enormous Seders, kept a kosher kitchen, and pushed us to date fellow Jews. She was a leader at our synagogue and in the Jewish communities of Haverhill and Bos-ton, alongside my father. And like him she worried about the flattening of Jewish culture that seemed to be under way in America in the 1970s and '80s, which was brought into stark relief in 1990 by a national study showing that the intermarriage rate had reached an alarming 52 percent.

Today, Boston finds itself on the cusp of a wave of Jewish renewal. It has articulated more clearly than any city in America the three foundations of the new Jewish identity: learning, spirituality, and social justice. It is backing its talk with bold action, from pioneering a two-year, hundred-hour program of adult education that is reaching thousands, to engineering a Jewish secondary school that proves Reform, Conservative, and Orthodox youth can thrive in the sort of pluralistic setting that too often eludes their parents. Synagogues are collaborating with the Jewish federation rather than quarreling with it the way they do in so many American cities. Rabbis are embracing converts and potential converts, along with gays and grays. Even as Jews continue moving to outlying suburbs, many are reengaging with the inner city and launching alliances with blacks, Irish, and Hispanics.

Why there, and why now? It is partly the unusual coming together of creative, articulate leaders at colleges, communal institutions, and synagogues. But over time every city gets the leaders it deserves, and that one, with its heritage of experimentation and rootedness in education, has demanded creativity and vision as a condition of employment. The setting also helps. Boston is big enough to pull together the people and money needed to test new ways of defining Judaism, yet small enough to avoid the rancor that can make the Jews of New York or Chicago seem more like a series of factions than a unified community. The thousands of Jewish students who pour into Boston every autumn keep its wider Jewish community thinking and acting young. And having so many breathtaking beaches and compelling cultural offerings was a big reason why people like my parents stayed, while being more than a bit arrogant makes the city's Jewish community, like all its others, simply assume it belongs at the cutting edge.

What Boston Jews are aiming for, as Brandeis historian Jonathan Sarna says, is to weave together what is best of Boston and Judaism— of Athens and Jerusalem. "The problem in the American Jewish community," he explains, "is that the great causes of the twentieth century are now behind us, whether it is fighting anti-Semitism, defending immigrants, bringing Jews out of the diaspora in places like the Soviet Union and Ethiopia where they were in big trouble, and most important, sustaining the State of Israel.

"Boston is way ahead of the curve in trying to find alternative sources of meaning. There is an explosion of learning here at all levels, a real sense that meaning is to be found internally, that the future begins at home. Synagogues allow for the full range of expressions of Judaism, from spirituality and *havurah* and new age all the way to the traditional. You get a good sense of all the options in Judaism today by looking here in Boston."

* * *

In its early days the Boston Jewish community was defined mainly by what it was *not*.

It was not big, which is surprising. The first Jew landed in 1649, but Solomon Franco lasted less than three months before heading back to Holland. Others came over the next 200 years, but like Franco they seldom stayed long. The problem was that Boston's agricultural economy had little to offer commerce-minded Jewish immigrants, its Puritan founding fathers did not welcome other religions, and while Boston was the most populous city on the Eastern seaboard until 1760, it was not a major stop on the transatlantic trade route that immigrants tended to follow. The result: during the 1700s and early 1800s, when Jews were settling in coastal cities like New York and Newport, Savannah, Baltimore, and Charleston, Boston was the only major colonial seaport that did not have a permanent Jewish community.

Boston also was not very German. When enough Jews did come to form a real community in the 1840s there were far fewer Germans, proportionally, than in places like New York and San Francisco. They largely bypassed Boston because its politics and neighborhoods seemed to belong to the Irish, it was still recovering from the War of 1812 and the Revolutionary War, and the wide-open West and South were more alluring to Jewish peddlers and merchants. Most Jews who arrived in the mid-1800s were Polish, coming especially from Posen, a part of Poland annexed by Prussia. Most were also poor, which meant Boston lacked the cadre of well-heeled German Jews that had formed by then in places like New York, offering forceful leadership and the money to back it up.

But their small numbers and the lack of a large German base meant that when Jewish immigrants from Eastern European began to flood there in the late 1870s, Boston did not have nearly as many of the internal tensions that plagued Jewish communities from Paris to Atlanta. The new arrivals generally spoke Yiddish like the old arrivals, and shared an East European outlook, so it is not surprising that the 5,000 Jews who were already there rallied more quickly than in many places to help the 35,000 who arrived during the last two decades of the nineteenth century. The Eastern Europeans were also typically quicker to embrace Zionism than more established German Jews, which helps explain why Boston emerged as an early center of American Zionist activity and engendered little of the anti-Zionist sentiment seen in cities with bigger German-Jewish populations.

That does not mean that Jews had an easy time of it in Boston. As the community doubled from 40,000 in 1900 to 80,000 in 1920, and grew again to 115,000 on the eve of World War II, conflicts emerged. Larger numbers meant less unity, and antagonisms inevitably arose between rich Jews and poor ones, as well as among Reform, Conservative, and Orthodox. The most troubling tensions of all, now that Jews accounted for just over 10 percent of Boston's population, were the ones between the "Israelites" and the Gentiles who surrounded them in the city of the bean and the cod.

The Yankees, for one, were hardly welcoming. Men with chiseled faces, Protestant faith, and Anglo-Saxon surnames like Lodge and Cabot, Forbes and Peabody, ruled the city's social, financial, and cultural institutions. They saw Boston as the "City on the Hill," a shining beacon for colonial America. They may have been forced by the sheer power of numbers to cede control of politics to the Irish, but that merely hardened their resolve not to relinquish other perquisites of power to the newer immigrants, especially Jewish ones. So they closed ranks and erected barriers. They saw to it that Jews were not admitted to their country clubs, allowed to check in at their country inns, or added to their social register. They promoted literacy tests for immigrants and opposed Brandeis's nomination to the Supreme Court. They kept Jews out of banking and bow-tie law firms, consolidated their power in state government, and retired to the privacy of their social clubs to make critical decisions about everything from Boston real estate to Boston finances and Boston charities. Not all the Yankees were anti-Jewish, of course, but a surprising number were who should have known better. Essayist Ralph Waldo Emerson depicted Jews as usurers and conspirators, writer and critic James Russell Lowell worried that they were plotting to take over the world, and, while he later learned better, poet Oliver Wendell Holmes grew up in a home where it was believed that the Jewish people were "a race lying under a curse for their obstinacy in refusing the gospel."

Boston was not alone in its anti-Semitism, but its version was especially virulent. No less an authority than soon-to-be Justice Brandeis, upset by his exclusion from several of Boston's prestigious clubs, observed in 1914 that "anti-Semitism seems to have reached its American pinnacle here."

One need look no further than Harvard, that most Brahmin of Boston institutions and Brandeis's alma mater, to understand what the esteemed jurist was upset about. The ranks of Jewish undergraduates grew steadily, from 7 percent in 1900 to 21.5 percent in 1921, as they were welcomed and nourished during the forty year reign of President Charles Eliot that ended in 1909. Yet that surge in Jewish enrollment worried many, including Eliot's successor, A. Lawrence Lowell, who in the early 1920s pushed for restrictive quotas. "Hebrews" applying to transfer to Harvard should "be rejected except such applicants [as] be possessed of extraordinary intellectual capacity together with character above criticism," Lowell wrote, while for normal applications "all doubtful or line cases shall be investigated with the nicest care, and that such of this number as belong to the Hebrew race shall be rejected except in unusual and special cases." Although most of Lowell's head-on attacks were headed off, the admissions committee turned to geographic limits and special scrutiny of "character" to keep out the Jews it had targeted with religious quotas.

"I played football and we all were buddy-buddy, Jews and non-Jews—but only until five-thirty," at which point each went his own way to eat and socialize, recalls Irving Rabb, who graduated from Harvard in 1934 and eventually joined a family supermarket business that grew into the huge Stop & Shop chain. David Pokross, who graduated in

1927, says he and his fellow Jewish students knew that President Lowell was laboring to limit their numbers, and that Jews could not be elected to class offices or class committees. He also knew it was no accident that "when I came to Harvard I was assigned four roommates, all Jews." Pokross, who went on to Harvard Law School and a partnership at Peabody & Brown, a leading Boston law firm, adds that "all my friends at Harvard were Jewish, all my activities were with Jewish friends. I had Jewish girlfriends at Radcliffe. I had very little, if any, contact with non-Jews. There were very many non-Jewish clubs that Jews couldn't get in; on the other hand, there were at least four or five Jewish fraternities. You had these two worlds, Jewish and non-Jewish, going on all the time."

Interactions with the Irish were even more problematic. The main battle line in Boston back then was the one between the Yankees and the Irish. Jews and Irish, by contrast, were listed side by side among those who "need not apply" to Brahmin bastions of ascendancy, and they often lived in the same tenement-studded sections of the city, which could have bred intimacy and camaraderie. More often it meant a fierce friction. They competed for turf and put one another down as they tried to pull themselves up in this not-always-golden land of opportunity. Most of all they fought over faith, with all the emphasis on the differences rather than the similarities between Catholicism and the Judaism that spawned it. Yet while antagonisms ran high on both sides, it was not a fair fight since the Irish generally had arrived in Boston earlier, outnumbered Jews by about a five-to-one ratio, and controlled such critical institutions as City Hall and the police and fire departments. The Irish knew their real enemy was the Yankees, but they were tough to strike out at, so Irish Bostonians often took out their frustrations on the more easily accessible and more vulnerable Jews.

"We were an enclave surrounded by Irish," journalist and author Theodore H. White wrote of growing up in Boston's Dorchester section in the 1920s and '30s. "To the south of us, across the railway tracks, lived very tough Irish—working-class Irish. The local library lay in such an Irish district, and my first fights happened en route to the library, to get books. Pure hellishness divided us, but after one last bloody-nose battle, I was given safe passage by the Irish boys whenever I went to the library."

White may have made his peace, but tensions between Boston's Irish and Jews became even more inflamed during the Depression, thanks in part to Father Charles E. Coughlin, the radio priest from Royal Oak, Michigan. Just as Hitler was undertaking his *Anschluss* in Austria in 1938, Coughlin was emerging as America's most vociferous and venerated Jew-baiter. He published selections from the anti-Semitic *Protocols of the Elders of Zion*, defended Nazi assaults on Jews during the infamous *Kristallnacht*, blamed Jews for imposing communism on Russia, and launched his own quasi-military, pro-fascist organization called the Christian Front. While the priest's appeals were nationwide, Boston, in the eyes of its own mayor, the legendary James Michael Curley, was "the strongest Coughlinite city in America." And while not all Boston Catholics or Irish followed the anti-Jewish cleric, his newspaper, *Social Justice*, was sold outside many Boston churches, and police there not only tolerated the anti-Semitic tirades of Coughlin's followers but at times they actually joined in.

Pokross, who is now ninety-three, recalls the Coughlin era as "one of the most horrendous periods of my life. My wife and I used to listen every Sunday to broadcasts of his tirades. I remember so vividly how I was trembling. I was actually trembling. I felt this terrible man was rousing people and we could have manifestly overt action against Jews. He was horrible, but he was a very, very effective speaker, unfortunately."

In the late 1940s Boston got its own version of Coughlin in the form of a Jesuit priest from Cambridge. Father Leonard Feeney stirred up his loyalists with sermons on the Boston Common deriding Jews as "degenerate, hook-nosed perverts," and he encouraged attacks against young Jews in Dorchester. But the times had changed, and Feeney attracted a considerably narrower following than Coughlin had. It was partly that the spirit of conciliation between Catholics and non-Catholics simply had too much momentum by then. Even more telling, Richard Cushing, Boston's charismatic new archbishop, was making ecumenism a centerpiece of his reign and was not about to be derailed by the emotionally unstable priest from Cambridge. The cardinal saw to it that Feeney was banished from the Jesuit order and later excommunicated from the Church. Cushing, an Irish-American from the heavily Irish neighborhood of South Boston, did not stop there as he opened dialogues between Catholics and Jews, urged an end to anti-Semitism, touted the fact that his own sister had married a Jew, whom he called "the best Christian I know," and helped defuse decades of antagonism between Boston's Irish and Jewish communities. By the time Cushing died in 1970, relations between Jews and Irish in Boston, and Jews and Catholics generally, were being cited as a model for conciliation rather than a case study in conflict.

The rise and fall of anti-Semitism was one in a series of developments that substantially reshaped life for Boston Jews during the 1900s. Another was their movement first within the city, then between city and suburbs, migrations that transformed not just where they lived but how.

It all started in the South End, adjacent to the Boston Common and just down the street from the State House, in what today is the high-rent theater district. In the 1840s it was a nondescript neighborhood with just under 20,000 residents, most white and native-born, who barely noticed the hundred or so Jewish peddlers and merchants settling in after arriving from Germany and Poland. They chose that spot because it was close to the city center and inexpensive, and in 1843 they inaugurated Boston's first Jewish congregation, Ohabei Shalom. Two more synagogues sprouted in the neighborhood over the next twenty years, as the city's Jewish population swelled to more than 2,000. Some Jewish South Enders had begun to prosper, especially those in the clothing trade, and as always prosperity made it tempting to move away from the unwashed immigrants who were moving in and escape to quieter, more refined surroundings. In this case that meant a mile up the road to the "upper" South End, a neighborhood bordered by the Back Bay, South Boston, and Massachusetts Avenue and featuring brick bowfront town houses that until recently had been occupied by the city's Yankee elite. It was there that the Central Europeans built more ornate houses of worship commensurate with their rising status and launched the Boston Young Men's Hebrew Association, which served as everything from health club to job service and social center.

Across town in the North End a very different Jewish community was taking shape, made up mainly of Russians and East Europeans. In 1880 the neighborhood of tenements and narrow, crowded streets was still mainly Irish, but by 1895 it had 7,700 Italians and 6,200 Jews, along with a melange of Germans, Portuguese, and Poles. The streets sounded like a Tower of Babel as mothers leaned out of windows, hollering to their children in a medley of languages. The smells were as perplexing as they were appetizing, with Old World aromas wafting out of restaurants and apartments. A passerby might be tempted by barrels of ripe apples and pickles, or turned off by carts of foul-smelling fish. Looking back it seems alluring, but to the newly arrived Jewish immigrants it often felt confusing and frightening. They responded by founding institutions that made them feel at home. They opened Orthodox shuls and burial societies, brought in kosher butcher shops and a Matzo Baking Co., and organized sewing circles and basketball teams. Over time prosperous North Enders did what their fellow Jews in the South End were doing: they moved up but not very far out, to the adjacent and less huddled West End. By 1905 the North End's Jewish population had slipped to 4,700, and by 1920 almost everyone was gone. In the West End, meanwhile, the numbers were climbing, surpassing the North End as Boston's biggest Jewish district by 1895 and reaching 24,000 as of 1910.

Moves like those were not unique to Jews. The Brahmins also were picking up and moving, as were the Irish, Italians, and blacks, sometimes in search of greener and more homogeneous surroundings, sometimes because they were pushed out by those waiting to move in. The Jews, however, migrated more than most. While they might pass Brahmins or Irish on the road, they were headed to different places, ones with a distinctively Jewish flavor. That is what happened with the next great migration to the adjacent neighborhoods of Roxbury, Dorchester, and Mattapan, which in those years were "streetcar suburbs" but today are considered inner city. The move began in the late 1890s and picked up steam just after the turn of the century, fueled mainly by Eastern European Jews anxious to escape the congested neighborhoods of the North and West Ends and the equally bustling streets of Chelsea, a working-class city north of Boston. By the late 1920s there were 77,000 Jews in the Roxbury region, or half the entire Jewish population of Greater Boston, and as of 1950 there still were 70,000. Grand new synagogues were constructed, kosher butchers and bakers lined the wide and grand Blue Hill Avenue for three long miles, and, even more than the earlier enclaves of the North, West, and South Ends, Roxbury-Dorchester-Mattapan was a vibrant, close-knit world where Jewish cultural and religious life thrived as never before in Boston.

That golden era was short-lived. Wealthier Jews had moved there from the center city in search of single-family homes and a more serene middle-class existence. As their less affluent coreligionists followed, the large homes were transformed into tenement-like apartments, quiet streets gave way to bazaars selling everything from herring to unplucked chickens, and what was suburban looked more and more urban and less and less appealing. Some left as early as 1920, although the mass exodus did not begin for another thirty years, with the Jewish population slipping from 70,000 in 1950 to 47,000 in 1960, 16,000 in 1970, and just a few hundred by the late 1970s. Rather than being the ultimate destination that its early inhabitants dreamed of, Roxbury, Dorchester, and Mattapan became, as historian Gerald Gamm notes, "the belt that connected Boston Jewry's immigrant past to its suburban future." Many older Boston Jews still mourn that movement, feeling they were forced out of their homes and neighborhoods as large numbers of blacks moved in. There is a common conception that real-estate agents and bankers conspired to push blacks into Mattapan as a way of scaring off Jews and leading to a massive, profitable turnover of their housing—and that certainly is part of what happened with the older and poorer Jews still there in the late 1960s and early '70s. But by then most of the rest of the Jewish community had gone, nearly all of them voluntarily. A better way of understanding Roxbury, Dorchester, and Mattapan's transformation, Gamm says, is to see it as "a prototypical characteristic of American Jews that makes them different from other diaspora Jews: the disposability of Jewish communities. They live in one place, then move into better neighborhoods. They shut down one synagogue and build a new one."

The next big move was out to the real suburbs, and the first one they picked was Brookline. It was a natural choice, lying just half a mile east of Fenway Park and a few feet from Roxbury, with good schools, tree-lined streets, and, according to a 1907 edition of the *Boston Evening Transcript*, qualifying as "the richest town in the entire world." The migration there began as a trickle at the turn of the century, with just 1,000 Jews in 1920, but by 1940 there were 14,000 and in 1960, 26,500. Jews also were relocating to Allston and Brighton, two Boston neighborhoods adjacent to Brookline that had 4,000 Jews in 1930 and 14,500 by 1960. The flow to affluent Newton began a bit later, although by the

1930s it was at least as much a magnet as Brookline and Brighton for middle- and upper-middle-class Jewish families who wanted a way out of Roxbury, Dorchester, Mattapan, and Chelsea. In 1960 Newton had 27,000 Jews—500 more than Brookline and almost twice as many as Allston and Brighton. The dispersion continued outward during the 1960s, '70s, and '80s, with tens of thousands of Jews moving north to communities like Swampscott and Marblehead, west to Belmont, Lexington, and Framingham, and south to Randolph, Milton, and Sharon.

The move to the suburbs was more than just a change of scenery. Jews went from living in close-packed urban neighborhoods to widely dispersed residential ones. Where Roxbury-Dorchester-Mattapan was once home to one in every two Boston area Jews, Newton at its height housed just one in seven. To sense his Jewish surroundings, all a Jewish immigrant in the North End in 1900 had to do was stick his head out the tenement window or stroll up the street past Jewish vendors and Jewish buildings. In Newton, by contrast, he would need a car and several hours to reach the Jewish butcher shop, bagel factory, and book store on Harvard Street in Brookline, to stop by the synagogue in one part of Newton and the JCC in another, and to drop his children off at their grandparents' in Malden or stop by the federation building in downtown Boston. The migration to the suburbs brought space and comfort, but it also brought fragmentation and disconnectedness.

Herb Savitz was part of that migration. He was born in Chelsea in 1925, and grew up in a world where "being Jewish just hit us in the face, we took it for granted. We thought everyone there was Jewish in the thirties and forties, we had no Gentile friends. We walked to Talmud Torah where we went to Hebrew school. We could walk easily to five synagogues, they were all around us. There were Jewish markets, places like Promisel's grocery store, and there must have been twenty-five kosher butcher shops. The corner druggist was Jewish, the mom-and-pop store was Jewish." In Newton and Brookline, where Savitz lived from 1951 to 1962, there again were lots of Jews but not the same Jewish street life. The tony suburb of Weston, his next home, had neither. "A lot of my friends told me not to move there because they heard people in certain areas of Weston wouldn't sell to Jews," recalls Savitz, who is now seventy-five. "I was a little concerned."

Were Jewish continuity and community possible in the new sea of suburbs? That is a question Jews there have been asking ever since their early migrations from one inner-city neighborhood to another, and that assumed new urgency after the move to and from Roxbury-Dorchester-Mattapan. The answers they arrived at, through a combination of careful planning and patching together solutions as they went, helped define Boston as a Jewish community unlike any other.

Part of the solution lay in centralized institutions, although they never have been a central part of the American Jewish tradition. There are no chief rabbis like in Europe and much of the rest of the diaspora to lay out rules or clarify rituals, no archdioceses like Irish Catholics count on to coordinate or help pay for opening or closing houses of worship. Faced with that vacuum, and with a swelling tide of impoverished immigrants, Boston Jews filled it in a way that became a model for Jews and non-Jews nationwide. In 1895 they consolidated the Hebrew Ladies Sewing Society, Free Employment Bureau, Charitable Burial Association, Leopold Morse Home for the Aged and Infirm Hebrews and Orphanage, and the United Hebrew Benevolent Society. The new entity, called the Federation of Jewish Charities of Boston, launched the movement of federations that now exist in every major Jewish community in America.

Looking backward the logic of joining forces seems compelling, if only to eliminate duplication, coordinate the painful process of raising money, and present a common front against the Brahmins and Irish. But each group had its own leaders and distinct constituents, and giving all that up was anything but easy. It happened mainly because Boston's neophyte community of Jews, 14,000 of 20,000 of whom were new immigrants, was too poor to keep going the way it had been and was small enough that the leaders of individual agencies already knew one another. Even so, the new federation at first served just German Jews. It would take decades of fence-building—along with crises like the Great Chelsea Fire of 1908, which scorched 492 acres, destroyed 2,822 buildings, and left 5,000 Orthodox Jews homeless—to convince the Germans and East Europeans that their common Jewish background was more important than their distinct geographic beginnings. As the federation's membership expanded, so, too, did its mission. It began as a way to help new arrivals assimilate and survive, but kept enlarging to take on pioneering roles in supporting and occasionally rescuing international Jewry, funding community education along with synagogue activities, and responding creatively to such modern-day challenges as intermarriage.

Hundreds of other communal groups formed to pull Jews together around other issues. There were unions for tailors, textile workers, and other disproportionately Jewish trades, and settlement houses for those out of work or in need of vocational training. There were Jewish social clubs, the Elysium for Germans and the New Century for Russians, along with Jewish clubs for bachelors and debutantes. Local chapters were formed of national civil rights groups like the American Jewish Committee and fraternal groups like B'nai B'rith, along with home-grown self-defense groups like the Jewish Community Relations Council of Greater Boston. Publishers opened newspapers like the *Jewish Chronicle*, the *Hebrew Observer*, and the *Jewish Advocate*, the only one that still exists. College students started groups, too, including the Harvard Menorah Society, which tried to meld Jewish life into university life and evolved into the Intercollegiate Menorah Association. Most important of all in bringing the Jews of Boston together, there was Zionism.

Boston was a critical center of Zionism in America. It was not that it had more organizations than other cities, or more members, although there were ten different groups at the turn of the century, from the Lovers of Zion of East Boston to the Boston Daughters of Zion. The city's real contribution was in ideas and leaders—from Louis D. Brandeis, who championed the notion that Jews can hold dual loyalties to place and helped legitimize the movement in America when he took over its leadership two years before joining the Supreme Court, to activist Laurence M. Ring, who made clear that Zionism was not an abstract ideal for Jews like him but a real-life solution. Scholars at Brandeis, Harvard, and other Boston-area universities set out historical and philosophical underpinnings of the relationship between Israel and the United States in terms that let Jewish leaders explain—then sell—that relationship to Congress and the American people. And a Gallup Poll on the eve of World War II found that more than 90 percent of Jews in Boston and the surrounding region embraced Zionism, which was more than anywhere else in America.

But while the work of Brandeis and the others was well known to

Jews nationally, the spirit and soul of Boston's brand of Zionism were embodied in the behind-the-scenes exploits of Dewey David Stone. A diminutive but elegant figure, Stone had no choice but to tread softly. In the 1940s he was masterminding the purchase of arms for Palestine's secret Palmach army and assembling a secret fleet to smuggle to the Holy Land thousands of European Jews threatened by Hitler's executioners. Stone was recruited to the task by David Ben-Gurion, the labor movement leader who later became Israel's first prime minister and defense minister. Ben-Gurion turned over large sums of precious cash, which Stone used to charter or buy ships. His most famous procurement was an old United Fruit vessel dubbed *Exodus-1947*, which won international sympathy when the 4,200 Jewish refugees on board were turned back from Palestine by a British blockade; after returning to Hamburg, those who refused to get off were clubbed and hosed by the Nazis. Stone himself became the center of attention when a crate of guns from one of his boats spilled open on a loading dock in Hoboken, New Jersey, prompting the FBI to bug his phones and monitor his movements.

Stone was steeped in the Zionist cause from birth, the way many Bostonians back then were. His parents started out in a small town near Warsaw and although their escape route led to America, their hearts had been captured by Theodor Herzl's vision of rebuilding a Jewish homeland in Zion. As a youth all he could do was deposit his nickels and dimes in the blue *"pushke"* box that was a fixture in Jewish kitchens, with the dollars raised finding their way to Palestine. But as he got older he got more sophisticated in how to make his contributions count. He had seen the economic and social opportunities Jews had in Boston, which helped him grow a highly successful bleach and dye business. But he also saw the way Jews had to strike out on their own to overcome barriers that limited their rise in Gentile firms, and how cash was the route to influence in politics.

"He made up his mind that if there was going to be a voice to his convictions, he had to buy his rights to speak and be heard," recalls his nephew, Steve Stone, himself a successful Bay State businessman and backer of Jewish causes. Dewey used that voice to aid his friend Chaim Weizmann, who later became Israel's first president, in getting President Harry Truman to back the creation of the Jewish state in 1948. "Dewey was attending some damn thing around New York, and one of his acquaintances came up with the fact that he was personally acquainted with Eddie Jacobson, Truman's old business partner in Kansas City. Dewey borrowed a nickel, got to the phone booth, dialed Eddie, and handed the phone to this guy. The guy persuaded Eddie to ask Truman, as a personal favor, to please see that Chaim Weizmann had his audience with Truman, and I'm sure that made some difference. Truman gave presidential instructions to his representative at the United Nations to throw the American vote for Israel."

Dewey Stone was back again to help Israel round up the other UN votes it needed for statehood, and years later to help rally to Israel's cause freshman U.S. senator John Fitzgerald Kennedy. Stone chaired the United Jewish Appeal, the United Israel Appeal, and the board of governors of Israel's Weizmann Institute of Science. But as his nephew notes, Dewey remained a Jew of the diaspora despite his ties to the Jewish state. "He was part of a group that could not honestly and consistently subscribe to the Zionist principles, key among which was the notion that Zionists commit to move to Israel and help redeem the land. That notion of moving to Israel they couldn't accept."

While big causes like Zionism and central institutions like the federation were part of what distinguished Boston Jewry, even more critical were the intimate worlds that were forming there, starting at the level of the synagogue. Their physical settings were perpetually shifting as congregations moved from the lower South End to the upper, and in and out of Roxbury. All that activity suggests instability along with impermanence, but synagogues were actually one of the few stabilizing influences in the migratory world of Boston's early Jews. They were changing homes and changing communities, moving away from the social institutions, neighborhoods, and neighbors that had defined their sense of Jewishness and cohesion. The only things that moved with them, and provided continuity, were their rabbi and many fellow congregants.

The role of the synagogue became even more critical in the second half of the twentieth century as Jews moved from the city and close-in suburbs to far-flung and fragmented communities thirty minutes to an hour's drive from Boston. The temple started out as the only Jewish institution in town. It was where families attended services on the High

Holidays and where children formed basketball and baseball teams. It was where the community held Torah study and bar mitzvah classes, hosted speakers and sponsored dances, mourned the dead and celebrated births. The centrality of the synagogue in Jewish life is a national phenomenon, one that has distinguished Jews in America from those in places like Argentina and France. But in Boston the distinction assumed a finer point. Synagogues there were generally smaller and less glitzy than the monster ones going up across the Midwest, and there were more of them, which at first was an attempt at intimacy and a desire to be with others who shared a particular religious orientation, and later was an accommodation to being in increasingly remote suburbs where there were not many other Jews. Even today Boston Jews have one of the lowest levels of membership in Jewish organizations of any city studied—but a relatively high level of synagogue membership and a lot of synagogues, with nearly 200 in the city and across the state.

Having all those synagogues sprouting across Boston, and later in outlying towns, was in keeping with the New England tradition of every neighborhood and small town having its own church, community center, and other critical institutions. And just as those towns were ideal laboratories for experimentation and innovation, so the shuls of the North End and Roxbury—and later of Sharon and Winchester, Medford, Malden, and Marblehead—offered their own particular ways of pushing the envelope on all that it could mean to be Jewish. The titanic temples of the Midwest and South might have to move toward the center, and the conventional, to accommodate their thousands of members, but in and around Boston there typically were more rabbis, more congregations, and more chances to try new things.

Many of the innovations worked and were widely copied. As early as the 1850s Boston Jews initiated a tradition of breakaway congregations, some of which struck out on their own simply to preserve distinctions like those between German and East Europeans, while others insisted that there be a greater focus on the young, progressive interpretations of Judaism, or the synagogue as the center of Jewish life. Another Boston tradition was transforming churches like the West End's Twelfth (Colored) Baptist into shuls; the practice came full circle when the Twelfth Baptist congregation moved into the old Temple Mishkan Tefila in the upper South End. In 1908, the Yavne group in the West End launched "the only Zionist congregation in the country," which sought to bridge gaps between denominations by appealing to a sense of Jewish people-hood. In the 1950s Brandeis University opened Jewish, Protestant, and Catholic chapels that were the same size and general design, forging a metaphor for the sort of religious pluralism the school was promoting through its research and teachings. Boston was back on the front lines in the 1960s, pioneering a *havurah* movement of informal religious communities that brought Jews together for fellowship, prayer, study, and celebration—all without a rabbi, congregational structure, or formal synagogue, much the way the early Jews had practiced their faith more than 2,000 years before. The Orthodox were also opting for informality, converting houses into shuls in Brookline and Newton, although unlike the *havurah*, what went on in the Orthodox homes was highly structured and traditional.

Experimentation like that is part of the culture of Boston. The city gave birth to the American Revolution, jump-started the nation's public school system, and inaugurated a series of other innovations, from subways to anesthesia, playgrounds and parks to public housing and public water supplies. It was only natural, then, that the Jewish community of Boston should take on the character of the world around it much the way Jews have done since they were exiled to Babylonia. Boston Jews had been, and still are, on the forefront of everything from designing a more scientifically based social welfare program to kicking off a student movement to save Soviet Jews. "Boston is not happy unless it's first, either first to do something or first to change something," explains Ruth Fein, the first woman to chair Boston's Jewish federation, the first to run a federation annual campaign, the founding president of the New England Holocaust Memorial, and the first and only female president of the American Jewish Historical Society. "There's a sense of both the special uniqueness of the place and a desperate need to start things, to be first. The Jewish community has that in spades."

That obsession with needing to believe it is first, even if it means embellishing to make it so, is one of several less endearing traits that the Jewish community has picked up from the surrounding community. The Jews of Boston are "more Brahmin than the Brahmins" in terms of their tightfistedness, says Fein, who ran a fund-raising campaign there and can compare it to work she did for the Jewish communities of Washington and Baltimore. That is why, although the Boston area was the natural spot to locate Brandeis University, it was just as natural that much of the money to start the school in 1948 came from New York. Boston Jews also took on tones of their overwhelmingly Irish surroundings. That made it easier for them to support Israel without having their loyalties questioned, since Irish-Americans had been doing the same for Ireland for generations. But the sense that they were interlopers in an Irish-run city made Jews in Boston less comfortable with publicly parading their Jewishness than their cousins were in places like New York, where Jews accounted for twice the share of the population. Only one Jew ever held a statewide office in Massachusetts—George Fingold, who served as attorney general in the 1950s—although Jews have consistently played critical behind-the-scenes roles in city and state politics. Jewish doctors had an even harder time, finding it difficult to get staff privileges at Boston's prestigious teaching hospitals, which is one reason Jews opened Mount Sinai Hospital in 1902 and Beth Israel fifteen years later. Even the incessant infusion of new blood has come at a price, for Jews as it did for non-Jews: the newcomers were unlikely to have had relatives who lived in the North End or Roxbury, to have roots in one of the newer suburban synagogues, or otherwise to share a history that can help define a community and bind it together.

Steve Stone, the eighty-two-year-old retired chairman of the Converse shoe company, lived through dark sides of the Boston Jewish experience even as he partook of its privileges. "I remember as a kid of twelve or thirteen when a neighboring kid said he'd take me down to his Boy Scout troop and get me in," says Stone. "The troop met in a very prestigious church in town. I came in with this guy and could hear whispering around me and people raising hell with my friend. 'What'd you bring the Jew for?' they wanted to know." But World War II changed all that, he adds: "The war was like Joshua blowing his horn. The walls came tumbling down. Jews worked into positions of responsibility and wealth. It's embarrassing to see how much our average income is now."

One thing that never proved embarrassing to the Jews of Boston, and never required embroidering, is the claim that they have been at the cutting edge of intellectual leadership and scholarship in ways that have profoundly influenced the world of ideas in America and beyond. Greater Boston has more college students per capita than anywhere in the country, and more good colleges, including Harvard, MIT, Tufts, Northeastern, Wellesley College, Boston University, and Boston College. So it is not surprising that it is also home to America's premiere Jewish-focused university, Brandeis, and to top-notch Jewish studies programs at places like Harvard and BU. That culture of rewarding intellectual achievement has spread well beyond campus life, putting even more of a premium on education than in other Jewish communities, for adults as well as children. New generations of Jewish youth gravitate to today's prized professions of biotechnology and computers the way their parents did to law and medicine and their grandparents did to shoes and apparel. Intellectual achievement is the kind of marker of success for Jews in Boston that financial fortune is in New York and political power is in Washington, D.C.

There are many ways to measure the results, starting by counting all the national Jewish figures who have lived in Boston. There are inspired rabbis of old like Solomon Schindler of Temple Israel and Louis M. Epstein of Kehillath Israel, and of recent times, like Samuel Chiel of Temple Emanuel and Bernard Mehlman of Temple Israel, along with scholars of old like philosopher Harry Wolfson of Harvard and cybernetics guru Norbert Wiener of MIT, and ones of new like MIT linguist Noam Chomsky and Harvard Law constitutionalist Laurence H. Tribe. There are inventors like Edwin Land, whose Polaroid revolutionized picture taking; historians like Oscar Handlin, who taught us that the story of America's immigrants is the story of America; and philanthropists like Lina Hecht, who proved more than a hundred years ago that with the proper training those unwashed immigrants could become "wage earners, breadwinners and self-respecting intelligent citizens." And, of course, there is America's most famous and most controversial lawyer, Alan M. Dershowitz. Such a list could consume an entire chapter, but a better way to assess the "smart set" of Boston Jewry may be, as historian Stephen J. Whitfield suggests, to see the unexpected places it has turned up. Start with Moe Berg, who, when he was not crouching as the catcher for the Boston Red Sox, was earning his doctorate in philosophy and law, studying at the Sorbonne, and teaching romance languages at Princeton. Or Edward A. Filene, the only department store magnate ever to reflect "an aura of intellectuality" through his writings on topics like business ethics and his launching of the Twentieth Century

Fund, which supports research on economic and social issues. And, writes Whitfield, while "theoretical physicists are usually not treated with the indulgence of celebrities . . . when Albert Einstein came to Boston to solicit funds for the Hebrew University on Mount Scopus (bringing Chaim Weizmann and other Zionists along with him), the German scientist's train was met with a brass band in the morning and with a kosher banquet in the evening."

Some of its brightest scholars were born here; others made Boston home in later life. Still more, from Henry Kissinger to Elie Wiesel, have passed through, generally as part of a teaching stint. The city's elite universities also ensured a nonstop supply of bright students, many of whom have stayed on and all of whom have infused Boston with a youthful energy and infusion of ideas that acted as an antidote to the inbred, old-boy feeling that seeps into all Jewish communities and is especially tempting in a city so self-satisfied that it refers to itself as the "Hub of the Universe."

No one was better at shaking Boston Jews out of their complacency than Rabbi Joseph B. Soloveitchik. The latest in a long line of distinguished Lithuanian rabbis, Soloveitchik came to Boston from Berlin in 1932, a year after he completed his doctoral degree and a year before Hitler came to power. He took a rabbinic post in Roxbury but his influence was soon felt across the community and the country. He argued that Jews should stop sending their children to public school and, despite angry calls that it was un-American and would re-create a Jewish ghetto, he founded the Maimonides School, the first modern Jewish school in New England. He knew the yeshiva tradition of separating boys and girls, but insisted that at his school they learn together. He realized that Orthodoxy was considered passé and that many believed it would die out with the immigrant generation, but he believed it could be revived if Jews grounded themselves in ancient laws and traditions, then embraced the best from the modern worlds of science and society. And while his lectures on everything from Jewish law to the human condition were so brilliant that he became the spiritual mentor for generations of Orthodox rabbis at New York's Yeshiva University, Conservative and Reform scholars also acknowledged his genius and were among those who packed his Saturday night talks at Maimonides.

Nationally, Soloveitchik was known as "the Rav," or teacher, and as the father of centrist or modern Orthodoxy. He looked the role, his white beard long but more manicured than the ones favored by Brooklyn's Orthodox Old Worlders, his hair short and topped by a modest yarmulke instead of a high-topped one or a black hat, and his suits more suited to today's temple boardroom than yesterday's yeshiva. In Boston— where he exercised the authority of chief rabbi although he never held the title—he had a legacy even more profound, though it was also more mixed. On the one hand he helped ensure that Boston's small Orthodox community remain middle-of-the-road politically and religiously, which meant it was able and willing to talk to and work with the Conservative and Reform. Yet sadly, Soloveitchik, much of whose life was devoted to change, was so revered that innovations he instituted at Maimonides and other institutions became inscribed as if in stone and have had difficulty changing along with the times.

*   *   *

No one ever mistook Shmuel Halpern for modern Orthodox. My mother's grandfather wore a crownlike yarmulke and a full gray beard, walked with a gold-headed cane that was more a matter of style than support, and had the magisterial bearings of a proud East European. He had a lot to be proud of as a rabbi learned enough that other rabbis, including Soloveitchik's father, consulted him, and a heritage that included being the eighth in a line of such intellectual rabbis—or rebbes—dating back centuries. My great-grandfather also had a lot to fret over in his last years, convinced the lineage of Jewish learning would die with him.

Shmuel grew up in Lithuania, in the village of Ostrovnia. He was an orphan, but managed to find local sponsors and attend the yeshiva. He was ordained a rabbi and kept studying, but to earn a living he had to work on a large Christian estate where he surveyed the forest and supervised the cutting of trees. In the late 1890s he married Dinah Meller from the nearby community of Abel. Life was good for Dinah and Shmuel. They were surrounded by Jews, and her father, who was in the liquor and lumber businesses, had the biggest house in Abel, two and a half stories with a wrap-around balcony and a hall huge enough to host weddings. But the serenity was short-lived. First came the pogroms, then World War I, which forced the family to seek temporary refuge in Russia. On the eve of the war Dinah and Shmuel's oldest child, Rose, who was sixteen and a beauty, left for America, drawn by stories from a U.S. relative who had visited, and nudged by her parents, who felt America would offer more opportunities for education and an advantageous marriage. She landed in New York, made her way to Boston, then settled in Portland, Maine, where she had relatives who arranged a *shiddukh*, or contract marriage, with a handsome, gentle young man named Selmour Rubinoff.

Rose and Selmour, my maternal grandparents, ran a grocery store. Rose salted away nickels and dimes to ship bundles of food to the family she left behind in Europe and eventually to bring her father, then her mother and two younger siblings, to America. Getting Shmuel in was not easy in those days of strict immigration quotas: Rose and Selmour had to get a shul in Portland to attest in writing that it would hire him as a rabbi, which it had no need for and no intention of doing. Once he arrived in 1923 he stayed for three years in Portland, a city religious enough to be dubbed Jerusalem of the North and observant enough that anybody who dared drive on the Sabbath would take convoluted detours to avoid going by the synagogue. My relatives went even further in their piety, saving wrappers from oranges to use as bathroom tissue on Saturdays so they would not have to tear off regular toilet paper, a violation of the Sabbath invocation against work; arranging for a "Sabbath goy" to turn on or off the lights and stove; and holding Seders where no words of English were uttered and the children were so bored they quickly fell asleep. In 1926 Shmuel landed the sort of jobs he had dreamed of since his days as a forester in Lithuania—first as a rabbi at a midsized synagogue on Erie Street in Dorchester, then at the majestic Crawford Street Synagogue in Roxbury.

This is where my great-grandfather's story begins to mirror that of the wider community of Boston Jews, and where it suggests the strains and stresses that simmered just below the surface in so many immigrant families. The synagogue built by the Beth Hamidrash Hagadol congregation on Crawford Street was a sprawling state-of-the-art brick structure that seated nearly 1,200. It was also a monument to the power of a building to inspire a community, as one of its early rabbis, Louis M. Epstein, observed: "The Crawford Street Synagogue is an illustration of the fact that not always is a synagogue built where the Jewish community is, but that sometimes the community is built where the synagogue is. Our synagogue has in a great measure been the making of the Roxbury Jewish community." While that was a bit of an embellishment, since Roxbury already was flourishing as a Jewish community by the time Crawford Street was completed in 1915, the shul did become a center of activity. By the time my great-grandfather arrived in 1926, it was abandoning the Friday night services, choir, youth services, hymnals, family pews, and other reforms instituted by its middle-class founders, and returning to the traditional patterns of worship favored by its newest members, working-class Jews from Eastern Europe.

That was just fine with Shmuel, who was an East European and a traditionalist. But it probably did not affect his day to day life much since he was what they called a "downstairs rabbi," who serves scholars seeking interpretations of Talmudic text, as opposed to the "upstairs" one who services the public. It was just as well that he was not inter-acting with the wider congregation, especially American-born members, for while this meticulous man in the long frock coat was fluent in four languages—Yiddish, Lithuanian, Russian, and Hebrew—he could not speak English.

Communication also was difficult with his children, or at least for six of the seven, although with them it was not a matter of idiom. Shmuel was resolved to preserve the order of things that prevailed back in Abel, from adhering to cherished rituals to seeing that his children were prop-erly deferential to their elders. They had begun rejecting that order in the old country and were even more resolved that it had no place in the new. The result was conflict, followed by alienation. "My father was very, very, very religious. He was a fanatically religious man," recalls Irving Halpern, Shmuel's youngest and only surviving child. "I guess there were a lot of people like that among the Jews. My father looked very askance at any anyone reading anything but Jewish literature. When my brother David refused to go to shul there was hell to pay, there were real fist-fights. When we came to the United States I had to go to public school, then go to Hebrew school afterward. My father had me study an hour of Hebrew with him, so I didn't have the chance to play with any other kids. He used to set the clock for an hour, but my mother would turn the clock forward to make the time go by faster."

Looking back it is clear that the conflict was as much of his children's making as Shmuel's—and, even more, it was a product of the profoundly unsettling changes they all were living through. All but my Nana Rose were rebels. Most sympathized with socialism and several actively embraced communism. "The newspapers," Irving says, "always accused the Jews of being communists in Russia and all over the world. They were, but it was because they were oppressed that communism appealed to them." That rebellion may seem logical in the forgiving light of history, yet to Shmuel it was a repudiation not only of the American democracy he adored but, much worse, of the religion he had held on to even as his world was uprooted in the moves from Ostrovnia to Abel to Portland to Boston. Jewish law told him which prayers to say when he got up in the morning and before he ate each meal, which garments to don as he dressed, and how to honor the Sabbath day of rest and reflection. It was how he made his living and made sense of his surroundings. It defined his relations with Jews and Gentiles, in commerce and communal affairs, and gave him comfort when he contemplated his mortality. It defined how a father would honor his children, and be honored by them, or at least it did until those children decided these were not the laws they would live by.

Rose was the exception. She kept a strictly kosher house, which was not easy after her husband died at the young age of thirty-six of brain cancer, following a long battle that impaired his speech, blinded him, and kept him from really knowing his four children, who ranged in age from one to twelve. She kept the grocery business going for several years, but although everyone presumed she was a rich widow she discovered that Selmour had let too many poor customers buy on credit to ever fully recover. She moved to Brookline in 1942 to be closer to her mother and her older children, and because she felt her two daughters who were still at home would get better schools and a better chance to meet eligible Jewish men. She lit candles every Friday night and served a Sabbath dinner, even though there was never enough money to lay out the lavish table she felt her children deserved. She would not drive, shop, or do anything else that resembled work on Saturdays or holidays, although she once gave her younger daughters 25 cents each to buy fried chicken dinners at the newly opened Topsy's, their first parentally sanctioned nonkosher meal. She sent my mother and her three other children to Hebrew school, taught them to speak Yiddish, and instructed them that when their public school classmates sang Christmas carols they should "sing them, too, just don't say the word 'Jesus.'" She consoled her son when neighborhood kids called him a "Christ killer" and her daughters when they were called "dirty Jews." She collected for the Jewish National Fund, enough to win awards from the Zionist group, although if she had not been so proud she could have qualified for charity herself. And she worshiped her father, to the point where her daughters found lipstick marks on her picture of him.

Shmuel was devastated by what he saw as his rebellious children's desertion of him and their heritage, but he was forever proud of his Rose. Just how devastated became clear in writings he left that were uncovered decades later in which he mourned the fact that the line of eight generations of rabbis would be broken with him. Just how proud became clear when, before he died in 1941 of a heart condition, he penned a letter in Hebrew saying, "When I die, hold my funeral up only for my beloved Rivka."

The particulars were different, but the outlines of life were much the same for my father's family—the Tikotskys. They came from Kosovo, a town 160 miles west of Warsaw that now is part of Belarus but has been claimed at times by the Germans, Poles, Russians, and Latvians. Kosovo was a classic shtetl with ten kosher butchers, four synagogues, three Jewish grammar schools, and the bad luck to be in Hitler's path as his troops stormed across Poland. The Nazis rounded up all they could find of Kosovo's 3,500 Jews, took them outside of town, and shot them. Most of my family, I am thankful, had escaped decades before. My great-grandfather, another Shmuel, bought and sold chickens, milk, and other farm goods in Kosovo, and he was good at it. But like thousands of his coreligionists he had big dreams and in 1903 he set out to realize them in America. He was joined two years later by my grandfather, Joseph, who along with two brothers took a train, a small boat, an ocean liner, another boat, and another train to get to Haverhill. On the transatlantic trip he danced along the steerage deck until first-class passengers tossed down quarters, dimes, and nickels, using the change to buy his first bananas—although, as his baby brother, Sam, recalled eighty years later in a recorded interview, it took Joseph and him a try or two to realize that the fruit had to be peeled. During the last leg of his sea trip my grandfather celebrated his bar mitzvah.

Shmuel, Joseph, and the rest of the family settled in Haverhill, which is where my father and I were born. It was one of several New England cities that considered itself the shoe capital of the country, and along with nearby Lawrence and Lowell it laid claim as the birthplace of America's industrial revolution. Haverhill now is part of the outer orbit of Boston but back then it was economically thriving and self-sufficient, enough so that in 1880 it enticed my distant relatives and other Jews from Boston to settle there permanently. By the time my great-grandfather arrived, Haverhill, like most modest-sized Jewish communities in the diaspora, had two synagogues, one catering to Ashkenazim and the other to Sephardim. Rabbi Jacob Joffee, who officiated at both temples, earned his living by taking up a collection among his congregants.

Shmuel could barely speak English so he made a living going house to house teaching children to speak Hebrew—at the rate of 50 cents per student per week—and helping them prepare for their bar mitzvah. He was not an ordained rabbi, but was a scholar and continued to keep kosher, wear a yarmulke, attend synagogue, and, in an image befitting his piety, maintain a long white beard. His son Joseph, my grandfather, went to work almost immediately, selling newspapers, fixing sewing machines, and eventually moving into the lady's shoe business, where he stayed for more than half a century, manufacturing, selling factory rejects in a retail store, and in the end going on the road to sell ribbons and bindings.

My grandmother, Minnie Kahn Tikotsky, was born in 1893 in Jefferson, Texas, a town of 3,000 just outside Shreveport, Louisiana. Her family was among the tens of thousands of Russian Jews who landed in the Southwest, steered there in part by a New York Jewish community troubled by the flood of refugees to the East Coast. The Kahns were a classic case: once the first came, others traced their steps. My great-grandfather ran a saloon in Jefferson until the hatchet-wielding prohibitionist Carry Nation closed him down. In 1905 he moved the family to Boston, where there were relatives and, they hoped, more economic opportunities. The Kahns settled in Roxbury, which was becoming the center of the city's Jewish life, and my grandmother attended Girls' High, then Burdett Business College. The major milestone in her early life came on that suspenseful day when a meeting was arranged, much the way it had been for my maternal grandmother, with the man picked to be her husband.

Minnie and Joseph married in 1916 and settled in Haverhill, near his family. She hired a tutor to help him write and read English but all he mastered were the funny pages of the newspaper, and even there his children were convinced he was guessing what the script said by studying the illustrations. He could read Hebrew, although after years of saying the same prayers twice a day, every day, he probably knew them by heart, and like many of his contemporaries there was only one Hebrew word that he could translate: *Adonai,* or God. The Tikotskys had three boys—Mauray, Raymond, and David—all of whom trudged alongside their parents through the city center and up the hill to the shul on Mount Washington for High Holiday services. They prayed to get out as early as possible, but they knew that, despite their mother's insistence that "the kids have to go to bed," Joseph would see to it that they were the last ones out.

The boys also learned at a young age that simply walking home, from shul or anywhere else, could be dangerous. "I remember coming back from my dad's shoe store in Lafayette Square and you had to walk by the Acre, near St. James Church," says my uncle Raymond. "A bunch of guys came by taunting us with 'you Jews, you sheenies.' My dad, who had huge hands, grabbed a board from a picket fence and went after them. They took off." The message to Raymond was clear: "My father showed me then that you don't sit back and take it, you do something about it." Minnie agreed, which is why she trimmed Tikotsky to Tye.

Whatever their name, Joseph and Minnie's identity remained avowedly Jewish. To him that meant keeping milk-based foods separate from meat-based ones, and keeping pork and other nonkosher items out of the house. It meant going to shul every Saturday morning, davening so often that his prayer book had frayed pages and a cover that was crumbling in its binding, and both loving and fearing a God who he never really had the time or inclination to contemplate. It also meant making sure that his children and grandchildren knew all the learned rabbis who were part of our extended family, including the revered Talmudic scholar Avraham Yeshayahu Karelitz, better known as the Hazan Ish. My grandmother, who was as much a part of the New World as he was of the old, read a different meaning into her God and faith. She kept a kosher house out of respect for her hardworking husband but when they went to restaurants near their cottage in Salisbury Beach she ate lobster, and she taught me and the rest of her grandchildren how to pick apart the shells, separate out the gooey green stuff, and dig into the tender white meat. She never questioned the existence of God but felt that was different from embracing ritual. She belonged to a Jewish bridge club and all her friends were Jewish but she was adept at negotiating her non-Jewish surroundings. Most of all she taught her children and grandchildren to be proud of their heritage and, living to be a hundred, she was able to pass down the same lesson to her great-grandchildren. I also suspect that, if her husband would have gone along and the option had been available at the time in Haverhill, she would have switched from their traditional synagogues to a Reform or Reconstructionist one.

"She didn't feel that the name change was giving up her heritage," says her middle son, Raymond. "She believed that you had to be very proud of being a Jew."

*   *   *

If she were around today my Nana Minnie would have lots of help filling in her Jewish identity, and she might even be tempted to change her name back to one that is more patently Jewish. That is because Boston, as much as any city in America, is no longer leaving it to chance—or to individuals—to understand its Jewish past and carve out a dynamic Jewish present and future. It is developing a whole new Zeitgeist for how to be a Jew. And it all centers on the new definitions being applied to three age-old precepts that are chiseled into the outer wall of the federation building in downtown Boston: Torah, the service of God, and acts of loving-kindness.

Start with Torah, which is a shorthand way of saying education about Jewish laws and texts, heritage and culture. Community leaders in Boston have watched for generations as their constituents attended select schools like Harvard and Brown, MIT and Tufts. They could understand quarks and quantum physics, had read Plato and Kierkegaard, and knew the difference between Henry James and William James. But they could not tell Moses from Maimonides, and did not know or care that there are two Talmuds, one from Babylonia and the other from Jerusalem. Studies confirmed that the 233,000 Jews living in Greater Boston near the end of the twentieth century were better educated secularly than those in any comparison community in America—but the studies also made clear that when it came to things Jewish, far too many Boston Jews were illiterate.

The Boston brain trust is not alone in this realization. The two Shmuels, my great-grandfathers, bemoaned their offsprings' ignorance of their faith a century ago, the same way other Jewish grandparents across the diaspora have for millennia. What is unusual about what happened in Boston, as federation chief Barry Shrage says, is that "we've decided that serious engagement with the question of Jewish cultural and religious renaissance can't begin with children. It has to begin with adults. You have to say that you won't allow your child to grow up and be an illiterate Jew, that it doesn't matter if you have to sell the family jewels, move to a new community, whatever you have to do you will do because you believe that child's happiness, not to mention the ability to earn a living, depends on it. Until recently it wouldn't have occurred to anyone that their child would be spiritually or intellectually cheated if they didn't know about Talmud or Mishnah. What's happening in Boston is that it's beginning to occur to people. They know they can give their kids just about everything—money, power, great jobs. This is a great country. But it's beginning to dawn on them that the one thing their children and grandchildren need the most, a sense of community, of values, of identity, it is occurring to them that their children will not have the benefit of those things if they don't make it happen."

That dawning did not drop out of the air and it was not cooked up by abstract academics. It began with the logical presumption that parents and grandparents themselves had to become Jewishly literate to appreciate the value of a Jewish education for their offspring. Experienced teachers and real students then undertook a series of experiments, some invented from scratch while others were variations on themes developed elsewhere. All had the same goal: getting adults, from recent college graduates to retirees, to recognize the gaps in their Jewish learning and get excited about filling them in.

Did it work? There are 1,500 reasons to think so. That is how many adult Bostonians have graduated from a high-level learning program called *Me'ah*, which means 100. One hundred is the number of hours of classroom study each participant does over two years, which boils down to about two and a half hours a week over a twenty-two-week academic calendar. The first year focuses on the Hebrew Bible and literature of the Talmudic periods, starting with the creation of the world and ending with an exploration of Rabbinic interpretations of the Sabbath and festivals. Year two covers medieval and modern Jewish experience, from the Middle Ages through the expulsion from Spain. The teachers are top-notch Judaic scholars and rabbis from Brandeis, Harvard, and other area schools, including Hebrew College, which launched and coordinates the program. Students include stockbrokers and doctors, lawyers, housewives, and senior citizens. Most are Reform or Conservative, although there are some Orthodox, and most do not know much about their Jewish background but all wish they knew more. "The only thing we assume is that people understand that to make a commitment for two years is a serious thing," explains Rabbi David Starr, who used to have a congregation but left to found and run the program. "If they are bullshitting themselves about their ability to do that it means they are taking a spot from someone else. What we can do best, and what most adults want, is not to be pandered to or proselytized to. They want somebody to help them get into the Bible. We can help raise questions for them. The answers will be better if the questions are good."

Me'ah is one of scores of adult education programs launched across the diaspora in recent years, but it differs in several critical ways from the lunch-and-learn programs popular in places like Atlanta and bids by Hollywood to glamorize mystical Kabbalah by linking it to pop stars like Madonna. *Me'ah* is carefully conceived and structured to provide a framework for understanding Jewish texts and culture, values and rituals. It is not aimed at giving participants a particular spin, or to be all-inclusive, but rather to teach them how to keep learning on their own. It is run out of synagogues and community centers because that is where Jewish life is centered in Boston, it is paid for in part by Combined Jewish Philanthropies because it has the money, and it is coordinated by Hebrew College, which has the expertise. Participants have to be deeply enough committed that they will keep attending classes over the two years, and do all the reading and thinking that comes with them. While it was inspired by several national models, it was crafted to the needs of Boston and is still supported by centralized and grassroots forces in the community, which see it as a concrete way to strike back against the Jewish illiteracy that threatens Jewish continuity. It also builds community by creating a common foundation of knowledge, of language, of conversation.

The program's success is measured not just by the hundreds of people who continue to sign up, but even more by the number who continue to learn after they graduate. More than half are participating in other Jewish adult education programs. Many synagogues offer an additional two years of formal instruction. And Jewish communities from Cleveland to Orlando are replicating the *Me'ah* curriculum developed in Boston.

"I was raised in an Orthodox family in which Jewish education was not offered to girls. I learned ritual, but not why. I took *Me'ah* because I was smart enough to know what I didn't know," says Judy Chudnofsky, a fifty-four-year-old businesswoman from suburban Needham who was part of the second class ever taught. "I understood that we had a First and Second Temple, and then all of a sudden there was a Holocaust, but I knew very little about what happened in the middle. *Me'ah* gave me a time line and told me where I fit in." As its founders had predicted, *Me'ah* inspired Judy not only to keep learning but to get others to do the same. When she would get home from classes just after 10 P.M., she and her husband, Jason, would stay up three more hours talking about what had transpired. Now both of them take a weekly Torah studies class. Several of his colleagues at Ziff Davis Publishing have started studying with them. Their younger daughter now lights Sabbath candles, and if she has children, she plans to send them to Jewish day school, while their grandchildren, nieces, and nephews are captivated by Judy and Jason's increasingly Jewish home when they come for Shabbat dinners or Seders. The Chudnofskys also gradually began adhering to Jewish dietary laws, first giving up shellfish, then banning all nonkosher foods, and finally keeping separate dishes for milk and meat.

"*Me'ah* attracts a certain type of person," says Judy, "and this person belongs to a nucleus of Jewish adults who are saying, 'I'm Jewish. I'm here. I have a stake in this and want to learn more.' As a result of *Me'ah*, people are saying to their congregations, 'I'm not going to settle for less than I want—for myself, for my children and grandchildren. I want better classes for adults and children, and I'm willing to sit on committees to make it happen.' It's a metamorphosis that will take a few more years to come to full fruition. People are filtering their kids into Jewish day schools. I am tremendously, tremendously optimistic."

Me'ah is a fitting metaphor for the hundreds of other cutting-edge ways of Jewish learning being tried across Boston. Brandeis is teaching journalists how to get to the crux of Jewish issues, college and graduate students how to run Jewish organizations, high schoolers how to appreciate Jewish history and arts, the public how to understand contributions of Jewish women, and communities how to test the effectiveness of ongoing initiatives to get Jews to care about their Jewishness. Hebrew College is redefining Jewish education to mean nothing less than transforming the life of the community by reaching out to grandparents and high schoolers as well as college-age kids; offering classes in music, film, and storytelling as well as the Bible; and using the Internet and summer camp to reach new students. Synagogues, JCCs, and other communal organizations are pioneering their own programs on everything from the evolving nature of U.S.-Israel relations to how to celebrate the Sabbath. Combined Jewish Philanthropies' comprehensive community survey in 1995 suggested all those efforts already were bearing fruit, with 26 percent of adults saying they had participated in some form of Jewish education the previous year compared to just 20 percent a decade earlier, and the numbers almost certainly have continued to climb.

That swirl of interest in education also is being felt among Jewish youth, the way community leaders hoped it would. Sometimes it has been informed parents pushing their children to learn, other times it is knowledgeable kids who embarrass their parents into heading back to school. Whatever the cause, the effect is that attendance is on the rise at Jewish day schools and exciting experiments in learning are under way at places like the New Jewish High School in Waltham.

The idea for "New Jew" percolated up from the grass roots, in this case from parents in Newton who saw the growth in Jewish elementary schools and worried that the only option at the secondary level was the Maimonides School, which was too Orthodox for them. So in 1996 they hired Rabbi Daniel Lehmann as headmaster even before they had a school for him to head. A year and a half later he opened an institution built around the principle of pluralism. Sixty percent of its 220 students are from Conservative backgrounds, 20 percent Orthodox, 10 percent Reform, and the rest are impossible to pigeonhole. Each day begins with prayer services, with choices ranging from a traditional minyan to meditation. Students come from as far west as Worcester, as far south as Sharon, and as far north as Maine, with some traveling more than an hour each way each day. Teachers and lecturers range from leading scholars at Brandeis to playwright and filmmaker David Mamet, from a gay Orthodox rabbi to a right-wing newspaper columnist. Students use the library and gym at Brandeis, which is just a mile away, and many spend a semester during their senior year studying in Israel. They learn to read Jewish texts, preferably in the original Hebrew and Aramaic, learn to sing a cappella and dance Israeli-style, and participate in prayer vigils for imprisoned Iranian Jews and protests against China's refusal to allow democracy. Their parents pay about $13,000 a year, with a third of students getting scholarships. And while their curriculum is decidedly unconventional, it includes enough algebra and physics, literature and writing, to help them get accepted to first-rate colleges like Harvard, Amherst, Bryn Mawr, and Bates.

"We want them to be able to have conversations about weighty issues of Jewish life with Jews who have vastly different focuses or orientations," says Lehmann, whose background is Orthodox but whose whole approach is aimed at building a comfortable middle ground where Reform, Reconstructionist, Conservative, and Orthodox can study, work, and live together. "I use the word 'experiment' a lot, and people have a positive feel for what it means to experiment. It's not a negative thing where we don't know what we are doing. Probably something better will come out of experimenting."

The second leg on which Judaism stands is the service of God. In Boston that centers on the Hebrew concept of *chesed*, or caring, in this case by building strong, coherent, loving communities of Jews. While praying is important, the concept of spirituality is being expanded to include feeling, caring, and touching. And although lots of institutions play a part, the central one is the synagogue, which is charged with everything from encouraging worship and healing to clarifying Jewish values and lifestyles. Jews have been attending synagogues in Boston since they arrived 150 years ago, but it is doubtful those early settlers would have understood or even recognized the way God is served today at a place like Temple Beth El in the western suburb of Sudbury.

Beth El's rabbi and cantor stand in the midst of the congregation rather than high on a pulpit. Levi's and Nikes are as common as ties and dresses. Some worshipers are from surrounding communities, but the membership roster includes fifty different zip codes in three states. God is still there but seems more down-to-earth and accessible these days, and is no longer just a "he." Even the building looks different. The stately brick structures of old have yielded to a gray wood facade that is easy to mistake for a country inn, and, even more unorthodox, the inner walls and pews are free from the donors' plaques that have become part of the furniture in so many American synagogues. Indoors, laughing and crying fill the sanctuary along with davening and *shukkl*ing. Sometimes congregants are laughing with the rabbi, Larry Kushner, such as during a Torah study discussing the sensuality of the Song of Songs when he observed that one way to tell whether the discussion was getting anywhere was "if you have to go home and take a cold shower." More often it is just the tone Kushner helped set, a tone that brings together an overflow crowd of teenagers, thirty- and forty-somethings, and graying grandparents on a rainy Saturday morning in April to talk about Old Testament verses. Most stay for a bar mitzvah even though many have no idea who the bar mitzvah boy is. And there is a waiting list of would-be worshipers hoping that someday they will be allowed to join.

"Beth El is one of the most spiritually alive places I have ever walked into," says Anita Diamant, author of the bestselling, biblically inspired novel *The Red Tent*. That is why she is willing to drive twenty-five minutes to get there from her home in Newton, where there are a dozen synagogues that would be flattered to have her as a member. "Beth El provides community, that very slippery, much-talked-about item. I have learned that what community really means is that you don't have to love everybody. You inherit a whole bunch of people, some of whom you'd choose and some you wouldn't have connected with at all. Beth El is a great place to grow and to be challenged, to learn and to laugh. It's a very lighthearted place as well, a place for serious spirit seeking. That's one of Larry's great successes. We laugh, we cry, we do everything."

Diamant's husband, Jim Ball, was brought up Presbyterian, toyed with the idea of becoming a minister during high school, watched as his mother became a born-again Christian, and decided to convert to his wife's Jewish faith after his first meeting with Kushner in the early 1980s. "Larry opened the door," Ball says. "The more I learned, the more I started eating it up." He has subsequently served on Beth El's board, been the synagogue's vice president, run its outreach committee, and taken courses with Kushner on topics ranging from Martin Buber to Moses, Abraham Joshua Heschel to the biblical prophets. Now, frustrated with having to read other people's interpretations of Jewish texts, Ball is studying Hebrew.

Those are the kinds of upbeat testaments one seldom hears about synagogue life, or at least, that used to be the case. People attended services out of a sense of duty or guilt, because their parents expected them to or because they were trying to set an example for their children. They read responsively when asked to and stood when the rabbi signaled. Men played with the fringes on their talliths, fiddled with their yarmulkes, checked their watches. Women fiddled with their husband's or brother's talliths, smoothed their dresses, checked their watches. "American synagogues are boring, secular, and irrelevant usually, don't you think?" says Kushner, a published author on topics ranging from mysticism to prayer. "People just don't go and if they do, it's not because they like what's going on. To quote [rabbi and humorist] Moshe Waldocks, nobody walks out of a bar mitzvah and says, 'That was great. I'm coming back next week.' " The punch line, of course, is that that is precisely what worshipers say when they walk out of a bar mitzvah at Beth El.

Kushner's formula is straightforward and centers on creating what he calls "Jews by surprise"—ones who join a temple so their daughter can be bat mitzvahed or their son can be circumcised, then discover they like the Jewish experience and want to stick around. There are no brotherhoods or sisterhoods, no bowling leagues or dinner societies—but there are three different Torah study groups every Saturday morning that relate the text to people's everyday lives. There are special programs for very young children but no children's services, mainly because children are invited to every service and they come, newborns, toddlers, and youngsters of all ages. Rather than just dropping off their kids for Sunday school, parents are encouraged to stay and take special classes for adults;

and rather than just the children studying for a bar or bat mitzvah, there are six months of classes where the parents join in the learning. The congregation calls itself Reform, but it sings Hasidic songs and worships with the kind of bowing and swaying that would make old-time Orthodox feel at home. On Simchat Torah, the holiday celebrating the completion of a year's reading of the holy scroll, Beth El members unroll the entire Torah, which helps them see all they have accomplished and understand what they are celebrating. As for dress codes, sweatshirts are fine, mink coats are not. There are no *macher*s there the way there are at most synagogues, getting rooms named after them for making big donations. That simply would not wash in a ruthlessly egalitarian congregation like this one, where lay people are as likely to conduct a service as the rabbi or cantor. Gender preferences also are out, which is why women are as likely to don talliths as men, and why in 1980 the congregation published what Kushner calls "the only gender-neutral liturgy anywhere in the world."

Beth El's prayer book returned much of the Hebrew that other Reform congregations had taken out, long before such restorations became the fashion. It expanded the Sabbath morning service and added brief readings for Sukkoth, Simchat Torah, and other festivals. It eliminated the traditional verse "Blessed art Thou, Lord our God, King of the Universe"—which it said conjured up an image of "the Creator as a hoary old king seated on the throne of mercy"—substituting "Holy One of Blessing, Your Presence fills creation." It stripped all prayers of male-dominated text. "We have dealt with these limitations in two ways," the Beth El authors explain in an introduction to the ninth printing. "By addressing the Holy One as both He and She, we hope to broaden and enrich our concept of God while learning to pray neither to Him nor to Her but to the Holy One, Creator of all. In most cases, however, we have chosen to address the Holy One as You rather than He or She. Not only does this avoid the need for either masculine or feminine pronouns, but it encourages a more personal bond between us and our God who is immanent as well as transcendent."

Kushner left in the summer of 2000 to teach full-time, after twenty-eight years at Beth El, and his congregants already miss him. But they are confident the reforms will stay along with the exuberance. "I think the culture of the place is established. Larry fostered a kind of independence among the congregation," says Diamant, who is on the committee searching for a rabbi to replace Kushner. "Congregations get the rabbis they deserve. We are looking for someone who is not another Larry, but is a great teacher and visionary in his own way, who is comfortable with the customs of the place. Beth El has been a leader in this style of worship for a while and it has caught on; it's less fringy than it used to be. At one point what happened at Beth El was considered kooky and it's not anymore. It is mainstream, or at least where the stream is headed."

Diamant is right. You can see it at synagogues across the Boston area. Rabbis have gone from being illustrious but Olympian orators in the mode of Temple Israel's Joshua Loth Liebman and Roland Gittelsohn, to bringing the *bimah*, or pulpit, down to their congregants the way Kushner did. Synagogues have been transformed from sterile sanctuaries devoted to restrained worship, to spiritual centers where members go for counseling on being gay or single, old or young, in mourning or getting divorced. Children are no longer whisked out of the sanctuary the first time they open their mouths, and a growing number of worshipers actually understand the Hebrew words they are uttering. Perhaps most surprising of all, women are being steered back to *mikvahs* by Reform and Conservative rabbis as well as Orthodox ones, with the ceremonial baths now used to celebrate the birth of a child or grieve over a miscarriage instead of just being a place for married women to purify themselves after menstruation. Rabbis now are involved in all aspects of congregants' lives, and synagogues are becoming the vital centers of community that their founders dreamed of, a place to go to out of choice as well as out of duty, with many Jews shopping around for one that fits their personality rather than signing up at the one that is nearest.

It is not just synagogues where spiritual life is blooming. Jews are meeting on their own to study the Talmud and Torah, to celebrate, mourn, and do all the other things that traditionally in America were done in synagogues. Boston has its own forty-year-old tradition in which pious Orthodox, along with countercultural *havurah*, meet in small groups and at members' homes. Today, nearly one in ten Jews there belong to a *havurah* or to a minyan group, either within a synagogue or independent of it. Sometimes, as with Shaarei Tefillah of Newton, a congregation launched by a handful of families in 1983 to celebrate a single holiday slowly changed shape—moving from home to home, building a house, hiring a part-time rabbi, and, in 1995, bringing on Benjamin Samuels as its first full-fledged rabbi. Even as it has grown to 145 families, the congregation remains cutting-edge and at times controversial, with the Orthodox Samuels reaching out to his coreligionists by teaching at Reform and Conservative synagogues and at the JCC. It also remains highly educated, with Tefillah-watchers joking that "if you don't have three degrees they won't let you in."

The Newton Centre Minyan is equally open-minded, but it has decided to remain as close to its nonhierarchical roots as when it started in 1979. That means no rabbi or other professional leader telling anyone when to sit or stand, no ownership of a building, no debt or fund-raising campaigns, no attempts to recruit members, and no pressuring or interfering with other members' ways of expressing their Jewishness. It does not call itself a shul because that implies more services than it can offer or wants to, and it does not call itself a *havurah* because that implies a '60s sort of clannishness. The service has aspects of the Orthodox with a full Torah reading every Shabbat, and of the Reform with lots of singing, women reading from the Torah, and regular references to matriarchy. Setup, cleanup, and whatever other work needs to be done are distributed among the 137 households that belong, decisions are made in the fashion of a New England town meeting, and a hall to hold services is rented at the First Baptist Church. Members also join together for social action projects and to help one another through periods of loss. The minyan's founders simply wanted to have a service that was authentic, sincere, and free from the strictures of the suburban synagogue, with no notion of going beyond its limited summertime and occasional holiday existence. But like many ad hoc communities around Boston, it simply was too successful to die and too popular to remain small. It now celebrates the full cycle of holidays, offers members access to a cemetery, has a *mohel* as a member, and has even applied to join the Synagogue Council of Massachusetts.

"People are taking responsibility for their own religious growth," explains Sherry Israel, who teaches at Brandeis, is Boston's leading Jewish demographer, and, along with her husband, Richard, was there from the beginning at the Newton Centre Minyan. "This kind of activity was a rarity outside the Orthodox community until recently. One thing that makes it possible in Boston are the tremendous Jewish resources here. A minyan at the level of our minyan has to consistently have lots of people who are Judaically knowledgeable, and Boston has that."

The last critical element of the Jewish experience is *tzedakah*, or acts of loving-kindness. As with the first two—Torah and serving God—loving-kindness is being given an expansive new meaning these days in Boston. It implies reaching within the Jewish community to help those in need. It also means reaching beyond, building partnerships with non-Jews to promote wider goals of justice and righteousness. Both forms of outreach have been going on in Boston for nearly 150 years, and in Judaism for 3,500 years, but in the 1990s they were defined more clearly than ever as a central mission of the organized community and of thousands of individual Jews.

That mission is apparent in the 650 Jewish volunteers who each week tutor children in fourteen inner-city schools in Boston and Cambridge, Brockton and Framingham. Some tutors are as young as twelve, others as old as eighty-five. "I felt this was something I could give. It wouldn't be sitting in an organizational board meeting and nodding my head 'yes,' but something I could actually do," Susan Ansin says of her three years volunteering with the Greater Boston Jewish Coalition for Literacy at the Lucy Stone School in Dorchester. She reads to students, has them read to her, and shows that an adult is willing to take the time. Her students are eight years old and younger; she is fifty-nine. They are black, Haitian, or mixed-race kids from the heart of the city; she is a white grandmother from prosperous Weston. She is Jewish, and most of them never really knew a Jew before. But "they reacted fabulously to me, truly," she says. "I may be kidding myself but I think that the black and white thing, the Weston-Dorchester divide, disappears when I am working with that child. It's an adult working with a child who thrives on having a one-on-one with an adult.

"I feel like I am engaging in something that is very Jewish by working with these kids. There's something spiritual to me about taking what I've always thought of as a Jewish value of helping out, and going out there and doing it."

Hundreds more Jewish volunteers are lobbying the Legislature for affordable housing, coaching teens on how to interview for summer jobs, teaching people of all ages how to battle pollution, and helping immigrants learn English. The Anti-Defamation League, under the leadership of the late Leonard Zakim, started the biggest black-Jewish Seder in the nation, launched one of America's largest antibias program for teens, and developed or refined national models for attacking anti-Semitism and racism. It built bridges with African-American, Irish, and other communities that historically had tense relations with Jews, trumpeting the message that Boston Jews care about more than their self-interest. The 1,800 people who turned out for Zakim's funeral in 1999—Jews, white Catholics, black Baptists and Muslims, the powerful and the powerless—made clear that his message was heard. Other organizations, from the American Jewish Committee to the American Jewish Congress, are defending public education, opening dialogues between Christians and Jews, and promoting the separation of church and state.

The agenda is not just domestic. Boston's sister-city program is helping Rabbi Shmuel Kaminezki rebuild the battered Jewish community in Dnepropetrovsk, in the process demonstrating that American Jewry's obligation to Russian Jews did not end with the fall of the Soviet Union. Another partnership links Boston with Haifa on initiatives like battling domestic violence.

While there is more going on today in the realm of social action, the challenge has grown, too. Boston-area Jews are more segregated than ever residentially and socially, economically and educationally. Most live lives that have little or no overlap with the city's poor or with blacks, Hispanics, Asians, and other minorities. That is partly a product of the move to outlying suburbs and partly a function of the Jewish community's enviable affluence. Traveling twice a week to the inner city to tutor or otherwise help is important, as Ansin says, and real connections are being forged. But there are limits to how much true knowledge that can yield of how others live, or true collegiality. *Tzedakah* is proving to be an even more imposing challenge for the Jews of Boston than Torah and *chesed*.

Nancy Kaufman understands the impediments but is not deterred. She runs the Jewish Community Relations Council of Greater Boston, an umbrella group that coordinates social justice and outreach activities of everyone from synagogues to communal groups. It was formed in 1944 in reaction to the failure of the organized Jewish community to save more Holocaust victims, and was reenergized in 1990 when Kaufman took over and vowed to reinvolve Jews in the inner city and social action. "Coming together as Jews can be very dangerous, and not in the interests of the community, if we only focus on ourselves and on building a strong, insulated Jewish community," she says. "I, Nancy Kaufman, can choose to send my child to a Jewish day school, which I did. But that doesn't mean that I, Nancy Kaufman, don't care deeply about the quality of public education. As we start removing ourselves from PTA meetings and neighborhood associations and health centers, because we are living in a different orbit, a different life, a different environment, we run the risk of not really being in touch.

"If Jewish continuity is not about social justice, what is it for? If we are going to be Jewishly literate, what are we being Jewishly literate for if not to make the world a better place? Along with strong day schools and strong synagogues we have to have a commitment to building justice for all."

The renewal under way in Boston and other U.S. cities is not the first time the America Jewish community has undergone a broad-based and deep-seated awakening. Something strikingly similar happened a century ago, in the fading years of the nineteenth century. Then, as now, change came in response to a perceived cultural crisis and a loss of faith in old norms and institutions. Then, as now, the new approaches were fueled by the young and the optimistic, and by a shift toward the spiritual and emotional. Likewise, Boston is not alone today among American Jewish communities in redefining itself and recommitting to the principles of Torah, spirituality, and social justice. But Boston has gone further than just about anywhere in the diaspora in pushing the limits of those concepts—and Jews there talk more about self-renewal, which critics see as self-promotion, boosters see as introspection, and actually is a bit of both.

One key to Boston's success in defining a new paradigm is its leadership, starting with Barry Shrage, the head of Combined Jewish Philanthropies. Leaders of Jewish federations typically are consumed with raising money to support other people's visions for their community, but Shrage, who came from Cleveland in 1987, has been instrumental in setting the vision and explaining it to everyone from rabbis to lay leaders, the press to the political establishment. Where most communities still use old hot-button issues like Israel and the Holocaust to solicit donations, in Boston leaders talk about the vitality of the Jewish community, the need to enhance learning, and other forward-looking themes. Where the federation, synagogues, social activists, and educators often are warring in other diaspora communities—as are the Orthodox, Conservative, and Reform—in Boston, after a series of initial skirmishes, all sides are learning to respect and even like one another, and to join forces against the shared enemies of assimilation and apathy.

"The debate here no longer is about what other people are going to do to Jews, but what Jews are going to do about being Jewish," says David Gordis, president of Hebrew College and one of those who has helped shape Boston's new spirit and template. "There's nothing surprising about the assimilation that is going on; everyone always has predicted that. But there is something quite unexpected about all this reengagement. My feeling is, 'Let's give it a shot.' "

What Gordis and others are up against may be clearer there than anywhere in America because over the years Boston, with all of its scholars and its penchant for research, has been studied more often and more carefully than any other Jewish community. The last survey of the Greater Boston area, released in 1995, spelled out the hopeful signs. Membership in synagogues and other Jewish organizations was up slightly since the previous poll in 1985, as was the frequency of attendance at services, and the trend toward decreasing participation among younger Jews had ended. More Jewish children were getting some sort of Jewish education, and of those more were in a day school or other intensive program. More Jews also were volunteering for Jewish organizations, although giving to Jewish causes was down. The total population of the community was stable, and educational achievement and income both were on the rise. Denominational breakdowns were unchanged, with Reform accounting for 41 percent, Conservative 33 percent, and Orthodox just 3 percent. That makes Boston's Orthodox community one of the smallest, proportionately, of any city in America and may explain why it has had so little of the interdenominational tension that characterizes communities with larger and more rigid Orthodox populations.

The report also set out the challenges. Intermarriage continued to be of concern in Boston, as everywhere in the diaspora, with 34 percent of Jews who were wed between 1991 and 1995 marrying spouses who were not Jewish—nearly quadruple the rate among those wed before 1975. About one in five spouses who were not born Jewish had converted or considered themselves Jewish, with the rate of formal conversion slowing slightly. Nearly three-quarters of Jews married to non-Jews said it was extremely important to keep alive memories of the Holocaust, 42 percent said it was very important to be Jewish, but just 20 percent said it was critical to have Jewish grandchildren. Only 8 percent of childless mixed-marriage couples belonged to synagogues, although once they had children the membership rate rose to 26 percent A more recent study out of Brandeis finds that among children who are raised and educated Jewishly, involvement in Jewish activities slowly declines to the point where, by twelfth grade, nearly half are no longer involved with the community. The dropout rate is highest where one parent was born non-Jewish, which suggests that, according to study author Leonard Saxe, "they had a bar or bat mitzvah because the grandparents think it's an important thing to do but never integrated Judaism as a central part of their lives. It's clear to me that intermarriage is a major issue, that it is increasing, and that it is changing the nature of the community."

One way to fight back, Saxe says, is to find those adolescents jobs at institutions like Jewish day-care centers rather than at places like Burger King, to create Jewish versions of everything from SAT preparation courses to athletic clubs, and to otherwise show them, at their impressionable age, that spending time with other Jews can be a good thing. Another way is through one of the fifty-five outreach programs that the Reform community runs across Greater Boston, touching 1,000 or so people a year. There is "A Taste of Judaism: Are You Curious?" a three-session series that gives the unaffiliated and interfaith a sense of what is special about this faith and an invitation to take the next step. There are "Yours, Mine & Ours" for partners in mixed marriages, "When Your Son or Daughter Falls in Love with Someone from a Different Faith" for parents who face that situation, and a sixteen-week "Introduction to Judaism" that looks at traditions and holidays, symbols, liturgy, and music.

"I'm realistic," says Paula Brody, who runs the outreach efforts. "The intermarriage rate is not fueled by people losing touch with their Judaism. It is fueled by Christians being open today to intertwining their lives with Jews, which wasn't the case fifty years ago. What we really need to do is train, train, train rabbis, educators, clinicians, and other Jewish professionals to understand the incredible complexity of this issue and what is involved in terms of really working with people successfully. What are the messages that we as a Jewish community want to give out? The message we need to give out is, 'We want you at our Seder, come, fall in love with Judaism, understand the history of the Jewish people, make it part of your memory system.' People need to gradually grow into Judaism. If we do our work they definitely will have a Jewish family."

Penelope McGee Savitz heard that message two years ago when she was getting ready to marry Andy Savitz. "First of all I fell in love with a Jew. He didn't ask me to convert but he wanted his children to be Jewish. I wanted our whole family to be Jewish. I didn't want to be at my son or daughter's bar or bat mitzvah and not be an active participant," she says. So the pair took weekly tutorials with a rabbi at a Conservative synagogue in Brookline, spent two hours a week reading about Jewish history and culture, began going to services, and started observing the Sabbath at their home in Cambridge. Today they have Shabbat dinners every Friday night, complete with candle lighting and challah, blessings over the wine and prayers in honor of their infant son, Noah McGee Savitz. They go to synagogue most Saturday mornings, then come home and spend the day walking and reading, reflecting on the week past and enjoying a day away from their high-pressure worlds of work.

Penelope, who was raised Catholic, is now an informed and active Jew. Andy has undergone a transformation almost as profound, making clear that when the Jewish community welcomes intermarried couples it can bring the Jewish partner back into the fold along with the non-Jewish one. "Before I married Penny I was what they call a 'revolving-door Jew,'" he explains. "I belonged to my parents' synagogue in Wellesley and would go to services with them on the High Holidays, although many years I didn't get there even then. But as our rabbi told us in conversion class, 'a religion that demands nothing gets nothing.' Before I was a very enthusiastic secular Jew but after Penny's conversion I am an enthusiastic secular Jew and an enthusiastic religious Jew. I'm also a more informed Jew. When I was a kid I rebelled against everything, including the idea of going to Hebrew and Sunday schools. I've learned a lot more as an adult. Next year Penny and I are going to chair our synagogue's membership committee."

*   *   *

My family has felt the same pushes and pulls as the wider community— pushed by forces of assimilation to wander from Jewish practice and even belief, then pulled back by a sense that Judaism is where we belong. It had happened in my grandparents' generation, and happened again in my parents'.

My father had two brothers, both of whom married Jewish women. My mother had two sisters and a brother and they did the same. They did it because they were part of the generation that was reaching adulthood just as the world was finding out about the Holocaust, and Jews who survived felt they had to carry on for those who perished. They did it because their world was more Jewish then, from friends and neighbors to sweethearts. They did it because the other worlds they intersected with—especially those of the WASPs and Catholics—were less welcoming then and sometimes were openly hostile. They did it because that was how they were brought up, and at that point in their lives they did not think much about it.

Over time, however, each had to come up with his own answers. "If you had your life to live over you'd say, 'Why couldn't I be part of the majority rather than a minority?' " says Raymond Tye, my father's brother, who had to face down anti-Semites as a boy in Haverhill and as a young man in the Military Police during World War II, as a junior executive in Boston in the 1950s and as one of the city's business wisemen over the following forty years. His experience in the military taught him that "no matter where you are, being Jewish brings problems." His experience as head of New England's largest liquor distributorship taught him that "the Christian business world did business with Jews but when it came five o'clock, they went their own way and we were not included. I called it the five o'clock shadow and in some ways it still exists." But he adds that "while it was difficult being a Jew, I had a firm conviction that we had to be proud of it because of our history. Because every possible impediment was put before the Jews. My commitment to Judaism went from anger at what could happen to us as Jews, to a pride."

That pride played itself out not by his attending synagogue, which he did only on the High Holidays or when it was required for family reasons, but by helping form the Hillel House when he was at Tufts, helping build the Anti-Defamation League in Boston into one of America's strongest chapters, helping Dewey Stone raise money to buy arms for Israel in its prestatehood days, helping his friend Cardinal Cushing understand why he needed to befriend the Jews, and how he could, and helping every Jewish cause that beseeched him for support over the next five decades. As for Israel, he says, "the Law of Return didn't apply to me. I felt that my country was America and I would live or die as a free person in America. But I did believe there was a need for Israel and I contributed to it very substantially. There was a need for the identity of a homeland where there was a right of return for anybody who wanted to be there."

His own Jewish identity came into focus when, years after he and his first wife divorced, he settled into a new marriage with a woman who was Catholic, a woman who had spent seven years in a convent and left the night before she was to take her final vows as a nun. He was secure in his own Jewishness but this marriage raised all sorts of issues of practice and perception, of whether his wife would share his religious commitment and how much he could share hers. Eileen, Ray's new wife, ended up embracing Jewish rituals and customs, but the issue was not really decided until years later. "When Ray was in the hospital once I went to the rabbi and said, 'I have been practicing Judaism for the eight years we have been married but my big concern is, if anything happened to my husband or me, we're prohibited from being buried together,'" she recalls. "I asked if a formal conversion would make a difference, and he said it would a make a big difference." So she converted. "The real reason for converting is that I believe strongly there's only one God," adds Eileen, whose Jewish name is Meira. "And I want to worship that

God with my husband and be buried with him and just have a life that isn't torn two separate ways."

Living a Jewish life that felt consistent also was a concern for my mother's brother, Maurice Rubinoff, but his struggle took a decidedly different form. He grew up in Portland, Maine, in a home that was Jewish in ritual and culture. Milk and meat were served in separate dishes, and were eaten while reading Yiddish papers like *Morgen Journal* and *Der Tag*. He went to Hebrew school, but remembers the stink bombs he tossed through the window to disrupt classes more than anything he learned sitting at his desk. He would have been bar mitzvah, but his father died when he was twelve and the family was too preoccupied. That death, however, brought him closer than ever to his religion. He attended shul every morning for nearly a year, paying tribute to his father and, in the process, learning to don tefillin, becoming familiar with the liturgy, and even leading the services, although the old men with whom he prayed could not resist teasing him for showing up without jacket or tie and sweating profusely after making a last-minute dash to be on time.

Death welded him to his faith a second time, at the end of World War II. He was a twenty-six-year-old ordnance officer in General George Patton's Third Army and his unit swept into the Buchenwald concentration camp just five days after it was liberated. "Some thousands were still alive, but would have been better dead," he recalled fifteen years later. "I saw piled-up stacks of bodies, with twitching limbs the rule, not the exception, piles of white ash with pieces of unburned bone protruding, spic and span crematoriums, immaculate execution chambers—products of the orderly Hitlerian German mind. I recall thinking to myself that such people could live under the same sun, moon, and stars was not only unbelievable, but an insult to the theology of God!"

While most soldiers in his unit headed home with their tortured memories, Maurice was assigned to stay behind temporarily in Bavaria. One Friday night, after Sabbath services at his base, he and five friends drove to the tiny town of Amberg to check out rumors that there were death camp survivors there. He found seventy-five of them, from Poland, Russia, and Germany—all patients in a United Nations–run sanatorium, all "well labeled by the tattooed numbers on their arms and by their striped concentration camp jackets," and all people who, but for their early escape from Abel, could have been his sisters or cousins, his aunt or mother. Over the next seven months my uncle became those survivors' savior. He woke early to get his army duties done, spending afternoons and weekends in Amberg. He "borrowed" supplies the Army did not need, pestered Jewish and secular relief agencies, and rallied his wife, Leah, to undertake a collection of food, clothing, and medicine back in Portland. He wrote to B'nai B'rith and the Joint Distribution Committee, to the *Jewish Advocate* and the *Jewish Daily Forward*, begging them to help the Jews of Amberg track down surviving relatives. He led the way in rebuilding Amberg's synagogue, which the Nazis had used to stable cavalry horses, and transformed the upstairs into living quarters, a mess hall, a library, and a workroom. He led worship services and helped the worshipers slowly build back their faith.

"I would like to express my deepest thanks and daily blessings to an American Jewish Sergeant by the name of Maurice J. Rubinoff, or as he himself asked to be called, Moishe," read a 1946 letter in *Der Tag* from Gershon Jakob Mintz, who identified himself by the number the Nazis seared into his arm, 15917. "He reunited me with the only twig which remained after the Hitler flood. And besides that he also strengthened my will, consoled me and gave me hope. And this he did not only for me alone, but for all the other Jews who were left alive." Intrepid investigative reporter I. F. Stone also wrote about Amberg, recalling a visit to the synagogue shortly after it was reconstructed: "In the office of this center there were two pictures. One, a small one, was a picture of Theodor Herzl, the Viennese journalist who founded the Zionist movement. The other, a very large picture, was a picture of their hero and messiah, Sergeant M. Rubinoff of Portland, Maine."

Back in Portland, Maurice settled into a more mundane life, one where he worked in and eventually took over his father-in-law's wholesale candy business. That meant going on the road to sell nearly every day, which did not leave much time for things Jewish. But he slowly began to find the time, agreeing when Jews in the small town of Berlin, New Hampshire, asked him to be their Hebrew teacher on days when he was there selling. They gave him use of a small house so he and Leah could come back weekends and he could officiate at bar mitzvah and other services. Later he taught Hebrew in Portland and ran the Hebrew school at Temple Beth El, helped build a new home for the Shaarey Tphiloh Synagogue, and, after turning sixty, finally got the bar mitzvah he had been deprived of as a youth. Until his death in 1998, Maurice led services, delivered sermons, and blew the shofar at Congregation Etz Chaim, the intimate Orthodox shul where he had worshiped as a child. He was, in effect, the rabbi of that congregation much like he had been the messiah for the survivors of Amberg, but he still lacked confidence next to his ancestors. "I felt like a nothing or a nobody in terms of Jewish intellectual background," he told interviewers in 1977. "Of course, you have to understand, a generation back this was the standard that they used. Today the standards are quite different. But in those days knowledge and understanding was everything and I am a part of that generation. I felt this inadequacy, and subconsciously, maybe, I always felt that I had the need to acquire a greater understanding and a greater knowledge."

That sense of not quite measuring up was not unique to my uncle Maurice. My parents and their siblings all felt it to some extent, which was natural given how learned their forebears had been. My grandparents were part of what I think of as a lost generation of immigrants. Forever struggling just to learn the language, earn a living, and educate their children, they never really felt a part of this strange new land. But their ongoing bond to the shtetl world they had left behind was in a strange sense freeing. It freed them of the self-doubts their children would feel about whether they were becoming too assimilated—too *Americanisher*—and whether they somehow were letting down the proud line of Jewish intellectuals from which they sprung. By contrast, my aunts and uncles, my mother and father, were successful Americans, all of them. They were also active Jews, ones who took leadership roles in their communities in and around Boston, and later in more far-away places. Yet only my Aunt Sylvia and Uncle Arnie kept on keeping kosher, with the smells of chicken soup and tzimmes filling her kitchen every Friday night, and only they kept going to synagogue every Saturday morning, becoming fixtures at Temple Emeth in Brookline and in the process honoring their parents and grandparents. Everyone else could rightfully say that they knew more than their ancestors about Jewish communal life, but they knew far less about its texts and laws, which was the direction all committed American Jews seemed to be headed in the 1960s, '70s, and '80s.

Mauray and Dorothy Tye, my parents, were a case in point. He was president of Temple Emanuel in Haverhill and the conscience of the congregation. She was the first president of its sisterhood and a firebrand for everything Jewish in town. Together they founded the synagogue's Social Action Committee and cofounded the region's Catholic-Jewish Dialogue, were driving forces in B'nai B'rith, the American Jewish Committee, and the Anti-Defamation League, and endowed a scholar-in-residence program that brings leading Jewish figures to Haverhill for a weekend of contemplation with the community. They believed in, gave money to, visited, and read everything that was written about Israel, but also believed in the diaspora and felt totally at home there. They saw that my brother, sister, and I went to Hebrew school and Sunday school, kept kosher when we were young in deference to my father's parents, hosted enormous Passover Seders for an extended family and friends, and conveyed to us a sense of how special being Jewish was. It was all they could do, and more than most did. The result was that our Jewish knowledge, like theirs, was deep and rich when it came to contemporary issues—but razor-thin in terms of understanding the Hebrew we read in synagogue or knowing the Torah, Midrash, and other sacred literature that had been so essential to our grandparents.

What did that mean to my generation, to me, my brother and sister, and fifteen first cousins, all now between thirty-five and fifty-five years old and many raising children of their own? The trend seemed to be toward further assimilation, much as was happening across Boston and the Jewish diaspora. The Holocaust did not resonate for us quite the way it had for them, nor did ties to a Jewish state that less and less depended on our help. Most visited Israel but never dreamed of moving there. Most never lived in a kosher house, never read Jewish newspapers, never thought twice about eating lobster or even ham, and never understood the Yiddish our parents would use when they wanted to share secrets. I grew up knowing the hurt of having the door slammed shut on Halloween by neighbors saying they did not give candy to Jews, of being glared at or whispered about as we walked to High Holiday services at Temple Emanuel. But anti-Semitism faded as I aged, and it simply was not the defining force for me that it was for my parents. Add it all together and the result, inevitably, was that we would be a bit less Jewish than our parents and grandparents, the same way they had been less than theirs.

But something unexpected happened on the way to conformity. My sister and brother-in-law were looking for an alternative to the under-funded public schools for their daughters and, with encouragement from my father, they slowly warmed to the idea of a Hebrew day school. Since there was no such school in or near Haverhill they helped found one, and each daughter spent four years there. The result was "to make Judaism a significant, vibrant, and fundamental part of me early in life," says my niece Rachel, who graduated from college a year ago. "While I was a student at the Solomon Schechter School I lived and breathed Judaism. I had no consciousness of any alternate mode of existence. Half of my day was in Hebrew and half was in English, and that was normal. I spent all of my days in the synagogue and all of my friends were Jewish. I didn't have to be consciously Jewish during those days—that's just how life was."

Things got more difficult later, when she transferred to public school, then a private high school and Brown University. She grappled with her Jewish identity and whether she believed in God. She explored and rejected the campus Hillel program, and explored and rejected Buddhism. She attended synagogue irregularly and made lots of non-Jewish friends. Just when she seemed to be moving away from her religion, however, "I realized that even though I don't go to temple regularly I have internalized the prayers. I feel comfortable in synagogue in a way that not even my parents do. And I do experience some form of spirituality, even if I don't necessarily feel the presence of God. . . . Jewish day school made me Jewish in a very effortless way, and I don't think I will ever totally lose that."

Something similar happened to Rachel's younger sister, Andrea, who is carrying on the family tradition by attending Tufts. "Schechter made me comfortable with my religion," she says. "It made me feel so involved in my religion, so proud of it, that I decided to have my bat mitzvah in Israel. Most people my age just wanted to have a party here with all their friends."

Rachel and Andrea were not the only ones touched by the Jewish day school experience. My sister, Suzanne, grew up feeling that "religion was required. We were told what it was and how to define ourselves within that context. I was sort of on automatic pilot." Then she watched her children attend a Hebrew day school, seeing them appreciate the history that had escaped her and learn to translate the Hebrew that she had been reading without understanding all those years. "They belonged in that temple in a way that I didn't," she says. Through all of that she was too busy with her job as a social worker, and together with her doctor-husband Norman raising two children, to really figure out what Judaism meant to *her*. But now she has reconnected with several of her friends from the Schechter days for informal Jewish studies classes. She and Norman attend meetings of the American Jewish Committee. They have begun hosting the dinner to break the Yom Kippur fast and, in the year 2000, had the first real Seder at their home. Suzanne is even thinking about being bat mitzvah, which was something girls in Haverhill did not do when she was growing up. "I'm searching," she explains. "I'm in the formative stages of figuring out what Judaism means to me."

My brother, Donald, is at a similar stage, finding himself drawn back to Judaism not by his parents or grandparents, but by his Israeli-born wife and his children. In his case they are sons, aged six and nine, both of whom attend the Solomon Schechter school in Newton. Ariella, a psychologist and Hebrew teacher, had the children speaking Hebrew as well as they do English before they started school, and she and Donald look to Schechter to fill in Elan and Eitan's Jewish identity and become the family's center of Jewish community.

"It was a joke when I was growing up, and now I take it seriously," Donald, a Boston attorney, says of his religious education. He has attended parent education classes at the children's school, learning a bit about the Talmud and prayer, Jewish literature and Jewish thought, and he reads the school newsletter to find out about that week's Torah portion. He also joined the board of the Jewish Family and Children's Service, a Boston-area welfare agency. "I read Hebrew at our Seder this past Passover in Israel and my kids laughed at my pronunciation," adds Donald. "I am envious of my kids' fluency in Hebrew and of their knowledge of Judaism. I have promised myself that within the next year I will participate in the *Me'ah* program, where I will study for a hundred hours about Judaism. If I am not able to speak with them in Hebrew, at least I should understand better what they are learning in school."

My fifteen first cousins offer an even better control group to explore the prospects for Jewish continuity, and, at first glance, the situation does not look promising. They are a diverse group that represents every element in American Jewry, with professions ranging from health care and real estate to the food, liquor, and printing businesses. They cover the landscape geographically, with some spreading out to San Francisco and Phoenix, Denver and Aspen, while others stayed closer to home in Boston and Portland. As for religion, of the ten who are married five married non-Jews, and of those who are single most say they would like to date Jews but often do not. Taken together, my cousins seemed to embody that elusive 50 percent of the unaffiliated or uninvolved that show up in every poll of Jews today—the ones community leaders are most worried about because religion and culture do not play defining roles in their lives, and who journalists have the most difficulty tracking down because they seldom show up at synagogues or other Jewish settings.

A closer look suggests Judaism is more important to nearly all my cousins than it seems on the surface, which is often the case in the diaspora. "The children know they are Jewish," says one female cousin who married a Catholic and named her two children after Jewish relatives, including my father and Nana Minnie. Her family celebrates the High Holidays and Passover, and lights four menorahs on Hanukkah, but also celebrates Easter and Christmas. The children will attend Hebrew school when they get older, and the family will pick a synagogue of its own instead of just going to her father's. This cousin, like others, answered a questionnaire I prepared that was modeled after the one Combined Jewish Philanthropies gave to Jews across the Boston area, and I promised her and the rest of my relatives anonymity in return for candor. She said her children, who are five and six, ask so many questions that they know more about Judaism than she did at their ages, even though she was raised by two Jewish parents. She also said, "I am not going to deny them a Catholic education . . . after all, they are OUR children."

Another female cousin recently married a man who is Catholic, and who she says "has been studying on his own to learn more about the

Jewish culture, history, etc. We plan to take classes together at the Reform synagogue so that he may convert sometime soon. In the meantime we maintain the Jewish customs, traditions, philosophies, and values as a family." When she has children, she adds, "they will be brought up Jewish." As for prospects for Jewish survival, she says they are "great" since "when there is interest, something does not die." A third cousin, also married to a non-Jew, is less sanguine. While Judaism "definitely is a part of my identity," she says it also is "not observed very much. . . . If I'm an example of the majority, then I would say we're in great trouble."

Other cousins carry scars from the anti-Semitism they suffered growing up, or the rejection they felt from other Jews, especially if they married a non-Jew. "I can remember for seven years being called a 'kike' at Eastern Slopes Inn, and in the seventh grade I was beaten up by a gang that called me a 'fucking Jew.' I remember going into a pizza place in Newton Corner and a kid saying, 'Are you going to get a bagel pizza?' " says one male cousin. "It's all based on having dealt with anti-Semitism at a young age. It's something that still haunts me. I don't want to associate with New York Jews, I don't want to be associating with whining Miami Jews. Yet at the same time, if someone made an anti-Semitic comment, I'd be the first one to jump up and want to fight." Another cousin, who married a Catholic woman, celebrates Jewish and Christian holidays, is raising his children as Jews, sends them to Hebrew school, and says they probably will be bar and bat mitzvah. "The [Jewish] culture and traditions are wonderful," he says, "and are clearly part of who I am. But, sadly, our response to the Holocaust and anti-Semitism may be more definitive than the richness of our religion, traditions, culture, and history. It defines how we deal and respond to everyone, Jew and Gentile, in every situation. Please do not interpret this as a minimization of the Holocaust or any other events. It just [is] very sad that we were brought up, as were our parents, to circle the wagons. Although I'm not sure how to get past that, I know that it's not the answer."

What about my cousins who married within the faith? One belongs to a Renewal congregation "with a social consciousness," along with a "loose *havurah*," and celebrates major Jewish festivals, contributes to Jewish charities, sends his children to Jewish day camp and Hebrew school, sent them for a couple years to Yiddish culture Sunday school, and plans on their being bat and bar mitzvahed. "I like to think of my Jewishness as a source of being aware of ethical obligations and as a reminder to respect minority viewpoints," he says. His wife adds, "As a child of two Holocaust survivors, who was raised pretty much without any religious upbringing, social or cultural traditions, my identity and desire to connect with [my] heritage came later—in college. Then with children came the desire for perpetuation/survival." Another cousin in similar circumstances belongs to a synagogue and a JCC, lights Sabbath candles several times a month, celebrates all the big holidays, and contributes to Jewish charities. Yet he says his children know less about Judaism than he did at their ages because he grew up "in a Conservative congregation with more observant parents," while his children "are involved in a Reform congregation with less observant parents. . . . The links in the culture chain to our ancestors are weakening, and it bothers me to see that what has always been so important to my parents and their parents (and consequently, important to me as a matter of respect for them) is somehow, in some measure, getting lost. . . . I'm not quite sure what the solution to this problem is—either at a personal level, or more generally; but you have me thinking about it again, at least for a bit, and that's probably a good thing." Another cousin who married a Jew says they and their two children are "highly assimilated." He applauds religion's role in providing spiritual fulfillment but says that it can also "isolate that group from the population at large and declare all those not adhering to the chosen religion inferior."

The best defense against assimilation like that is supposed to be a deep and varied Jewish education of the kind many young people are getting today. That is a compelling theory, yet I wonder what the theorists would make of my cousin who got the best Jewish education of any of us when he was young, including Hebrew day school, Jewish day and overnight camp, study of the Talmud and other texts, and a religious piety that included praying when he got out of bed, at each meal, and in the evening and nighttime. "I was on top of the world," he says, recalling his commitment at age thirteen. He went on, decades later, to marry a Catholic woman who was equally steeped in her religion. Today their life seems like a series of contradictions to anyone looking in from the outside, with a framed Catholic marriage contract on one wall, a Jewish *ketubbah* on another. There is a mezuzah on the door, Jewish songs often can be heard in the home, and his two young children celebrate Jewish holidays, are beginning to learn Hebrew, occasionally attend synagogue, and probably will be bar and bat mitzvah. They also celebrate Christian holidays and are being educated in Catholicism. My cousin still loves his religion and still conducts services at a Jewish old age home, but he deeply resents the harsh judgments that Jewish friends and relatives have made of his choices and the way he is raising his family. "I practice my Judaism privately and with my family," he says. "I don't want or need to compare notes or be grilled by others. . . . The hatred and discrimination I grew up with—non-Jew against Jew, Jew against non-Jew, even rich Jew against poor Jew—that really turned my stomach."

Of all my relatives, the most avidly Reform was my mother's younger sister, Judy, who grew up in Portland and Boston and now lives in Scarsdale. For more than thirty years she and her husband have been active members of the Westchester Reform Congregation, one of America's most cutting-edge Reform synagogues. She grew up with what she calls a Conservadox background, adoring and admiring her grandfather the rebbe, but she also loved and admired her husband, who found in Reform as much ritual or tradition as he wanted or needed. Judy and Len were more surprised than anyone when their son Scott became an Orthodox rabbi and scholar in the tradition of his great-grandfather and the seven generations of Litvak rabbis who came before.

"I remember as a child every Friday night we'd light the *Shabbes* candles. First of all my mother would get a little teary-eyed, wistful, and nostalgic, because the candles would bring out memories of her parents and grandparents," says Scott, forty-one, who lives in Brooklyn with his wife and seven children, and now goes by his Jewish name, Zalman. "She lost her father when she was only one, so her grandfather Shmuel became a sort of surrogate father. She remembers him being very gentle, warm, and fatherly, and he was Torah literate, learned, and observant. She always wanted me to be like him. As I was growing up that was the only aspiration she ever expressed to me. She did not want me to be a doctor or lawyer; she wanted me to become a rabbi like *zeydeh* Shmuel. I always cherished my mother, I cherish her to this day, and that certainly resonated with me. But that's only the beginning of the story."

The story picks up in Israel, first with a family trip there after his bar mitzvah, then a semester there during his sophomore year at Wesleyan University, when he participated in an archeological dig that brought home just how old and inspired Jewish traditions are. A chance encounter with a cousin introduced him to the Orthodox yeshiva movement called Ohr Somayach, which offered intensive study programs aimed at non-Hebrew-speaking North Americans like him. He returned and enrolled after graduation, studying mornings, afternoons, and evenings for nine months. "They would teach me how to learn. They gave me the keys to do it on my own," he says. He used those keys to open doors to the world of his rebbe ancestors, but also remained very much a part of this world, first drawing on his dual training as psychologist and rabbi to extract young Jews from Christian cults, and now selecting and accompanying to Jerusalem scores of promising Jewish college students who will study, as he did, at Ohr Somayach.

"I look at pictures of my great-grandfather Shmuel, and of our son, and they're both wearing yarmulkes, both wearing tzitzis," says Zalman. "With ritual we create a sense of connections with every generation."

As for his mother, Judy, she has come to respect Zalman's Torah-observant beliefs and behaviors even as she clings to her Reform ones. She tells stories of her grandchildren and their friends sitting around the pizza shop after school, the way all teenagers do, except these teenage girls are wearing ankle-length skirts, the boys are wearing tzitzis and *payess*, and the shop is closed on the Sabbath and serves only pizza that meets the strict standards of *glatt* kosher. She loves the way her four-year-old granddaughter, Shoshana Rivke, called the other night to tell her, "*Bobbeh*, I love *Shabbes*." Most of all Judy cannot get over the way her son has rebuilt the broken chain to her grandfather.

"I know how heartbroken my grandfather was when he died that no one was able to carry on the traditions. His children were all intellectuals and socialists," she says. "I also know how much my mother adored Scott. Somehow, in my gut, I love the idea of how proud they would be of him carrying on. It was supposed to die because my grandfather's children didn't take it on. I was the only one of my mother's children who went Reform, because of my husband, so I was the least likely to produce a hero of traditionalism. Why did it happen? That's the miracle. It's a special gift to my mother and my grandfather, and I hope he is watching somewhere."

Chapter 4

BUENOS AIRES:

An Explosive Awakening

It has been more than seven years now. But every Monday morning of every week that passes, 368 Mondays and counting, they come to pay homage and plead for justice before the austere walls of Argentina's Supreme Court. A young widow implores prosecutors to find and punish the murderers of her husband, who perished along with 85 others when a bomb ripped through the Jewish communal complex in 1994. A community leader sounds the sacred shofar, hoping the piercing pitch of the ram's horn will rouse those in the nearby courthouse much the way it tumbled the walls of Jericho more than 3,000 years before. Throughout the courtyard 200 others stand in mute demand for action.

So far, no one has answered their call.

The government vowed swift action in the wake of the bombing, the second in two years against a Jewish target. But the investigation has called into question the state's competence and its possible complicity. Only low-level functionaries have been arrested, evidence of links to the police and other powerful interests has been buried, and prosecutors concede they probably never will resolve who ordered and paid for the attack against the Argentine Israelite Mutual Aid Association, or AMIA. When the president and 150,000 other Argentineans took to the streets to denounce the bombing shortly after it happened, many Jews thought they really could feel at home in that decidedly Catholic country. The apathy ever since has made them think again.

Some within Buenos Aires's 170,000-strong Jewish community have responded by steering clear of connections to their faith and culture. Being Jewish, they concluded, simply is too dangerous. They already identified themselves as Latin along with Jewish, taking pride in the fact that their grandparents had helped settle Argentina a century before, so they simply started emphasizing the secular side of their identity and being more circumspect about their ethnicity. The explosion also laid bare the Jewish community's economic woes, causing umbrella organizations like AMIA to teeter and forcing synagogues and social clubs to spend millions of scarce dollars hiring security guards and erecting car-stopping concrete barriers. And the recent violence has resurrected grim memories—of how Argentina became the Nazis' escape route of choice after World War II, and how thirty years later Jews made up a disproportionate share of the *desaparecidos,* or disappeareds, when Argentine generals waged their Dirty War against supposed subversives.

Those are the responses that world Jewry knows about and that prompted it to elevate Argentina to the top of its list of distressed diaspora communities. But a look behind the dramatic press accounts and desperate pleas from communal leaders makes clear that the AMIA attack set off stirrings of a very different sort for large numbers of Argentina's Jews. Rather than scare them away, the bomb has served as a rallying cry. Anti-Semites, these Jews reasoned, had shown that they did not distinguish a Jew who is practicing from one in denial, so why not learn more about what this 3,500-year-old religion stands for and why their ancestors clung to it despite the perils and pitfalls. The government would not move on its own to track down the bombers, so Jews would have to stand together to make it move—and what better way to do that than by turning up each Monday in front of the Tribunales building, paying tribute and demanding answers.

That is not the reaction the bombers had counted on or that even the most prophetic Argentine Jew could have foretold. It saw one of the diaspora's most isolated and assimilated communities pushed to the brink by the deadliest assault ever against Jews in the Americas—but rather than retrenching these Jews have come out fighting, vowing to stand up to their enemies and reconnect with their landsmen. What is happening is nothing short of a seismic event in Argentine Jewry's 200-year history, nothing short of amazing in the annals of a Jewish diaspora filled with amazing stories. And it offers a resounding message to the world: What really counts are not a community's central structures or financial fortunes, both of which are in disarray in Argentina. What matters most are the connections that real people forge at the grassroots level with one another and their faith.

"When the problems around us are bigger, each one of us has more need to know where he comes from, where he goes, and who he is," explains esteemed Argentine poet Eliahu Toker. "Before the bombing many Jewish writers like me didn't want to be stamped as Jewish. After the bombing I don't know that we would say our works are Jewish, but we recognized ourselves as Jewish.

"The community organizations were ill before the bombing and afterward the illness is much clearer. But that is the organized community, it is central institutions like AMIA. Then there is the living community, the people. Many people feel nearer to that living community after the bombing."

Debi Pinson, a seventeen-year-old with blond hair and topaz eyes, is one of those people. Like scores of young Jews from Dnepropetrovsk to Boston, she was looking for an intimate community to give her life grounding at a time when the world was moving toward the global. She found it in a small synagogue on the outskirts of Buenos Aires, where she serves as cantor many Friday evenings, sings in the choir, and helps run the children's program. And like so many fellow Jews from Düsseldorf to Jerusalem, Debi says the fact that terrorists are trying to scare her into abandoning those ties only makes her more determined to hold on.

"The people who put the bomb, what they want is for me to leave the shul, to say, 'Yes, Judaism here is finished,' " she says. "I will not give them what they want."

*   *   *

Incongruities like those, where a brutal bombing ultimately pumps life into a Jewish community, have long been part of the lure of that singular land. To understand them it is necessary to go back to the beginnings, to see why Jews ever ventured to the southernmost tip of South America and to understand how they formed the largest fraternity of Jews between Texas and the South Pole.

The first to come were the Marranos, or secret Jews, who fled Portugal more than 400 years ago just as it was entering a loose union with Spain and redoubling its drive to convert or expel its Jews. They were part of a group of "New Christians" who had converted to Catholicism to stay alive and blend in, yet these daring few quietly sustained Jewish rituals like kindling Sabbath candles and forgoing pork. The very name their contemporaries gave them—"Marrano" derives from the Spanish word for pig, or the Aramaic-Hebrew for "Mr. forced convert"— suggests the contempt in which they were held. The city fathers of Buenos Aires were suspicious enough of the underground religious observance, and alarmed enough by the commercial competition, that they convinced the Viceroy of Lima to dispatch a Portuguese inquisitor to the colony that is now Argentina. Today the Marranos are lionized for having held on to their Judaism in the face of the Inquisition and are a source of inspiration to contemporary Jews concerned about continuity, but the Marrano community in Argentina never was more than marginal and most traces of them had evaporated by the early eighteenth century.

The real roots of today's Jewish community in Argentina are considerably more recent, although almost as romantic. Jews seeking their fortunes began arriving from Western Europe in the early 1800s, at a time when there were no inquisitors to hunt them down. But the laws of the newly independent nation ordained that only Catholics could marry, register the birth of a child, or officially bury their dead. It was not until 1860 that the first Jewish wedding was recorded, it took until 1882 for Argentina to get its first rabbi and first Jewish congregation, and it was not until 1888 that legislation was passed securing the rights of Jews and other non-Catholics.

Around that time desperate circumstances in Europe and Asia combined with an opening in Argentina to attract the first large-scale Jewish immigration. Pogroms were making life unbearable for Jews in Russia and Romania, while the accession of a new ruler of the Ottoman Empire led to upheaval in the eastern Mediterranean. Argentina, meanwhile, was so eager to attract settlers to its open, unsettled landscape that it sent

recruiting agents to Europe. Their pitch was straightforward and compelling: free passage, temporary shelter at hostels, and, best of all, an
implied pledge to set aside age-old anti-Semitism provided the Jewish
refugees would work the land. History is filled with instances of nations
taking extraordinary steps to rid themselves of their Jews; seldom had
one gone to such lengths to entice them. Most would have preferred the
more familiar destination of the United States, but that often was not
an option and, in the boom years between 1901 and 1914, 87,614 Jews
officially entered Argentina. By the eve of World War I, Argentina's
Jewish community had grown to more than 100,000, which made it bigger than Palestine's.

One of those who appreciated the fortuity of the situation was Baron
Maurice de Hirsch, the descendant of a distinguished family of bankers
to the German nobility. Hirsch dreamed of rescuing his fellow Jews in
Eastern European by resettling them in North America and, even better,
along the southern edge of the New World. But his dreams assumed an
unexpected contour: the only way for Jews to truly be free, the cosmopolitan philanthropist believed, was to take up a life as "free farmers on
their own soil." That happened to be precisely what Argentina had in
mind for its vast grass-covered pampas, where the production of export-
able crops was spiraling upward but there was a shortage of hands to
harvest them and to tend the herds. The result was a series of agricultural
outposts, beginning with the now-enshrined Moisesville, where 20,000
Jews from Europe who were used to a life of commerce settled on the
land. It made for quite a sight: bearded Jews riding the range, pausing
to pray outside their barns, and occasionally succumbing to the drunkenness and lawlessness that threatened to ensnare gauchos, or cowboys,
of any faith. The new arrivals proved almost as adept in adapting to life
on the plains as the natives, in the process creating a culture that colonist
and journalist Alberto Gerchunoff immortalized in his 1910 book *The
Jewish Gauchos of the Pampas.*

Most Jewish cowboys eventually hung up their spurs and headed to
the city, settling into the more predictable lines of law and medicine,
manufacturing and finance. Yet that image of the hardworking pioneer
rooted in the rich soil remains critical to the sense of connectedness of
today's Jewish community in Argentina. Anti-Semites might characterize

them as predators leaching off the hard work of others, but Jews there know better. They proudly point to their forebears' role in settling the most remote lands, which they feel gives them as legitimate a stake in the country as any of their countrymen, 85 percent of whom also came from Europe and 90 percent of whom are Roman Catholic.

There are other images of their ancestors that Argentina's Jews would prefer to forget. In the late 1800s Polish-born Jews became major players in the field of white slavery, importing prostitutes to service the mainly male immigrants to Argentina, operating brothels and bribing officials. They even founded their own synagogue, cemetery, and communal institutions when they were shunned by the rest of the community. Jewish socialists and communists, who were far more plentiful, posed challenges of a different sort, taunting the observant by eating just across from the synagogue on the fast day of Yom Kippur and clashing with Zionists. Anti-Semites did not really care about politics, but they pretended to when they went after Jews, casting as anti-Bolshevik pogroms like one they launched in 1919 that lasted a full seven days, saw Jewish homes and shops looted and hundreds of Jewish workers hurt, and came to be known as Tragic Week.

While such incidents were relatively rare back then, the hardships were real enough that during the early 1900s one Jew left for every five who came, a rate of departure nearly three times as high as in the United States. But those who remained settled in to become Latin America's most vibrant Jewish community and, with about 300,000 members by the mid-1900s, its largest. More than two-thirds lived in Buenos Aires. In a bid to make their surroundings seem a bit less foreign, they sought to re-create the social, cultural, and political institutions they had left behind in places like Poland, Germany, Syria, and Morocco. There were a hundred or more Jewish periodicals, in Yiddish, Hebrew, and Spanish, along with stores whose New Year's cards were geared to the Jewish calendar rather than the Roman one. There were five Yiddish theaters, which was more than anywhere else in the hemisphere outside of New York, along with language schools to help the newly arrived learn Spanish and cooperative credit associations where they could get loans. The socialists organized trade unions, opened libraries, and published newspapers. Zionists did the same, as did communists and anarchists. Most early immigrants took up the trades they knew from the Old World, peddling wares on the installment plan, setting up simple shops selling basic goods, or plying needlework, baking, and other crafts.

Some of those institutions stubbornly hung on, but most were gradually transformed by their Latin environment. Yiddish and Hebrew periodicals disappeared, one at a time, as Jews learned to read Spanish. Same with the Yiddish theater, although an actress as elegant as Cipe Lincovsky managed to transpose her talents to the German theater, then to film. Pessimists worried that accommodations like those meant assimilation, which they oftentimes did. Yet just as often the result was a new way of defining Judaism, a distinctively Argentinean way that distinguished Jews there not only from their grandparents in Europe, but from their cousins who settled in places like New York and Boston.

Consider the more marginal role that synagogues have played in Argentina. Most Jews there approach their Judaism in secular rather than religious terms. The early arrivals from Germany, France, and England had long since left the ghetto and taken on the Enlightenment dream of full participation in the wider society, while the multitudes who followed from Russia and Poland had traded in the yeshiva for the new faiths of Zionism or Bundism, a Russian brand of socialism. Even among the Orthodox, which remains the biggest denomination, a special term was coined to explain their peculiar reluctance to keep kosher, attend shul, or observe Sabbath etiquette: SNOX, or strictly nonobservant Orthodox. A triumverate of traditional rabbis was sufficiently troubled by that pattern, and by the widespread practices of intermarriage and quickie conversions, that beginning in 1927 it issued a proclamation banning *any* conversions in Argentina and requiring those who wanted to convert to travel to Jerusalem and apply to a rabbinic court there (the ban was intended to last "until the end of time," but it has been widely circumvented since the 1960s). In the wider community synagogues always were more social than religious and never played the defining role that they do in North America, which helps explain why more Argentine Jews belong to Jewish sports clubs than temples.

The situation with Jewish schools was just the opposite. At their peak in the late 1960s, 20,000 students—about half the Jewish school-age population—attended one of the seventy full-time Jewish kindergartens or elementary and high schools. That is five times the rate in the United States and a bigger share than just about anywhere else in the diaspora.

In cities like Boston, each group of Jewish immigrants wanted its own synagogue where it could set the rules on the way religion would be practiced and who would worship there. In Buenos Aires, they wanted their own school. Zionists might knock on your door in the morning, trying to sign up your sons and daughters. The Orthodox would make their case in the afternoon, with the socialists and anarchists coming by in the evening. Each offered a pitch suited to its political or religious bent—for the Orthodox that meant boys only—and each warned parents that public education meant not just reading, writing, and arithmetic, but also religion as it was espoused by the all-powerful Catholic Church.

In America, successful synagogues often generate their own schools. In Argentina, the school typically came first and, once it got going, parents would open an adjoining shul. Schools offered Argentine Jews a way to preserve and pass on their religion and culture, a means of reinforcing their separateness from the consuming credo of Catholicism, and, perhaps most important, a place their children could get a substantially broader, more worldly education than the public schools offered. And the Jewish schools were good enough that their graduates have gone on to run education and other communal programs in Jewish communities from Bulgaria and Cuba to Israel and the Upper West Side of Manhattan.

Sports and social clubs were almost as central to their Jewish identities as the schools. Visit Buenos Aires on a Sabbath morning and it is there, rather than the shul, where you will typically find Jews, young and old. The clubs have everything a Jewish community center has in America, from swimming pools to gymnasiums, cultural centers to a theater, library, and restaurant. But they have lots more, as is evident from a visit to Sociedad Hebraica. Its 12,000 members and 1916 founding make it the oldest and biggest of Argentina's forty-three Jewish social clubs. The fourteen-story downtown facility has all the normal athletic offerings, along with classes in bar and bat mitzvah, baby-sitters and courses on baby-sitting, programs for singles and seniors, as well as a welfare office that helps poor Jews find jobs, get prescription drugs, and sort through their legal woes. Its suburban complex is part country club and part resort, and the 321 acres take nearly an hour to tour. It includes 550 housing units, most of which are used only on weekends and some of which are stately single-families costing $200,000. There are twenty-four tennis courts, four soccer and two rugby fields, an eighteen-hole golf course, and three swimming pools. Hungry? There is a kosher pizza bar. Want to test your athletic prowess? There are jogging groups and leagues for nearly every sport. For an average family, membership runs about $2,500 a year—three times the cost to an average JCC membership in America and a sign of just how much Jews in Argentina value belonging.

But Hebraica and the other social clubs, which together have more than 70,000 members, are about more than just entertainment. They echo Latin American culture, where sports is a passion. Italians, Syrians, and other national groups all field their own teams in Argentina, so it is only natural that Jews do, too. Jewish clubs allow for the mingling of Ashkenazim and Sephardim, of Bundists and Zionists. They cement ties with Israel through nursery school classes that feature Israeli singing and adult lectures on Israeli politics. And as with Jewish schools, they let participants connect to their heritage from the safe vantage point of secular society. Just being around other Jews makes these Jews feel better, in part because in the wider Argentine society many have been wary of fully letting down their guard.

As for religion itself, Jews in Argentina never felt comfortable with it, especially with the Orthodox forms they brought over from Europe where the rebbe was the wellspring of leadership and legend. But they never felt comfortable abandoning it entirely. So they did the next best thing, tinkering until they came up with a form that suited their new surroundings.

The most creative Argentine reformulation, ironically, came from a Conservative rabbi from Connecticut. Marshall Meyer came to Argentina in 1959 looking for adventure, although he never envisioned it lasting twenty-five years. He and his wife, Naomi, had just completed their university classes, his parents had recently died, and Buenos Aires was looking for a rabbi. Meyer understood that Argentine Jews were different from those he had studied with at Dartmouth College and the Jewish Theological Seminary in New York. They were living in a physical isolation unknown to the thriving Jewish communities of North America. They had nostalgic memories of Europe, but after sixty years had at least as much in common with Latin mores and attitudes. They not only were more secular than Jews in Europe and the United States, but more political, with a stronger tilt to the left. They had a rich Judeo-Argentine literature that, like those who read it, was preoccupied with the struggle of blending a Jewish identity with an Argentinean one. And with a community of close to 300,000, they were understandably tired of being seen as junior partners to their powerful neighbors to the north.

Meyer gave them the chance to be served by rabbis who looked and sounded like them. When he arrived every one of their spiritual leaders came from places like Germany and Poland, Switzerland, Turkey, and Israel. Spanish was a second language for them, Latin America was a foreign culture, and women were not allowed to read from the Torah. So he founded a seminary that trained enough rabbis, male and female, to fill the need locally and export them to Chile and Peru, Paraguay, Bolivia, Mexico, and even New York and California. Those who remained not only spoke Spanish to their congregants, they, like their mentor, greeted them with the soothingly familiar *che*.

Meyer also offered Argentine Jews a new, indigenous denomination. Before they had a simple choice: Orthodoxy or nothing. Now they could connect to a religion that offered transliterations and translations of a Hebrew language they could neither read nor understand, let men and women pray together, welcomed the young with music, food, and warmth, and while Conservative in name, looked to American Jews more like Reform. He gave them his mentor, Abraham Joshua Heschel, along with philosophers Martin Buber and Franz Rosenzweig, all of whom saw spirituality and human relationships as at least as important as ritualistic observance. Most of all, Meyer preached that Judaism requires its adherents to promote social justice. When the Jewish university student Graciela Narcisa Sirota was kidnapped in 1962, then had a three-inch swastika branded on her right breast, he pushed the Jewish community to organize a nationwide strike. When journalist Jacobo Timerman was arrested and tortured by the military junta, he visited Timerman in jail, the only Jewish leader to do so, even though it meant undergoing a humiliating strip search. His was an activist religion ideally suited to the activist 1960s and '70s. It offered those angry at the generals a way to hit back. It gave the young a way to relate to religion, and they brought their parents back to the synagogue. It captured the spirit of the Catholic Church's liberation theology, developed by liberal priests in the 1970s to serve Latin America's poor, only Meyer got there a decade before. It made clear that Argentina's Jews finally could feel at home in Argentina.

"For us as Jews the synagogue was the course of our grandfathers, not of us. It was a room for making bar mitzvah, not to be at every Friday," recalls Dr. Daniel Colodenco, a pulmonologist who teaches Jewish history in the rabbinic seminary Meyer set up. "Marshall attracted a lot of young people to the synagogue service by making it more socially relevant. He confronted people with a line of thinking not seen before in Argentina. We in Argentina had had just two kinds of Jewish education: classical Orthodox and Zionist. He brought insights of the American academical establishment, of Bible criticism and modern Jewish philosophy.

"For me it was a revolution, it opened a new way of thinking. He was the first rabbi, the first Jewish leader, who mixed a political opinion about human rights and politics with a Jewish position about this. Until now the Jewish positions were only toward Jewish interests, and those interests were primarily anti-Semitism and anti-Israel."

That sort of preoccupation with anti-Semitism was common across the diaspora—but Argentine Jews had more reason than most to be anxious. Ask most Jews there today and they will cite convincing facts and figures to prove there is less hostility to Jews in Argentina than, say, in the United States. Old-timers remember growing up with taunts of "Jewish shit," of learning to box and wrestle so they could defend themselves from Catholic gangs. But they also remember a trend of things getting better. Successive popes urged greater tolerance toward Jews and other non-Catholics, and public schools were secularized in 1954. Legal restrictions limiting Jewish participation in other public arenas also were eased over time, educators increasingly tried to tone down religious and racial stereotypes, and society seemed to be moving to a social pluralism that made room for Jews.

The progress, however, was anything but steady in a country that seesawed between democracy and dictatorship, pluralism and chauvinism, violence and calm, and welcoming its Jews as opposed to wishing they would go away. The most dramatic in a series of jolting interruptions came in the early 1930s, when nationalist and anti-Semitic voices were amplified by the locally powerful branch of the Nazi Party and by anxieties generated by the Great Depression. The mass immigration of

Jews had been slowed temporarily during the 1920s when Argentina, like America, feared an influx of revolutionaries from Europe. It ground to a near-halt in the late 1930s as laws were rewritten to make clear that political refugees like the Jews fleeing Europe were not the sort of immigrants Argentina was looking for. The 1920s saw nearly 75,000 Jews enter the country, but during the war years of 1933 to 1943, when European Jews were desperately trying to escape, Argentina let in fewer than 30,000. In 1947 Jews made up just 600 of the 116,000 legally admitted immigrants.

No such limits applied to Nazis and ex-Nazis. Argentina was not alone in recruiting German scientists, engineers, and other professionals anxious to escape their war-ravaged land; America, Great Britain, and Canada conscripted them for the Cold War against the Soviet Union. And not all the Germans who came, nor all 250,000 already there, were Nazis. But Argentina had been helping Axis leaders in Germany, Italy, Romania, and Vichy France plot escape routes ever since it became clear they would lose the war. After their surrender, President Juan Perón opened two offices in Europe to entice German scientists, and between 1946 and 1955 Argentina admitted nearly 40,000 Germans, along with Ukrainians, Croats, and others known for their brutal treatment of Jews. Perón and his compatriots were willing to ignore the new arrivals' Nazi pasts, which is how Argentina ended up with more than 180 war criminals. Among them were the notorious Martin Bormann, "Hitler's evil spirit," who issued the orders on concentration camps and killings; Adolph Eichmann, known for his masterful efficiency in executing those orders; and Dr. Josef Mengele, the "monster of Auschwitz," who supervised cruel experiments on twins and dwarfs. Whereas the ex-Nazis who escaped to most Western countries lived out their lives in low profile, the ones in Argentina penetrated the country's most powerful elites, from the presidential staff to parliament and the police. Some, like Mengele, felt so safe they shed their aliases. They also adopted Bariloche, the international ski resort, as their exclusive retreat.

Argentine Jews responded the way Jews have across the diaspora, by banding together to maximize their clout. A relatively weak confederation of twenty-eight Buenos Aires–based groups was launched in 1933 to protest the persecution of German Jews, and over the next several years it was expanded to include 130 organizations from across the country even as its mission was broadened to battling racism and anti-Semitism at home and abroad. The Delegation of Argentine-Israelite Associations, or DAIA, gave Argentina's Jewish community an unprecedented political voice but it did not end the ravings of Argentina's anti-Semites.

That hysteria occasionally erupted into violence. Neo-Nazis took to the streets with fire bombings and beatings in 1960, after Israel kidnapped Eichmann, and again in 1962, when it executed him. In 1967, when the military was running the country, 142 of the 313 anti-Semitic incidents reported worldwide took place in Argentina. Nazis and their sympathizers were a problem, but the Arab League posed an even greater threat with its ties to Middle East militants, its generous foreign financing, and its nonstop assault of anti-Jewish propaganda. One result of the hatred was that, in the 1950s and '60s, Argentine Jews moved to Israel in even larger numbers than Jews from the United States, where the community was ten times larger.

Such festering anti-Jewishness traces partly to the Catholic Church and partly to the "small but powerful segments of the elite that were anti-Semitic and even pro-Nazi," says Beatriz Gurevich, a Jewish historian and author who has spent ten years researching the Nazi influence in Argentina. "We can't speak of Argentine society as pro-Nazi; that's absolutely unfair. General discrimination against Jews was more extensive in the United States than in Argentina. But there were some very powerful elites that were pro-Nazi, small ideological groups that held power."

Just how powerful—and perfidious—those elites were became apparent during the Dirty War, which lasted from 1976 to 1983. The generals who seized control borrowed Nazi techniques of paramilitary policing and vicious torture, which is not surprising since much of the military was German-trained. They also echoed the Germans' targeting of Jews: among the 20,000 or more Argentineans killed by the junta, Jews accounted for nearly 10 percent, or more than ten times their share of the population. Thousands more left the country, joining thriving communities of Argentine Jews in Israel, the United States, Spain, Mexico, and Sweden, and the American Jewish Committee closed its Buenos

Aires office in 1977 because of "repeated acts of intimidation and threats to the lives of its representatives." Some analysts attribute the generals' attacks against Jews to the overrepresentation of Jews among the union leaders, university faculty, social workers, intellectuals, and other "leftist" groups being targeted. That explains part of it, but equally critical is that the military and its right-wing supporters, including many high-level churchmen, were virulently anti-Semitic.

Jews who stayed in Argentina during those years suffered more than most outsiders realized, even if they were entirely apolitical. There were "at least three to four bomb attempts per month, at least one per week," recalls Mario Ringler, president of the rabbinic seminary founded by Meyer. "They were especially menacing toward Marshall Meyer. I remember once, when I was vice president of the seminary, calling Marshall and telling him he better leave the country. They had sent him a snapshot taken with a Polaroid showing him shaving himself at his home in Belgrano. They said, 'The same way we took this picture of you, we can shoot you.' "

Jacobo Timerman, the most famous Jew arrested by the generals, also had vivid memories of that era: "The police and the military were permanently looking for Jews. When they would grab someone else they'd say, 'It's a pity it's not a Jew.' " Timerman, who wrote about what it was like being tortured and locked in isolation in his 1981 book *Prisoner without a Name, Cell without a Number,* spent the 1990s in self-imposed isolation in Uruguay recovering from heart troubles. Shortly before his death in 1999, in what he said was the first in-depth interview he had done in a decade, he made it clear that he was as anguished as ever by his fellow Jews' timidity toward the junta, which blended bids at quiet persuasion with a campaign to keep world Jewry from criticizing the generals for fear it would spur even more hostility. As for Argentina, Timerman wearily concluded that "this is permanently an anti-Semitic country, although Jews are ashamed to say it."

*   *   *

The July 18, 1994, bombing of the AMIA building seemed to prove Timerman right. It stripped away Argentine Jews' sense of security and prosperity, suggesting they were as vulnerable as ever. It showed that the institutions of government might have been democratic in name, but they were as subject to corruption and as unaccountable as in the bad old days of the dictatorship. It revealed that the community structures Jews relied on during times of crisis were themselves crumbling. And it pushed some of Argentina's 200,000 Jews to try and merge into the wider society, although over time it convinced many more that it was time to revisit the faith of their fathers.

The explosion occurred at 9:53 on a Monday morning, just as the city was gearing up for the workweek and only two months after Jews there celebrated one hundred years of organized community life. The blast blew out doors, windows, and walls along a full block in the congested garment district and could be heard five miles away. The seven-story AMIA headquarters on Pasteur Street, erected half a century before, collapsed like a castle of sand. Dozens were buried in the rubble, including young people registering at a community job bank and old ones collecting pensions. The bomb killed Christians along with Jews, ripping five-year-old Sebastian Barreiro from his mother's grip as the pair walked past the building and tossing his body halfway across the street. Survivors had to pick their way through the ruins and jump onto nearby terraces to escape. Specially trained soldiers from Israel flew in with rescue dogs and electronic sensors to help search for survivors, but all they dug out were remains of victims, including the driver of the van that carried the bomb. Rabbis held hands with relatives of those trapped in the building as they tried to keep up hope, accompanied them to the morgue to identify what was left of their loved ones, and presided over what seemed like a never-ending series of shivahs.

The final toll: 86 dead, 236 wounded, and a stretch of the city left looking like a war zone. The explosion also expunged much of the community's memory of itself, destroying thousands of books and records that documented, in Spanish, Yiddish, and Hebrew, more than a century of Argentine Jewish history. Even as he sifted through the rubble, one Argentine Jewish leader recalled the prophetic words spoken fifty years earlier by his grandfather, Moises Senderey, who in overseeing construction of the AMIA building was sufficiently alarmed that he installed a granite wall with heavy iron gates and told his family that "some day our Jewish building will be attacked."

The first focus afterward understandably was on the bombing itself, the deadliest terrorist act in Argentine history. Who did it, the Jewish community and the nation demanded to know? Why? Was it linked with the bombing two years earlier of the Israeli Embassy, which had killed 29 and wounded 252? When would the bombers be brought to justice?

More than seven years later the answers remain incomplete. It is known that on July 10, 1994, eight days before the bombing, an Argentinean man delivered the white Renault van used in the attack to a group of Buenos Aires police officers. It is known that those policemen were part of an extensive network of corrupt officers. It is known that the bombers used an explosive mix of ammonia nitrate and aluminium, more than 600 pounds of it, loaded into plastic bags in a way that ensured the explosives would wreak maximal havoc. It is known that critical suspects urged their colleagues to stay silent, that millions of dollars turned up in the bank account of one key figure while others received help with their legal defense and public relations, and that critical evidence simply vanished. In the end, twenty people face charges, fifteen of them policeman.

The rest are suspicions. Those following the case suspect that military officers, past and present, were involved, along with anti-Semitic elements among Argentina's million or more Arabs. They suspect the bombers knew that Mondays, the day of the attack, was when researchers from Project Witness met at AMIA to pore over government files on Nazis given refuge in Argentina, although they probably did not know that that week's meeting had been canceled because of a school holiday or that the records were stored in an adjacent building. They suspect that the AMIA case is intimately linked to the embassy one, based on the nearly identical ways the bombers behaved in the days before they struck and their use of nearly identical explosives. They also suspect that Iran was involved, along with the Iranian-backed Hezbollah terrorist group.

Such suspicions, unfortunately, are not enough to bring the suspects to trial. And while the established facts may yield convictions against underlings, that would not satisfy anyone. Which is why the Jewish community these days is investigating the investigators, and asking why—after more than seven years and promises of quick action by former

President Menem and others—there has been so little progress on either the AMIA or the embassy case.

The answer is partly that the probes, especially the AMIA one, have been halfhearted. For the first three years only eight policemen were assigned to the case, compared to the thousands who investigated the 1995 bombing of the Alfred P. Murrah Federal Building in Oklahoma City. Argentine law hamstrung investigators by limiting the suspects they could interrogate and their use of informants. The police who were arrested were held in custody by former colleagues, which made it easy for them to conspire on their stories and otherwise thwart the inquiry. The most glaring deficiency of all was the lack of political will to track down the culprits, who clearly had political connections. The fear seemed to be that getting to the bottom of the bombings would require unearthing too many nasty secrets about how illegal goods enter Argentina, how police and politicians are on the take, and how remnants remain of the old network that aided and abetted the Nazis.

"From the beginning what I felt was that there was no political decision to solve this case," says José Barbaccia, a thirty-six-year-old prosecutor who was on duty the day the bomb exploded and has stuck with the case ever since. Barbaccia, one of two prosecutors who has been assembling evidence, sits in his cramped office in the federal courthouse trying to explain why so much still is not known despite his best efforts. "We asked for help. . . . The president always said you will get all you need, just ask," he says, referring to Menem. "But the facts are very other. In the government there is no need or urge to solve the case." Will it ever be solved? "I don't know," the young lawyer sighs. "It's difficult to answer that, it's very difficult. It depends on many things, including luck."

The demonstrators who gather every Monday in front of the Supreme Court are not willing to trust to luck. They meet under the banner of an organization called Memoria Activa, which means "keeping alive the memory." Some come because they are family and friends of bombing victims; others, Jews and Gentiles, believe the AMIA attack reveals a malaise infecting all of Argentine society. Whatever attracts them, they are united by a determination to catch the killers. At a time when a variety of Jewish groups are embracing decidedly different strategies toward that end, that collection of rabbis and relatives, attorneys and artisans, delivers the most unambiguously combative message and captures the most press and public attention.

"We are here every Monday because of our need to sustain the claim for justice," explains Laura Ginsberg, whose husband worked for AMIA for fifteen years and, at the age of forty-three with two young children at home, was killed during the bombing. "We have no answers. At the present moment we believe there is not a political decision to solve the bombing, to find all those responsible. We blame the government and the organized Jewish community, especially DAIA. Two years ago, when we blamed the government, DAIA went to the [Argentine] White House to apologize."

DAIA is the Jewish community's political arm, and the incident Ginsberg refers to happened in 1997, at a rally outside the bombed-out building on the third anniversary of the attack. It drew 10,000 demonstrators, along with Argentina's ministers of foreign affairs, justice, interior, and labor. When Ginsberg got up to speak she neither masked her anger nor minced her words. "I accuse the government," she said, "of approving impunity, of approving the indifferent approach of those who know the truth but keep silent, of approving an absence of security . . . of covering the local connection that was used to kill our loved ones." The crowd reacted with a ninety-minute outpouring of insults against the assembled government officials, and particularly Interior Minister Carlos Corach, a Jew. Corach was sufficiently bruised that he called in the leaders of DAIA and AMIA, demanding—and receiving—a public apology.

But it was too late. By then the communal organizations no longer spoke for a large segment of the Jewish public, and the communal leaders' apology to Corach further eroded their authority. Ginsberg's outburst, meanwhile, marked a milestone in the Memoria Activa movement: fingers now were pointed not just at the bombers, but at the Argentine power structure and the Jewish establishment that was backing it.

That was a dramatic turnaround from the way Argentine Jews, and the rest of the nation, had rallied around AMIA and DAIA in the immediate aftermath of the bombing. Nearly 150,000 Argentines gathered in front of the Congress Building to proclaim that the attack had wounded Argentina as well as its Jews, and then-president Menem promised Jewish leaders that he would put "all the state's resources" in the hands of investigators. Menem had built trust in the Jewish community when he visited Israel earlier in his tenure, the first Argentine head of state to do so and a gesture made more dramatic because his parents were from Syria, which remains in a state of cold war with Israel. The logical way to reach out to Jews in the aftermath of the bombing, Menem and others believed, was through DAIA, which had led the battle against anti-Semitism since World War II, and AMIA, the umbrella group that ran everything from welfare programs to the Jewish cemetery. That was the same logic the bombers had used in selecting the AMIA-DAIA building to reach out with their deadly message of hate.

Yet just as Menem's words rang hollower with each year that passed without the bombers being caught, so did the Jewish community's faith in its communal institutions. The men in charge of DAIA and AMIA were pushing behind the scenes, but they worried that if they pushed too hard, too publicly, they would compromise their valued ties to Argentina's rulers and aid the forces of reaction that always waited in the wings. While Memoria Activa members repeatedly compared the lack of progress in solving the AMIA bombing with Oklahoma City, where both bombers were in custody within a week, DAIA chieftains insisted the more apt comparison was with terrorist attacks in Israel and France, where it often takes ten years to bring the guilty to justice. Whatever the merit of their arguments, Jewish leaders failed to recognize how alienated their constituents were becoming. The message finally got through via Ginsberg's speech, at which point DAIA president Ruben Beraja, who was on the podium with her, pocketed his prepared remarks and improvised a stinging indictment of Iran as the presumed sponsor of the bombing. But he was booed and hissed—partly because it was clear he was responding under pressure, and even more because his response stopped with the easy target of Iran and did not criticize the Argentine government for failing to search out proof of who ordered and carried out the attack.

Rather than changing tactics, Beraja and his colleagues simply stopped inviting Memoria Activa to official events, reasoning that it was a fringe group. They also found other less voluble and confrontational allies, including a group called Friends and Families of the Victims, which holds its own vigil on the eighteenth of every month, reading out the names of the eighty-six victims, lighting eighty-six candles, and planting eighty-six roses in remembrance.

The DAIA leaders might have prevailed if a second crisis had not intervened so quickly. This one came by way of Mexico and Asia, and involved money. The collapse of the Mexican peso in 1997, along with the ongoing Asian financial crisis, made international investors question their holdings across Latin America. Those shock waves, and the aftershocks of Brazil's devaluing its currency, propelled some banks in Argentina to merge and others to close. One institution done in by nervous depositors was Banco Patricios, which had a modest half billion dollars in assets and was owned by a Jewish family named Spolsky. Patricios was absorbed in March 1998 by Banco Mayo, which was headed by Beraja and, with twice the assets, seemed substantially more stable. But just seven months later Mayo could not pay its bills and was purchased by a consortium led by Citibank. In December the nation's last Jewish-owned bank, this one in the outlying province of Cordoba, went under.

The demise of the Jewish banks dealt a devastating blow to Argentine Jews. Beraja had headed the politically powerful DAIA for six years, and had always linked his bank's fortunes with the community's. Now prosecutors in three different courts were trying to trace Banco Mayo money that had allegedly gone missing. Banco Patricios director Sergio Spolsky likewise held a top job in the Jewish community, as treasurer of AMIA, and he, too, came under investigation, this time by a special ethics tribunal set up by the Jewish community. The back-to-back bank failures created crises of confidence within Argentina's Jewish world and without. Many Jews had seen their personal holdings threatened by the demise of the Jewish banks, especially if they had stocks and bonds that were not fully insured, and they feared that the bankers had been equally slipshod as stewards of community holdings. Anti-Semites, meanwhile, salivated at the opportunity to cast the Jewish bankers as conniving conmen who had duped their working-class depositors, with some equating Beraja to Hitler and others lashing out at the "ethnic banks."

The bank failures also ended a proud tradition of Jewish leadership in Argentine finance—and of the philanthropy that went with it. Patricios and Mayo, like the Jewish-owned cooperative banks they had absorbed, gave to schools and sporting clubs, the Israelite hospital, the

Jewish retirement home, Aleph TV, and Jai radio. They also made loans at highly favorable rates to AMIA and to individual Jews. Which meant that, when the banks crashed, the community as a whole was rocked. To the newly opened Bar-Ilan University it spelled a loss of revenue so substantial that it almost forced an immediate closing and contributed to its later demise. To Jewish day schools it compounded a crisis that already had seen their share of the community's children fall from about 50 percent at its peak in the 1960s to 35 percent. A textile merchant in the traditionally Jewish Once business district was so devastated after losing all his savings that he killed himself.

Nowhere are the hard times easier to add up than at AMIA. The organization, which has just $40 million in assets, is $25 million in debt. That is by far the biggest shortfall in its history, and it comes at a time when the banks that might have bailed it out are themselves out of business. Seventy of its 300 staffers already have been dismissed, while the rest have seen their pay cut by 30 percent and paychecks delayed three months or more. It has pared back subsidies to Jewish schools and religious movements, and is hard-pressed to continue providing welfare services to the 1,500 needy Jewish families who depend on it. It cannot afford the studies that social scientists say are required to assess the community's wants and needs, or to tell how many Jews there are in Argentina (community leaders say there are 200,000 in Buenos Aires and another 20,000 in the rest of the country, but Sergio DellaPergola, the Jerusalem-based demographer, insists there are no more than 170,000 in Buenos Aires and 200,000 in all of the country). Even more troubling is the way AMIA's credibility has been undermined: the organization had stood at the center of Jewish life in Argentina, playing a role in everything from weddings to funerals; today few Jews care what it does and most think it has nothing to do with them.

Part of those troubles can be traced to the bombing, which shook AMIA's confidence and forced it to divert millions of dollars to hire guards and plan intricate security systems for synagogues, social clubs, and other institutions that suddenly felt exposed. The bank failures also played a role, robbing the community of its chief financiers and philanthropists and forcing it to select new leaders. But the root causes of the troubles facing AMIA go back decades, and have to do with how the community governs itself and how it failed to adapt to changing circumstances.

One problem is that Argentine Jews are not used to donating to Jewish causes the way their grandparents did and their counterparts do in North America. Getting people to pay their dues to synagogues and communal groups is difficult enough. Getting them to dig deeper, the way they must to dig out of the current crisis, so far has proved impossible. That is partly because they could always rely on the heads of Jewish-owned banks and credit cooperatives to kick in funds for schools and synagogues. But over time that dependence spawned a complacency, a stinginess even, as well as a disengagement from what the communal institutions were doing.

Many Jews today have another reason for not giving: too little money. They played leading roles in making and marketing furs, shoes, clothing, and other textiles, and were the first ones hurt when the textile trade moved to China and Brazil. They are doctors and architects at a time when patients can no longer afford private doctors and there are few new buildings for architects to design. There are lots of ways to measure the effects of that growing impoverishment on the community. Of 370 children attending the Jewish day schools at Temple Bet El in the fashionable Belgrano neighborhood, 170 get partial or full scholarships and more than a dozen have had to drop out. At the Hebraica sports club 20 percent of members are subsidized, twice as many as in recent years, and housing values at its suburban country club are half what they were a few years ago. Jews are applying for help in record numbers at Jewish welfare agencies, Jewish professionals are driving taxis, and many who would like to be buried in Jewish cemeteries no longer can afford to be. The most telling sign of all is the rate at which Jews, mainly young ones, are moving to Israel, America, and other places where it is easier to find work: nearly 1,000 made aliyah in 1999 alone, 27 percent more than the year before.

Yet money is not the only reason AMIA is in crisis. Its confusing setup of Zionist-based political parties and proportional representation is every bit as unworkable there as its sister system is in Israel, and its elections are so incomprehensible and inconsequential to most Argentine Jews that only 3,505 of 20,518 eligible members voted last time. Its decisions on which schools to fund, and which religious movements,

(*top*) Helen Israel, a Holocaust survivor, cradles a photograph from sixty years before of her with her young son Lech, who soon after was killed by the Nazis at Auschwitz.

(*bottom*) Paul Spiegel, who was hidden by a Catholic family during the Holocaust, today is president of the Central Council of Jews in Germany. The post carries with it a government bodyguard, shown here helping Spiegel out of his government-supplied Mercedes.

Rabbi Shmuel Kaminezki says the daily prayers at home in Dnepropetrovsk with two of his daughters.

A grandmother prays at the modest shul that elderly worshipers managed to keep open throughout the Soviet era. The elderly still come each day to pray and to get a free kosher meal.

The author's family gathers for an evening out, some forty years ago, near their summer home in Seabrook Beach, New Hampshire. Seated around the table are, *clockwise from lower left*, Suzanne, Donald, Larry, and Maıray Tye, Rose Rubinoff, and Dorothy, Minnie, and Joseph Tye.

The author's great-grandfather, Rabbi Shmuel Halpern, joins others in the family in playing with his granddaughter Sylvia, seated on the table. The others are, *from left to right*, Dorothy, Selmour, Maurice, and Rose Rubinoff.

Rabbi Alejandro Avruj leads young worshipers in a march around his shul, which lies in the shadow of Buenos Aires's slaughterhouse district. The Torahs are held high to celebrate Simchas Torah, the holiday commemorating completion of the yearlong reading of the holy scrolls.

Friends and relatives gather in front of Argentina's Supreme Court, the way they do every Monday, to keep alive the memory of those killed in a 1994 bomb attack on the Jewish communal building in Buenos Aires.

Ben Briscoe *(left)* and his brother, Joe, in the Irish Parliament in front of the family crest designed by their father, Bob. The coat of arms incorporated the emblem of Dublin along with the Star of David.

Shopkeeper Linda Levine readies a package of meat in the kosher butcher shop and grocery on Clanbrasil Street in Dublin.

Sabbath dinner with the Ohana and Kac families. Michael Ohana holds the kiddish cup, standing next to his mother, Nicole, and father, Sydney.

The sexton at an Orthodox synagogue just outside Paris, wearing the traditional Napoleonic hat favored at Jewish houses of worship across France.

Elise Eplan *(left)*, her sister, Jana, and brother, Harlan, with their families, join in a Rosh Hashanah tashlikh ceremony where worshipers toss bread into the water to ceremonially cast off their sins.

A portrait of Leon Eplan, the family patriarch, who arrived in Atlanta from Odessa in 1882.

Grigory Korol, chairman of the religious community in Dnepropetrovsk, emigrated to Israel in 2000 to be near his children and grandchildren.

Phil Warburg with his wife, Tamar, and their daughters, Tali *(left)* and Maya, pictured near their home in Israel.

have been highly political and alienated those whose institutions were not selected. It already owned the land for its new nine-story headquarters, and had $15 million from the government and private insurers to help build it, yet it pushed itself even deeper into debt by diverting some of that money to fund its deficit. It accepted questionable investment advice from financial officers with clear conflicts of interest. It sponsored theatrical productions and launched journals, yet refused to listen to researchers who were warning of ominous demographic trends.

Those demographics also help explain AMIA's troubles. It relies on its Jewish burial services for more than two-thirds of its income. Yet spiraling poverty has meant a doubling of subsidized burials and a 70 percent reduction in revenues. An intermarriage rate of nearly 50 percent has hurt, too: the Jewish cemetery will not accept non-Jewish spouses, which has led many Jewish partners to decide not to be buried there and not to pay their AMIA dues. And many AMIA members today think that burials are the only service the group offers, making them less inclined to pay the annual dues that account for 20 percent of its budget and ignoring its vital roles in everything from welfare to schools.

"AMIA has had a confused mission, confused strategies, confused everything," concludes Gabriel Berger, a respected consultant who spent one year running Hebraica and another running AMIA. "The social contract that should be the basis of a community has been lost here."

Things are even worse at DAIA. Its mission was to defend the community against anti-Semitism and forge links to the government and public, and under Beraja it achieved unprecedented influence. He brought it out from under AMIA's wing and forged an identity for the Argentine Jewish community that is distinct from those in Israel and the United States. He opened doors at the Argentine White House and other palaces of power, and poured his bank's funds into the organization. But he also compromised DAIA's independence. Beraja was so tied to the president and other senior government officials, who propped up his bank with $300 million in loans, that he could not conceive of condemning that government for failing to catch the AMIA bombers. And DAIA was so tied to Beraja's bank that, when the bank went under, even Beraja knew he had to go as DAIA chief. Anxious over the loss of credibility at the once-proud organization, representatives of the

Hebraica sports club, the Reform congregation of Temple Emanuel, and other Jewish institutions have been boycotting DAIA board meetings. DAIA, they charge, has become infected with the same questionable ethics that made so many Argentines, Jews and non-Jews, give up on their government.

"If the anti-Semites will plan how to destroy the Jewish community they couldn't do it better than AMIA and DAIA have," says Yaacov Rubel, a Jewish author and demographer who has done extensive research on the community. Others agree, recounting a sad joke that is working its way through the community: If a plane carrying the leaders of DAIA, AMIA, and Argentina's major Zionist organization were to crash, who would be saved? Answer: the Jewish community.

While some have insisted that the only solution is to let the communal organizations wither away, others have said they could be rescued. AMIA showed hopeful signs in the late 1990s and into 2000, paring back its budget by nearly 30 percent, reducing its debt by $7 million, and selling two big buildings, including the one it used as its headquarters after the bombing. It vowed to be more evenhanded in how it funds competing schools and synagogues, and to help them cut costs and consolidate operations. It stopped spending money it does not have and refinanced its indebtedness. And in 1998 it hired as its executive director Enrique Burbinski, the respected head of one of Argentina's biggest Jewish community centers and a committed reformer, who began showing up every Monday at the Memoria Activa demonstrations and stopped acting as an apologist for the government. The new president of DAIA also said he knew change was needed, and said he would be more independent of the government, although his close ties to Beraja made some skeptical that he could deliver on the reforms.

The road to reform has turned out to be a dead end, or so it seems. The AMIA board members who penned most of the new ideas resigned late in 1999 when their ideas were being ignored. Burbinski was stymied, too, and his contract was not renewed. The director of burial and membership services, a key post, was fired and replaced by a crony of the AMIA president. The new DAIA president died and was replaced by a Beraja ally. Most disconcerting of all, while the new ethics tribunal did its job in pinpointing parties responsible for recent breaches of community trust, AMIA and other communal authorities failed to execute the recommended punishments. The lesson is clear: AMIA may be learning how to better manage its finances, but it still does not understand how to handle its ethical duties, which is one reason members continue to resign.

* * *

At the very moment when AMIA and DAIA's credibility was crumbling a curious thing was happening back on the streets of Buenos Aires. The bombing was bringing Jews back. And the crisis in communal leadership was pushing them to refocus on the grass roots, which they felt was an easier place to reconnect with their religion and culture.

Nowhere is that return to the fold clearer and more compelling than in the Mataderos, the old slaughterhouse district just a thirty-minute ride from the heart of downtown but a universe away from its centers of power and money. Jews in the rest of the city might recall that there once was a congregation there, with a couple of Jewish schools and five or six shuls. But they also knew it withered away thirty years ago, when the district was so depressed that even the slaughterhouses were moving out and Jews were leaving for better neighborhoods. Tfilat Shalom, the major synagogue, erected in the 1940s by a wealthy leather manufacturer, still stood but its stucco walls were cracking and the roof was crumbling, garbage had been left upstairs to rot, and, as in the shuls of the old Soviet Union, it was mainly old *zeydeh*s who stopped by to pray.

What most Jews of Buenos Aires do not know is that Tfilat Shalom is back and booming. You can feel the energy on a Friday evening, as the choir belts out the *Magen Avot* to the pop rhythm of the Carpenters' "On Top of the World," and *Adon Olam* mixes Hebrew lyrics with a Paul McCartney melody. You can hear it on Saturday afternoons as people who make their living as plumbers and carpenters, or licking stamps at the rate of 4 cents an envelope, sit in a circle debating the weekly Torah portion. And you can count it at the Havdalah service to ring out the Sabbath. A decade ago it barely attracted the minyan of ten needed for a quorum; now it fills scores of brown-and-black plastic chairs in the main hall, with adults huddling near the electric heaters in the back as their children flock to the *bimah*.

They were lured in by Alejandro Avruj, their sorcerer of a rabbi. Or at least he someday hopes to be a rabbi. When he first came in the late 1980s Alè, as he is known by everyone, was just seventeen and studying at a Jewish high school. A handful of worshipers invited him for the High Holidays, and he knew enough to chant prayers and lead them in songs. The old men loved that he could read Hebrew. The children were mesmerized by the chestnut brown hair that reached to the middle of his back and made him look like Jesus or, as they learned more about their own religion, like Samson. So Alè, who by now had enrolled at the rabbinic seminary, came back the next two years for Rosh Hashanah and Yom Kippur and ran an occasional service on the Sabbath.

It was not until the summer of 1994 that enough worshipers started coming to call it a community, or to even suggest a rebirth. Every thriving community across the diaspora can point to a seminal event that sparked its renewal: in Düsseldorf it was the arrival of the Russians, in Dnepropetrovsk the fall of the Soviets, in Boston and other U.S. cities the 1990 shocker that the intermarriage rate had topped 50 percent. For Jews in the Mataderos it was the broken bodies left behind at the AMIA building.

"I thought that after the bombing no one would come, that they would be afraid," Alè recalls. "But during the High Holidays, which were just two months later, the synagogue was full of people. It was incredible. I stopped everybody and said, 'Now we are crying and our kids are beautiful, what is the deal? Will no one come again until next year, unless a bomb explodes?' I said that I will open the doors to the shul next Shabbat and asked people to raise their hands if they would come. It began with a few people. Now we have a hundred every Friday evening."

The children came first, the way they have in so many communities, forming a choir and learning enough Hebrew and ritual to make their bar and bat mitzvahs. They asked Alè why the bombers hated Jews and what was in the Torah. The mothers were next. They stopped by the shul to pick up their kids and were struck by the stench and rot, by cakes stored in cupboards and cockroaches that were feasting on them. They told Alè they would take care of it, and they did, sweeping out the building and sewing curtains on the ark, painting, repairing, and putting the cakes in the refrigerator to keep away insects and rodents. And as they began to develop a stake in what was happening they occasionally dropped by with their husbands for a service on Friday night or Saturday morning.

"It was very slow. There was one bar mitzvah, another bar mitzvah. Little by little people were doing things," recalls Horacio Carlos Pinson, who runs a modest household goods business and wanted to rediscover the lost connection to his grandfather, a rabbi in Russia. "At the time of the AMIA bombing people began to come here out of the necessity of being in a temple. There were a lot of different reactions to the bombing but most people wanted to get more connected. We then had the opportunity to get young people. Everyone wanted to get with other people who had suffered by the explosion."

His wife, Liliana, was one of the mothers who refurbished the synagogue. Now she cooks for the card games Tfilat Shalom uses to raise money and supplement its sliding scale of dues, which can be as much as $20 a month or as little as nothing. Their daughter Debi had the first bat mitzvah in the reopened synagogue. The Pinsons live just nine blocks away, but like most neighbors they had no inkling that the nondescript green building tucked in a row of houses was a synagogue, and like most Jews who stayed in the neighborhood they did not realize how many other Jews were left. They and a few other families eventually became so committed to the community that they put up the mortgages on their own houses as collateral to raise the money needed to rebuild.

"I live here. Everything important to me is here," Debi explains as she sits in the makeshift Kiddush room off the sanctuary during the break between morning and afternoon Shabbat services, her gray sweatshirt and blue jeans characteristic of the informality of the place that has become a home to young people like her. She sings in the choir and helps match popular melodies to traditional Hebrew songs because, she says, "it's an easier way to get the people in." She serves as cantor many Friday evenings and helps run the children's program, which now has nearly a hundred participants. She took the special security course required of all teachers in Jewish schools in Buenos Aires, and even held her fifteenth birthday party at the shul. "My friends said to me, 'Aren't you afraid to be here so much because of what happened with the bombing?'

I'm not afraid. And if something will happen here, I prefer to die here and not in another place."

That willingness to back their belief with their life, which is eerily similar to the attitude of young Israelis, comes partly from "the fact that we built this temple with our hands," explains Marcos Perelmutter, nineteen, who sings beside Debi in the choir and, like her, is a youth leader and part-time cantor. "We washed the floors. We helped to paint. We put our love here. We feel a very, very, very big feeling of pertinence, of belonging." For Marcos the AMIA attack, which killed his aunt, transformed Judaism from an identity he inherited to a cause he could commit to. He took his cue from Alè, enrolling at the rabbinic seminary, offering his services to outlying congregations, and even letting his hair grow over his shoulders. "Asking me what it is like being a Jew," he says, "is like asking me what it is like being a human being. I am a Jew, that is my life."

It is not just the young who feel that way. Raul Gulman attends services at Tfilat Shalom every Friday night and Saturday morning, and returns Monday nights for board meetings. It is a thirty-minute drive. There are six other shuls within a few blocks of his home, and he is seventy-four years old. But after a lifetime helping with Jewish causes ranging from AMIA to the United Jewish Appeal, Gulman says none has touched him like helping rebuild the synagogue in the Mataderos. "Before this I felt that my life was finished," he says. "One son is a rabbi, another is a doctor. Everything was okay and I said, 'That's it.' But I didn't know that in this circle of life a little part was needed to complete it. When I came here I found a synagogue that was destroyed. We had a little minyan with ten *zeydeh*s. But we started to rebuild it step by step. We began to have services for Purim, to have bar mitzvahs, and I saw my friend's son go to another province and lead a service in our name.

"I feel that I come here and it lets me live the rest of the week. Two weeks ago my son came to services here from Mexico, where he's an Orthodox rabbi, and told everyone, 'Thank you, you brought my father a new life.' "

Gulman is attracted by the same things that appeal to those who are a quarter of his age: the synagogue's energy and authenticity. They like its social programs—it launched an envelope-stuffing and -stamping business that gives work to those who have none. They like its religious rituals—it offers Torah study groups that probe such real-world issues as prostitution and intermarriage. They like that women make up 80 percent of those attending afternoon *Minchah* services, and that young people—Gulman calls them "our kids"—play critical roles in the services and the community.

And the upstart synagogue a few blocks from Buenos Aires's most destitute slums—where the rabbi is not ordained and the cantor is a teenager, the organ pipes out Beatles melodies, and few if any are rich—has a message for the rest of Argentina's Jews: Judaism is alive and thriving at the grass roots, where it matters most.

The Mataderos synagogue is not the only one sounding that theme these days. Far from it. The deeper the crisis becomes at the communal level, and the more word spreads across the diaspora that Argentina's once-vital Jewish community is on the brink, the more individual congregations there, Orthodox as well as Conservative and Reform, are raising their voices to make clear that this is not the full story.

To get the other, more hopeful side you have to talk to their children, say leaders of Temple Bet El, Argentina's first Conservative synagogue and still the largest, with 3,000 people packing its High Holiday services. Conversations with those young people, especially ones who attend Bet El's day school, suggest they know considerably more about their Jewish histories, in Argentina and before, than their parents or grandparents did. They also know about Jewish rituals and Jewish morals, with one after another saying that a Jew "must be a good person." They are proud of their Judaism—nearly all say it is more important to them than being Argentine or being school children, than living in Buenos Aires or identifying with any other group—and they are determined to sustain it. "It's very important to stay Jewish," explains Brian Reznik, a sixth grader. "If nobody defends Judaism it will disappear. If we are strong it won't disappear."

But these children see what is happening around them. They lived through the AMIA attack and saw the four-foot-high concrete-filled yellow barrels go up on the road outside their synagogue and school (later replaced with more aesthetically pleasing pyramid-shaped barriers). They watch as Bet El's plainclothes guards inspect the bags and pat down the bodies of strangers, then roam the corridors with Secret Service–like earphones and walkie-talkies. They know that the coaches of many non-Jewish soccer teams canceled games with Jewish teams, for fear they might be putting their children in peril. These young Jews understand that they are at risk, even if they do not understand why. "It's not fair. We are normal people, it's only that we are Jewish," says twelve-year-old Natali Lisman. While she is proud of her culture and religion, she adds, "in the street I don't say that I am Jewish because it's dangerous."

The way to keep those children involved is to show them that Judaism is relevant to their lives and a positive force in the world, say the leaders of Bet El. That is why they run breakfasts for the elderly, hold bar mitzvah classes for young people who have Down's syndrome or are deaf and dumb, reach out to non-Jewish spouses of mixed marriages, and provide food, medicine, and jobs to poor non-Jews as well as Jews. They are proudly antiestablishment and persistently ecumenical. "We must be with the Torah in one hand and the newspaper in the other," Bet El's rabbis say, echoing the words and ideology of Marshall Meyer, who founded the synagogue and forged its course of social activism.

As for the crises at AMIA and DAIA, "a crisis is the moment when you can choose your priorities," says Lydia Azubel, Bet El's president. "We used to grow with the help of the banks. Other institutions grew with the help of AMIA. Now that we have no help we have to come back to our roots. When the Jewish community of Argentina started, it was a very rich community with very poor people. The poor people built very strong institutions. When the Jewish people started to be richer we started to think less about our organizations and they became poor and some disappeared. History has come full circle. Now we are at the bottom again but we are coming up.

"We will remain Jews and I think we will be a spiritually stronger community, although poorer in economic terms. We will grow, and we won't depend on anything but our own efforts."

That bullish approach is sufficiently compelling that it has caught on thousands of miles to the north in Manhattan's Upper West Side. Conservative Congregation B'nai Jeshurun, New York's oldest Ashkenazic synagogue, was revitalized by Marshall Meyer when he returned to New York from Buenos Aires in 1985. Today its two rabbis (Rolando and

Marcelo) are from Argentina, as are the cantor and the director of family life. And it offers precisely the sorts of socially conscious, spiritually enlivened programs—for parents pushing strollers and singles toting briefcases, gays and lesbians, the truly observant and barely religiously literate—that are working so well in Argentina, which helps explain why it is the hottest Jewish house of worship of its kind in New York City and possibly all the United States.

Back in Buenos Aires, Rabbi Sergio Bergman is taking the Meyer legacy in a slightly different direction. While he, too, grew up with Meyer's ethos of social responsibility, he says today's circumstances require a repositioning of Jewish experience away from the synagogue and into the home. And although his congregation at Temple Emanuel is nominally Reform, he advocates a return to ritual and tradition.

As with so many Argentine Jews, Bergman's conception of his faith was defined in large measure by the AMIA explosion. The bombing happened just three days after the birth of his third daughter. "My wife, Gabi, was giving milk to the baby then and I didn't sleep a lot in my own house because I was in the morgue, working with families, trying to recognize victims," says the youthful-looking rabbi, who was trained in Reform and Conservative seminaries. "Because of the bombing we made a family decision to get involved with a project, a life project, a creative project, an affirmative project to give a different kind of signal of what the community here is. If I couldn't do that I would have left the country. I had a choice then to come to Israel and get a Ph.D. or to work in a community center here in Argentina."

Bergman's new paradigm of practice borrows from the Orthodox, who understand how rituals like keeping kosher can define and enrich the Jewish experience. "We know that ninety-five percent of our families think the sacredness of McDonald's is above the sacredness of the Torah," he says. "That's a tragedy for us. So the Reform/Liberal community, which two hundred years ago had to change traditions to adapt to the modern era, now has to reform the Jews. It has to give them back their own vocabulary, the Jewish terms that they lost." But, like American Reform rabbis who advocate a reembracing of ritual, Bergman insists it is vital to preserve the freedom of choice that is central to the Reform movement and distinguishes it from Orthodoxy. "We will never tell anybody that if he doesn't eat kosher he doesn't belong to the Jewish people or isn't a good Jew. Our goal is, for example, that they should go to the McDonald's near the Once neighborhood, which is the only one in the diaspora that is kosher. This is a process. It's the door to reentering the Jewish tradition."

There are other doors that Emanuel helps open—encouraging members to light candles and gather as a family on Friday nights, teaching them how to don tefillin, getting them to send their children to its Jewish school and to practice *tzedakah*, or charity. The synagogue itself remains important, but rather than being the primary place congregants come to feel Jewish, it is now where they come to learn how to bring Judaism into their homes and lives. For such lessons to be conveyed the synagogue is being reoriented away from the large and centralized to the local level and small numbers, that let people easily interact with one another. And it is through such transformations at the grassroots level, adds Bergman, that communal institutions like AMIA and DAIA will be transformed and reformed. "Change," he says, "never comes from the central structures. It starts low down and percolates up."

That sort of gradual embracing of tradition, of relearning her heritage with the help of Bergman and others, is how Lili Esses, who is forty-two, came back to Judaism and introduced it to her nine-year-old daughter. "I light Sabbath candles and I keep kosher since a week ago," explains the artist, who attended synagogue with her Orthodox grandparents until she was six, then switched to the Conservative Temple Bet El, then got involved in leftist politics and gave up on religion. The AMIA bombing is bringing her back, step by step. "After the bombing I said I really want to know what a Jew is. I did my bat mitzvah then, and studied, and every Saturday morning I came to the synagogue.

"For me, Jewish life here can be divided into after and before AMIA."

*   *   *

Having the grass roots as the locus of innovation and inspiration would not be surprising in the United States or most of Europe, where Jewish organizational life typically has been localized and fragmented. But things were different in Argentina. The Jewish community was as cohesive and centralized as anywhere in the diaspora, which it had to be to respond to recurrent anti-Semitism and tended naturally to be because it was so concentrated in one city, Buenos Aires. All of which makes the current focus on individual congregations and local activities nothing short of a revolution.

Will the revolution prevail? Some insist not, and predict that Argentine Jews will continue to abandon Judaism and Argentina, drifting off to secular society and to North America and Israel. But Haim Avni, a history professor at the Hebrew University of Jerusalem and Israel's leading expert on Latin American Jewry, says he has heard such predictions before: "Back in 1962, when I was preparing to travel to Argentina for the first time, everybody told me, 'You're crazy. They are all coming here and you are going to Argentina? It's done. It's over.' It was 1962, a moment of great crisis in Argentina, and boatloads of immigrants were arriving in Haifa. It gave the impression, at least in Israel, that sooner or later Argentina was going to be absent from the Jewish road map. I doubted it at that time and I doubt it now, too."

In fact, there are more reasons for hope today than there were in 1962. So many different models are being tried—from Emanuel's home-based approach to Bet El's social activism—that if one fails, there are others to fall back on. More than ever before in Argentina there are articulate leaders—lay and religious, Orthodox, Conservative, and Reform. Most encouraging of all, individual Jews seem willing to lead and be led, in synagogues and, it is hoped, at some later stage, at the level of floundering communal institutions. Argentine Jews seems to be saying that, in the era after the AMIA bombing, they can find greater strength and security by coming together and rediscovering their roots than by abandoning them.

"The bombing had a stripping effect, it revealed what was underneath people's clothes," says Alfredo Neuburger, whose lifetime of work with the community includes seven years as executive director of DAIA. "You can cover things up in normal times, but when something traumatic happens the deep feelings of people come to the surface. Some people left the community totally because of the bomb. Something happened inside them saying, 'It's dangerous to be Jewish in this country.' Others, however, came back. They felt they had to belong, they had to participate. In traumatic situations good people become better and bad people become worse.

"I have seen a lot of very good things happening in this community the last couple of years because of people who rededicated themselves. This community is in transition from an anachronistic model, a model that was brought from Central Europe in the 1930s and '40s that is struggling not to die, to a new model of the future that is struggling to live. It's regrettable that we needed a bomb to bring all this out."

Chapter 5

DUBLIN:

Who Ever Heard of an Irish Jew?

Bob Briscoe was sure his time was up now. It was 1922, the Civil War was in full swing, and he had just been cornered in his hotel room by a pair of pistol-packing troopers loyal to Michael Collins, head of the newly declared Irish Free State. As a leader in the rival army of anti-partition Irish nationalists, Briscoe knew that detention meant execution. But as he was being marched away one of his captors looked at him quizzically and asked, "Are you a Jewman?" When the broad-nosed Briscoe indicated he was, the trooper turned to his colleague and said, "Hold on! He's only a Jewman. We'd be wasting our bloody time with him." And so, Briscoe recalled years later, the soldier "gave me a great kick in the pants that sent me flying down the stairs and out the door."

The troopers can be excused for their ignorance, of Briscoe and the special role that Ireland's tiny community of Jews has played in its country's history. Bob himself had long been a prized player in Ireland's battle for freedom from Britain, to the point where Collins and his commanders were so familiar with his looks and heritage that they never thought to add "Jewish" to his orders of capture. But most Irish were and are unaware that there are any Jews in that most Catholic of countries, not to mention a community that at one time reached 5,400, and fewer still off the Emerald Island have ever heard of an Irish Jew. Bob went on to become the lord mayor of Dublin and a member of Dáil Éireann, the Irish parliament, with his son Ben taking up both assignments after him.

Yet even as the Briscoes' proud history reflects the romance of Ireland's 120-year-old Jewish community, the family's contemporary situation reflects that community's current crisis. Ben moved away from organized Jewry when it refused to welcome his wife, Carol, who was raised Catholic but embraced her husband's faith, and only one of their four children considers herself unabashedly Jewish. Ben's older brother, Joe, is a venerated member of Dublin's Jewish community, but that community has shrunk to about 1,000. While Joe's sons strongly identify themselves as Jews as well as Irishmen, like most of their generation they do it from afar, with one son ensconced in Boston and the other raising his young family outside Tel Aviv.

As for the Dublin Jews who stayed, they are defined partly by their romantic quirkiness. They take pride in James Joyce's lonely yet luminous Leopold Bloom, and in the fact that the first real-life Jews arrived on their shores as far back as 1079. Synagogue elders don the black top hats favored by English nobility, a sign of their continued bonds to the British Isles. Worshipers chant the *Aleinu* with a tad more eihhh than normal and a nuuh that seems never-ending. The kosher butcher and Lubavitch outreach office, the Hebrew school and shuls, coexist next to edifices and inhabitants more comfortable with confessionals and catechisms. And on an island infamous for its clashes between Catholics and Protestants, Jews have found a haven they insist is free of anti-Semitism.

That does not mean their lives are free of angst. Far from it. They feel a powerful allegiance to their Irish homeland yet struggle, as Jews do across the diaspora, with how to balance that against equally compelling bonds to the Jewish people and Jewish state. They are troubled by soaring rates of intermarriage and torn by the divergent worldviews of their Orthodox and Reform members. Most also accept the portentous predictions of demographers that Dublin's Jewish community will continue to shrink and shrivel the way comparable communities from Liverpool to Glasgow are.

But not all Jews in Dublin accept their sentence of death. It is partly a matter of semantics, of understanding just what it means for a people to die. Some Irish Jews are vanishing into the wider population, assimilating to the point where they no longer recognize their own Judaism and where others assume they are no longer Jews. More often, however, young Dublin Jews so cherish their faith that they are severing their equally deep Irish roots by moving to places like Manchester, Tel Aviv, and Boston, where they can find Jewish mates and more easily embrace their religion and culture. Wherever they end up, they hold tight to their uniquely Gaelic brand of Judaism in a way that suggests that even if the Jewish presence in Dublin ends, the community of Irish Jews around the world will carry on.

For Joe Briscoe the quarrel is more basic. He simply refuses to believe that the recent past has to be a prelude to the future, and refuses to let go of his conviction that there are ways to reverse the dire decree imposed on his community. "It's my feeling that in the not too distant future, a lot of Jewish people around the world will realize that Dublin is a good place to live and bring up their children," the retired dentist says.

"I think there's going to be a reversal of the tide of emigration to one of immigration and, to put it in a nutshell, there will be a renaissance or rebirth. But having said that, it is not enough for people like myself or anybody else in the Jewish community to sit back and wait for this to happen. We've got to do something to make it happen."

* * *

Things began happening for Jews in Ireland as far back as biblical days, or so legend has it. One story says that Noah's granddaughter Cessair was the first colonist to set foot on Irish soil. Others link the earliest Irish to Moses and King David. The *Annals of Inisfallen*, an ancient text, offers the most definitive early evidence of Jews arriving, in 1079, apparently as a delegation to secure the admission of other Jews. Their reception was frosty: "Five Jews came over sea with gifts to Tairdelbach [King of Munster] and they were sent back again over sea."

They returned in small numbers during the twelfth and thirteenth centuries, and again in the sixteenth and seventeenth. Hebrew studies began to be taught at Trinity College in 1591 and by the late 1600s an actual community had taken shape in Dublin. It had its ups and downs over the next 200 years, sinking so low in 1790 that the synagogue had to be closed but reviving in the 1820s with the arrival of Jews from Germany, Poland, and England. Yet as late as 1881 there still were just 472 Jews in all of Ireland, most living in Dublin, and even there the congregation was hard-pressed to assemble a Sabbath-morning minyan.

The pogroms of 1881 in southern Russia changed everything. The czar eventually quelled the violence but he also cracked down on the Jews, imposing the May Laws that limited Jewish settlement and commerce and convincing 2 million Russian Jews to look for homes elsewhere. Most went to America, Palestine, or Great Britain, but some landed in Ireland, where they reinforced existing Jewish communities in Dublin and Belfast and founded new ones in Cork, Limerick, Waterford, Londonderry, Dundalk, and Lurgan. In 1891 there were 1,779 Jews nationwide, by 1901 the total had climbed to 3,769, in 1926 there were 5,315, and in 1946 Ireland's Jewish population reached its peak at 5,381, of whom 3,907 lived in the twenty-six counties that made up the Irish Free State.

Most ended up there by accident. Some were bound for America but got off when their boat docked in Ireland because they were seasick, or in response to warnings that red eye and other supposed maladies would prevent their admission to the United States. Others were tricked into believing they had arrived in America by ship captains eager to take on extra fares for the last leg of the voyage. Language also created confusion: Ireland sounded so much like *heymland*, the Yiddish word for destination or homeland, that many Yiddish-speaking Russians thought they had reached America when they stopped off in Dublin, while Cork sounded all too much like New York to those unfamiliar with English and relieved to have arrived.

Whatever brought them, life was good enough once they settled in that most sent for their families and planted roots. The Jewish community in the early 1900s was concentrated on Dublin's south side, around the South Circular Road in an area dubbed Little Jerusalem. Most Jewish children attended Protestant schools, which were more interdenominational and less religious than the Catholic ones, but after school they studied Hebrew, played cricket or tennis at the Jewish sports club, or stopped by Baron's Deli for a soft drink and a bit of schmooze. At shul men sat separately from women and most congregations called themselves Orthodox, but as in Argentina it was a brand of Orthodoxy that allowed for driving on the Sabbath, did not require married women to wear wigs, and generally looked like what Americans think of as Conservative.

The Sabbath meant a series of warming rituals. The oldest son would pluck a hen from the coop in the backyard, bring it to the slaughterhouse where its throat would be slashed according to Jewish law, then bring back the carcass so his mother could inspect it for lumps, red marks, and other impurities. If she found any, he would lug the chicken off again, this time to the rabbi, who would check to see whether it qualified as kosher or had to be given away. The eldest daughter would spend her afternoon dashing to the kosher baker for a challah or to the butcher for a treat of chicken livers. Then the family would sit down to light the candles and sip Kiddush wine, with the *Shabbes* goy stopping sometime later to stoke the fire and switch on or off the lights.

As for their social life, that was "no problem," says Nick Harris, who was born to a strictly observant family in Dublin in 1915, with the help of a Jewish midwife. "We ran dances every month in the 1930s and the place would be pretty full," he recalls. "Girls would be on one side of the room and boys on the other. If any girl wasn't dancing we'd make sure someone danced with her. And we'd exchange visits with young Jews from Glasgow, Manchester, and Belfast; there were regular ones with Belfast because it was so near by train. Those really were marvelous years in Dublin."

Marvelous, yes, but not without incident, especially for someone as easily excited as Harris, who like many young Jews found it useful if not vital to learn to defend himself with his fists. "One night I was going to a dance on the north side of the city and decided to meet two friends at a pub in Dublin on the way out," he remembers. "I got there first and was waiting to be served when I heard someone say from the small end of the pub, 'I'd love to kill a Jewman.' I told the barman, 'Would you mind telling that fellow that there's one here, and he can start with me.' I found the man and said, 'You're the fellow who'd like to kill a Jewman?' He said he didn't mean me, then everyone intervened and pushed him out."

Life for Dublin Jews then, as for their coreligionists across the diaspora, consisted of learning when to live within walls and when to try to topple them. Their community generally consisted of the area within walking distance of whichever of eight shuls and synagogues they belonged to, and taking a wrong turn could bring trouble. On Lombard Street, as Dermot Keogh recounts in his seminal work on Irish anti-Semitism, non-Jewish youths might interrupt a game of marbles or relievo to taunt a Jewish child with this doggerel: " 'Two shillies, two shillies,' the Jewman did cry. 'For a pair of fine blankets from me you did buy. Do you think me von idjit or von bloomin' fool? If I don't get my shillie I must have my vool.' " To which the Jewish kids had a trenchant retort: " 'Two pennies, two pennies,' the Christian did shout. 'For a bottle of porter or Guinness's stout. My wife's got no shawl and my kids have no shoes, but I must have my money, I must have my booze.' "

Jews knew which social clubs would not welcome them, but they had their own. Nine out of ten of their neighbors practiced a religion that centered on the mass and allegiance to the pope, and ate at restaurants that featured pork puddings and bacon breakfasts. But Jews generally remained true to their ancient ways of praying and eating, celebrating the Sabbath a day early and forgoing meat and shellfish when dining out. Then there were the perils of choosing between the propartition treaty forces and the rejectionists, showing too much loyalty to Britain or Israel, and navigating the other confusing cleavages of Irish society. So most Jews kept their heads down and steered clear of politics. There was one pitfall, however, that they could not get around: looking and acting differently in a land where nearly everyone else shared a culture, heritage, and gene pool.

James Joyce understood that minefield better than most. Asked to explain why he had chosen a Jew like Bloom for his protagonist in *Ulysses*, he explained that it was "because only a foreigner would do. The Jews were foreigners at that time in Dublin. There was no hostility toward them, but contempt, yes the contempt people always show for the unknown."

That contempt generally was confined to name-calling of the kind Bloom had to endure, but in 1904 in Limerick it boiled over. It started with an ugly sermon by Father John Creagh, head of a 6,000-strong religious order that catered to the poor. Jews already "were sucking the blood of other nations," Creagh said, and recently "they have, indeed, fastened themselves upon us, and now the question is whether or not we will allow them to fasten themselves still more upon us, until we and our children are the helpless victims of their rapacity." He called for and got an economic boycott of Jewish businesses that occasionally included violence and spelled the end of a community of Jews that traced its roots in Limerick back to 1861.

The other low point in Irish-Jewish relations came before, during, and just after World War II. Ireland failed miserably in its bids to save Jewish refugees who would become victims of the Holocaust, admitting what Keogh calculates were as few as 60 and, most tragically, not following through on a pledge to rescue 500 orphaned children. In the early years of hostilities the island nation feared it would be invaded by the Nazis, and Jews living there were so worried that many made plans to hide their babies with trustworthy non-Jewish neighbors. After the war Ireland admitted far fewer Jews than the Jewish community volunteered to support and that justice seemed to dictate. Their wartime experiences convinced many in Ireland's Jewish community that it was not the Germans they had to fear. Their own government, they believed, was brimming with anti-Semites and entirely untrustworthy, a suspicion that was reinforced when prime minister and founding father Eamon de Valera visited the German envoy in Dublin on May 2, 1945, to express his condolences on the death of Adolf Hitler.

"That de Valera, as head of a neutral country, should be the first to go to the German Embassy to pay his respects on Hitler's death, this was shattering. It was unforgivable and utterly insensitive to the Jewish community," recalls Hubert Wine, who served for sixteen years as a district judge and for fourteen as head of the Jewish Representative Council of Ireland.

While the wartime wounds and the earlier ones from Limerick still fester, over time far more has united than has divided Jews and Christians in Ireland—which is not surprising given all that the Jewish and Irish peoples have in common. Both are known for their gab, guilt, and good humor, and both hold deep religious beliefs. Both have a heritage of oppression and a history of reaching down to aid the underdog. Both had to battle the British on the way to statehood, and much as the Jewish state revived the ancient language of Hebrew the Irish Republic breathed new life into Gaelic. Both have seen scores of their brethren exiled around the world but remain hopeful that many will return to their now-thriving homelands of Israel and Ireland. And for every Irish Catholic who attacks Jews as unscrupulous moneylenders, there are many more who credit them as unusually generous employers.

"The Irish are just a good people," Chaim Herzog, the former president of Israel who was born in Belfast and grew up in Dublin, said in an interview shortly before his death in 1997. Like many Irish-born Jews, Herzog considered his Irishness a defining part of his identity, no matter that he left for Palestine in 1937 when his father took over there as chief rabbi. "I was brought up in a very religious home. I was first and foremost a Jew," said the silver-haired Herzog, who never lost his Irish brogue. "But like everybody we were very loyal to Ireland. The truth is we loved Ireland. This rose up from people like Bob Briscoe; their identity with the Irish struggle made us part of the struggle." As for the mutually reinforcing Irish and Jewish senses of humor, Herzog recalled a story his father passed down from his days as chief rabbi of the Irish Free State: "There was a state dinner at Dublin Castle and my father wouldn't eat the food. The cardinal turned to him and said, 'Why don't you have some of our delicious ham?' My father looked at him, smiled, and said, 'Let's discuss it at your wedding.' "

Rabbi Herzog was one in a line of distinguished rabbis to serve Ireland. The best known of his successors was the late Lord Immanuel Jakobovits, who was appointed as Ireland's chief rabbi in 1949, served as rabbi of the esteemed Fifth Avenue Synagogue in Manhattan starting in 1958, and was Great Britain's chief rabbi from 1966 to 1991. Ireland has acknowledged the importance of the office of chief rabbi by making him one of just three clergy to administer the oath to the Irish president, and the president attends the induction of the chief rabbi.

All of which helps explain why Chaim Herzog, like most Irish Jews, adored and romanticized his Irish lineage. Whereas Jews living in Düsseldorf seldom call themselves German Jews, and those living in Buenos Aires sometimes hesitate about putting their Argentinean identity on a par with their Jewish one, in Dublin the two typically hold equal standing. It is partly because the whole Irish experience tends to produce passion, and because Ireland has opened so many doors to its negligible and shrinking Jewish minority.

"I'm Irish and of the Jewish faith," says Mervyn Taylor, the first Jew to hold a federal cabinet post when, in 1993, he became Ireland's first Minister of Equality and Law Reform. "All my constituents want to know is how well I am performing on their behalf. Whether I'm a Protestant, Catholic, or Jew is neither here nor there as far as they are concerned. There used to be two Jews who lived in my district but they moved. Now there are none at all."

Jews have always fared well politically in Ireland—better, in fact, than in a place like Boston, where they make up a substantially larger share of the population. The Irish Republic and Northern Ireland both seem to delight in bestowing honors on their Jewish citizens, and the honors have actually increased even as the Jewish presence on the island is diminishing. As far back as 1874 Lewis Harris, a Jew, was elected an alderman in Dublin and, if he had not died in 1876, he was due to be appointed lord mayor. In recent years Jews have held judgeships and distinguished professorships, risen to prominence in medicine, law, and finance, written acclaimed books and produced important films, and no fewer than twenty-one Jews have represented Ireland in the sports of rugby, football, cricket, fencing, and golf. Jews also served in the honorific but esteemed post of lord mayor in Cork and Belfast.

No Jewish family has better captured the fancy of Ireland and the world than the Briscoes. The very notion of Bob Briscoe, a Jew, being elected lord mayor of Dublin was as counterintuitive as for a Catholic to have become mayor of Tel Aviv. The romance of it ensured it would be enshrined in history texts as well as in the good-natured jokes Briscoe inspired everywhere he traveled during his graying years. "Did you hear they elected a Jewish lord mayor in Dublin?" New York Yankee legend and master of the malapropism Yogi Berra asked a pal. "Only in America." And in Boston then-mayor John B. Hynes introduced Bob by saying, "We have here with us two fine fellows—an Irishman and a Jew. I give him to you now, Lord Mayor Robert Briscoe."

But back in Ireland Bob Briscoe's story was not always a joking matter, and while he was an original, his life also reflected the story of the wider community of Irish Jews. His father, Abraham William Briscoe, was an Orthodox immigrant from Lithuania who hired a Protestant minister to teach him English, scratched out a living as the Irish version of a Fuller Brush salesman, and ended up a partner in one of Dublin's leading furniture businesses. Ida Yoedicke Briscoe, Bob's mother, traced her roots to Russia, was living in Germany, and, after Bob brought her to Dublin, wrote poetry and taught in the Hebrew school. Bob was born in a suburb of Dublin in 1894 and says he was raised with two values above all others: a love of Ireland and an allegiance to the Jewish people. The former he carried to heights that his father never envisioned and, had he lived to see them, would have made him anxious about his daring offspring. As for his Judaism, Bob was not nearly so pious as his parents but he neither forgot nor forsook his Jewish roots, believing it better to prove his loyalty through the rough-and-tumble world of action than by attendance at synagogue and adherence to ritual.

His résumé as a patriot rivals that of any of Ireland's legendary leaders. He signed up early to battle the British and was dispatched by Michael Collins to Germany to buy arms and munitions. Operating under the alias Captain Swift, he became one of the IRA's wiliest and most accomplished gunrunners. Later, when de Valera and Collins split and Civil War broke out, Briscoe joined with de Valera in rejecting the treaty partitioning the island and became one of the future prime minister and president's most trusted emissaries and advisers. In 1927 Bob was elected as the first Jewish member of the Irish parliament, holding the seat until 1965. After nearly twenty-five years on the Dublin City Council he was elevated to lord mayor in 1956, and again in 1961.

The skills he fine-tuned fighting for Ireland he later applied battling on behalf of Israel and European Jews entrapped by the Holocaust. He was an ardent backer of Vladimir Jabotinsky, who founded the Haganah in Palestine and later served as supreme commander of the more radical Irgun movement that advocated armed retaliation against Arab attackers. Briscoe taught Jabotinsky how Ireland had trained its Republican army and waged its guerrilla campaigns, and he tutored the Zionist fighter on ways to exploit Britain's vulnerabilities. Bob traveled across North America and South Africa raising money to buy ships to smuggle Jewish refugees to Palestine from Poland, Bulgaria, Hungary, and other lands threatened by the Nazis. And he led the largely futile struggles before, during, and after the war for Ireland to rescue more Jews at risk, actually using the word "holocaust" in a letter he wrote in 1936, years before most of the world recognized Hitler's evil designs.

Years later, when it came time to design a coat of arms, Bob once again reflected his loyalties to both country and people. His crest incorporated the emblem of Dublin along with the Star of David. "He did that because the Nazis had forced Jews to wear the star as a sign of contempt," says his son Ben. "He wanted to show that Ireland was a country where you could wear it without any embarrassment."

Bob was not all saint, to be sure. He entrusted his wife and nurses with most child-rearing responsibilities and never hid that Joe was his favorite. He had more failures than successes in business, to the point where his wife, Lily, had to sell a piano to pay one of her children's college tuition, and he loved to gamble, to the point where one family member joked that he would wager on two flies crawling up the wall. He also had little patience for what he saw as the petty concerns and hypocrisy of the organized Jewish community—although he remained the go-to guy for Irish Jews who had a beef with their government, needed a helping hand, or were looking for a role model of how far they could rise in that Catholic country.

"Bob Briscoe was a wonderful man for us, a wonderful spokesman and a great Jew," says Gerald Goldberg, who was born in Cork in 1912, became its lord mayor in 1977, and was one of the last Jews left as the new millennium dawned. "He is the one who made me go into politics."

Others wonder why Briscoe, after almost fifty years of loyal and effective service to Ireland and to de Valera—never was named a cabinet minister or even parliamentary secretary. "De Valera, it seems, wanted to promote him but did not do so because he felt that the appointment would provoke opposition," concludes the historian Keogh. "This pointed to an undercurrent of hostility towards Jews in the country, which even de Valera disappointingly adjudged better left unprovoked."

Bob's children, all of whom remain loyal to their Irish birthright, have their own stories of occasionally experiencing that hostility and ignorance up close, despite their father's prominence. Joan, the eldest, recalls that when she was six, a classmate at her Catholic school was weeping "because she was afraid I would go to hell because I hadn't been baptized." Brian, the gentle middle child, who went to a Protestant school and later became a doctor, remembers how a handful of schoolmates, angry after being trounced in rugby and searching for a scapegoat, stamped his torso and limbs with black swastikas. The headmaster was prepared to expel the ringleader, but Bob said an apology to his son and the school would suffice. Ben has several disturbing memories—of his classmates' locking him in the school toilet and saying it was a concentration camp, of being called a "greasy Yid," and, worst of all, of punching in the nose a boy who called him a "dirty Jew," then the teacher's calling him in front of the class. "He looked me up and down— I was wearing a scruffy jacket with stains, like any kid—and he said, 'You are a dirty Jew, aren't you?' "

With Ida, the next-to-youngest, anti-Semitism took the form of being told by her school's headmistress that she could not even be considered for election as class monitor because " 'we can't have a Jewish girl as head girl.' When I went home I said, 'Daddy, I would have been head girl if I weren't Jewish.' He looked so sad and he said, 'Don't they accept my money the same as anyone else's?' I think what hurt him worst was the fact that I accepted it so readily. He accepted the fact that he was minority and that the majority doesn't have to change to accept the minority, but he felt that it doesn't have to discriminate, either."

But to America and the rest of the world, Bob Briscoe's experience in Ireland sent a decidedly more upbeat message. The fact that a Jew could rise to the rank of lord mayor of Dublin demonstrated just how tolerant and broad-minded the Irish were, which was a welcome relief from the widely held view of that nation as an island of ancient animosities and sectarian strife. "The Irish were absolutely thrilled because they had always been thought of as a narrow, bigoted crowd, and now they could show that that was only a myth," explains Joe Briscoe. "And Jews everywhere were absolutely thrilled because they were proud that another Jew, somewhere in the world, had made history."

*   *   *

Today it is the future rather than the past that is engaging the Jews of Dublin. And a single question is proving all-consuming: Can we survive?

The numbers seem to say no. The decline in Dublin's Jewish population has been steady since the mid-1900s—from 3,512 in 1946 to 3,063 in 1961, 2,451 in 1971, 1,950 in 1981, 1,385 in 1991, and just over 1,000 as of the year 2000. The pace of decline also has picked up—from 1.2 percent a year from 1946 to 1961, to 2.1 percent from 1961 to 1981, to nearly 3 percent between 1981 and 1991. Most alarming of all is the changing age profile: in 1926 the under-twenty-four age group accounted for 53 percent of the Jewish population in the Irish Republic, but by 1991 that young group made up just 27 percent. Those over sixty-five, by contrast, made up a scant 3.3 percent in 1921—and a full 25 percent by 1991.

Statisticians are not the only ones sounding alarms. Stop any Dublin Jew coming out of shul and she has a story of young people in her family, or a friend's, leaving Ireland in search of education, professional opportunities, and, most important, a Jewish spouse. Left behind are parents and grandparents who have homes, careers, and other ties that make it difficult to leave. The problem, of course, is that those who are left typically have had all the babies they are going to, and the young people who are leaving typically do not return once they have children.

"I took off from Ireland myself and when I got back all my Jewish friends had gone," says Carolyn Collins, who is Jewish, works in real estate, and has two teenage children. "But in my day we all did our primary university degree here, we didn't leave as soon as they go now. Now, as soon as they finish high school they go to universities abroad. My daughter wants to study medicine but it's very difficult to get into the University of Dublin. There's such a shortage of space." While she would like her daughter to stay, Collins adds, "it's absolutely more important that she marries Jewish than that she lives in Ireland. I recognize the fact that once she goes, it's very unlikely that she'll come back."

Mervyn Taylor's family is characteristic of Irish Jews: one son lives in London and another in New York, and his daughter is in Tel Aviv. It was not that they lacked status or opportunities in Dublin. Taylor was the first Irish Jew to become a government minister, a position he used to issue a landmark report on the rights of the disabled, to crack down on domestic violence and protect children, and, even more transforming, to legalize divorce in that land where the Church has long opposed it. Regardless of how ennobled the family, Taylor says, "if people decide they are going to immigrate to Israel, what can you do about it? If my son goes to America and meets an American girl, what can I do? There is a sort of emigration ethos in Ireland. It is not just a facet of the Jewish community but of the country at large, hence there are huge Irish communities in not just the United States but Britain and Australia."

Taylor is right, or at least he was. Ireland had been losing its best and brightest youth for generations, due in large measure to the dearth of economic opportunities at home. In the 1840s there were 6.5 million people in the part of Ireland that became the Republic, but famine and emigration whittled that down to 2.8 million by 1968. Through the 1990s, however, the Irish economy was the fastest-growing in the European community and became known as the Celtic Tiger, Ireland began importing workers and exporting software, the population ballooned to 3.6 million, and Irish youth came to understand that their best prospect for a good, high-paying job was in Ireland.

For young Jews, the situation is more problematic. They were leaving in search of not just jobs, but other young Jews, so they have continued to go. The result has been a slow erosion of all the Jewish institutions built up in Dublin over the previous 120 years. The Maccabi sports club, once the largest in Europe with more than 2,000 members, was forced to close in 1998. Gone, with it, are Jewish rugby and cricket, wrestling and tennis. At the end of World War II there were two Jewish day schools with class sizes as high as sixty; today there is one, Stratford College, and only 40 percent of its students are Jewish. The only kosher bakery closed, although bread is available at a general bakery, and the only kosher butcher died in 1998, although the community has kept his shop open. Activities on behalf of Israel have slowed to the point where, in 1999, the Israeli ambassador worried that "Christians are more involved in Israeli affairs than Jews." Finding rabbis willing to come has become more difficult each time there is a vacancy, and the days are long gone when Ireland could boast of such eminent chief rabbis as Isaac Herzog and Lord Immanuel Jakobovits. Most heartbreaking of all, a city that once supported eight Orthodox synagogues and prayer halls was down to two at the end of the 1990s and, in the summer of 1999, it shuttered and sold the elegant redbrick synagogue on Adelaide Road, whose opening in 1892 was said by the then–chief rabbi of the British Empire to symbolize the haven Ireland was offering the refugees flocking to its shores. "You have come here, my foreign brethren," Rabbi S. Hermann Adler added at that consecration ceremony, "from a country like Egypt of old to a land which offers you hospitable shelter."

One hundred and seven years later, former judge Hubert Wine, the honorary life president of the Adelaide Road Synagogue, was called on to give its deconsecration address. "This ceremony of deconsecration of this magnificent and august synagogue, now in its one hundred and eighth year, is one of the saddest days of my life," Wine, who began attending services there when he was four years old, told his overflow audience. Rabbi Ephraim Mirvis, who presided over the congregation in the 1980s, offered equally somber words of send-off: "I, too, have participated in the ups and downs of many communities. But my friends, the honest truth is, in all my experiences, this is the saddest synagogue service I have ever attended."

Dr. Michael Solomons has watched the decline of Dublin Jewry from the vantage point of the community's Reform congregation, called Dublin Jewish Progressive, where he served two terms as president. It was founded in 1946 by Orthodox Jews who felt Orthodoxy was behind the times. Members of the Reform congregation say that over the years the Orthodox repeatedly tried to squelch them by denying them access to the Orthodox cemetery, rabbi, and other communal structures. Today Dublin Progressive has ninety families and has settled into an uneasy coexistence with its more traditional fellow Jews. Solomons, whose Irish roots trace back to the 1850s, often comes to the synagogue alone these days now that his four children have left for England, New Zealand, and America. And he says they "will never come back, although they love to be here for the holidays. They enjoy being with us here, and they are very happy to be considered Irish. I'm the last of the Mohicans among the Solomons in Ireland."

That feeling of watching a community slowly dissolve around them is familiar to Jews across the Irish island. Kilkenny's Jewish community dissolved as far back as 1901. Limerick's lasted into the 1930s, peaking at about 200, but as of 1999 there were just two Jews there, both married to Roman Catholics. The census in Waterford showed four Jews in 1971 but none in 1981.

What happened in Cork is typical of such small towns. In 1901 it had 359 Jews but that dropped to 252 in 1946, 75 in 1971, and in 1999 there were just 8. Even at its height, Jews were an isolated minority in that city of 175,000 on the southeast coast. But that did not keep them from developing a thriving cultural and religious life, especially on the south side of the River Lee in the area that Jews and Gentiles still fondly refer to as "Jewtown." The fact that their community was small, and that most of its original settlers came from the same villages in Lithuania, also did not keep the Jews of Cork from developing the schisms that seem to form in every Jewish community, in this case leading it to build two synagogues and hire rival religious leaders.

What was it like living as a Jew in a place as remote as Cork? "No work was available for Jewish boys and girls in the non-Jewish community, which was understandable because the Irish were brought up with the tradition that we were everything that was wrong culturally and religiously. So we didn't seek to mix with Irish people at the outset of our lives," recalls Gerald Goldberg, who was born in Cork in 1912 and was still living there at the turn of the century. "We had an annual Hanukkah dance, a special table at Yom Kippur, a kosher butcher shop, and a man who made meat kosher. We had a cheder. Every morning I lay tefillin, which I still do."

Fred Rosehill, who was born in Cork fifteen years after Goldberg, fills out the picture: "We always were a little frightened of the Gentiles. We kept our heads down, kept quiet; no one would bother us if we didn't bother them. Our parents were artisans and peddlers who grew into small-business people. My father and everyone else's worked six days a week to send their children to the university. Our fellows qualified and went into the professions but none of them ever came back to Cork. Most of the professional people went off to America as doctors, lawyers, and dentists."

Over time the barriers between Jews and Catholics began to crumble. It started with children playing soccer together in the streets and spread to the world of work. Golf clubs eventually let in Jewish members, as did the rowing club. Relations became sufficiently easy that, in 1977, Cork elected Goldberg its lord mayor. "My wife and I both were welcomed among the Irish people like nobody on Earth," he says. "They never interfered with the practice of our religion or sought for us to be otherwise." Rosehill agrees, saying his election as president of the Cork Rotary Club was almost as telling a rite of passage as Goldberg's as mayor: "It was absolutely marvelous growing up Jewish here. Judaism is my religion but Ireland is the country where I was born and that gave me everything I've ever known. I look to Jerusalem in my prayers but I look to Ireland as the country I live in and the country I literally would die for. One is spiritual, one is national.

"I'm a Corkman, an Irishman, and a Jew in that order," adds Rosehill. "In fact we made a video of Gerald that is called 'A Corkman, an Irishman and a Jew.'"

As for the future, Rosehill is not willing to give up on Cork. On

Passover he ran a community Seder that attracted fifty-two celebrants, some from Cork and Kerry and others visiting from Israel and America. He uses CD-ROMs to teach Jewish history and traditions to his grandchildren, whose mother is Jewish and father is not. Every two weeks he opens the old synagogue for tours and he already has guided through 2,000 people, explaining the heritage of Cork's Jewish community and what being Jewish means. For the High Holidays he invites several Hasidic Jews from London who help open the shul and sustain the service.

"Why bother?" he asks out loud. "Because we have a history, we have a background, we're one people. Judaism is everything from Yom Kippur to chopped liver. It's from a social background, a religious background, an ethnic background, a racial background. It's in us. It's intangible but it's there. The future for this community lies in the concept that the old days of Orthodoxy are long gone. One must embrace a Conservative type of Judaism, an interfaith, outreaching Judaism that takes in all shades and makes it possible for visitors to feel comfortable and come and pray with us in any manner that is acceptable to them."

Belfast Jews also are looking for a way to sustain their community in the face of declining numbers and physical isolation. The first arrived from Germany in the 1840s, while the descendants of most of the Jews in Northern Ireland today came from Russia between 1880 and 1919. They were poor and did not speak English, but over time they set up a social club and dance hall, a restaurant, tennis courts, football fields, burial grounds, and an Orthodox synagogue that holds hundreds. They also made their influence felt in the wider community, providing it with doctors and dentists, lawyers, merchants, and, like Dublin and Cork, a lord mayor. At its height in the early 1970s the Jewish community in Northern Ireland numbered about 1,500, most of whom lived in the north of Belfast. Today there are barely 250.

The Jews of Belfast have been exceedingly skillful in negotiating their society's most treacherous divide, the one separating Catholics from Protestants and Republicans from Unionists. They did it by not taking sides, determinedly so, to the point where they earned the respect of both sides. The Catholic cardinal now boasts of his warm relationship with Belfast's Jews at the same time that leading Protestants, especially evangelical ones, feel an affinity with those they call the Old Testament's chosen people. And the Jewish community is using its neutrality to bridge gaps the way it has since the Troubles started in the early 1970s. "In the early days, when there was total chaos and no one knew what the hell was going on, the premises of the synagogue were practically the only safe meeting point in the whole of North Belfast for opposing factions and for clergy trying to hold things together," recalls Cyril Rosenberg, a longtime leader of the Belfast Jewish community. "It let them meet in an atmosphere where each felt they weren't in the other's territory."

That neutrality is captured in a joke that every Belfast Jew knows, and retells, mainly because it is so revealing of the pressure on everyone in Northern Ireland to choose sides: A Jew is approached on the street and asked his religion. "I'm Jewish," he answers. "Ah yes," the inquisitor says, "but are you a Catholic Jew or a Protestant Jew?"

It will take even greater political acumen to fashion a future for Belfast's shrinking community of Jews. It recently sold off many of its facilities, partitioned the synagogue so it has half as many seats, and has to work hard every day to get the ten men needed for a minyan. What it has not done is come up with a way to replace the dozen or so mainly young Jews who leave each year, giving it a birth rate that has dropped to near zero. Most who go are bound for England, Israel, or America in search, like their cousins from the south, of spouses, education, or jobs. The Troubles also have played a role, limiting Jews' opportunities to safely congregate in public the same way they did everyone else's and raising the same doubts about whether it is wise to fashion their future around Northern Ireland.

"We all tell ourselves that if we really and truly get a peace here, and a lot of money from the European community and America, industry and commerce will grow and somewhere in there Jewish people may come as employees of international companies," says Rosenberg, a retired jeweler. "But how many will that be? And they have got to be young married people who will produce families. We don't need any more old people or even middle-aged ones."

What about Dublin? Conventional wisdom argues that the community will continue to shrink over the next twenty years to the point where there are only a few hundred, mostly elderly Jews left, where it is increasingly difficult to sustain institutions ranging from the synagogue to the kosher butcher, and where the community itself becomes a museum offering a taste, but no more, of what Jewish life used to be like in Ireland. That, after all, is what is happening today to scores of small Jewish communities across Europe, and especially in Great Britain—which makes Dublin Jews sad and leaves most resigned to their fate.

"When Limerick had no shul my father would take me down to Cork, and now it has all its problems," says Joe Morrison, who was born in Limerick in 1915, was the last Orthodox Jew to leave in the late 1930s, and now lives in Dublin. "I've seen two shuls, two minyans, and two Orthodox communities disappear. Unless some unknown factor arises, I'm pessimistic about Jews existing as a community in Ireland."

Zvi Gabay, Israel's first full-fledged ambassador to Ireland, who returned to Israel in 1999, also is an expert on disappearing Jewish communities. He saw it happen in Iraq, where he grew up and where the community shrank from 150,000 to fewer than 100, and he witnessed it again in Egypt. Ireland, he says, had a unique opportunity to take in as many as 20,000 Jewish refugees following World War II "but the government closed the gates. I don't believe that there'll be another chance for the growth of this community. It is diminishing by its numbers and by its activities as a Jewish community."

But others see the crisis confronting Dublin Jews as an opportunity. The sales of the Adelaide Road Synagogue and Maccabi sports club have netted more than $10 million, making Dublin one of the wealthiest Jewish communities of its size in the world and giving it resources it could use to attract and support Jewish immigrants. The consolidation of the Adelaide Road and Terenure congregations—and plans to construct a new Jewish community center complete with a synagogue, meeting rooms, and a restaurant—offer an unusual chance to match physical structures to whatever vision the community charts for itself. Ireland's red-hot economy should make it easier to keep young members of the community, or even to bring back those who left. Membership in the European community, with its ease of movement for residents of member states, could present a way around the country's infamously restrictive immigration laws and let in more Jews from other European states. And Ireland's projected need for as many as 200,000 skilled workers from abroad has inspired the Dublin Jewish community to begin a drive to fill some of those spots with Jews from South Africa, who share the English language and culture, are leaving their land in droves, and had the way paved by other South African Jews, including the cantor at Terenure.

None of that will be easy. Most Jews who are thinking about leaving their homelands have no idea there is a Jewish community in Ireland, most are from parts of the world like the former Soviet Union and Africa from which it still is nearly impossible to gain entry to Ireland, and most could not begin to afford Dublin's skyrocketing housing costs. Equally difficult are the multiple layers of divisions that have grown up within the Irish Jewish community. Less Orthodox, older families from the Adelaide Road Synagogue are having a very hard time feeling comfortable with the more observant, more recent arrivals from Terenure, with whom they seldom mixed before. Even more imposing barriers exist between those Orthodox congregations and the Reform one. Then there is the split between those who say it is okay to live in a shrinking but close-knit community provided it plans for its more modest future, and those who dismiss such thinking as defeatism. Even if a consensus were to emerge on a plan to save the community, it could be too late if young people continue leaving at the rate they have been.

"We've got to do something soon," Gavin Broder, the controversial South African–born chief rabbi of Ireland, warned in an interview in 1999. "In theory it seems that the community will dissolve, but I wouldn't be so quick to presume that. You have married people with children here and I don't see them leaving. They have all the facilities here. Foodwise, from a religious perspective, it's not a problem. Education is not a problem.

"What excites me is really filling in the void that has been here. I want to make people stop talking about what Dublin used to be, what it was when they had four, five, or six kosher butchers versus what it is now. I want to try and get rid of that stigma. There are wonderful opportunities here because at the moment our economy is working, young people are doing terrifically, it's a wonderful place to live," said the rabbi (who himself left Ireland in October 2000). "It would be wonderful to turn around and, say, bring in fifty families, refugees or whatever. It's a nice idea. But it's a slow process, whether it is done through advertising or whatever. I believe it to be possible so long as something is done. We have to be proactive in trying to create the interest."

Carolyn Collins, the property manager with two children, is equally upbeat as she imagines the Dublin Jewish community preserving its vitality even if it remains small: "It would be very comfortable to have one shul, a rabbi, a hazan, and a school in twenty-five years. If you look at the statistics of the community there are nineteen Jewish children now in the fourth year of school, and not every single one of them will move away. Also, some of us are talking very seriously about looking for Russian immigrants. Some say it's not worth it, that they won't get work permits, but there's definitely a case being made to do that. And I suppose some people will come back to Ireland after they're educated abroad."

What if the optimists are wrong, or if they never get a chance to test their vision of renewal? The death of the Dublin Jewish community might not be as onerous as some imagine—and it would not be a demise in the way we normally use the word. Faced with what they see as a choice between giving up Ireland or forsaking their Jewishness, large numbers of young Irish Jews have left their cherished homeland in order to maintain ties with their 3,500-year-old religion. They have gone searching for spouses and more vibrant Jewish worlds, and when they found them they planted roots.

The result is that the Jewish communities of Dublin, Cork, and Belfast have shrunk, but Israel has a 300-strong community of Irish Jews. Manchester, Boston, New York, Sydney, and Johannesburg have their own substantial enclaves. Those transplants, like other Irish who have migrated across the world, continue to honor what is special about Ireland—but they have something extra to hold on to, the unlikely hybrid called Irish Jewry. They celebrate Passover and St. Patrick's Day, they hold up as heroes Chaim Herzog and Michael Collins, and, like Fred Rosehill of Cork, they consider Israel their spiritual home and Ireland their national one. Many are so torn by having to leave that they have linked up with hundreds of other Irish Jews around the world via e-mail—they call themselves Irish JIG, for Jewish interest group—to share rich stories on growing up Jewish in Ireland, take virtual tours of today's world of Dublin Jewry with Joe Briscoe as their guide, and otherwise remind themselves and their children of the heritage they still cling to. Which is precisely what their ancestors did when they settled in Ireland in the late 1800s. They were building new lives, but wanted to sustain the Yiddish of their native Lithuania and Poland along with the dietary laws and other customs of their ancient texts.

Yes, the community of Dublin Jews is shrinking—but far from dying, it is moving as a way of staying alive, the way diaspora Jews have for thousands of years.

The Briscoes, the first family of Irish Jews, offer a case in point. Only two of patriarch Bob's seven children still live in Dublin, and only one of them, Joe, is still deeply involved with his religion. That probably is not surprising, given that Bob and Lily lived too far out of town and were too turned off by religious bureaucracy to ever become actively involved in the organized Jewish community. But they took the lead in Jewish causes ranging from saving wartime refugees to ridding Ireland of any vestiges of anti-Jewish or anti-Israel sentiment. They made sure the boys became bar mitzvah and that the family celebrated the High Holidays and Passover. And they taught all the kids to be at least as proud of being Jewish as they were of being Irish.

Ben, who took over his father's seats in parliament and the Dublin City Council, broke with the organized Jewish community after what he felt was the cruel refusal, even by the Reform, to reach out to his second wife, Carol, who was raised Catholic but was deeply interested in Judaism. "The only time I go to synagogue now is for state functions such as the installation of a new president," Ben says. Still, he has been a steadfast supporter of Israel and other Jewish causes during his more than three decades in government. And he insists that, even if he does not attend temple, Judaism "is in my genes. It's a personal conviction that I identify with now, a sense of belonging. It's knowing that there were so many Jews who in the Second World War thought it wasn't them that the Germans meant."

Only one of Ben and Carol's four children devotes much energy to Judaism, but she is deeply devoted, having lived in Israel, studied Hebrew, had a Jewish boyfriend, and celebrated countless Sabbaths with her uncle Joe and aunt Debbie. Carol also has embraced Judaism, writing her undergraduate thesis on the effect of World War II on Jewish children in Ireland, working on a master's thesis that looks at how Jewish families made the transition from shtetls in Eastern Europe to cities in Ireland, trying to expose her children to Jewish culture and, when asked if she considers herself Jewish, replying, "Yes, because of my sympathies. Maybe it's osmosis. I suppose it's not even the traditions, just the values. The values and the culture. I'm talking about family values, the values of what's right and what's wrong, what's decent. The way that children were talked to, were encouraged, were listened to, were part of the family. When I was a child I remember being told that children should be seen, not heard, not brought places. You could visit relatives but never really would be part of that big, bustling, argumentative family. Yes, that's distinctively Jewish, I have never seen it with anybody but my Jewish friends.

"I would have converted at the time when we were married had it not been for that," Carol says of the community's presumed coldness to her when she married Ben in 1967. "I just said, 'If that's the way the community feels, there's no point.' I am accepted now but it has taken thirty years to feel that way."

As for Ben and Joe's siblings who left Ireland, Joan, the eldest, moved to Canada in 1947 and was married a year later, to a Catholic. Her four children all were raised Catholic, although one son was made an honorary member of the Jewish Students Union at the University of Alberta after he helped with a letter-writing campaign against a Holocaust denial teacher. "All my friends know about my Jewish background," Joan Briscoe O'Reilly adds. "I am very proud of it."

Ida Gressis, Joan's younger sister, lives in Ohio and recalls that growing up in Ireland "Catholicism always was more familiar to me than Judaism. We didn't live in the Jewish quarter, my nurse was a Roman Catholic, and I went to Protestant school. I have to be honest, I always felt a little bit embarrassed. I was a little self-conscious. I always said that I was Jewish, I didn't hide the fact, but maybe I did a little." Ironically, it is now—after marrying a Catholic and raising her children in Catholicism—that Ida says she feels most comfortable with her Jewishness. "People know what Jews are in the United States," she explains. "Being Jewish in America is a lot easier than being Jewish in Ireland. I've been here longer than anywhere else; people are interested, they're fascinated by Jewish people. My kids? I think they like being Irish and Jewish, I believe that."

His mother is right, says Ida's younger son, Robert, a graduate student in philosophy at the University of Michigan. "I do feel a connection to my Jewish ancestors. I feel proud of it in a strange sort of way. I don't know why I feel proud but it kind of makes me different, just because I have this ancestry. I feel a pull to learn about Judaism, I feel a responsibility to do that. I visited Dublin in 1998 and while there I toured the Dáil with my uncle Ben Briscoe. He would introduce me not as Robert Gressis but as the next Robert Briscoe. I thought it was pretty neat. I thought maybe I should have a political career in Ireland. I felt an instant connection with the legacy."

He may have been Robert Briscoe for a day, but he has a cousin who carries that name permanently. Robert is the oldest child of Brian Briscoe, Robert and Lily's middle child. Brian married an Italian Catholic and, like his sisters, he raised his children Catholic. But he never stopped going to shul on Yom Kippur, celebrating Passover, or "always being very much aware that I was a Jew." Some of that rubbed off on his son Robert, who has gravitated to his Irish roots and his Jewish ones. "I graduated from college in 1993 and it is since then that I have considered myself Jewish," says Robert, a Ph.D. student in philosophy at Boston University who spent four months studying in Israel. "When I have imagined children I have thought it would be nice to celebrate *Shabbes* on Friday nights, although not to raise them religious. I really do like celebrating the Sabbath on Friday nights. I have Jewish friends and we do that." As for Brian, a radiologist who lives in Baltimore, he defines his identity in terms that his father the lord mayor could relate to: "I am an American citizen and proud to be an American citizen. But I also am proud to have been of both Jewish and Irish heritage. I am proud of all three."

Joe, the retired dentist, is whom journalists, students, or others from outside the community or the country are referred to if they want to know about Irish Jews. He also is a critical link in the international Irish-Jewish e-mail network. All with good reason. He always had an affinity for things Jewish growing up, and when his father died he acquired an affinity for the synagogue, too. In keeping with the Jewish tradition of honoring the dead Joe attended services every morning and evening for a full year, which he says "obviously was an education. I became a bit more knowledgeable about the ritual, if nothing else, and it brought me in contact with many more people in the community. My two sons, who were very small at the time, on most occasions accompanied me to synagogue on Shabbat. For that particular year we were very observant. After that year we continued, although not quite with the same intensity."

Joe and Debbie's two children, not surprisingly, are the most committed to their Judaism of any of that generation of Briscoes, although they are not practicing it in Ireland. The older son, David, who was born in 1959, lives outside Boston and is a pediatric kidney specialist at Children's Hospital. He says he came to America purely to pursue his career in academic medicine, and that Judaism remains a critical part of his world: "It's very important, very, very important in my personal life. I'm not a religious Jew, if you know what I mean; in fact I probably would be considered by some to be very nonreligious. But in terms of my activities—my children, their morals and outlook on life, the cultural tradition, my wife, my kids—we love it."

David's younger brother, Daniel, lives just outside Tel Aviv, where he is an eye surgeon and an active participant in Israel's large community of Irish expatriates. That takes various forms, from the annual St. Patrick's Day gathering at the Irish Embassy to theater groups that meet throughout the year and informal gatherings of friends around the bottle of Paddy Whiskey that Daniel always has on hand. "The Irish-Jewish community," he says, "is very alive outside Ireland as well as inside."

While he would rather see his children close by in Dublin, Joe says Jews have been moving for so many centuries that "it is part of our psyche. It's not something we can just switch off. I hope this ebb of Jews from Dublin reverses and becomes a flow back. But I think the Jews who are leaving have absorbed all the good qualities of the wider society they lived in and are taking those with them. There is a uniqueness about being Jewish and Irish."

Chapter 6

PARIS:

Getting Along, Getting Ahead

His parents told him he was going on vacation. No matter that news of the trip to Paris came out of the blue, that he was just fourteen and had flown in an airplane just once before, or that only he and two younger brothers would be going, with his father, mother, and the three little kids staying behind in Casablanca. He tried not to think about all that, or connect it to his girlfriend's mysterious disappearance a few months before. The trip was sure to be an adventure and Sydney Ohana convinced himself, the way any teenager would, that fun was reason enough for his parents to whisk him off to the City of Lights in 1965. He kept believing that until he was greeted at the Paris airport by his twenty-year-old cousin.

"He told me, 'You will never go back to Morocco,' " Ohana recalls thirty-five years later. "I asked what would happen to my father, mother, and the smaller children. He said, 'Don't worry, they'll leave Morocco by car. They'll go through Spain to France. They're obliged to leave everything in Morocco, to take nothing with them. They couldn't tell you because it was dangerous.' "

His cousin was right: the Paris excursion was not at all out of the blue and while Sydney did eventually go back to Morocco, it was not until he was twenty-five. Meyer Ohana, his father, had been planning the escape for a full nine years, since the family made its first exodus to Paris in 1956. Sydney was just five then, and did not understand what Moroccan independence from France meant or why Jewish families like his were fleeing. To outsiders, an Islamic land like Morocco might seem an even stranger home for Jews than Catholic Ireland. But Jews had lived in Morocco longer than Muslims, and into the 1950s there was a community of 220,000 deeply observant Sephardic Jews that prospered under the protection of the supreme leader, Sultan Muhammad V.

The Ohanas had come to Paris at the first sign of an Islamic backlash in 1956, then returned to Morocco when things settled down. But Meyer knew it was just a matter of time before they would have to leave again. So he began sending money to France and making plans through his two sisters there, quietly arranging for the day when his family would pack up for good. The car was too small to fit everyone, and he felt Sydney and his brothers were old enough to travel on their own even if they were too young to be entrusted with their trip's true purpose. So he sent them off by air as he and the rest made their getaway by land, their small car loaded up inside and out. Meyer was preoccupied with having to leave behind all he had worked so hard to build, including a successful freight company, but the main thing on young Sydney's mind was "that I would never see my girlfriend again, or all my friends. And I was afraid of my new life in France."

His fear was well founded. The Paris that greeted the Ohanas had one of the world's oldest and largest Jewish communities and might have been expected to embrace them, the more so because of France's half century of imperial ties with their native Morocco. But the young Jews Sydney met made clear from the start that while davening three times a day, laying tefillin, and adhering to every nuance of the ancient laws of keeping kosher might be the way Jews did things in Morocco, it was not how people behaved in a civilized society like France. In Paris, Sydney learned about Israel and the Holocaust. He discovered that being Jewish did not necessarily mean being religious, and it definitely did not mean living in the kind of Jewish enclave where he had grown up in Marrakech. He also found that although France's religious leaders were grateful for the 220,000 new arrivals from Tunisia, Morocco, and Algeria, who doubled the size of Paris's Jewish community and infused it with confidence and vitality, most French Jews did not appreciate the North Africans' swarthy complexions or their openly Orthodox habits. And they certainly did not want their Ashkenazic sons and daughters marrying the Arabic-sounding Sephardim.

Yet just as the evolving lives of the Briscoes evidenced the changing nature of Irish Jewry, so the Ohanas today reflect the brave new world of French Jewry. Sydney married the daughter of a leading Ashkenazic family and their children barely acknowledge the old divisions. Like many around them, the Ohanas question the renewed assertiveness of the Orthodox and, while they were among the first families of the city's oldest and most elegant traditional synagogue, La Victoire, they opted to have their daughter's bat mitzvah at a Reform temple. They worry whether the Paris Jewish community will be able to sustain its enormous numbers and other signs of success, but are heartened by the fact that their twenty-three-year-old son recently quit a high-paying job to run a national student organization aimed at ensuring that his generation learns from the Holocaust and from mistakes of other eras.

This is the other half of the narrative of contemporary European Jewry—the hopeful half, reflected in growing, dynamic communities like Berlin, Warsaw, and, most of all, Paris. The Ohanas—and their Parisian Jewish community—are the story of life that balances the oft-told stories of presumed death represented by Dublin, Glasgow, Liverpool, and all the other European cities whose Jewish communities are dwindling.

Signs of that life are everywhere in Paris. Start in the overflowing synagogues, which have a peculiarly French flavor, with ushers wearing the sleek, curvaceous caps favored by the Little Corporal, Napoleon Bonaparte, and congregants reciting the Shema prayer by puckering their lips to form the proper "une"s and "dieu"s. Back on the street there are 500 kosher restaurants, groceries, and bakeries to choose from, more than anyplace on earth with the possible exceptions of New York and Tel Aviv. Europe's largest community of Jews is also among the diaspora's most ardent backers of Israel, although French Jews, like their counterparts in Dublin, also pledge a heartfelt allegiance to their homeland. All told, a Parisian Jewish community that just sixty years ago was ravaged by the Holocaust today stands as the clearest testament that Hitler failed in his bid to stamp out European Jewry.

Parisian Jews continue to face challenges, of course. Profound ones. They are troubled by soaring rates of intermarriage and wide gaps between their traditional and less observant members. They have struggled for half a century to accommodate their strange blends of Ashkenazim and Sephardim. And today many worry that assimilation and ambivalence will eventually cause their community to slowly shrivel, although others see signs of revitalization that make them more upbeat than ever about surviving and thriving.

While those struggles are painful and leave some French Jews feeling disconnected, they are also yielding original answers that can offer models for the United States and Israel, where the same fault lines run even deeper. They are prototypes for models of pluralism, of how to bridge ethnic divisions within a community the way the Ohanas did within their family. There are also models of how to accommodate seemingly split loyalties to France and Israel, to country and culture, that could inspire struggling democracies in the Balkans as well as burgeoning Jewish communities in the former Soviet Union. French Jews, once a case study in assimilation, are now an object lesson in how to compellingly redefine Jewish identity for a new millennium.

Soon after coming to France "I discovered a new way to be Jewish," says Sydney Ohana, one of Paris's best-known plastic surgeons. "I discovered Israel. For us in Morocco, Israel was only a dream. And I discovered all that happened during the Second World War. I began to have contacts with non-Jewish people. I go to meetings of the Jewish community, meetings like B'nai B'rith, meetings to help Israel or to help the Jewish community. I opened my eyes and saw that religion is just one part of our Jewish life and that there are ways we can be Jewish beyond only the biblical traditions."

*   *   *

The history of French Jewry over the last 1,200 years reads as if it was written by Robert Louis Stevenson. At times France assumed the demeanor of the novelist's Dr. Jekyll, allowing its Jewish residents unprecedented freedom and prosperity. Then, without warning, it metamorphosed into the nefarious Mr. Hyde, mercilessly persecuting the Jews within its borders.

The reign of the Carolingian kings, and especially those who ruled in the ninth and tenth centuries, was France at its most generous. Jews administered the affairs of Catholic institutions and sold the wine used in masses. They held ambassadorial posts and served as tax collectors. They had equality in the courts and bids to pass canons hostile to them were turned back.

Then came the Crusades and their angry aftermath, running from the end of the eleventh century through the beginning of the sixteenth. There were murders and forced conversions, blood libels like the one in Blois in 1171 where thirty-one Jews were burned at the stake, and acts of brutality as when King Philip Augustus imprisoned all of Paris's wealthy Jews in 1181, freeing them only after they paid huge ransoms. Expulsions also were the order of the day, first from the relatively small French kingdom, then from one outlying region after another. Jews were fined and their properties seized, local populations were incited to rise up against them with massacres, burnings, and beatings, and they were made to live in ghettos and wear badges identifying themselves as Jews.

On the eve of the French Revolution there were close to 40,000 Jews living in the land, mostly in the northeast regions of Alsace and Lorraine. But while they lived under French rule most did not consider themselves French. Their language and dress, commercial enterprises and adherence to ancient laws and customs marked them as Jews, with the same separate communal structures that characterized the shtetls of Eastern Europe.

The revolution changed everything. As part of the wider leveling of society Jews were granted equality and citizenship, the Sephardim in 1790 and Ashkenazim the following year. It was the first time that had happened anywhere in Europe, and it placed French Jews in an unfamiliar position at the cutting edge of the Jewish diaspora. On the one hand they finally were free to escape their ghetto existence and become full participants in their nation's economy and politics. But freedom, as is clear today, brings with it the challenges of how to resist assimilation and retain what is special about being a Jew, which was precisely what the architects of the revolution hoped would happen. And as with the rest of the changes sweeping across France, the toppling of the old order in Jewish settlements led first to anarchy, then to a general uncertainty about who was in charge and how the former ghetto residents were supposed to behave.

Napoleon quickly stepped in to end the disorder in a way that was a storybook blend of Jekyll and Hyde. He set up under the Ministry of Religions a centralized hierarchy called the consistorial system, responsible for everything from collecting dues to paying rabbis' salaries, enforcing government edicts, and regulating religious affairs. The state for the first time recognized Judaism as a legitimate faith, but it was determined to control its choice of leaders and the direction of communal life. The diminutive emperor also imposed a series of economic orders, dubbed by Jews the "infamous decree," that limited the professions they could enter and places they could live. Napoleon presumed that Jews were greedy and duplicitous, and set up an ambitious program of social engineering to remake them into worthy participants in his new social order. While the edicts no longer prevail, the consistories do, as one is reminded by the Napoleonic hats that sextons still wear in some synagogues across France. More important than the structures was the slow process Napoleon launched of elevating civil law and secular identity over Jewish law and Jewish separateness. French Jews were for the first time emancipated—but their part of the bargain was to think of themselves as Frenchmen first, with their Jewishness narrowed to the private sphere of religious worship. They might choose a synagogue while their Catholic neighbor worshiped at a church, but once they stepped outside both would share a national identity.

The changes launched by the French Revolution and institutionalized by Napoleon, as historian Paula E. Hyman writes, "would gradually transform the descendants of Yiddish-speaking village peddlers into comfortable members of the urban French bourgeoisie." The reforms also set a pattern of voluntary assimilation that would be repeated everywhere from Weimar Germany to modern-day America.

France's transformation was not trouble-free, however. By the end of the nineteenth century French Jews were becoming more confident members of French society. They moved in even larger numbers to Paris, which was the center of French culture, and began reaching out to defend fellow Jews worldwide through the newly formed Alliance Israelite Universelle. But the arrival of more than 40,000 immigrants from

Eastern Europe between 1881 and 1914 challenged the old orders in France the same way it did across the diaspora. And French Jews' sense of belonging, of being part of the noblest experiment in emancipation in their people's 2,500 years of exile, was dealt an unexpected blow by the arrest on October 15, 1894, of Jewish army captain Alfred Dreyfus.

Dreyfus, born into a wealthy manufacturing family and the only Jew on the French General Staff, was charged with treason. A court-martial found him guilty based on a piece of yellow paper listing French military secrets retrieved from a wastebasket at the German embassy in Paris with handwriting that distantly resembled Dreyfus's. His rank was reduced, his epaulettes were ripped off, and his sword broken in a public ceremony, and he was banished to the notorious penal colony on Devil's Island in South America with orders that he remain until his death. Convincing evidence that he had been framed emerged two years after his conviction, but it took another ten years for him to be fully rehabilitated and awarded the Legion of Honor. The whole affair gave grist to anti-Semites, with thugs shouting "Death to the Jews" as they smashed Jewish storefronts and right-wing elements in the army and Catholic Church casting doubts on the loyalty of all French Jews. In the end, however, Dreyfus's mistreatment helped to bring the liberals back to power and, in 1905, led to the legal separation of church and state. While Dreyfus himself never lost faith in the country he called "this noble France," his mistreatment reminded the world that hatred against Jews was rampant even in the land of *liberté, egalité*, and *fraternité*.

A half century later disturbing new questions would be raised about the nobility of France and the honor of its leaders. France fell to Germany in the summer of 1940, with the Nazis occupying the northern three-fifths of the nation and the Vichy French regime ruling in the south. Over the course of the war 75,000 of France's 325,000 Jews were deported and exterminated. Thousands more were interned in labor camps on French soil. Survivors tell of grandparents being sliced to death with a garden hoe or sold out to the Gestapo for two kilos of sugar. Jewish businesses were seized and often sold, Jews were excluded from posts in education, civil service, and the press, and an anti-Jewish police force was established. Jews also were banned from public establishments, allowed to shop for just one hour in the afternoon, subjected to curfews, and required to notify authorities before they could move.

After 150 years of emancipation, Jews slowly were stripped of their rights as citizens. After 150 years of being encouraged to blend in, Jews were compelled to advertise their religious identity by carrying cards bearing the stamp "Jew" and sewing large yellow Stars of David onto their jackets. And while the crackdown came first and more ferociously where the Germans ruled directly, nearly all the indignities eventually spread to the Vichy zone.

It took another half century for France to publicly face up to its complicity during the Vichy era—to the painful realization that Frenchmen had been victimizers as well as victims—and even then it was not a matter of choice. There simply were too many carefully documented, widely distributed indictments of the regime in film and print. Too much evidence had been presented during the trials and convictions of Gestapo officer Klaus Barbie and Vichy officials Paul Touvier and Maurice Papon. "Even the Jewish community, after the war, accepted the French version that France had a knife on its throat and was obliged to do what it did," explains Serge Klarsfeld, a survivor and France's best-known chronicler of the *Shoah*, which is Hebrew for Holocaust and France's preferred way of referring to the genocide. "But in the free zone where there were no Germans, the French arrested more than 10,000 foreign Jews and hundreds of children and they arrived a few days later in Auschwitz. They were the only Jews in Europe arrested in zones without any Germans. French children like me were more afraid of the French policemen than German soldiers."

While he and his wife, Beate, have spent their lives amassing evidence against the guilty, Klarsfeld also acknowledges "the miracle" of the French who fought back against Vichy collaborators and, in the process, helped ensure the survival of three of every four French Jews. "The intervention of the French population and the churches in August and September of 1942 is what prevented the Vichy from giving more Jews to the Germans," he says. "French people living in the free zone denounced the rape of the French tradition of honor, of hospitality, then the Vichy started to cooperate less intensely in arresting Jews." Other Frenchmen went further, helping Jewish neighbors get false papers, hiding them, assisting in smuggling their children to Switzerland, or aiding Jewish men and women in joining the resistance, de Gaulle's Free French forces, or the Foreign Legion. The odds of escape were greater if the

Jew in question happened to have deep roots in France, which meant he probably had better contacts, more money, and was less affected by the new anti-Jewish laws, at least at first, than more recent arrivals from places like Poland and Algeria.

Its Holocaust history continues to have a profound impact on French Jewry today, more so than with any Jewish community outside of Germany itself. That is partly because it raised such troubling questions of French complicity, and whether or not France can be trusted in the future to safeguard its Jewish citizens. Even more important is that France had more Holocaust survivors than any nation occupied by the Germans, and those survivors passed down to their children and grandchildren a resolve to remember even when they themselves could not speak about the horrors they had endured.

Nicole Kac-Ohana, Sydney's wife, grew up knowing that the *Shoah* was gnawing at her parents, both of whom had lived through it. But it took until the late 1970s—when Nicole was twenty-five, and had just given birth to a child of her own—for her mother to find the words to tell her story. Stella Szternblytz was sixteen when the Nazis stormed into Lublin, Poland, and she knew the only way to avoid a death camp was to obtain the identity papers of a non-Jew. She met a smuggler at the train station and paid him the necessary bribes. Yet just as the transaction was being completed, her cousin approached, shouting, "Esther," her Jewish name, and asking in Yiddish for news from the family. Stella froze, fearing the police would overhear and arrest her for trying to swap identities. But quick reaction by the black marketeer saved the day, the exchange eventually was consummated, and Stella Szternblytz became Helene Galand, a Catholic Pole. The near-disaster at the station taught Stella how easily a slip-up could happen and she put the lesson to use during her eight months at the Halendorf slave labor camp in Germany, which housed primarily non-Jewish Russians and Poles. Stella made herself think and behave like her Catholic alter ego, Helene, knowing that if she revealed her Jewish upbringing or, as she feared most, uttered a Yiddish word in her dreams, the game would be up and her life could be over. Exhibiting the kind of self-control no teenager should ever have to know, Stella lived to be liberated.

Michael Kac, Nicole's father, spent the war practicing a different but equally harrowing sort of deception. He escaped Poland in 1936 bound for Palestine but only made it as far as France. At first he peddled gloves and socks out of a suitcase; then he opened a successful leather shop. But the outbreak of war ended the good times for him as for other Jews in France. Unlike the others, Kac refused to wear the yellow Star of David and, when the French police came to arrest him at his apartment building, he pretended to be someone else and managed to get away. The game of cat-and-mouse continued for the entire war, with him fine-tuning his skills at locating hideouts and narrowly escaping each time the Nazis closed in. After the armistice Michael met Stella, who was twenty years his junior and had only recently arrived in Paris, and she agreed to marry him if he agreed to help track down any of her relatives who had survived.

That focus on family, on rebuilding what they could of their old lives and holding those they loved close for fear of losing them again, was the preoccupation of an entire generation of *Shoah* survivors in France. But not all wanted to hold on to their Jewishness.

Some sought to strike back against the Nazi insistence that they were different by becoming more French than ever, the way Napoleon had hoped they would. During the war that meant signing up to fight not in the special Jewish units of the resistance, but as communists, Gaullists, or whatever other affiliation they chose. Afterward it meant doing whatever it took to prove they were authentically French, and neither mentioning the nightmare of the Holocaust nor praying to a God they felt had abandoned them. Many went a step further, disguising in public or discarding altogether their Judaism and insisting that their children do the same, for fear they could come under attack again. The numbers of conversions and name changes rose in the postwar years, as did the number of Jews who refused to circumcise their baby boys.

To others, however, Hitler offered the most compelling argument imaginable against assimilation: no matter how they defined themselves they would forever be Jews in the eyes of their tormenters. The war, and especially the behavior of the Vichy collaborators, also had convinced them it was only with other Jews that they could ever be truly secure. So, like their grandparents, they associated mainly with their coreligionists. They began supporting the Representative Council of Jewish Institutions of France, or CRIF, founded in 1943 for the sole purpose of politically defending the Jewish community. Regardless of how they felt about their religion and culture, they clung to their Judaism as a way of honoring the victims of the Holocaust and defying its Nazi perpetrators.

"We are for freedom of religion but also for freedom of people who do not want to be religious. We want the right to consider ourselves Jewish even if the rabbi says we are not Jewish," says Max Sarcey, a defiant survivor who spent the war years in the resistance, then in Auschwitz. Sarcey says he does not believe in God, is only moderately interested in Israel, and finds it "very hard to define" just what parts of Judaism he does embrace. But the embrace is there, for him as for so many who lived through the war. "Our culture," he explains, "is French but our home is Yiddish. We're French and Jews, Jews and French."

That attitude of denying the primacy of their Judaism—but somehow knowing they are fooling themselves by trying to deny it—was pervasive enough in the postwar generation that it gave birth to a joke still told in Jewish circles in France: It was 1948, just after Israel's founding, and a Jewish politician from France named Daniel Mayer was visiting Israeli prime minister David Ben-Gurion. Mayer said, "Mr. Ben-Gurion, I want to be clear first and foremost that I am French, second I am a socialist, third I'm president of the League for Human Rights, and only fourthly am I an Israelite." Ben-Gurion, who had been taking notes, answered, "It doesn't matter because in Hebrew we read from right to left."

Michael and Stella Kac were less conflicted about their Jewish identities. He kept his promise of reconstructing her family, helping relatives from as far away as Brazil relocate in Paris, paying for their apartments, and finding them jobs. She never stopped believing—in God or the Jewish people. Together they built a Jewish home, schooling their three daughters in Jewish history and customs, teaching them to cherish the Sabbath and its *brochas*, and instilling in them a commitment to Zionism as well as to France's quirky brand of Judaism. The girls remember their father arriving home Friday evenings with an armful of bagels and salmon, gefilte fish and challahs from Goldenberg's restaurant in the Marais district. What they did not know until years later was that before he got home, he had made stops at the apartments of aunts, uncles, and distant cousins, dropping off parcels of food and drink with the concierge so the relatives would not feel obliged to say "thanks." He gave money to Israel, anonymously—as Jewish law prescribes—and during the 1956 Sinai Campaign he had flown to the front hundreds of fur-lined leather coats to warm the soldiers during the cold nights. And he assisted the Jewish refugees flooding into France after the war, supplying them with jobs or, when needed, forged immigration papers.

What Michael and Stella could not do was talk about their wartime traumas. "I wanted to preserve my daughters from the bad things in life. I have always been afraid and frightened, and didn't want to transmit the fear to my daughters," explains Stella. Decades later, however, she decided she had to tell them: "I was conscious that something very important happened in my life and that I had never shared it with my daughters. It's important to share things when they are grown up, when they are having their own children."

Even before they heard the stories the girls had gotten the message. "What they cared about after the war was the solidarity of the Jewish people, to be together, to be helped," says Nicole, the youngest of the three. "I don't think it was to preserve the culture; that's our problem now. At that time, because a lot of people had died and others felt culpable being alive, it meant that they had to gather together. My parents didn't have any goy friends, they just didn't feel easily with the others. The place where we were living, the places where we met our friends, the friends of our parents, all that was Jewish. We always were surrounded by Jews, always."

And there were other, unstated lessons her parents passed down, adds Nicole. Like her mother's "*complexe de perfection*, her complex of per-fection. For her not to be denounced in the work camp she always had to look at every part of her body and her mind. It was much more than self-control. It was a question of death. There was no room to be herself. And she wanted her children to grow up in the most perfect way. There was no other way. I remember when I was young, around seven years old, I always thought there was a camera in my room looking to see if I were doing things correctly."

Other middle-aged Parisians tell similar stories of their survivor parents—of feeling that it was okay to be Jewish at home but dangerous to be openly Jewish in public, of learning what their parents had endured not from them but from distant relatives. For Nicole, the most confusing legacy was when her father simply stopped talking five years before he died in 1999 at the age of ninety. He was not senile and not angry. He would read, listen to others talk, and sip vodka with old friends, but he uttered barely a word. "We tried to understand," says Nicole. "He was a strong man, very authoritative. When I told him I needed to talk, that he still had a lot of things to tell me, he said, 'I already told you all what I had to tell you.' It was a lesson of finishing life with serenity and quietness, of waiting for death without fear, without violence, without being sick." And, she might have added, for a man whose young life was filled with the horrors of the Holocaust, it was a lesson that he had found peace in bearing silent witness to how his family and his people were thriving.

The French Jewish community as a whole settled into a serenity of sorts in the 1950s, or at least that was how optimists saw the bids to expand Jewish education, strengthen political institutions, and generally battle back against absorption. Pessimists were convinced that assimilation was winning and that the determination "never to forget," while compelling to some survivors, was not enough to motivate the young or ensure continuity. Luckily, the question never had to be tested because the community was about to be rocked by a revival that seemed to come out of nowhere.

It actually came out of Africa. Much the way Düsseldorf saw its size and vitality soar during the 1990s with the arrival of Russian Jews, so France in the 1950s and '60s was reinforced by Sephardic Jews from Algeria, Tunisia, and Morocco. A total of 220,000 came between 1950 and 1970, the most Jewish immigrants taken in by any nation other than Israel during that period, swelling the population of French Jews to 535,000 and more than doubling the number of Jewish communities to almost 300. But whereas the Russian Jews had little Jewish background and were attracted mainly by Germany's promises of social services and political freedom, the North Africans were substantially more steeped in Judaism than their French hosts and were motivated to flee in part by a craving to practice their Judaism freely.

Jews had a long and often exalted history in North Africa. In Algeria, records of Jewish settlement date back more than 1,300 years, and by World War II, the community was 118,000 strong. Morocco's is even older, with legend having it that Jews arrived before the destruction of the First Temple in 586 B.C., and by 1948 the Jewish population had reached

265,000. As for Tunisia, from the eighth to the eleventh centuries Kairouan was the liveliest center of rabbinic culture outside of Babylonia, and in 1946 there were 71,000 Jews living in the country. While all three communities of North African Jews had sunk deep roots, all were threatened by their homelands' moves to independence and the nationalism and anti-Semitism that accompanied them. Feeling compelled to move, they had two choices: Israel, which would take anyone who wanted to come, and France, where all the Algerians and about half the Tunisians and Moroccans already held citizenship. Many poorer and more observant Tunisians and Moroccans decided on Israel, but the rest—along with almost all 110,000 Algerian Jews—opted for France. It offered greater economic opportunities and, since they already spoke French and thought of themselves as part-French, the language and cultural barriers seemed less imposing than in the Hebrew-speaking Jewish state.

The new arrivals to France stood out from the old in lots of ways. They were more likely to keep kosher, don tefillin, and abstain from working and driving on Shabbat, and that observance was more tied to family than synagogue. They knew more about Torah and less about Jewish history, Jewish intellectualism, and the State of Israel. They were better versed in Arabic languages and not at all in Yiddish, and were less likely to have been touched by the horrors of the Holocaust, although the Germans or Vichys did crack down on Jews in all three North African lands. Tunisian and Moroccan refugees married outside the faith just 5 percent of the time through the mid-1970s, compared to 40 percent among French-born Jews (the rate among Algerians, who always had been more drenched in French culture, was 48 percent). And the North Africans, many of whom had grown up in all-Jewish villages, were much more open about their Jewishness, whether that meant wearing a yarmulke in the street or reacting with outrage to perceived anti-Semitism, which was how French Jews had been nearly two centuries before, when they lived in Jewish ghettos. To the new arrivals it was a matter of pride; to the old it seemed a provocation.

The old Ashkenazic majority had reason to feel threatened given the way the Sephardim were redefining French Jewry. Some secular Jews saw the boom in synagogues, and in Orthodoxy, as reminiscent of Israel's Meah Shearim neighborhood and the intolerance they associated with it. Other old-timers pined for the days before the arrival of the

Sephardim when, as they put it, there was "less intense practice and prejudice." While the Tunisians, Moroccans, and Algerians at first were shy about joining communal projects and taking on the old-timers, they eventually began participating and quickly assumed control. The last two grand rabbis of France have been North African, as are the director of the umbrella social services agency and the president of the Consistory of Paris. All of which sidelined many of those who had overseen Jewish communal affairs for so long that they assumed it was their birthright and resented being voted out by the new majority of what they saw as fanatic Sephardim.

"Now people want those communal jobs and they're willing to fight for them. You have a completely new type of person coming forward and it means that the establishment, which doesn't need to prove anything, is just not interested anymore in serving these entities," says Baron Eric de Rothschild, a scion of the banking family that personifies that establishment and has underwritten and overseen Jewish charities in France for nearly 200 years. "Everything gets mixed up and everybody is stepping on each other's toes. The cacophony is absolutely appalling, but it's the reality of the community today. My family is still very central but the visible levers of power have passed into other people's hands, actually some of them with rather disastrous results."

Moise Cohen, president of the Consistory of Paris, sees the same events in decidedly different terms. The North Africans "gave a new vitality to French Judaism. The community here was disappearing," says Cohen, who arrived from Morocco in 1958. "When I came there were only three kosher restaurants; now within the Paris *bet din* there are one hundred and fifty, which is more than in any other city. We have more than seventy kosher caterers and something like five hundred kosher points of sale, with groceries, bakers, and so on. It is absolutely fantastic. The people coming from North Africa were so active, so energetic, so enthusiastic, so dynamic. They began to make synagogues around Paris, Marseille, Lyon. Then community centers, and *mikvah*s, and schools. The movement is increasing and increasing in a fabulous manner."

Sydney Ohana lived through all those changes and understands why some resent them while others celebrate. In Marrakech and later in Casablanca "we lived in a Jewish community with many synagogues and a very good religious life," he recalls. "It was like living in a ghetto. We were very close to one another and we never married non-Jews. There were very good Jewish schools and we were very Orthodox. We had to do prayers morning, afternoon, and night. And we knew when we were eighteen we would leave Morocco; every Jewish boy and girl left to study in France." But Sydney never made it to eighteen, leaving first in 1956 at age five, when his family fled the country for the first time, then departing for good when troubles flared up again nine years later.

Being in France "opened my eyes," he says. "I discovered the world. In Morocco for many centuries all the Jewish life was around the religion. In France the religion is just one part of our life and one part of our Jewish life." After a couple years in France, he also began to see that "French Jews were afraid of the Sephardim, they were afraid of our way of life. We were not ashamed to be Jewish. For us it was normal, but they thought we were Jewish too openly. I knew that my father-in-law and mother-in-law wanted my wife to be married with an Ashke nazic, not a Sephardic. I think for them we were a little bit Arabic people in the beginning.

"Today, things have completely changed. At the beginning Sephardic Jews were poor people; twenty years later there were enough rich ones to live in the same quarters as Ashkenazic. In the beginning there were no doctors, lawyers, and politicians from the Sephardic community," adds Sydney, whose wife, Nicole, also is a doctor. "Now most of those Jewish professionals in France are Sephardic. Most of the great professors in hospitals in Paris are Sephardic, most of the big lawyers in Paris are Sephardic, and there are many weddings between the two communities. Nobody asks anymore if we are Sephardic or Ashkenazic. It is not so important."

*   *   *

One reason the barriers fell is that Sephardic and Ashkenazic Jews realized that whatever divided them paled next to the ongoing fissures between Jews and non-Jews in French society. That was especially apparent during the Six-Day War in 1967, which rallied the support of Jews from Boston and Berlin to Buenos Aires. But in Paris the specter of Arab armies massing on Israel's borders drew a particularly heated response—in part because France's many Holocaust survivors feared that Israel could be exterminated the way much of European Jewry had been, and even more because, after years of supporting Israel, the French government suddenly was tilting to the oil-rich Arabs and cutting off arms for Israel. French president Charles de Gaulle stirred the cauldron when, at a press conference six months after the war, he suggested that French Jews who had backed Israel were guilty of divided loyalties. Jews generally, he added, were "an elite people" and "domineering," and through history they had "provoked, more precisely given rise to," their own persecution.

In the old days a fence-mending visit like the one de Gaulle made to the chief rabbi might have kept the community calm, but the community itself was changing beyond recognition in the late 1960s and early '70s. The Jews who had arrived recently from Algeria, Tunisia, and Morocco were far less shy than their French-bred cousins about expressing their Jewishness and their anger. At the same time young Jews born in France since World War II could not understand why their war-weary parents and grandparents were so anxious to blend in, and the ongoing student protests taught them how to make their voices heard. New evidence of Vichy complicity in the Nazi nightmare prompted still more Jews to question France's loyalty to them, while a new generation of Jewish intellectuals suggested that rather than Jews heeding Napoleon's call to merge into the wider society, society should recognize that Jews and other minorities had the right to be different.

The end result of developments like those within and without the Jewish world was that "the Jewish community of France was being very much politicized," says Henri Hajdenberg, who in the 1970s led the Jewish Renewal movement and today runs the Representative Council of Jewish Institutions of France, the community's political arm. "It's still politicized, maybe more politicized than the American community. We are the most politicized Jewish community in the world. Israel is the big unifying factor. The feeling when I was young of most Jewish leaders was not to make too many waves, but now we can speak loudly."

That newly confident voice continued to be called upon through the 1970s and into the '80s and '90s as anti-Semitism continued to surface. Sometimes it took the form of terrorist attacks, like a car bomb in 1974 that exploded in front of the United Jewish Philanthropic Fund's Paris office, and failed strikes the next few years against the chief rabbi of Paris, the Marseille synagogue, and the Jewish Union for the Resistance and Mutual Aid. Over time the bombers improved their accuracy: in 1979 they injured thirty-two at a Jewish child-care center, during the High Holidays in 1980 they killed four and injured ten outside the Reform synagogue on the Rue Copernic, and in 1982 they tossed a hand grenade into Jo Goldenberg's restaurant in Paris's Jewish Quarter, then sprayed diners and passersby with submachine gun fire, killing six and wounding twenty-two. There also were desecrations, such as in 1990 when thirty-four graves were vandalized in a cemetery in the southern city of Carpentras and the body of an old man was dug up, impaled with a parasol, and left with a Star of David on his stomach. Even more worrisome was the rise during the 1970s of the Holocaust-denial movement and the increasing popularity of the far-right National Front movement led by Jean Marie Le Pen, which by the mid-1990s was drawing 15 percent of the vote nationally. Then there were the restrictions on immigration, imposed in the mid-'70s, that twenty years later would keep out ex–Soviet Jews even as they were pouring into Germany. Other restrictions, never codified but apparent to all who tested them, made clear that while Jews could work in most areas of government, ongoing tensions over Israel would make it difficult for them to be accepted in the military, the secret service, or the Ministry of Foreign Affairs.

Even when the government tried to be sensitive it often misread Jewish sensibilities and dug itself into a deeper hole with the community. That is what happened after the 1980 synagogue bombing when Prime Minister Raymond Barre went on television to condemn the bombers, whom he said intended to hit Jewish worshipers but instead "made victims of innocent Frenchmen walking along the Rue Copernic." The wording was almost identical to what an Argentine leader would say fourteen years later in distinguishing Jewish victims from non-Jewish ones in the bombing of the AMIA communal building, and the implication was equally offensive: the non-Jews were "innocents," but Jewish victims somehow deserved their fate.

But as happened centuries before, each Mr. Hyde–like act of contempt against the Jews was followed by gracious gestures worthy of the good Dr. Jekyll. And rather than retrenching as they might have in earlier days, French Jews drew strength from the slights and solidified their position as the most secure and successful Jewish community in Europe.

Numbers, as always, tell part of the story. There are the numbers of

Jews that demographers say were living in France at the end of the twentieth century: 521,000, which was almost twice as many as in the United Kingdom, and three times more than in Germany, Italy, Belgium, Denmark, and Spain combined. Looked at another way, one in every hundred Frenchmen is a Jew, and France's Jewish community is the world's third largest, behind the United States and Israel and ahead of Canada and Russia. Paris alone has 310,000 Jews, ranking it seventh among cities worldwide and, outside of Israel, trailing only New York, Los Angeles, and Miami–Fort Lauderdale. And if you believe France's communal leaders, Paris's Jewish population actually is on par with Jerusalem's while France's has reached 700,000 (that still would be less than a quarter the size of its Muslim community). Another number French Jews are proud of is 25,000, which is how many children attend the 110 full-time Jewish schools nationwide. That is nearly 25 percent of school-age Jews, and another 50 percent attend Hebrew or bar mitzvah courses, youth movements, or other programs where they receive a Jewish education.

French Jews also have achieved prominence and prosperity. They have held the most senior posts in government—from minister of finance to minister of culture and even prime minister, with Léon Blum being elevated to the office by the Socialists in 1936 and Pierre Mendès-France of the Radical Party starting his service in 1954. Simone Veil, a Jewish Holocaust survivor, was minister of health and president of the European Parliament, and is said to be the most popular woman in France. There are Jewish movie stars, soccer players, and Nobel laureates, game show hosts, talk show hosts, and TV news hosts, most of whom proudly proclaim their Judaism. There are festivals of Jewish film, klezmer music is a part of popular culture, three radio stations offer Jewish programming, tales of the *Shoah* are regularly featured on television, and vacationers can find "Jewish vacation packages" complete with kosher meals. As for Israel, almost as many French Jews make aliyah each year as Americans, and France has become the top destination for Israeli travelers.

"French Jewry has a connection to Israel like no other diaspora country is connected to Israel," says Jean-Jacques Wahl, director general of the Paris-based Alliance Israelite Universelle, the world's biggest organization devoted to Jewish education. "It's partly that it's very near, just three to four hours flying, the same as England. But here in France you probably will not find any Jewish family involved in Jewish life that doesn't have a brother, sister, aunt, or uncle living in Israel. It's because of our Sephardic Jews. Most families split when they came and today there are more and more mixed Sephardic-Ashkenazic marriages, so every family today has some relatives in Israel."

Synagogue life never has been central to French Jews, but more of them are attending services today than ever at the city's mainly Orthodox houses of worship. That trend is especially visible among the Lubavitch movement, which has forty full-time representatives in and around Paris. They have opened ten Chabad centers, enrolled 1,300 children at their schools and 1,500 at their day camps, and drawn 20,000 Jews to their annual Hanukkah candle lighting. Untold others participate in their Torah studies in the Alps, log on to their Web site at www.lubavitch.fr, call their Torah phone to hear a Jewish story or Jewish song, or contribute to the luxury *mikvah* they are building in a high-rent neighborhood of Paris. "France as a country is the most advanced in a lot of details and concerning a lot of developments in Judaism," beams Rabbi Mendel Azimov, who along with his father launched the Lubavitch program in Paris. "It is the most advanced in Europe."

At the other end of the spectrum are the Reform, who have just two big synagogues but fill them with hundreds of worshipers every Friday night. There is only one Conservative temple, a new one, but as in much of the diaspora the Reform synagogues along with scores of "Orthodox" ones hold services that look like what Americans think of as Conservative. And in a country where there is a group representing every interest, not to mention a Jewish community awash in more than a hundred organizations, France even has L'Association de Juifs Laics, or the Association of Nonreligious Jews.

While French Jews are proud of their achievements, one stands out as an inspiration for the diaspora and the Jewish state. More than any diaspora land, France reflects all the cleavages of Israeli society—Sephardim versus Ashkenazim, overbearing Orthodox versus stubbornly secular, more poor Jews than anyone likes to admit along with plenty of rich ones, political parties urging toughness vis-à-vis the Palestinians arguing with those urging compromise. But whereas in Israel those divisions often prove paralyzing, French Jews have found ways to work through them. There are enough Orthodox safeguarding religious traditions that secular Jews in France feel freed of any guilt that they are jeopardizing the continuity of those traditions. Some Ashkenazim with deep roots in France undoubtedly still resent the more recently arrived Sephardim, but it is tougher to sustain those resentments when a generation of social and political mixing makes it difficult to distinguish a Spanish Jew from a German one. And the fact that Jews in France do not have to worry about making a government function, or making peace with their blood enemies, relieves them of the stresses that cause divisions in Israel to fester.

"France is the reverse of Israel where you have embittered Sephardim pointing their fingers at the Ashkenazic elite, which is not relenting," explains Alexandre Adler, a Paris-based historian, TV commentator, and foreign-policy columnist for *Le Monde*. "In France things run quite smoothly because we all feel that as Jews, we are confronting the rest of society."

Historian Diana Pinto is even more taken by French Jews' achievements. The fact that they are "voluntary Jews," vigorously affirming their group identity as Jews in societies that are bullishly individualistic and indifferent to religion, offers what Pinto says is a model for Jewish continuity in an era when the Holocaust and anti-Semitism are fading as reasons to stay Jewish. Even better is French Jewry's "pluralism," the way it lets people choose whether to define their Jewishness in terms of religion, politics, culture, ethnicity, intellectualism, or some mix of those. Then there is the way that France accepts the notion that its Jews can be loyal French citizens at the same time that they are deeply committed to Israel, which Pinto says is an object lesson for the treatment of Albanians in Serbia, Turks in Germany, and the multiple layers of ethnic and religious minorities in the former Soviet Union.

Not everything in the world of French Jews runs smoothly, to be sure, especially when it comes to the centralized institutions that oversee religious life. Joseph Sitruk, the country's chief rabbi, has become a lightning rod for critics who resent his iron hand on everything from religious conversions to the brand of toothpaste they use, blame him for doing away with organs and mixed-sex choruses, and say he has rebuffed women and the Reform. Sitruk's defenders call the Tunisian-born rabbi the "locomotive of the Jewish community in France," crediting him with increasing tenfold the number of Jews studying Jewish texts, bringing others back to Shabbat, and reaching out to the masses with videotapes on topics ranging from Israel and God to violence and peace.

But that debate seems abstract and irrelevant to the average French Jew, and even to the future of the community. A far more critical and imposing challenge is how to reach the 50 percent or so of French Jews who do not attend synagogue, keep kosher, observe the Sabbath, send their children to Jewish day schools, or adhere to other traditional ways of defining Judaism. They help explain an intermarriage rate that now tops 40 percent, and lead some to worry whether France's enviably successful Jewish community can sustain itself.

"Religion is much less in the mainstream of life today. It's losing clout," worries Michael Ohana, Sydney and Nicole's twenty-three-year-old son. "I know my work will take me a lot of time, and I won't be able to spend more time on my Judaism if I want a life with my friends and family. Judaism's part is going to decline." Yet if his words suggest despair, Michael's actions offer hope. After graduating from business school he took a high-powered job in London with the international consulting firm McKenzie & Co., but that quickly proved unsatisfying. So he returned to Paris and assumed the leadership of a student-based organization called Souviens-toi de ton Futur, or Remember Tomorrow. The group is aimed at ensuring that the generation coming of age in the twenty-first century learns the lessons, good and bad, from the hundred years just passed. To get that message across, Michael organized a trip in March of 2000 for 170 French students, mostly non-Jews, to the Auschwitz and Birkenau concentration camps in Poland, where they lit 2,000 candles of remembrance along the railway tracks near the crematoria.

Michael also brought along two special visitors: his mother and grandmother. Standing together, the three generations sent a powerful signal not only of honoring the dead and remembering France's role in the Holocaust, but of Jewish continuity. Young French Jews like Michael Ohana may not keep kosher, but they feel a pull to the *Shoah* and want to have their grandparents buried in Jewish cemeteries. Some have given up on synagogue, at least for now, but others are going back and dragging along their parents and grandparents, the same way young Jews are in Buenos Aires and Boston, Düsseldorf and Dnepropetrovsk. Assimilation still is a worry in France, as in every Jewish community, but it is less so than it was 200 years ago, when Napoleon made his Faustian bargain to grant French Jews their freedom in return for their blending in. Anti-Semitism is a concern, too, but it pales next to the threat of half a century ago, when Stella Szternblytz, a.k.a. Helene Galand, worried that dreaming out loud in Yiddish would sentence her to death.

"Seeing my mother between Michael and me there at the camps, it was a very nice picture," says Nicole. "It was really the first time my mother gave all the details of what the Nazis did to her. She began to tell how when they went to the toilet, they had to get permission from the capo. She was so amazing that the journalists who were with us put a special microphone on her jacket, they followed her with microphones the whole day. This was an important way of showing the students how in the diaspora, Jewish people want to maintain the history of their people.

"I don't want to be a Jewish mother, but I am very proud of what Michael is doing with this. Judaism is all these values, it's all this history. These are the most important things. The religion is one thing, but the values that come through the minds of the people, that is something much more important to me. Being a Jew is about culture, about history, about a way of feeling. Being a Jew is having doubts, it's having questions."

Chapter 7

ATLANTA:

Hebrew with a Southern Accent

At the beginning the Atlanta Jewish community was an amorphous collection of pilgrims and prophets. There were clusters of refugees from Hamburg and Budapest, Constantinople and Kiev. A few hundred pioneers fled poverty and persecution in the Old Country, arrived in the New, and somehow wandered south in search of a more forgiving climate and more fertile economic opportunities. As the hundreds became thousands they gave birth to businesses and planted synagogues, kept alive rituals and put a singular southern stamp on their age-old faith. All without anyone noticing. Most northern Jews refused to even step below the Mason-Dixon line, certain nothing there was worth seeing.

But in the waning years of the twentieth century Atlanta's Jews came into their own in a way that finally would make their contemptuous cousins up north take notice. It started in 1996 and it centered on money. The Jewish community, numbered at 75,000, decided to raise $25 million. It was the first time community leaders had tried that sort of solicitation for bricks-and-mortar projects, which are not easy to sell to donors worn down and tapped out from the annual fund-raising drive. For it to work, professional consultants told them they would have to collect from not only fellow Jews, but from Presbyterian bankers and

Methodist businessmen who would blanch at the thought of Jews supping at their social clubs or squiring their daughters to debutante balls.

So what did Atlanta's Jewish kingpins do? They made it even harder by nearly doubling their goal to $45 million. That, after all, was closer to what was needed to refurbish the old-age home, build a new community center, and reconstruct other critical Jewish institutions. And the volunteer fund-raisers vowed not to accept a dime unless the donor agreed that giving to the building fund would not mean giving less to the annual campaign.

It took just two calls to know it would work. The cofounders of the Home Depot hardware chain committed $15 million outright, along with a $5 million challenge grant. The campaign chairman and his sister, three honorary chairs, and five other wealthy Jews each kicked in $1 million. The best part was the $4.7 million contributed by Coca-Cola, the banks, and other bastions of the Protestant power structure. The fund-raising was so successful that, barely eighteen months after it began, it ended with $50.3 million—twice what the consultants had predicted and $5 million more than the quixotic goal set by its bullish leaders.

Money too often is used as a measure of a Jewish community's strength but it does matter, more so in Atlanta than anywhere. What the community raised will let it reach out to new arrivals, who have more than tripled the city's Jewish population over the last thirty years. The ease with which it was raised has given Atlanta Jews a new confidence, one that is seeing synagogues and other institutions chart ambitious and expensive new visions of their own. As word spreads of its fund-raising prowess, other Jewish communities are looking to Atlanta for hope that, in an era awash in stories of vanishing Jews, growth is possible and productive. And the rest of American Jewry finally is acknowledging that the South, where few knew there were viable Jewish communities and most never would want to be, has the second-biggest concentration of Jews in the country and is growing faster than any other region.

"That campaign was a coming-of-age," says S. Stephen Selig III, a real-estate baron who was president of the Atlanta Jewish Federation back then. "We kept saying we were one of the great Jewish communities in America. We said that all the time about ourselves, but if we couldn't pull off this campaign we couldn't be a great community. We had to walk the walk, as it were, instead of just talking the talk. I was interviewing somebody yesterday about a position here in the Jewish community and he asked me what, other than money, bricks, and mortar, we got out of the capital campaign. I said that it basically had solidified our community."

But just as shrinking populations have carried a cost for old Rust Belt communities of Jews, Selig and others worry that growing is exacting a toll from Sun Belt cities like Atlanta. The main risk is that with all the new arrivals the Jewish community will forget its heritage of *mentshlicheyt*—the sort of small-town warmth and gentleness seldom seen in the East—and that today's Jews of Atlanta will not appreciate the way their forebears forged alliances with oppressed blacks and fashioned a role for Jews in a land famous for its God-fearing Christians.

"There was a southernness here which I'm not sure is here anymore," says Margaret Strauss Weiller, a fourth-generation Atlanta Jew whose grandchildren also live there. "That's a kindness, a neighborliness, a concern for other people. I think that's very southern. Whether it's southern-Jewish or just southern I'm not sure. I'm also not sure we can keep it as the community grows. Our southern heritage is being diluted.

"Ten years ago I knew half the people in every row of my synagogue, but at the High Holidays this year I don't think in every row that there was a person I knew. That's scary."

*   *   *

Atlanta Jews know they are a curiosity to the rest of American Jewry. They know that Jews from New York, Chicago, and Los Angeles think it is not quite the same being Jewish in Birmingham, Charlotte, or Atlanta. How could it be with the South's record of racial rancor? With its images of intolerance and insecurity? Even today, doubts resurface about how much the region really has changed every time the national news features such old southern war-horses as Senator Jesse Helms and Christian Coalition founder Pat Robertson. Then there is the way that Jews, like everyone else in Dixie, speak with a drawl that makes it difficult to distinguish "wheel" from "will," and use alien expressions like "I'll carry you to there" when they mean to offer you a ride.

Atlanta Jews agree that they are not the same—they say they are better. That attitude is apparent everywhere you go in the city, and generally is not born of hubris. It is partly the pride of old-timers like Weiller. It is that people are tired of having to explain and defend themselves to every supercilious aunt from New Jersey and insolent new arrival from New Rochelle. It is also the heartfelt belief that their community really has come of age as reflected not just in its fund-raising prowess and soaring population, but in the lunchtime Talmud study groups sprouting across the city, the new Jewish academies, and the growing number of national Jewish leaders coming out of Atlanta and the region.

Their modest and scattered numbers—their physical and psychological isolation from the hubs of Jewish life in America—almost ensured that Jews across the Deep South would be different. Visit a standard southern city like Anniston, Alabama, and tell anyone you are Jewish and they would automatically steer you to Hyman Gordon the jeweler and to Gershon Weinberg, owner of the barbecue joint on South Quintard. That was because there were only about a hundred Jews in the community of 25,000, and those were the two whose high-profile jobs ensured that everyone knew them. The Jewish community in Atlanta is substantially bigger, but even at nearly 100,000 it accounts for less than 4 percent of the population in the metropolitan area and just over 1 percent in the state, which means that even there, being Jewish is an anomaly.

It is more than their small numbers that makes Jews stand out in the buckle of the Bible Belt. Southern Baptists, United Methodists, Presbyterians, National Baptists, and other churches in the South approach their religion earnestly. The faithful attend services on Sundays, go back Wednesday evenings, and may stop by again on a Tuesday or Thursday, Monday or Saturday. They attend prayer groups and teen groups, singles groups and senior groups, all easily accommodated in gymnasium-like sanctuaries. Kids sign up for a week of Vacation Bible School in the summer, kneel to worship before the kickoff at football games, and, in some public schools far from the meddling eyes of the Supreme Court, use the loudspeaker to lead fellow students in a moment of Christian prayer. Their parents recite prayers before county commission and city council meetings, and in some communities the Ten Commandments are tacked to classroom walls next to the Magna Carta. While the religious landscape is beginning to change in bigger cities across the region, with growing numbers of Muslims and even some Hindus, the first question most southerners still ask when they meet a newcomer is, "Have you found a church home yet?"

For southern Jews, being so far out of that religious mainstream means they have to think harder about who they are and, if they decide the difference is worth preserving, to work harder at it. The same is true of the tiny band of Jews in Dublin, just as it is of Jews in Des Moines, Anchorage, and other outposts in America. But in the southern United States, whose dual lineage as oppressor and oppressed makes it especially wary of outsiders, being different poses a heavier burden.

"I grew up in Chicago, and spent time in Cleveland, and it was relatively easy to be Jewish in those communities," says David Sarnat, who ran Atlanta's Jewish Federation from 1979 to 2000. "In Chicago one high school was 99 percent Jewish, a public high school. We didn't have to go to Jewish day schools, we'd just walk down the street and there were fifteen synagogues. Just by osmosis we had some sense of what our Jewishness was all about. In Atlanta, being Jewish was a conscious act, it wasn't an osmotic happening. Part of it was the hostile environment. You were different. Growing up in Chicago you were just one of another ethnic group; everybody had some sort of hyphen in his name. Down here in Atlanta, you either were American or Jewish."

Proving that they are good Americans as well as good Jews can be stressful and at times means having to downplay their differences. That helps explain why there are fewer protests in Atlanta than there might be in Boston when colleagues put up Christmas decorations in the office, and less insistence on equal time for menorahs. For Elliott Levitas, who represented Atlanta for five terms in Congress and five in the Georgia House, it meant getting used to "playing the angels or Joseph in our school Christmas pageants. I was an angel and I think I was a monk. Most Jewish kids of my generation would sing Christmas carols until we got to the word Christ, then we'd mouth it or be silent. What we ended up with is a Protestantization of Judaism, taking on attitudes that make us more like the majority community, the way Jews have throughout the ages. But I personally think it also makes us more aware of our Jewish identities."

Aware, certainly, and proud—but also steeled for the periodic affront that stems as much from ignorance as an intent to offend. That is how David Alexander interprets his Methodist father-in-law's unease with him. "I have dark skin, dark eyes, dark hair. My wife, Deanna, was his favorite daughter and I was not what he wanted for her. He wanted a hunter-farmer," says the thirty-eight-year-old psychotherapist. His father-in-law's reaction helped prepare David for the reaction of his wife's young cousins in central Florida when they first met him: "They lined up to touch my head to feel the horns. They'd been brought up to believe it, the little kids honestly believed that Jews have horns."

The Atlanta establishment is more subtle. Jews have had a difficult time breaking in to banking, utilities, and other highly prized and paid fields, but those employers never advertised their reticence. It was the same with high-society cotillions: Jews did not have to be told they were not welcome. As for the restrictive covenants that kept them out of some high-priced neighborhoods, the law required that they be set down in black-and-white. "When I went on the bench in 1979 a judge currently on the bench who was a good friend said, 'Marvin, you're going to get invitations now to join the Capital City Club, the Piedmont Driving Club, and the Athletic Club,' which were prominent social clubs," recalls U.S. District Judge Marvin Shoob, the first Jew to sit on the federal bench in Atlanta. "I said, 'Great,' because there weren't any Jews in any of them. I discussed it with my wife and we decided I would accept the offers because they would open some doors. But the invitations never came. When I started serving as judge, they didn't extend those invitations."

Most barriers have come down over the last generation, but others barely budged. Piedmont has a handful of Jewish members, but most slid in through a non-Jewish spouse or other special circumstances. Jews sit on the boards of banks, but everyone can recite the list because there are so few. Jewish girls are accepted as debutantes but it is still not easy, and rabbis are among scores of Jewish members of civic societies like Rotary but they continue to draw stares and whispers. Interviews with second graders at a Jewish day school make clear that young Atlanta Jews do feel fully accepted by the wider society, but most also have tales of being teased for "having a Jewish nose" or "having someone say mean things about our religion." Jewish business titan Erwin Zaban tries to put those vestiges of anti-Semitism in context, saying, "The Atlanta Jewish community is accepted by the non-Jewish community in a way that they were not accepted in my father's generation." Yet Zaban, who was born in 1921 in Atlanta and has long been one of its most philanthropic Jews, adds that "outwardly I am accepted but I don't know whether inwardly I am. . . . I can't tell you there is no prejudice here. I am sure there must be."

For every sign of prejudice, however, there are many more of acceptance and even embrace. Many white Christians of the Old Confederacy are brought up to revere Jews as the chosen people of the Old Testament. Nowhere have Americans been more supportive of the Jewish state than in the South, where Israel is seen as an object lesson not just for fulfilling biblical prophecies but also for its military might and daring. Jews have been elected and appointed to a range of senior offices, from vice mayor and mayor of Atlanta to U.S. attorney, city councilor, state legislator, and congressman. "To the extent that I was an identifiable Jew, a member of the synagogue, and practiced my religion, it was a plus," says Levitas, who eventually was defeated by Patrick Lynn Swindall, an antiabortion, anticommunist Republican, in a campaign where Swindall touted his Christianity in a way that many Jews felt was anti-Semitic. "That's not to say that there weren't people in the legislature and the community who didn't like Jews and made no bones about it, but I never felt it was a negative factor overall.

"There is a group of very conservative Christians, the Jerry Falwells of the world, whose support for Israel is part of their messianic message that there have to be Jews around for Christ to come again. I don't consider that to be a positive reason. In fact I had a correspondence and several conversations with Menachem Begin when he was prime minister about his verbal support for the Moral Majority, for the Falwell types. He said, 'We have so few friends we have to take them where we find them.' "

If Atlanta Jews have been shaped in part by being minnows swimming in a sea of Christianity, they also have been swept up by the wider political, cultural, and economic waves crashing through their region. The most obvious is metropolitan Atlanta's phenomenal growth—from 2.9 million people in 1989 to nearly 3.9 million just ten years later. It was driven by a high-tech explosion that crowned Atlanta the "Silicon Valley of the East," a thriving economy that saw the city pace the nation in job growth, and an ability to attract world-class events like the 1996 Olympics. During the first half of the twentieth century, Atlanta recast itself from a sleepy symbol of the Old Confederacy to the hub of the New South; the transformation was completed during the second half as Atlanta made a convincing case that it was, as its boosters liked to say, "the world's next international city." But the new wealth and status has brought unwelcome side effects. The city has nearly as many cars now as people, and with its far-flung suburbs and drive-through dry cleaners Atlanta is every bit as bound to the automobile as smog-laden Los Angeles. Office towers are scattered across the urban landscape without proportion or planning. Housing prices are soaring. Worst of all, there is an erosion of the intimacy that made Atlanta a different kind of big city.

The Jewish community has shared in the ups and downs of Atlanta's boom, as was made clear in population surveys done for the Jewish federation in the late 1990s.

The good news is that Atlanta is one of the fastest-growing Jewish communities in America—and among big cities that are not merely meccas for retirees, it may be number one. In 1947 Greater Atlanta had just 10,000 Jews. By 1971 it had nearly tripled to 27,500, by 1998 it more than tripled again to 85,900, and at the turn of the century Jewish leaders were saying it was close to 100,000. Size is not the only thing Atlanta Jewry has going for it: It is among the most affluent Jewish communities in the country, with nearly a quarter of its households earning more than $100,000. It is among the youngest, with 25 percent of members aged nineteen and under and only about 14 percent sixty-five and older, although that elderly group is growing four times as fast. And it is remarkably well educated, with a disproportionate number of singles.

Their growing numbers and influence have given Atlanta Jews a heightened visibility and confidence. David Alexander sees it in his children. His parents' generation and his were circumspect in exhibiting their Jewishness, at least in public. His children are not, which is even more surprising since David's wife never converted and some members of her family regard Jews as oddities. "Every night when we sit down and have a meal we say the blessing over bread," says Alexander. "Now the kids will sing the *Hamotzi* at McDonald's and I'm the only one who is embarrassed by it. They did it at Arby's once, and a Jewish family three tables over was beaming and introduced themselves to us."

They may be less self-conscious, but the federation's exhaustive survey suggests that the Atlanta Jewish community today also is less Jewish, at least in the ways that is typically measured. It has one of the highest intermarriage rates of any sizable Jewish community in America, with 37 percent of Jewish weddings pairing a Jew with a non-Jew, and another 6 percent involving the conversion to Judaism of a partner not born Jewish. Intermarriage is also becoming more common, with a rate of 62 percent for weddings that took place within five years of the survey's completion, compared to only 16 percent for marriages twenty years or more before. Just under half of the children of intermarriages are being raised Jewish, and such couples are less likely to be involved with Jewish organizations or rituals. As for how the Atlanta Jewish community as a whole stacks up against comparable cities, Atlantans are less likely to keep kosher or light candles every Sabbath—and more likely to put up a Christmas tree.

That scarcity of observance can only be partly linked to their being in Atlanta or the South, since so many started out somewhere else. Just 26 percent of the Jews living in Greater Atlanta were born there, with another 22 percent born elsewhere in Georgia or the South. A full 18 percent are natives of New York, and another 12 percent were born in other parts of the Northeast. The trend of outsiders, and especially Yankees, flooding into the city and its suburbs is one that transcends religion and leads some to conclude that today's Atlanta is "a northern city surrounded by Georgia." The outsiders come, but they do not necessarily stay. Atlanta's Jews are among the most mobile in America, with 27 percent having arrived within five years of the survey and just 39 percent living there twenty or more years. That trend is almost certain to continue: 15 percent of respondents said they "definitely" will move in the next three years, 16 percent said "probably," and only 30 percent said "definitely not." In Boston, one Jew meeting another asks, "What do you do?" In Atlanta the first question is, "Where are you from?"

One effect of that coming and going has been to forge a community so diverse and cosmopolitan that, if you could parachute into all the city's churches on a given Sunday, you would hear people worshiping in 120 different languages. Diversity has brought with it a watering down of some of the city's more conservative, less tolerant instincts, as well as an opening up to different ways of living, working, and praying, which is good for an often marginalized, sometimes vulnerable minority group like the Jews.

But all that moving around also means that large numbers of Atlanta Jews do not feel a part of the local Jewish scene. Thirty-seven percent say they belong to a synagogue, which is one of the lowest rates in the nation, and a survey of synagogues found that the actual rate of membership is even lower: 27.5 percent. Membership in the Jewish community center also is low, with just 14 percent saying they belong and the JCC saying just 8 percent are members. Why the gap between reported and actual memberships? Some respondents feel so guilty for not having joined such organizations that they lie about it, surveyors say, and synagogue members are more likely than nonmembers to respond to such a survey. Atlantans also fall short on a series of other measures of participation. They have one of the nation's lowest rates of children enrolled in Jewish day or synagogue schools, although enrollment is growing. Ditto for denominational affiliation: 33 percent of respondents said that, rather than identifying with the Reform, Reconstructionist, Conservative, or Orthodox movement, they are "just Jewish," which is one of the highest levels of that ambivalent response in any large city tested. As for charities, only 36 percent of Jewish households make gifts to the Atlanta Jewish Federation, which is one of the lowest rates anywhere of such giving. It was only with the help of heavy hitters like Bernie Marcus and Arthur Blank of Home Depot that the federation was able to raise more than $50 million in its recent capital campaign.

There are several silver linings in the recent surveys, however. Fifty-seven percent of Atlanta Jews say that being Jewish is "very important" to them, which is considerably higher than the national rate of 44 percent and suggests there is an interest that could be tapped. Another 31 percent say it is "somewhat important," and only 13 percent say it is not important. Atlanta Jews also do better than the national average when it comes to celebrating holidays like Passover and Hanukkah that focus on the home rather than the synagogue, which implies that they care about the holidays but not about the synagogue. Forty-one percent of Jewish families in Atlanta have been to Israel, which is a higher proportion than in Boston, Detroit, Baltimore, Atlantic City, and other older, more stable Jewish communities. And Atlanta Jews are prosperous enough to be very charitable—and are giving at healthy rates to non-Jewish charities—which suggests that if the Atlanta Jewish Federation developed a more convincing pitch it could raise substantially more money.

If it were possible to put a face to all those disturbing trends it would look like Larry Levin. The fifty-two-year-old psychotherapist is a Jew married to a non-Jew and has two children. Like many Atlanta Jews he came from somewhere else (Philadelphia and Miami Beach), does not belong to the Jewish community center or a synagogue ("I never had a major religious experience in a synagogue"), celebrates Christmas along with Hanukkah ("Hanukkah comes in a real poor second"), gives to national Jewish charities (the Holocaust Memorial Museum) but not to the Atlanta Jewish Federation, has been to Israel but worries about its current direction ("the Orthodox Party and strange political system make it hard to want to directly send support"), has a mezuzah on his door but does not light Sabbath candles or fast on Yom Kippur, and had a bar mitzvah ("under protest") but doubts his children will ("my oldest went a couple years to Hebrew school but asked out and doesn't want to be bat mitzvahed, my youngest asks a lot of questions"). Answers like his to questions posed by the Atlanta Jewish Federation keep Jewish leaders up nights fretting and raise doubts about the continuity of this ancient faith. And he may prove the worriers right. But as with most "disconnected" Jews across the diaspora, when Levin has a chance to expand on his one-word answers it becomes clear that Judaism means more to him than it appears.

"Connected is a funny word, connected to what?" he asks. "Connected to the Jewish religion? Or connected to and identifying deeply with being a Jew in a non-Jewish culture, with what it means to be a minority and the burden of history that comes with it? I feel very connected with the latter, my kids do as well, and my wife has a tremendous appreciation of it." He experiences that connection by meeting every week or so with five other intermarried couples to celebrate holidays, Jewish and Christian ones, talk about issues, and enjoy one another's company free from the doubts that often seep in when just-Jewish couples mix with intermarried ones. He also makes his children's education a major (and expensive) priority, which he sees as a "Jewish value." He takes pride in accomplishments of other Jews and feels part of a "special race." And while anti-Semitism is less of a factor for his children than it was for him, he says "a 'never-forget' mentality is deep in me. I educate my kids around that stuff because I don't trust the world, and that's a very Jewish thing. I think any Jew who is not a little bit paranoid is nuts or shortsighted."

Is all that enough to sustain his involvement and his children's, and to sustain Judaism? Probably not. But Jewish leaders in Atlanta say it is a critical beginning. They regard Jews like Levin less as being alienated from Judaism generally and more as having not yet found a way to connect to the Atlanta Jewish community. The word they use is "unaffiliated," and based on survey results they attach it to about half their community's Jews. Finding creative ways to connect them up has become an obsession for everyone from rabbis to federation officials, and many of the answers they are devising could be models for communities from Boston to Buenos Aires.

Consider all that the Orthodox are doing in Atlanta. As in Boston they make up just 3 percent of the community's Jewish population, which is half the national rate and pales next to the 10 percent in New Orleans and 20 percent in Baltimore. But the fact that there are more than 1,300 families in Greater Atlanta who call themselves Orthodox and back it up with practice and piety is a big achievement, especially to Rabbi Emanuel Feldman, who knows how difficult it was to get there.

When he arrived at Atlanta's old Union Station in 1952, the congregation he inherited had just forty families. It was the most reverent of the city's shuls, but reverence had long since gone out of vogue as a generation of immigrants died out or blended in. Members who lit candles on Friday nights were considered ultra-Orthodox and the handful who also kept kosher were, as Feldman puts it, "fanatics." Almost no one donned tefillin or dunked in the *mikvah*, which was in a run-down neighborhood. Assembling a morning minyan might mean waiting more than an hour for the tenth old-timer to show up, and attending Jewish day school meant shipping your son to another city. The "synagogue" was a converted home and the first religious question posed to the rabbi was, "We just had a baby boy. What is the Hebrew name for Nicholas?"

Today Congregation Beth Jacob gets sixty or seventy worshipers at its minyan at 6:15 in the morning, which is ten more than came to its

Rosh Hashanah services when Feldman started. On Shabbat 400 attend services in a large, graceful synagogue that has about 3,000 members, half of whom keep the Sabbath by praying or spending a quiet day with their family. Everyone shows up on the High Holidays, some men in yarmulkes and others in black hats, with their wives and daughters sitting in a section that is separate but on the same floor and surprisingly close. Dozens attend nightly classes in Talmud and Midrash, hundreds of women regularly visit one of the city's well-maintained *mikvah*s, the synagogue sponsors golf tournaments to support its schools and "Taste of the South" Sabbath dinners to support its singles, and enough people keep kosher that the huge Kroger's and Harris Tweeter supermarkets stock items marked *glatt*, the highest level of kosher. Atlanta has an Orthodox day school and high school, and hopes to have a seminary soon. And Feldman's son, who succeeded him as rabbi in 1991, has ten rabbis helping him reach out to less religious Jews, with lunchtime learning programs, services in outlying suburbs, and other efforts to make less observant Jews more so.

"God is giving those of us who have the tools to reach people at a serious level another chance by slowing down this hellish race to oblivion," says the younger Rabbi Feldman, Ilan. "What really turned this place into a machine, and we *are* a machine now, is when we professionalized our outreach. We now have these ten rabbis doing this full-time and they're all Orthodox ordained rabbis. Their big key to success is that they study Torah with people, and through relationships forged over intelligent give-and-take over the Torah those people say, 'I like you, I like your wife, you're cool,' and so forth. I'm confident that people who are accessing what we are offering are in for lifelong changes."

His father is even more bullish. "I think Atlanta is on the cusp of being *the* major Jewish growth city," says the gray-bearded Emanuel Feldman, who now lives in Israel and serves as editor in chief of the quarterly journal *Tradition*. "There's a thirst for Jewish knowledge in Atlanta. It is *the* growth city—I'm talking spiritually, not in a business sense—of the twenty-first century. It has all the building blocks in order to take off. Those building blocks are good schools, good rabbis, good teachers, a high school, a *kollel*. A lot of stuff is happening right now that will act as a springboard for greater things down the line. It will bring more Jews in from out in the cold."

The Orthodox are not the only ones reaching out and pulling in. The Reform have been doing it for decades. At 34 percent they are the largest denomination in Atlanta, and their ten synagogues are double the number for any denomination other than the Orthodox, many of whose ten shuls are tiny. The Reform believe their more open, embracing brand of Judaism is more attractive to the adults in mixed marriages, and their children, many of whom are not Jewish in the eyes of the Orthodox and Conservative. Nowhere better captures that Reform spirit than Atlanta's oldest, wealthiest, most talked-about synagogue, a Romanesque redbrick and white marble structure popularly known as The Temple. More than a hundred years ago it embraced Napoleon's notion that religion was best kept minimalist and private, casting aside such traditions as candle lightings and circumcisions, bar mitzvahs, *kippot,* tallith, Hebrew, and even the singing of *Hatikvah,* the Israeli national anthem. Today some of the customs are back, much the way they are in Reform synagogues nationwide, but a first-time visitor can sense the same spirit of independence and even defiance. The rabbi wears a prayer shawl but not a head covering, while several women chanting from the *bimah* have both. There are readings in Hebrew but there also are transliterations for congregants unable to read the holy script. The Orthodox predict that Reform Jews are too watered-down to survive, but The Temple tenders proof to the contrary: A decade ago it did not even hold services on the second day of Rosh Hashanah. When it started to three years ago it had only enough celebrants to justify opening an auxiliary chapel, yet now it draws a crowd big enough to fill half of the 1,200-seat main sanctuary.

There is more to come. Inspired by the success of the federation's $50 million capital campaign, The Temple is raising money for a $20 million expansion aimed at accommodating the hundreds of recent arrivals who already use its facilities, along with those whom it is determined to bring in. It will open a nursery school, convert the existing social hall into a worship chapel and build a new social hall, and construct a four-story underground parking garage. Even before it has the space to handle them, it is trying to attract newcomers by visiting them at home, inviting them to Shabbat dinner, and taking them to services.

"We are hoping the nursery school will be the entry point. We're saying to the unaffiliated that there is something very important about bringing their children up Jewish and giving them a solid Jewish education," explains Alvin Sugarman, who in his bid to reach out is reaching beyond his quarter century as The Temple's rabbi to skills culled from an earlier life as a traveling salesman. "We want to create a welcome atmosphere. The unaffiliated community is a tremendous untapped market. Maybe I'm a cockeyed optimist, but if we develop meaningful relationships I genuinely believe they will connect."

The fast-growing Reconstructionist congregation is focusing its attention on a group that historically has felt disconnected from its Jewish roots: homosexuals. "Atlanta is in some ways the gay and lesbian haven in the South—I believe we're second per capita in the country, and I will do outreach to the gay and lesbian communities," explains Joshua Lesser, the city's first full-time Reconstructionist rabbi, who was hired in 1999 by Bet Haverim, the first Reconstructionist congregation. As part of that outreach, Sabbath services include a "Prayer for the End of Hiding" where worshipers "ask that our hiding draw to an end, that we no longer feel we have to pretend, to promise falsely, to renounce ourselves, and that our fullest creative expression as Jews and as gay people be among the blessings you bestow upon us." The fact that they represent only 1 percent of Atlanta's Jews inspires rather than discourages the Reconstructionists, just as trying to bring in homosexuals has not kept them from welcoming heterosexuals.

In the middle sit the Conservatives. They make up 29 percent of the community, have more liberal conversion and divorce policies than the Orthodox and more ritual than the Reform, and, like the other movements, recognize that their biggest challenge is finding and appealing to the unaffiliated. "Atlanta can best be compared to an adolescent boy who had a growth spurt and whose body has to catch up to the length of his arms," says Rabbi Arnold Goodman of Congregation Ahavath Achim, or AA, the Old South's biggest Conservative synagogue. To accommodate its 4,800 High Holiday worshipers, AA seats some in areas where they cannot see the pulpit and have to follow the service on a TV screen. The synagogue is so big, and so crowded, that during one recent Rosh Hashanah few were aware that a worshiper had suffered a heart attack during services, although five doctors sitting nearby responded in an instant.

"What makes Atlanta unique is that it's a growing community with more and more financial resources," adds Goodman, a born-and-bred New Yorker who delivers his sermons parading back and forth on the pulpit like a Southern Baptist preacher. He uses a microphone to project and regularly checks his watch to ensure the sermon and service end on time, not needing notes as he urges his flock to educate themselves as well as their children in the ways of Judaism. "There is a sense today that this Jewish community is perfectly comfortable being up front on all the issues that concern us," he says. "We don't duck."

Goodman is right. Atlanta has been unusually forthright in confronting the challenge of shaping its army of new Jews into involved, informed Jews, which is in part an outgrowth of its long history of adjusting to new circumstances. Sixty-five years after it was founded, AA shifted its allegiance from the Orthodox movement to the Conservative. Around the same time members of The Temple, who also had started as Orthodox, were experiencing an even more profound transformation from assimilationism to openly asserting their ethnic and cultural uniqueness. In the 1990s that process of accommodating to change meant forming alliances unimaginable in most of the diaspora.

Start with the way the different denominations work together. In most Jewish communities, Reform rabbis have a difficult enough time talking to Conservative ones, and the Orthodox only talk to other Orthodox. That used to be the case in Atlanta, and in the early 1990s a bid to start a synagogue council of lay leaders and rabbis was stymied by a dispute over whether to admit the Reconstructionist congregation, which openly appealed to gays and lesbians. But the rabbis continued meeting regularly on their own, and there never was the kind of backbiting and infighting that there is in most places, in part because Jews were such a small minority in Atlanta that they needed to stick together. In 1997, as the rancorous debate in Israel over who is a Jew was splitting the religious movements in America, the Atlanta chapter of the American Jewish Committee invited eight leading Reform, Conservative, and Orthodox rabbis to get together for three hours a month, behind closed doors, to quietly talk through any conflicts. The dialogue helped them plot common strategies for getting the unaffiliated to affiliate, and it forged bonds that led the rabbis to travel together to Israel in the summer of 2000.

"It wouldn't happen in any other community with the Orthodox joining a group like this, and if they did no one else would come," says Sherry Frank, head of the American Jewish Committee chapter and a central figure behind this and other outreach efforts. "There still are intractable differences that no one is going to bridge, particularly patrilineal descent. There is no way of getting around issues like 'who is Jew?' In this community we've put that down and said we'll reach out and educate on other issues. It was partly out of desperation; there is such an enormous number of unaffiliated." Sugarman, rabbi at The Temple, agrees that sharing a goal makes it easier to cooperate: "We want the same thing, survival of the Jewish people, even though we are taking different highways to achieve that."

The rabbis are not the only ones worried about Jewish survival. A youth leadership group called Access has 1,200 members in their twenties and draws hundreds more to series like one it ran on Jewish entrepreneurship. A two-year adult education program developed by the Hebrew University of Jerusalem has a long waiting list to get in. Jewish groups sponsor Asian-Jewish Seders, black-Jewish comedy nights, and initiatives to make the 3,000 refugees from the former Soviet Union feel at home as Jews in Atlanta. The federation has tried to pull together all the initiatives and plan new ones for seniors and singles, teens and the Torah-true. And new synagogues are going up in outlying areas from Sandy Springs to Snellville, Roswell to Alpharetta, which is where many new Jews are settling.

Robert Franco attends a weekly lunch-and-learn session with an Orthodox rabbi who "makes Judaism come alive like nobody else I ever heard. He puts in practical terms what the Torah means to your everyday life. As I look back I see that I'm the kid who in college sat out on the quad and listened to the Hari Krishna. Obviously there was a need for something spiritual, and I didn't get it from Hari Krishna or from the synagogue. These lunches have made the synagogue relevant to me."

Most exciting of all is the way new Jewish elementary and high schools are opening and expanding. That is partly because of the bad reputation of public schools, especially within the city limits, and because the main private alternative had been Christian academies or Episcopalian prep schools. But it also is because these days, many newly arrived

Jewish families feel that schools are a way to feel a bit less foreign in their new southern surroundings, while many older arrivals believe education is the way to assert their Jewishness in an overwhelmingly Christian context. And parochial schools do not have the stigma in the South that they do in other regions, probably because there are so many Christian ones and because religion generally is regarded more positively. Whatever the reason, students at places like the Epstein School are learning young all the good things it can mean to be Jewish.

"Judaism has a lot of laws of common sense, like 'don't kill people,' 'don't steal,' 'don't have any affairs,' " explains Shira Grossman, an eighth grader at Epstein, which is part of the Solomon Schechter network. There are lots of different ways to be Jewish, adds classmate Daryn DeVille, "it just depends how you choose to show your love for God." Belinda Sandalon explains that her mom asks her every day what she learned in school, so "I usually give her mini-Bible lessons. She grew up very reformed."

That is the pattern one sees today across the Jewish diaspora—children caring more and learning more about their Jewishness than their parents and grandparents—but it is particularly pronounced among children at full-time schools in Atlanta, which are particularly focused and creative. Eighty percent of Epstein's 670 students are from families that are Conservative, which is not surprising since the school was housed at Congregation Ahavath Achim before it moved to its sprawling campus in suburban Sandy Springs. In preschool and kindergarten they start to learn reading and math along with Hebrew and Jewish traditions. In grades 1 through 5 they spend half a day on things like science and social studies and the other half learning about Jewish history and holidays, along with concepts like *tzedekah*, or justice, and *tikkun olam*, which means "repairing the world." In middle school they mix music and computers with studying Rabbinic texts and doing mitzvot in the form of community service.

"We want to create the next generation of Jews by having them knowledgeable and connected. We want to work with the head and heart. We want them to be part of the culture and to make choices about their practice of Judaism that are based on information, not superstition or ignorance," explains Cheryl Finkel, who has run the school since shortly after it opened. "I was raised at a time when my *bubbeh* wanted us to be proud we were Jews, but she didn't know why. I learned about Plato, but not about Rabbi Akiva. Our generation and our parents' had the height of secular education but were illiterate in terms of Judaism, and there's no reason for that.

"We're laying things down for the long haul here, not just to make them look cute at their bar mitzvah. Our mission also is making sure the family catches fire along with the kids. They don't subcontract with us to teach their kids Judaism, this is a partnership. And it doesn't stop when they graduate in the eighth grade. That would be like stopping math just when they're really beginning the complicated part. We want them to get to the calculus, the trigonometry, and beyond."

Non-Orthodox day schools in places like Atlanta and Boston are new enough that it will take another generation and a lot more studies to know for sure whether they are promoting Jewish continuity the way Finkel hopes. But the early evidence is encouraging. Nationwide, studies suggest that young people who get an intensive Jewish education are more disposed to donate to Jewish charities, affiliate with Jewish institutions, and marry within the faith, although it remains to be seen whether they follow through on their good intentions. In Atlanta, meanwhile, each year more young people are enrolled in Orthodox and non-Orthodox Jewish day schools, to the point where there are now 2,000 students citywide from kindergarten through twelfth grade. Each year more kids from Epstein and other day schools are leading their family Seders and otherwise putting into practice their new Jewish literacy. Epstein takes all its eighth graders to Israel for two and a half weeks at the end of the year, and a surprising number end up going back to visit or study. And there are other gains that old-timers like Margaret Strauss Weiller can feel even if she cannot measure them, involving traditions she feared were lost but that are being reclaimed by her grandchildren, who attend Epstein and other Jewish schools. "My great-grandparents were moderately religious, but my family was not. I was confirmed at Sunday school but that was it," she says.

"I made the decision that I wanted my children to be raised Jewishly, and they have made a further decision to educate their children Jewishly in a major way. It makes me feel fabulous to see my grandchildren. It makes me feel so good that my efforts on behalf of my children ended up like this. I do a lot of talking to my grandchildren and I'm so jealous, they are fluent in Hebrew and it's just amazing to me."

The Eplans offer an even better case study of Jewish generational change. They are one of the oldest and most honored Jewish families in Atlanta, dating back six generations and playing founding roles in Jewish institutions ranging from Congregation Ahavath Achim to the young-adult group Access. And because they are neither overly rich nor inordinately famous, their story is especially representative and worth telling.

Leon Eplan is an urban planner and professor who, during the ten years he ran Atlanta's planning department, helped steer the city's Olympic preparations and shape its urban landscape. His wife, Madalyne, has taught school, launched a bed-and-breakfast reservation service, and raised three children. He was born in Atlanta in 1928, she was born six years later in Mobile, and they settled in Atlanta full-time beginning in 1959, lured in part by what they call the city's Jewish magnetism.

Leon and Madalyne knew they were making a controversial choice in 1965 when they decided to enroll their older daughter, Elise, in the kindergarten class at Hebrew Academy, which is highly traditional and was, back then, Atlanta's only full-time Jewish elementary school. They were proud of their Judaism and involved with the Jewish community, but their ties were as much cultural and intellectual as spiritual and ritualistic. They had equally deep bonds with Atlanta's non-Jewish world, which was why they had moved to an older neighborhood close to the city center while their friends stayed in outlying areas where there were more Jews and whites. "It was not in vogue to send your children to Hebrew Academy unless you were particularly religious, it was just not done," explains Madalyne, who had accepted a job teaching kindergarten at Hebrew Academy and wanted Elise close by. "All our friends knew we were committed to public education. These people said, 'You can't send your children there, they'll be unable to function with non-Jews.' We took a lot of grief."

The choice was even more difficult for Leon. "I had gone to public schools," he says, "and I was a public official. I had a very strong relationship to the city and its school system. I was very much involved with all the civil rights stuff, the non-Jewish stuff, and here I was removing my kids and putting them into a Jewish school. Where would they get that exposure? But we had a choice of sending our kids to public schools, which were rapidly deteriorating, private ones, which normally were tied to churches, or the Jewish school."

Those are the same dilemmas many Jewish parents face: how to accommodate their commitment to that most democratic of institutions, the public school, with their commitment to their Jewish roots and values, and how to blend their interest in raising their children in a diverse society with their interest in making them proud of their distinctiveness as Jews. The choice in some ways is easier today, as more non-Orthodox Jewish day schools have opened and the quality of many public school systems has continued to deteriorate, but it has also gotten harder because there are so many more good non-Jewish private schools in Atlanta.

Elise stayed at Hebrew Academy through the seventh grade, which was as far as it went, and her sister, Jana, who was three years younger, graduated three years later. In retrospect their parents know they made the right choice. For Madalyne the recognition came partly through her experience as a teacher: "I suddenly realized the oneness of teaching Jewish children. You're not in a school apart from what the child is outside the school. It's beautiful to behold." Leon agrees: "It was a great decision, partly because they got a very strong Jewish identity and comfort level being Jewish, and partly because it was an excellent education generally."

The kids were not the only ones learning new ways to relate to their Jewishness. After their daughters went off to college Madalyne and Leon decided to renovate their home, and the idea occurred to them of keeping kosher. Their parents had never done it. Neither had they, not even when their children pushed them. "One night it occurred to me that if I ever wanted to, this would be the time to keep kosher," Madalyne recalls. "But my next immediate thought was that I had never wanted to keep kosher. Why would we do that? I finally talked to Leon, who was out in left field on it. He said, 'Well, I think it's all right if you want to do that.' It was a commitment to make our house say something to our grandchildren, and I guess to ourselves. But our friends went berserk, they thought it was going off the deep end."

Elise made clear from a very young age that Judaism—especially the kind practiced in Dixie—was central to how she saw herself. She coordinated B'nai B'rith Girls for a region that extended from Baltimore to Miami, which let her see how similar Jewish life was in southern cities like Charleston and Augusta, and let her know the continuity that came from meeting children whose parents participated in the same organization when Leon led it thirty years earlier. She spent three of her four college years at Brandeis, writing her thesis on early Jewish life in Atlanta and experiencing firsthand how much less intimate the Jewish community was in a big northern city like Boston. After college her jobs shifted from politics to financing, from promoting public housing to codirecting the foundation set up by Arthur Blank, cofounder of Home Depot. But there was a common theme, starting way back, when at age twelve she set up a lemonade stand to raise money for antiwar presidential candidate George McGovern, and it revolved around *tikkun olam*, the Jewish concept that you can and should improve the world. She also kept kosher as soon as she was out on her own, and wherever she found herself she got involved in Jewish communal work. "I felt pretty good about myself as a Jew," Elise, thirty-nine, says looking back. "Education absolutely is the key. I can go to any synagogue and know how to daven. I know the stuff, I'm comfortable with Hebrew and with the prayers."

Today Elise is raising her two children—Hannah, who is five, and Max, two—to make Judaism even more central to their young worlds than it was to hers, and she and her parents are teaching her Boston-born husband about Jewishness southern-style. "It's much more beneficial to me to be in the South, to feel challenged to be a Jew, rather than being a lazy Jew in Boston," says Robert Marcovitch, a Harvard-trained attorney. "I didn't really have to try to be Jewish growing up in Newton, whereas here I got married to a woman who is more formally devout than I am, more literally believing than I am, who wanted a kosher house. I was happy to accommodate her. I feel great about all that my kids are learning, but I feel a little weird that they'll know Hebrew fluently and I'll not have learned a lick. I will try to fill in that learning."

Jana, who describes herself as "the sensory child" in contrast to Elise's intellectual bent, says she grew up "having a voice in me at all times saying, 'Being Jewish is great.' That didn't come from day school.

It was with me as a three-year-old." Now her five-and-a-half-year-old son, Gil, goes to Epstein and her toddler son, Tamir, will in a year or two, even though that means struggling to pay $17,000 or so in tuitions and driving them thirty-five minutes each way. "I'm doing it because I can't teach them to feel this way by myself, I can't teach them to feel the way that I feel about being Jewish. Now Gil is correcting us on our pronunciation of everything, every Hebrew word. I love it. Every time he says a Hebrew word I say that I got my six thousand dollars' worth. He says his prayers over his food, he does it every single day. There's going to be this used-to-it-ness, which is great."

Jana also has been doing her own back-of-the-envelope assessment of how Jewish day school affects Jewish identity, using six friends as a test group. All attended Hebrew Academy, some for as little as a year and others the whole way like her, and Jana has kept tabs on whether and how Judaism has stayed in their lives. The count as of early 2000: All but one is married or involved with a Jew, and that one has been president of her temple, is raising her kids Jewish, gave them her name because it sounds Jewish, and hosts the only Seder on the island where she lives off the coast of Maine. Another of the Gang of Seven, Jana says, "practically takes a second mortgage out to have her kids in Jewish day school," while a third, the only man in the group, "goes to Torah study weekly."

Jana's husband, Craig Frankel, also grew up in Atlanta, although in a Reform congregation that he says made it feel like intermarriage when he joined Jana's Conservative family. Now they build a ceremonial harvest hut in their backyard on Sukkoth, are part of a Shabbat dinner group, memorialize the Holocaust on Yom Hashoah, and keep kosher, all of which he says is "a thousand percent consistent with Reform. You're supposed to choose traditions, find those that enrich your life, adopt them and modify them, and reject those that don't fit your lifestyle. I'm not doing it because it's a commandment. I'm doing it because it helps my family feel Jewish."

Defining the role of Judaism in their lives and their children's, Jana and Craig say, means constant compromises and adjustments. They belong to his parents' Reform temple and her parents' Conservative one, the way lots of Jews who grew up in Atlanta do. They chose a Jewish school for their children, but like her parents and sister they chose to live in a racially and religiously diverse neighborhood and their children participate in sports, arts, and music in that neighborhood rather than at the school or Jewish community center. All this, Craig adds, "is not a perfect compromise but it's our solution now. Three to four years from now, we'll see if it works."

Harlan Eplan took a slightly different path than his older sisters. He went to Hebrew Academy only through second grade, then switched to the nondenominational, highly selective Paideia, a "very kumbaya school" where "they didn't mention the word 'religion.'" He did not return to Atlanta after college, does not keep kosher, speaks Hebrew but not as well as the girls, and does not observe as many Jewish festivals. But he was active in Jewish youth groups growing up, and is still moderately active now that he has graduated from Clark University and Yale Business School and settled in Manhattan. He keeps in touch with enough of his old friends in Atlanta to know that "pretty damn close to a hundred percent of them are more observant and better educated in terms of halakhic and religious issues than their parents. They had better Jewish educations."

Living in the Northeast for a dozen years also has convinced Harlan that southern Jews are right when they say they are different—and better. "It's the quality and the comfort," he says. "That's something none of my friends up north have. None of them from White Plains or Jersey, my best friends from college, none of them feel that kind of strong tie to their community. Perhaps that is because they were in environments where they had Jews around them all the time and didn't need that connection with the community. That inherent commonality is why people go back to Atlanta. It's the quality of Atlanta's Jewish community."

*   *   *

Harlan's great-grandfather was among the early pioneers who helped create that special quality of southern Jewishness and the singular character called the Dixie Jew. Leon Herman was twenty years old in 1881 and seemed on course to take over his father's successful bakery in Odessa, a port on the Black Sea. But the czar conscripted him into the Russian army, which was a dangerous place for Jews in that era of pogroms, and Leon decided his safest course was to escape to the west. So with the Cossacks on his tail he worked his way into France, along with a friend named Eplan. When Eplan died en route of a heart attack, Leon borrowed his passport—which had an entry visa for America—along with his last name. The newly minted Leon Eplan's first stop in the New World was New York, but finding it too big and impersonal he headed to Philadelphia, then Nashville, finally ending up in Atlanta, where he knew a man named May whom he had met on the trip across the Atlantic.

The Atlanta that greeted Leon Eplan in 1882 was one that his grandson and namesake Leon could easily mistake for today's Anniston, Alabama. It had the feel of a western boom town, with a handful of paved streets, a meager manufacturing base, and a modest population of 37,000, just 600 of whom were Jewish. The first Jews to come were Jacob Haas and Henry Levi, who had arrived thirty-six years earlier, just two years after the tiny terminus of the Western and Atlantic Railroad was incorporated as Marthasville and the same year it was renamed Atlanta. Haas and Levi, like most early settlers, were born in Germany, left to escape economic and political turmoil, and, once in America, peddled everything from clothing to canned goods until they built up enough cash and courage to open a store of their own.

The pioneers typically invested more of their energy in business than worship. They started to organize themselves in 1860, but the Civil War intervened and the Hebrew Benevolent Congregation—today known simply as The Temple—was not officially chartered until 1867. It took another eight years to begin building the first permanent synagogue. Those founding fathers did care about their faith, they just had different ways of showing it. They launched a Jewish burial society as early as 1860 and six years later started a social club called the Concordia Association, the forerunner of the prestigious Standard Club. Other communal institutions followed, for debaters, sewers, and even one catering to voracious readers.

Atlanta was progressing, but it seemed backward measured against Jewish life in other southern cities. A ship carrying forty-two Jews had docked in Savannah Harbor in 1733, just five months after Georgia's first colonists arrived. As of 1820 Charleston had 700 Jews, the most of any American city and 150 more than New York. The southern cities of Richmond, Baltimore, and Savannah were also among the six biggest Jewish communities in the country, and the South as a whole had more

Jews than the North. Over the next forty years, however, the flow of Jews to the South slowed relative to the rest of the nation. It was partly the inconvenience of getting there from the northern ports where they disembarked, while its rural character and suspicion of foreigners made it less attractive to many German-speaking refugees. Then there were the tensions over slavery and economics that, in 1861, led Georgia and its neighbors to secede from the Union and launch what southerners call the War between the States.

A few Atlanta Jews left out of opposition to slavery or other concerns about the war, but most stayed and many enlisted, the way they would in later wars. They wanted to prove their allegiance to their community and its cause, and their buildings burned along with everyone else's when Union troops under the command of General William Tecumseh Sherman torched the city.

The flames had long since subsided and the city and region had begun to rise again by the time Leon Eplan got to Atlanta. Over the next thirty years Atlanta's population would quadruple to 155,000 and its Jewish community would grow nearly sevenfold, to 4,000. Most new arrivals were, like Leon, from Eastern Europe. Some were steered there by New Yorkers overwhelmed by all the refugees and eager to farm them out across the expansive country; still more came on their own, pushed south by harsh northern winters to peddle their wares, or attracted, as Leon was, by a friend or relative who had arrived before.

Leon was a squat, powerful man who made a living by buying, on credit, loads of dry goods that he and his horse would cart across the countryside, leaving Atlanta on Monday morning and returning in time for Shabbat on Friday. Each time he saved a few hundred dollars he would send for another family member from Europe—first his wife, Rosa, and their son, Sol, then his brothers and sisters, bringing over more than a dozen in all, including his mother. Eventually Leon had enough cash to open his own business, one that an official family history calls a "wholesale men's clothing store" but was more like a pawnshop. It did well—and almost made him very, very rich. The opportunity arose not through the sale of clothes or lamps, but when a barrel filled with syrup broke in the shop upstairs, dripped through the ceiling, and ruined $500 worth of merchandise. Asa Candler, who owned the shop, apologized profusely, saying he had no money but would give Leon $500 in stock, which was almost half the capitalization of his newly formed Coca-Cola Company. Convinced the firm would flop, Leon said thanks, but no thanks.

As involved as he was in his work, Leon made time for his religion. In 1887 he helped launch and later served as president of Ahavath Achim, which back then was Orthodox. Twenty years later he broke away and helped start a Conservative congregation, Beth Israel, although it faced such pressure from the Orthodox that it had to fold after seven years. Leon resented that heavy-handedness and did not rejoin AA, but he remained active in communal affairs. He was a founder and first president of the Montefiore Relief Association, an aide organization that later became part of the Atlanta Jewish Federation, and it was on his front porch on Central Avenue that he and fifteen friends launched the Jewish Progressive Club, which for a while was the largest of three Jewish social clubs. He also helped inaugurate a new concept in finance called the Morris Bank Plan that let poor immigrants take out loans the primary backing for which was two people attesting to the borrower's "good character." Rosa, meanwhile, organized the Ladies Aid Society, which made sure that poor families had food for Passover, and ran a Wayfarer's Home to house and feed strangers. She got wealthy Jews to contribute carloads of coal that were stored on railroad sidings and dispensed it to the poor when it got cold.

While most of Leon and Rosa's contact with fellow Jews was reaching out and lifting up, there also was some separating and striking back. They were part of an Eastern European Jewish orbit that, as was happening from Buenos Aires to Boston, seemed a world away from the earlier-arrived, less observant, wealthier and stodgier German Jews. If AA was the base for the Eastern Europeans, The Temple was a bastion for the Germans. The former spoke Yiddish, the latter were embarrassed by it, along with the new arrivals' poverty, piety, and prostration before the twin credos of Zionism and socialism. At AA, congregants wore long black beards and fringed prayer shawls, the men prayed in the main hall and the women in the balcony, and everyone read Hebrew and knew how to sway and *shukkle*. The Germans knew about the ancient rites and rituals, but felt they were more suited to the Old World. Under the tutelage of their American-born and -educated rabbi, David Marx, members of The Temple were determined to belong, to blend in, to adjust to life in this land of Baptists, Methodists, and Presbyterians by not seeming "too Jewish." They picked up slow drawls, moved into white-columned mansions, and considered their southernness at least as central to their identities as their Jewishness—and they were not about to let all they had achieved be undone by their unskilled, unwashed coreligionists from the shtetls of Bialystok or Odessa.

So the two layers of immigrants created two layers of Jewish life in Atlanta. They went to their own synagogues and dated their own women. They joined separate fraternities, played basketball on different courts, and rang in the New Year, the Jewish and secular ones, with their own kind, the Germans at the meticulously landscaped Standard Club and the East Europeans at the less lofty but equally elegant Progressive Club. The Germans even invented different names for themselves and their poor cousins: the former were "Hebrews," the latter "Jews." And on one occasion, when the diminutive Rabbi Marx ventured onto East European turf at the Jewish Education Alliance, Leon Eplan "told him to get out. My grandfather was a big, big man," recalls his grandson, also named Leon. "He picked Marx up, took him to the front door, and left him there."

As if the community did not have enough factions, in the early 1900s about 150 Sephardic Jews arrived from Turkey and Greece. They spoke Ladino, had their own particular ways of worshiping, founded separate welfare agencies, burial societies and Sunday schools, and added a third stratum to the increasingly unsteady matrix of Jewish society.

The Leo Frank murder trial was the great leveler. The now-infamous case opened with the discovery of a grisly crime scene at three in the morning on Sunday, April 27, 1913. The night watchman at the National Pencil Factory was on his way to the "colored" toilet in the basement when he found on a slag heap the limp body of a thirteen-year-old employee, Mary Phagan. Her strawberry blond hair was stained a frightful red, the result of a blow that had punctured her scalp, dented the back of her head, and left her braids matted with dried blood. One eye was black and swollen, and her cheeks were slashed. Her dress reeked of urine and was raised high enough around her hips to reveal blood on the backs of her legs. Around her neck was a piece of jute cord tied so tightly it had sliced into her flesh, along with a strip of torn petticoat.

All the facts seemed to point to the twenty-nine-year-old factory superintendent, Leo Max Frank. He was the last person who acknowledged seeing Mary alive. He had given her an envelope with $1.20—her pay for ten hours running a machine that inserted erasers into the tops of pencils—when she stopped by the previous afternoon on her way to the parade honoring Confederate Memorial Day. He had carried Mary's lifeless body to an elevator and deposited it in the cellar, or so said Jim Conley, a black factory sweeper who told police that he had helped dispose of the body and later testified that Frank had a history of molesting young females. Frank, meanwhile, did not have convincing answers for any of the questions posed by police: Where was he when the murder occurred? Why did he choose that particular Saturday night to call to make sure everything was okay at the factory? What did he have in mind when he summoned the watchman early the day of the murder, then asked him to leave for two hours? And why were there traces of what police said were Phagan's blood and hair on the floor of the workroom opposite his office?

There were other facts that made little impression on anyone at the time, although they are the ones that in retrospect seem most telling. Some had to do with Conley. He had a history of petty thievery, disorderly conduct, and drunkenness. He reportedly was drinking whiskey and beer the morning of the murder. And he told several other factory workers that Frank was innocent. Police also overlooked evidence that argued against their fingering of Frank. They lost or ignored bloody prints on the victim's jacket and in the factory cellar that might have identified the murderer. They concluded without proof that the hair in the workroom was Mary's and that the red stain was blood. And they seemed unfazed by the fact that Frank's body was unscratched even though Phagan's fingers were out of joint and there was other evidence that she had tried to fight off her attacker. Most troubling of all was Conley's admission, ignored by both sides at the trial, that on the morning of the murder he had defecated at the bottom of the elevator shaft that he said he and Frank later used to transport Phagan's body to the basement. When police first arrived they climbed down a ladder to the basement and found the excrement undisturbed, but later, when they used the elevator, it smashed the feces. Conley, it was clear, had lied about at least one critical aspect of his comings and goings the morning of the murder.

In the end facts had less bearing on the case's outcome than the tone of the times. Phagan was the daughter of a dispossessed tenant farmer who, like many of his neighbors, had to take a job as a "lint-head" at a cotton mill. Their wives and daughters also typically were forced into the factories, although after Mary's father died her mother married a man who was sufficiently prosperous that Mary could have quit but chose not to. That she enjoyed her work and other particulars of her situation were of little interest, however, to the small-town southerners championing her cause back then. Mary Phagan's brutal murder already had risen to the level of epic, embodying not only the dark forces that had forced them from their farms but the very defilement of southern womanhood. Enraged, yet unsure who to blame, they could not have invented a more tempting target than Leo Frank. He was a college-educated Yankee from New York, a prosperous Jew whose thick glasses, full lips and eyebrows, and bowler hats cast him as a caricature of the outsider. He also was shy and suspiciously nervous. In case the public missed the point, the press offered daily reminders, branding him "the monster" and a "jewpervert" and inventing tales of a second wife back in Brooklyn whom he had murdered. Every day for a month jurors entering and exiting the courthouse had to wade through crowds screaming "The Jew is the synagogue of Satan" and "Crack that Jew's neck," while defense lawyers and the judge were warned they would not leave the courtroom alive if the "damned Jew" was acquitted.

The most astute analyst of the fervor that Frank set off was Mary Phagan's own pastor, the Reverend Luther Otterbein Bricker. "My feelings upon the arrest of the old negro nightwatchman, were to the effect that this one old negro would be poor atonement for the life of this innocent girl," Bricker, who ultimately became convinced of Frank's innocence, wrote a friend thirty years later in a letter that he allowed to be published. "But, when on the next day, the police arrested a Jew, and a Yankee Jew at that, all of the inborn prejudice against Jews rose up in a feeling of satisfaction, that here would be a victim worthy to pay for the crime."

Jurors took less than four hours to convict, and the following day a judge sentenced Leo Frank to hang. His lawyers appealed all the way to the Supreme Court, twice. When that failed they asked for clemency from Governor John M. Slaton, who was nearing the end of his term and knew that any intervention would doom his hopes for a U.S. Senate seat. He knew that, yet his review of the evidence and visit to the pencil factory convinced him the conviction was unjust, so he commuted the death sentence to life imprisonment. Most Georgia newspapers applauded Slaton for his courage but angry Georgians burned him in effigy. A mob of 5,000 took to the streets, armed with guns, dynamite, and a hanging rope, and chanting "Slaton, Slaton, King of the Jews." The demonstrators threatened to overrun the governor's mansion and were turned back only by an equally determined state militia. Jews knew that they, too, were targets. Some packed their children off to the safety of out-of-town relatives; others boarded up their shops and homes and checked into downtown hotels.

Frank was shipped to the state prison farm in Milledgeville and assigned to work in the fields with other convicts. Less than a month later a two-time murderer slashed Frank's throat with a butcher knife while he was sleeping. He survived, but a month later twenty-five men united under the banner of the Knights of Mary Phagan stormed the prison. The group, which included two former state supreme court justices, a clergyman, and an ex-sheriff, broke through the front gate, overpowered the warden and guards, cut phone lines, emptied gasoline from the cars in the prison garage, and dragged Frank away. They drove all night until they reached Marietta and, at a big oak tree not far from Mary's birthplace, they stood their prisoner on a table, blindfolded him, then kicked away the table and watched as the rope sliced through his recent knife wound and choked him to death. Even that was not enough. As word spread of what had happened, hundreds flocked to the tree, tearing away for souvenirs shreds of his nightgown and the hemp binding his feet, snapping pictures, and berating the bloodied swaying corpse. "Now we've got you," shouted one man. "You won't murder any more little innocent girls."

Like the murder trial of Italian anarchists Nicola Sacco and Bartolomeo Vanzetti in the 1920s, and the spy trial of Julius and Ethel Rosenberg in the 1950s, the Leo Frank case stands as a landmark in American legal and social history, one that scholars, journalists, and politicians return to every time the issue underlying it heats up. Here the issue was anti-Semitism, and what happened to Leo Frank is widely regarded as the worst case of its kind ever in the United States. It was the American Dreyfus Affair, minus Dreyfus's eventual liberation. And as happened nineteen years earlier in France with the spy trial of the Jewish army captain, the Frank case exposed the vulnerability of Jews in America and the need for them to defend themselves. The B'nai B'rith was just in the process of launching the Anti-Defamation League to battle prejudice, and the persecution of Leo Frank helped the new organization define its mission and energize its troops. Anti-Semites also drew inspiration from the murder case. The Knights of Mary Phagan breathed life into the moribund Ku Klux Klan, which within a decade was claiming 4 million members and was back to burning crosses, staging lynchings, and placing wreaths on Mary's grave, which to them was a sacred shrine.

The impact in Atlanta was more direct and debilitating. Frank's arrest, conviction, and lynching—and the public celebrations they spawned—made clear how precarious the Jews' standing was and made every Jew in Atlanta wonder whether it could happen to them. Historically, Jews there had been spared the sort of venom Dixie's ultraconservative, xenophobic elements directed at blacks, but that protection seemed to be eroding even before the Frank case, and afterward the Klan and its fellow haters openly argued that Jews and blacks were colluding to undermine the white race. The trial itself marked the first time anyone could remember when the testimony of a black man was enough to convict a white in Georgia. Benjamin Davis, editor of the respected black publication *Atlanta Independent*, noted the irony: "Under ordinary circumstances the public conscience is such that it is impossible to convict a white man upon the testimony of a Negro unsupported, and it is easily within the purview of reason that a native white man would not have been convicted upon the evidence of a discreditable Negro like Jim Conley." But as Davis implies, Leo Max Frank was a Yankee, a Jew, and a college-educated capitalist, all of which, in the minds of most white southerners, ruled him out as "native."

Hardest hit of all were the German Jews of The Temple. They had spent more than a generation blending in, adopting southern manners and a southern mind-set, and had convinced themselves they had more in common with southern aristocrats than with fellow Jews from Russia or Poland, Turkey or Greece. Now, when they were desperate for that white establishment's support and comfort, they got only isolation and shunning. "They were still 'the other' in the mind of white Christian Atlanta," Melissa Fay Greene writes in her book *The Temple Bombing*. "They'd been, collectively, like a drowning man to whom no one had bothered to toss a line. Upper-crust white Christian Atlanta had looked the other way when mobs and demagogues went after the Jews. It was a civics lesson not easily forgotten."

The temptation was to point the finger at their Yiddish-speaking cousins, but that would not work this time. Frank, after all, had been one of theirs, a member of The Temple and the Standard Club, a German Jew who married into one of Atlanta's most eminent German-Jewish families. They were taught a lesson that assimilated Jews in Germany's Weimar Republic learned thirty years later: Whatever subtle differentiation they drew between German, East European, and Mediterranean Jews, to their enemies—which during this hurtful period just before World War I seemed to include most of white Georgia—a Jew was a Jew. But rather than using that realization to heal the breaches with their fellow Jews, or to strike back at their accusers, they became more determined than ever not to be too pushy, too loud, or too vocal, taking their cue on all three counts from their short-statured, strong-willed rabbi, David Marx.

One effect of that assimilationist attitude was to make any discussion of the Frank case verboten in much of Atlanta's Jewish world for forty years or more, in the process impeding several attempts to clear his name. That is what happened in 1923 when a Canadian journalist working for the *Atlanta Constitution* found that X-rays of the tooth marks in Phagan's shoulder did not match X-rays of Frank's teeth; editors planned to published the findings but prominent Atlanta Jews convinced them it would stir up trouble. The Jewish community moved in again in 1937, keeping Atlanta movie theaters from showing a new Warner Bros. film on the Frank case. And in 1942, Marx said no to a Jewish graduate student who wanted to review his files on Jewish efforts to save Frank.

Samuel Leon Eplan, the eighth of Leon's nine children, was totally captivated by the Frank case. "Most of the Jewish community in Atlanta were afraid to walk the streets for fear of being killed," Sam recounted more than half a century later. But not him. He was in high school, it was summer vacation, and he managed to sneak out of the house and attend every single day of the trial. He also got to meet Frank at the state prison farm, recalling later, "I am satisfied that Frank was completely innocent. However, there never was a repudiation by Jim Conley of his confessions and the final determination as to the guilt or innocence of Leo Frank will never be known." In fact, Conley reportedly had confessed over the years to at least three different people—his lawyer, his girlfriend, and a convict with whom he served time and who gave a deposition attesting to the admission. And, writes *A Little Girl Is Dead* author Harry Golden, "a fourth person also knew Conley had killed the girl. That was a Negro friend who played checkers with Conley in the basement that morning of April 26, 1913. Whoever he was, he may well have witnessed the murder."

Even more decisive proof appeared seventeen years after Golden wrote his book, and eleven after Sam dictated his recollections to his son, who wrote it into a family history. In 1982 Alonzo Mann, a white-haired eighty-three-year-old, gave the Nashville *Tennessean* a dramatically different eyewitness account of events on the day of the murder than he had provided the Frank jury nearly seventy years before. "Leo Frank did not kill Mary Phagan," said Mann, who was a fourteen-year-old office boy at the pencil plant at the time of the killing. Saying he was coming forward now to "get right with the Lord" before he died, Mann told the newspaper that he had witnessed Conley carrying Phagan's wilted body to a trapdoor that led to the basement. He surmised that "Conley killed Mary Phagan to get her money to buy beer." Mann was afraid to tell the truth at the trial, he explained, because Conley had warned him, "If you ever mention this, I'll kill you." Buoyed by Mann's statement, and his passing lie-detector and stress evaluation tests, Frank's defenders petitioned the Georgia Board of Pardons and Parole. In 1986, the same year Mann died, the board awarded Leo Max Frank a posthumous pardon. It did not pronounce him innocent, noting that innocence beyond a reasonable doubt was a standard "almost impossible to satisfy," but it chided the state of Georgia for its "failure to protect Frank."

Jews in Atlanta, like others across the diaspora, knew long before the Frank case that even the friendliest of governments could not always be counted on to defend them. So they founded their own organizations to raise money for poor immigrants, safeguard their civil rights, ensure they had somewhere to gather for poker and baseball games, and, most important, raise money for what they hoped would be a Jewish state in Palestine. "My mother was a Zionist for fifty years before the establishment of the State of Israel in 1948," said Sam Eplan, who picked up his mother's passion and taught his children that Zionism was at least as critical to their faith as keeping kosher or observing the Sabbath. "I remember as a child on Saturdays, probably twice or three times a month, she would give me two or three dollars to go to the United States Post Office and buy a money order to the Moshav Zekenim, which was one of the old established Homes for the Aged in Palestine." He probably ran into lots of other Jewish youth running the same sort of errand for their mothers, but few if any would have been from The Temple. Rabbi Marx, understandably afraid that non-Jews would see loyalty to Israel as disloyalty to America, remained determinedly anti-Zionist and urged his congregants to emulate him, although by the time the Balfour Declaration was signed Rabbi Jacob Rothschild had taken over for Marx and joined the rest of the community in celebrating the new state.

Close bonds also were being formed during those midcentury years between the Jews of Atlanta and those in Raleigh, Charleston, Savannah, Macon, and dozens of other southern cities. All had similar immigrant grandparents who had started as itinerant salesmen, wandering from town to town until they found one that needed a dry goods store or otherwise seemed a good fit. All enjoyed the same sense of being out of sync with the community, nicely so, when they gathered for a Passover Seder or to break fast after Yom Kippur—and the same sense of loneliness when all their neighbors headed to church on Sunday mornings. The bonds were natural and were strengthened through Jewish fraternities like Alpha Epsilon Pi and groups like the Don't Worry Club and Just Us Boys, which let Sam Eplan participate in dances and debates everywhere from Savannah to Chattanooga. In later years, when the smaller towns lost their critical mass of Jews, it was natural for those who were left to consider moving to Atlanta, the way Sam's daughter-in-law Madalyne did, knowing that it had a thriving Jewish community that included lots of their old friends.

"Mobile was a small town really. The synagogue I grew up in was Orthodox and Ashkenazic, and was a very warm, emotional, loving situation," Madalyne remembers. "Ours was like a family in the movie *Avalon*. Everybody was so close, the men all knew Hebrew. But Jewish Atlanta became my world very quickly. When I was single I adored every single aspect of it, from the Jewish community center to the synagogue. It was just an exciting Jewish city for me because I'd never had it like that, and an exciting non-Jewish one because there was an openness that was different than Mobile."

The Atlanta that Madalyne encountered in the 1950s was growing fast, and so was its Jewish community. The city's Jewish population doubled to 4,000 between 1900 and 1910, and more than doubled again to 10,000 by the time Israel became a state in 1948. In the early 1960s, as the civil rights movement was picking up steam and business and civic leaders were promoting Atlanta as the "City Too Busy to Hate," that city had just over 21,000 Jewish residents and had just elected Sam Massell, a Jew, vice mayor.

Blacks and Jews always had a close relationship in Atlanta, although not always a warm one. Newly arrived Jewish immigrants typically lived in or near black neighborhoods, but they typically moved out as soon as they could afford to. Jewish store owners solicited black customers, extending them credit when other white merchants refused, and blacks accounted for a disproportionate share of the trade in Jewish-owned delis and lunchrooms, beer halls and fruit stands. But proximity sometimes meant tension, as Sam Eplan recalled regarding an incident in 1905, when he was just nine: "My brothers, Ike and Mose, were attending Crew Street Elementary School. There was a large Negro community living some distance away, toward Lakewood Park, and every afternoon, after school, a group of these Negroes, about seventy in number, would invade our neighborhood. It was the signal for the start of a rock-throwing battle.

"I would get home an hour or two before Ike and Mose returned from school, and it was my job (together with other boys of my age) to gather these rocks together and to pile them in strategic locations so that our side would have the ammunition to fight back and repel these black invaders. This kept on for several months, and many of our boys suffered injuries from these battles. When the fighting started, our older brothers would run us back home."

But like the Jewish community of which he was a critical part, over the years Sam built bonds with African-American Atlantans that made black-Jewish relations a quiet model for black-white relations—and gave substance to the hope that Atlanta could avoid the race war that was tearing apart so much of the South. Sam understood that one reason Atlanta Jews were partially spared attacks by white racists was that blacks made an easier target. He also understood that Jews, given their histories of being victimized by oppression and promoting social justice, had a responsibility to do what they could to advance the rights of blacks. So when Mayor William Berry Hartsfield was looking to integrate the city's golf courses in 1959, Sam was one of the whites he tapped to come along. When poor blacks needed legal help and had nowhere else to turn, some turned to Sam. And when fifty sticks of dynamite ripped apart the side wall of The Temple at 3:37 A.M. on Sunday, October 12, 1958, Sam was one of scores of Jews and non-Jews who rushed to the scene.

The Temple almost certainly was targeted because its new rabbi, the Pittsburgh-born, Guadalcanal-toughened Jack Rothschild, had been speaking out on civil rights since shortly after he arrived to take over for Marx in 1946. Rothschild endorsed the U.S. Supreme Court decision desegregating public schools, one of the first southern leaders to do so. He invited blacks to his home and onto his pulpit, more firsts, and generally pushed his reluctant congregants and coreligionists to realize their duty as Jews to stand against racism. The result, many feared in the wake of the bombing, would be another Frank case, another move by white Atlanta to distance itself from and silence its Jewish citizens.

Precisely the opposite happened. Mayor Hartsfield rushed to the bomb site and stood by its targets, saying, "Whether they like it or not, every political rabble-rouser is the godfather of these cross-burners and dynamiters who sneak about in the dark and give a bad name to the South. It is high time the decent people of the South rise up and take charge." President Eisenhower also expressed his sympathy and ordered his FBI chief, J. Edgar Hoover, to help. Pastors throughout the city denounced the attack from their pulpits that Sunday, politicians railed against it, schools offered use of their buildings while repairs to the synagogue were undertaken, and Ralph McGill, publisher of the *Atlanta Constitution*, warned that "when the wolves of hate are loosed on one people, then no one is safe," words so affecting that they, along with the rest of his front-page column, won him a Pulitzer Prize.

The explosion had every bit as profound an effect on the Jewish community as the Frank case had, but this time it was a healing one. "I was teaching in a public school then, in a very poor school on the other side of town," recalls Madalyne Eplan. "Everybody from the school I was in, the parents, were horrified. I was kind of stunned by it all; I didn't know these people but I was reassured. I was overwhelmed by the response of the non-Jews I knew." The Temple bombing and the reaction it engendered helped lift the shadow that Atlanta Jews had been living under for the previous forty-three years, since the lynching of Leo Frank, in much the same manner that the bombing years later of their communal headquarters would help unite the Jews of Buenos Aires. "Far from having plunged us into another era of darkness and fear," Rabbi Rothschild's widow, Janice, wrote nearly thirty years after the explosion on Peachtree Street, "this potential disaster of our own day had actually brightened the future for Jews and non-Jews alike and restored confidence to the hearts of those who still trembled with the memory of Leo Frank."

The Temple bombing had another counterintuitive outcome: at the same time that it made Atlanta Jews aware that involvement in the civil rights movement made them vulnerable, it made some realize that they had a responsibility to be supportive. It was more of a risk for them than for Jewish activists from northern cities like Boston, which did not have the South's tortured history of slavery and Jim Crow laws sanctioning segregation, were not subjected to school integration orders until years later, and were not targeted by lunatic bombers. Making things more difficult for the Jews of Atlanta was the fact that they owned Rich's Department Store and other businesses where blacks staged their first sit-ins. Even so, more and more Atlanta Jews worked behind the scenes on biracial committees, supported black candidates for office, and offered other forms of quiet support. "Jews in Atlanta realized that identifying with our cause made them a target," says Ozell Sutton, a black leader who has devoted his life to civil rights, starting in Little Rock and continuing in Atlanta. "But when the chips were down, they came forward, if you know what I mean. As far as groups outside our own, there was no greater support to be found than with Jews. It was far more than among Catholics or other white people. It wasn't the whole Jewish community that has been there with civil rights, but the whole black community hasn't been there, either."

Cecil Alexander has followed the civil rights debate from the other side of the black-Jewish divide. "I was the subject of hate calls," recalls Alexander, a prominent Jewish architect born in 1918, whose grandfather fought for the Confederacy, whose uncle was one of Leo Frank's lawyers, and who himself was at the forefront of the push for black rights. "I loved it. I felt it was something really worthwhile doing, although my brother-in-law from Montgomery held me responsible for the whole civil rights movement. We had a meeting here of American Jewish Committee representatives from all over the South during that period, and they were saying, 'Atlanta is a sanctuary. You're not exposed to the risks we in smaller towns are to our businesses, our lives, our families. You shouldn't tell us what to do.' The bombing of The Temple changed that attitude. They realized we weren't a sanctuary, that we were exposed here, too."

Sam Eplan was another Jew willing to take risks to promote civil rights, and he passed that passion on to his children, along with his special sense of what it meant to be a Jew in Atlanta. "My father said his father believed the diaspora was the greatest opportunity ever given to Jews," recalls Carolyn Goldsmith, Sam's daughter and the younger Leon's sister. Sam, who died in 1984, had a similar love for the New World he was born in, and especially for that city. "My father worshiped Atlanta," adds Carolyn. "Every time they paved a new street we had to get in the car and look at it. My father's attitude was, 'When you die, and you're good, you'll go to Atlanta.' Atlanta always had a certain softness and gentleness that you could see on the street, overlaid with the go-go attitude of the East brought in by immigrants.

"I consider myself a southern Jew, I'm an Atlanta Jew. I do worry that we are losing that sense. I worry about it when someone blows their horn at me. I put down the window and yell, 'We don't do that here.' "

*   *   *

Add that to the list of challenges facing today's Jewish community in Atlanta. It is not just a question of capturing all the new arrivals who are not participating in the city's Jewish life. It also means ensuring that they, along with the children and grandchildren of Jews from Atlanta, understand that being Jewish in Atlanta carries with it a special inheritance. It is the legacy of Leo Frank and the Temple bombing, of civil rights and self-help. It is knowing that Atlanta's Jewish growth was built in part around the slow decline of smaller Jewish communities in southern cities like Cleveland, Mississippi, and Demopolis, Alabama. It is sensing the place's intimacy and civility.

Atlanta Jewry's very success almost ensures the loss of some or all of that history. At the time of the Frank trial there were 5,000 Jews in Atlanta; today there are twenty times as many. Back then it was a close-knit community. Atlantans knew their neighbors, and Jews not only knew the people they sat near at shul but those who attended the synagogue across town. Today it is difficult to know where the city ends and suburban sprawl begins, and synagogues are springing up far too fast for even the most committed Jew to keep track.

"When I was growing up there were about 750 Jewish kids within five years of my age and I knew all of them. It was comparable to growing up in a small town where everybody knows everybody," says David Alexander, talking about an era as recent as the 1960s and '70s. "Now kids grow up in the Jewish community totally unaware of entire factions. Their sense of Jewish community depends on which piece they grow up in—they are part of the Hebrew Academy community, or Davis Academy, or whatever summer camp they go to. They have no sense of being part of one singular family that I had."

Jana Eplan, Leon and Madalyne's daughter, sees the same trend. The Atlanta Jewish community "already has stopped looking southern," she says, "but I don't know how much it matters. People who aren't from here don't want to hear about it from us; they think we're snobby and elitist. I don't think it's the southern history that gives us our foundation. I think it's that we are committed to this Jewish community."

Her aunt Carolyn understands that attitude but does not accept it.

She knows the forces pushing Atlanta to lose its southern character, but she sees other forces that might mediate against what she feels would be a major loss. "I watch people like my husband, Bob, who is from New York," she says. "Over a period of years they become more southern than any of the southerners because it's a pleasant way to be."

Epilogue

ISRAEL:

A Partnership of Equals

This chapter was supposed to be about us and them. The "them" was Israel, which I had planned to portray as a society admirable in many ways but arrogant in its attitude that it occupies the center of the Jewish world, with the diaspora pushed to the periphery. Israelis had made the desert bloom, as they reminded every Jewish tourist who passed through. They had stoutly and single-handedly defended Israel during five wars and ceaseless flare-ups. And they were not about to let a bunch of wealthy benefactors from a pampered diaspora tell them how to run their country. The "us" was that diaspora, which I saw as the browbeaten underdog. It was a critical core of world Jewry that too often let itself be pushed to the sideline and too seldom appreciated its own worthiness and permanence. It had fought its own wars against anti-Semites, had shipped hard-earned dollars to Israel year after year to help build the Jewish state, and was tired of being made to feel like a schlepper cousin.

Then I went to Israel, my fifth trip there but one quite apart from all the previous visits. I found that I knew very little about Israelis. I found that Israelis, especially young ones, are too busy thinking about themselves to think or care much about the diaspora. While I wanted to talk about their ties to Boston and Buenos Aires, they wanted to tell

me about Israel's vitality and self-confidence and make me understand
Israel's perspectives on security and peace. The hubris still was there,
but it seemed more like pride than insolence and more aimed at bucking
them up than putting down anyone else. Israel still has as many pressing
problems, internal and external, as any nation on Earth. But I also experienced a country that increasingly is at home with the world, via the
Internet, cable TV, a propensity for international travel, and vigorous
trade contacts—and at home with itself, as its economy hums and it
wrestles with the day-to-day issues facing any "normal" society.

What about the old Zionist ideals, the sense that any good Jew
belongs in Israel? Most still accept that, believing that Israel offers the
world's Jews security and backing that up by welcoming 850,000 Jews
from Russia in just the last decade. And Ariel Sharon, in one of his first
statements as prime minister in March 2001, called for Israel to continue
aggressively recruiting diaspora Jews and said the Jewish state is "the
only place in the world where Jews can continue to live as Jews and
withstand the danger of assimilation. Most Israelis, however, seem to
feel otherwise. Push them just a bit and they acknowledge that Jews can
live rewarding Jewish lives in places like New York, Paris, and even
Düsseldorf. They understand why Russians would flee economic hard-
ship but express wonder at American or French Jews voluntarily swap-
ping their comfortable lives for Israel and its stresses. They also are
coming to appreciate the strains, financial and environmental, that come
with too many diaspora Jews accepting their offer of return. As for the
old paternalisms—self-righteousness about their decision to make aliyah,
resentment about American Jews putting their cash on a par with the
blood Israelis have sacrificed to build the Jewish state—they seem stale
as well as old. These days the biggest threat to the Israel-diaspora relationship is not arrogance but irrelevance.

All of which echoes the questions being raised today across the diaspora. Israel still matters to Jews I met from Argentina to Atlanta, but
not in the defining way it did a generation ago. Most have come to see
the Jewish state as a symbol rather than a crusade, a source of pride but
not necessarily a place to send their dollars or their children. They still
rally around Israel during times of upheaval like those it has experienced
recently, and battle back against what they see as the media's one-sided
coverage of Middle Eastern tensions. Yet diaspora Jews have identified

equally compelling needs to keep Judaism alive in their homelands and in other far-flung lands. They still turn to Israel for haven, but now most go because it is their only choice rather than to fulfill some dream of returning to an ancestral homeland. The old insecurities also are evaporating: Jews everywhere are still proud of Israel's accomplishments but finally feel comfortable acknowledging that it has troubles, like any country. There is less talk about feeling guilty for not going. The diaspora is becoming normalized the same way Israel is. From Boston to Buenos Aires, Düsseldorf to Dnepropetrovsk, Jews are feeling more at home than they imagined possible.

Yet even as Israel and the diaspora are growing apart, the maturation under way in both places offers new and potentially more promising ways for them to come together. Both are troubled by questions of religious and cultural continuity. In the diaspora the wake-up call came in the form of surveys showing soaring rates of intermarriage and plummeting fertility; in Israel, it was studies suggesting that the young are so turned off by traditionalists' grip on religion that they regard their Jewish identity as a distant second to their Israeli one. Both are beginning to sense that, while the old ways of interacting are dangerously outmoded, a bigger danger is for Jews in or out of Israel to assume they can go it alone. So they are building bridges—from sharing solutions to discrete problems like violence against women and pollution, to bringing young diaspora Jews to Israel to experience life in a mainly Jewish world. Young Israelis are making return visits to see how the diaspora welcomes Reform and Conservative, feminists, gays, and others who feel as if they have been written out of the Israeli Orthodox establishment's definition of who is a Jew.

It is clearly more complicated trying to forge bonds between Israel and the diaspora now that both are more self-confident. But as both sides are beginning to sense, such a partnership of equals also can be more satisfying and long-lived.

"American Jews have to admit that Israel is a rich country and that helping Israel financially is the news of yesterday. We in Israel have to admit that making aliyah is not the only Jewish achievement," says Yossi Beilin, minister of justice in former prime minister Ehud Barak's cabinet and one of the architects of the new Israel-diaspora relationship. "We are equals, that's the new covenant. The idea is to sign a declaration of interdependence and to select some projects. My first idea was the Birthright idea, a visit of young Jews to Israel. There are many other ideas, like international TV, a Jewish TV channel. We have more of a common language than anytime in history, English. It is a small world with the Internet. We have many new vehicles to communicate with each other, from conference calls to just traveling from one place to another. We don't need ships and boats and weeks of traveling the way we used to.

"I think the time is right for this new partnership. The younger generation will accept it. I hope that my generation can accept it."

Nomi Friedman is part of that younger generation. The nineteen-year-old from Zichron Yaakov is a blend of all the rich diversity in today's Israel, with a Sephardic, Israeli-born mother and an Ashkenazic, American-born father. She spent seven years in the United States growing up, but today is an Israeli in citizenship and self-definition. She plans to spend a year in South America, Australia, or some other faraway land after she completes her two years in the army, but is certain that "I wouldn't want to live anywhere but in Israel." And even though her paternal grandfather and other relatives live outside Israel, she says that "there is some connection in theory to the diaspora, but it doesn't really matter to me. The connections that matter are to Israelis, whether they are Jews or Arabs. That is much more important than to Jews abroad."

Yet things could be different. She imagines her generation forming new ties to the diaspora that are just as meaningful as the ones her parents had. "A lot of young Israelis are not really connected to their Judaism beyond the tradition. For Israeli kids, Judaism is usually the ultra-Orthodox. That's why they are very much afraid of Judaism, they think it's dark and medieval," says Nomi, who goes to shul regularly but not every Sabbath, and keeps kosher but is unsure how she feels about God. "In the United States I saw a totally different kind of Judaism, one that has nothing to do with the ultra-Orthodox. Meeting Jews from America and other places, and learning different ways to relate to a Judaism that's not in the Dark Ages, can help a lot."

*   *   *

At the beginning, relations between the State of Israel and world Jewry seemed more clear-cut, almost defining themselves. When Nathan Birnbaum of Vienna coined the modern term "Zionism" in 1890 he was giving expression to a messianic vision and an urge to return that had been part of the Jewish consciousness for thousands of years. Theodor Herzl transformed that idea into a practical political movement. He imagined the establishment of an independent Jewish state—in Uganda, Argentina, or, as he finally came to believe, in *Eretz Yisrael*—as the only way for Jews to survive in the kind of anti-Semitism-infested world he had witnessed as a correspondent covering the 1894 spy trial of French army captain Alfred Dreyfus. When Herzl's dream was posthumously realized with the creation of the State of Israel in 1948, the role of world Jews in rallying around that Jewish state seemed self-evident.

But translating that support into action raised vexing questions, even at the beginning. Should the Zionist label embrace those who were collecting money and building support for Israel from afar, or only those who actually moved there? Was it time to reconfigure Zionism to take into account Jewish communities like those in America, where Jews were secure in a way Herzl had never imagined possible? What role, if any, should Israel's friends around the world have in deciding its fate? And, as Birnbaum himself wondered as he gradually withdrew from the Zionist movement, were not the Jewish people, wherever they resided, at least as important as the Jewish state?

The pendulum in answering those questions has swung back and forth. Before and after the Six-Day War in 1967, for instance, Israel assumed a new resonance for Jews across the diaspora, reminding them of its vulnerability when things looked grim on the battlefield, then generating an unprecedented outpouring of pride, celebration, and self-confidence when Israel won its stunning victory. Jews around the world not only sent money and pushed their governments for support, but thousands flew in to help, taking over for Israeli soldiers in the fields and the factories. A similar sense of pride and shared purpose arose with subsequent crises—from Israel's inspired signing of the Camp David Accords with Egypt in 1978, to its dramatic airlifts of imperiled Jews from Ethiopia in 1984 and 1991, to the violence and wrenching self-examination that have accompanied the on-again, off-again initiatives to forge peace with the Palestinians.

Beyond the abstractions, and the drama of intervening events, a reality was unfolding that defined the diaspora relationship to Israel from the 1960s through at least the 1980s. It was a reality that saw my family, at High Holiday services each year in Haverhill, Massachusetts, listen to rousing appeals to back "our beloved Israel" from Manny Epstein, perennial head of the Israel Bonds drive. We were grateful for any break from the long prayer service, even one that suddenly injected money into conversations about God and ethics. But each year my father and mother gave generously. They felt it was their duty, and they knew it was less about planting trees or building buildings than taking out an insurance policy just in case anything imperiled our seemingly secure existence as Jewish Americans. We and all the other Jews I knew listed Israel at the top of our list of what being a Jew was about, even if we never imagined moving there. We visited, in my case for the first time just after high school, the same way Jews did who grew up in Paris, Dublin, and Atlanta. We learned to read (but not understand) Israel's official language of Hebrew, and took pride in dancing Israeli dances (or at least trying to) at bar mitzvahs and weddings.

It all was part of a set of rules that diaspora Jews abided by even if they never wrote them down. You knew where your elected officials stood on Israel, and they knew that a pro-Israel position was a prerequisite for your vote. You donated your time and money to the Jewish state every year, and dug even deeper during every crisis. You never publicly criticized Israel even if you heatedly debated the wisdom of its actions with other Jews. I learned just how inviolate the last law was when I breached it in 1992 by writing a travel story in *The Boston Globe* that was 90 percent positive about Israel. A joke I told at the end about Israelis' not understanding the expression "excuse me" begot a column in Boston's *Jewish Advocate* that branded me a self-hating Jew.

By the mid-1980s cracks began to form in that solid wall of diaspora support for Israel, and the old rules of engagement began to break down. Jews in America and elsewhere increasingly were uncomfortable supporting Israel when they believed Israel was wrong. The New Israel Fund, Peace Now, and other Israel-based groups added to the unease by planting two heretical notions: that it actually was the responsibility of diaspora Jews to speak out for Israeli policies they backed and against those they opposed, and that world Jewry should earmark its Israel donations to pro-peace initiatives or other projects they endorsed rather than steer them to umbrella organizations like the United Jewish Appeal. Diaspora Jews also were losing patience with what they saw as a bid by the Orthodox to use the debate over religious conversions to repudiate the contributions of the Reform, Reconstructionist, and Conservative movements.

While those developments were difficult to measure because they happened piecemeal and over many years, the extent to which they had shaken the traditional Israel-diaspora relationship became clear in a 1997 survey of adult American Jews. It found that younger Jews are every bit as committed as their elders to God and religion, but they are considerably less committed to marrying other Jews, having Jewish friends, belonging to Jewish institutions, and, most important in this context, to bonding with Israel. Among those aged twenty-five to thirty-four, the youngest group surveyed, only 23 percent said they felt strongly attached to Israel; among those fifty-five and older it was fully twice as many. Overall, the connection to Israel and Israelis had eroded substantially since a similar survey just a decade earlier. A closer look at the results suggests that young Jews in America, as in France, Argentina, and other parts of the diaspora where they have been asked, are saying that they know Israel should matter to them, much the way the Holocaust should. But as with the Holocaust, their bonds to the Jewish people and the Jewish state increasingly seem more abstract than instinctual, and simply are not part of their personal experience the way they were for their parents and grandparents.

"The perimeter of Jewish life has shrunken such that the outer, public sphere has diminished in meaning for American Jews from just ten years ago. This includes politics, organizational life, philanthropy, and Israel," says Steven M. Cohen, an American who teaches at the Hebrew University of Jerusalem and ran the 1997 survey of American Jews. "What's left standing is a commitment to self. That means their parents, grandparents, spouses, and children. It also means the institutions that serve them and their family like the synagogue, their children's school, and the Jewish community center. All other organizations and ways of relating to their Judaism are details around that thesis."

It was not just young diaspora Jews who were becoming more inward-focused. The 1990 National Jewish Population Survey set off alarms among Jewish educators, rabbis, and communal chiefs with its report that, over the previous five years, the rate of American Jews marrying non-Jews had reached a staggering 52 percent. That was similar to what surveyors were finding in other diaspora countries. The immediate and understandable response by Jewish leaders was to become obsessed with the crisis of continuity inside their own communities and distracted from their historic focus on Israel, which is one reason why Jewish youth became similarly disengaged. Over time, however, many of those same leaders have come to conclude that rather than being a diversion, Israel can be part of the solution to their internal intermarriage-identity dilemma. Coming up with new ways to learn Jewish history and forge spiritual ties, the way Jews are doing from Atlanta to Paris, is critical to making new generations feel that their faith and culture are worth preserving. But the other half of the answer, diaspora leaders reasoned, is to reconnect with today's thriving Jewish state in ways that bring alive the history, culture, and spirit.

In Israel, meanwhile, long-simmering resentments were boiling to the surface with respect to diaspora Jews generally and those from the United States especially. Some disliked the way America was infecting Israel with its spin-dominated political campaigns and its fast-food culture. Others objected to the way U.S. presidents thought they could dictate to Israel its policies on everything from West Bank settlements to arms sales to China, and the way U.S. Jews thought their money bought them a say in internal Israeli affairs. Many of the gripes had been around for a generation but now, as Israel's economy was soaring and its sense of security growing, more Israelis felt it was time to vent their frustrations. Beilin, who was then the deputy foreign minister, did just that in a 1993 address to the Women's International Zionist Organization during its international summit in Tel Aviv. The Israel Bonds campaign—long the symbol of the diaspora's relationship with Israel— no longer mattered as much, he said. Such efforts amounted to less than one half of 1 percent of Israel's annual budget, he explained, and Israel could get along without them.

While his remarks touched off almost as many shock waves in Israel as in the diaspora, Beilin was merely giving voice to what for most young Israelis is the reality of their world. The old ways of relating plainly do not hold the same meaning. Two of every three Israelis today were born in Israel and they are less likely than their forebears to have siblings or other close relatives across the diaspora. They depend less on world Jewry for support, financial or psychological. Rather than rejecting the diaspora, they simply do not factor it into their thinking about themselves or their country. What growing numbers of them do reject is religion and a feeling of connection to a Jewish people outside of the one in Israel. Religion to them is too bound up in ritual, and they see Jews outside Israel as too bound up in the notion that Judaism is just about religion. They feel they have all the Jewishness they need by being part of a real Jewish state, celebrating the holidays of the Old Testament, speaking the Hebrew of the Torah, and putting their lives on the line to defend Israel and, by extension, Jews everywhere. Which makes them remarkably like their inward-looking counterparts in the diaspora.

As in America, a groundbreaking study brought the hazy trends into clearer focus. The author this time was Aliza Shenhar, who now is president of Emek Yezreel College in Haifa and when her report came out in 1994 was a top official at the University of Haifa. She and her colleagues found that government-supported schools were not teaching young Israelis about the way Jews live today in lands outside Israel, and were not exposing them to the Torah, Talmud, and other ancient texts, all of which constituted "a palpable threat to society in Israel." They fingered a series of culprits, from the moves to consumerism and professional specialization to growing tensions between the Orthodox and the secular.

The Israeli authors, like the Americans, said that much of the needed change has to come from within. Israel's education establishment has to be radically reshaped to include more Jewish history and culture and less "fanaticism" and "moralizing." But equally critical, Shenhar and her colleagues wrote, is that "Jewish history instruction should emphasize the destiny of the Jewish communities in the diaspora, their extensive cultural creativity and their attempts at coping with the challenges that the surrounding society poses. . . . We should emphasize the affinity and mutual responsibility that links Israel with the Jewish diaspora as an important component of Jewish identity."

Her greatest fear, Shenhar adds in an interview, is that "for the younger generation Jewish studies has become identified with religious studies. They are protesting against an Orthodox monopoly on religion by staying away. This process is very dangerous for the future of Israel and the Jewish people. The Jewish people have survived for 2,000 years because they always had connections between different communities and they always felt like one people. When a Jew was killed at Passover in

Casablanca, another Jew who lived in Berlin felt as if he had lost a member of the family. This sense of solidarity is disappearing, and if it disappears it will be the end of the Jewish people.

"It is not enough to be here in Israel. It is not enough to speak Hebrew. It is not enough to celebrate Jewish holidays. There should be something more."

* * *

To understand what more is needed, and how all those trends are affecting real Israelis, I met with Israeli relatives and friends of the families I focused on in my seven diaspora cities. Some are sabras, or natives; others made aliyah later in life. Some are highly religious, others hardly at all. Taken together they offer a firsthand look at why some Jews cannot imagine living anywhere but in Israel, along with a close-up take on the links that are being forged to replace those that are fraying between the Jewish state and world Jewry.

"I never thought about not living here," says Danny Lichter, Nicole Ohana's cousin, who was born in 1951 near the kibbutz outside Haifa where his Polish-born parents settled after World War II. He is drawn to Israel partly because "it is where I grew up. I have a very, very strong connection to my childhood, to the adventures that have happened here." As the child of Holocaust survivors, he also has a sense that "the most important thing for the Jewish people is to have a country for ourselves, a place where we can have a gun and aircraft and cannons, a strong country that can make sure the Holocaust will never happen again. If something happens in Paris, Boston, or South Africa, and the anti-Semites appeared again, Jews from those places can come here. They can work here. They can hold a gun and fight here. The Jewish people need a country and I feel that I am part of that country." Most of all, Danny chose Israel over all the countries he visited—including France, where Nicole and other relatives live—because of his three sons and a daughter, who range in age from eight to twenty-four. "What I am doing here," he says, "is not really for the Jewish people all over the world. It is for my children."

That sense that the children come first is a defining feature of life in Israel. It is why many of the early settlers came, why others followed, and why they stayed even though life there was difficult. It grows out of

Judaism's emphasis on the young, and Holocaust survivors' sense that they owed it to those who perished to build a better world for the generations to come. It is part of the psyche of the young state, part of its optimism. Israelis know that as soon as their sons and daughters turn eighteen they will begin potentially perilous service in the army, which makes it all the more important that their time before that be carefree. You can sense that mind-set on holidays like Lag b'Omer, when the young take center stage by lighting up the skies with bonfires and trading stories through the night. You can count it among the Orthodox, who average nearly seven children per family, and among the wider society, which accounts for just 37 percent of the world's Jews but a full 50 percent of Jewish children. You can hear it in the words of parents like Danny Lichter, who start out talking about grand visions of the Jewish people but end up with what really counts: his children.

The choice of staying in Israel is even clearer for Orthodox Jews like Yosef Yitzchak Kaminetzky, who like his baby brother, Shmuel, is a rabbi in the Lubavitch Hasidic movement. A grayer, slimmer, more scholarly version of Shmuel, Yosef, who spells his surname slightly differently, loves the work his brother is doing to rebuild the Jewish community in Dnepropetrovsk. He understands why his mother left Israel for Brooklyn, why his other brothers chose Melbourne and New York, and why his daughters are working with Chabad missions in Romania and Siberia. As a distinguished chronicler of Lubavitch history, Yosef could have gone to work at the movement's headquarters in Brooklyn, but he chose to remain in the tiny town of Kefar Chabad, not far from Tel Aviv. For him, there is no question that "a Jew who is really observant or *frum*, who keeps all the mitzvot, does better to come to Israel because it's much easier to live in Israel. It's better to live here. When I look out the window I see olive trees and palm trees. Things are much more pleasant in our little village than if I were in our Chabad center in New York. I live like I am in Paradise."

That sense of having made a conscious choice, and feeling sure it was the right one, surfaces repeatedly among these diaspora relatives, whether they mark their time in Israel in decades or days. That is natural, and the same conviction shown by Jews across the diaspora in explaining why they remain where they are. But there is something special with Israelis, particularly for those who uprooted themselves from more settled worlds to move to the unfamiliar land in the middle of the Middle East. Most were pulled by longing as much as reason, by an emotional attachment more than a practical weighing of pluses and minuses. Others were pushed by a sense that they could never entirely belong in an overwhelmingly non-Jewish world. What they got once they arrived often is difficult for outsiders to appreciate, but it is clear to them.

"The moment I put my foot on the ground here I knew this was it," recalls Daniel Briscoe, a thirty-eight-year-old eye surgeon in Tel Aviv who came for his first time when he was seventeen, spending two weeks on a kibbutz and two more touring the country. "I kept coming back every year. I just fell in love with the country. I wasn't at peace with myself until I came to live here. I couldn't fight it anymore. That is what is called getting the bug."

The Briscoes are among Ireland's first families, with Daniel's grandfather and uncle having served as lords mayor of Dublin and members of the Irish parliament. His father was a highly respected dentist, both parents were central figures in Dublin's Jewish community, and when Daniel left in 1988 the Irish economy was on its way to becoming the hottest in Europe. But as a Jew in an overwhelmingly Catholic country, he says there "always was a certain undercurrent of anti-Semitism" and a sense of "having to prove that, as a Jew, you also could be a good Irishman." In Israel, by contrast, "it's my country. Nobody asks me any questions about why I'm here or how I'm here. They accept that I belong here. I love Ireland very much. It's a very nice country to bring your kids up in, it's a country with a lot of very good values. But it's not my country anymore."

Nathan Greenbaum, now seventy-three, came when he was just fifteen. He had escaped the Nazis by fleeing from Poland to Russia, then to Iran, and finally to Palestine. He returned to Europe after the war as a recruiter for the Jewish Agency, trying to convince Jews in Displaced Persons camps that "the best place for them would be among other Jews in Palestine who are trying to build a new Jewish society and to establish an independent state." Many were won over but not his cousin Helen Israel, who with much trepidation decided to try and build a new life for herself in Düsseldorf. Greenbaum, a teacher and writer, lived and worked for several years in Canada and America but never was tempted to permanently relocate. "I still am convinced that the future of the

Jewish people is here in Israel," he explains. "If I were sent out today as a recruiter for Israel, my arguments would be somewhat different. But I still think anyone should come to Israel who has a Jewish touch, who wants his children to grow up in a Jewish environment and stay as a Jew, to be exposed less to the possibility of intermarriage. It is the place for anyone who wants the Jewish people to survive."

For Ben and Sonya Rabinowitz, coming to Israel not only meant leaving behind a lifetime of personal, business, and religious contacts in Atlanta; it meant saying good-bye to their children and grandchildren, as well as to cousins like Leon and Madalyne Eplan. They used to visit Israel regularly, then in 1992 decided to come for good. "A Jew can be a Jew here without any problem. I'm not talking about an observant Jew, a Jew period," says Sonya, seventy-one, as she sits in her cramped apartment in Jerusalem, explaining why she gave up an existence in Atlanta with three times the living space and considerably more creature comforts. "There's a relaxing that happens here. I'm not always aware of it until I get off an airplane in New York and all of a sudden my inside is tight again. There's a complete Shabbat feeling that you get here. Any Jew who prays says three times a day that they want to return to Jerusalem. I never dreamed that we would be able to do it."

Coming to Israel not only means giving up the easy living of a place like Atlanta, it also means taking on the burdens of that disputatious society. I get a sense of just how nerve-testing that can be as I make my way from interview to interview. In the car, the radio crackles with reports of the hastily executed troop pullout from Lebanon, with tensions building along a border that is less than a hundred miles away. Climbing the steps to the office of a professor at the Hebrew University of Jerusalem, I pass through a standoff between flag-waving Palestinian students and flag-waving Israelis. Every conversation I have with secular Jews ends with them bemoaning the growing power of the Orthodox, while every meeting with Orthodox Jews touches on their concerns about the lack of observance among the secular. The final reminder comes as I fly out of the country, passing over a towering landfill that creates an obstacle course for my plane and stands as a monument to Israel's worsening environmental crisis.

Danny Lichter has experienced battles like those all his life. Growing up on a kibbutz, he watched his parents paint over all the windows during the Sinai Campaign so enemy planes could not see lights signaling a settlement. He lived through the Six-Day and Yom Kippur Wars, and was part of an elite commando unit that operated deep inside Lebanon during the nearly twenty-year-long campaign there. He also knows better than most Israelis the continuing nature of the risk, from within and without, as he earns his living selling high-security fencing to the government and private companies. But as he explains from his patio in a comfortable neighborhood of Tel Aviv, "Even with all these difficulties I believe that this is my place and I have to be here."

Philip and Tamar Warburg did not have to be in Israel. My old friends from Boston moved there because it made them feel part of an intimate, vibrant country that was struggling to define itself and build a future. It gave them a sense of being Jewish without having to be religious, of being part of an important experiment and adventure at the same time they were building a strong community life and nurturing home for their young daughters. As for all the problems the country has, that is part of the challenge. Philip takes on polluters in his role as director of Israel's leading environmental law organization and Tamar focuses her architecture practice on designing energy-saving, environmentally sensitive structures.

"We decided to move to Israel in 1994, buoyed by the promise of the Oslo peace accords," says Philip, who has worked on a series of environmental projects with Jordanians and Palestinians. "Both Tamar and I felt we had something to contribute professionally, but much more important was the hope that we'd be raising our two daughters in an Israel that was building bridges with, rather than struggling against, its Arab neighbors. A healthy Israel isn't a 'stand-alone' society. It's a nation with real, affirmative ties, not just to the Jewish diaspora but to Arab societies that are so much a part of life in the Middle East. The challenge of building these ties feels overwhelming at times, but there's no other way to build a peaceful future for the Middle East."

Just as the Warburgs feel part of the struggle to construct a more peaceful Middle East, they also feel very connected to Israel as a modern society with its own particular norms and traditions. "A lot of the joy and meaning for us, living in Israel, comes from the present-day experience of actively contributing to a culture and society in formation," he says. "Our daughters are growing up with a strong sense of being 'part of,' rather than 'apart from.' They belong to a particular society where religion and history are certainly relevant but aren't the sole defining factors."

For many of today's refugees, coming to Israel was less a matter of what the Jewish state offered than of its being their only choice—and some are having second thoughts. Grigory Korol is typical of the nearly 1 million Russians who arrived over the last decade. He is old. He is poor. And Israel was one of the few countries that would take him. He loves the idea of being in Israel, and loves being surrounded by Jews, but he still would rather not have come.

"I came because my children and grandchildren live here. If it were not for them I would have stayed," says the seventy-eight-year-old, whose bushy eyebrows sit atop sad eyes that brighten as he talks. He looks like the Polish Jew that he originally was, his black yarmulke slanted to the side and sitting too far forward, his hands gesturing to add emphasis to his words as his wife sits behind him, nodding. Back in Dnepropetrovsk, Korol was chairman of the religious community and a critical force in the revival of Jewish life. He was one of a handful of Jews who kept the synagogue open during the Soviet era, and in the 1990s he was right-hand man to Rabbi Shmuel Kaminezki. He hesitated in coming to Israel at his advanced age partly out of fear of having to move into an unfamiliar apartment, learn to speak Hebrew, and settle into a new world. Those adjustments proved easier than he expected when he arrived in March of 2000. His apartment in Bat Yam, a community just south of Tel Aviv, has the same bland furniture, ersatz Oriental rugs, and cramped quarters as ones in Ukraine, and his building and the community around it are filled with fellow refugees from the former Soviet Union, all of whom speak Russian and many of whom, like him, speak Yiddish. Unlike them, Korol had something to keep him in Dnepropetrovsk: the mission of rebuilding a Jewish world that had disappeared. "The rabbi used to tell me that both of us will be the ones to stay in the community to see the last Jews leave," he says through an interpreter. "But I think all the youngsters who are being educated now in the community will stay and keep it going. The ones who are leaving are their grandparents."

Korol and his wife are unusual among the families I interviewed in doubting whether they belong in Israel, but nearly all expressed fondness for the diaspora communities they left behind or where their relatives live. "Argentina is not my home because I feel better here," explains Virginia Burdman, one of those who helped revive the old Tfilat Shalom synagogue in Buenos Aires's slaughterhouse district. She moved to Israel four years ago with her husband, Marcelo, and young son, Brian. Virginia was born a Roman Catholic. She was studying to become a priest in the Anglican Church when she met Marcelo, who is Jewish, and she eventually converted to Judaism. "Of course we miss Buenos Aires," she says, "but each one of us has to find his own place and Israel is my place. I have no regrets in coming, definitely not."

Marcelo is more torn. "It's hard," he says sitting in an ice-cream shop in the center of Tel Aviv's shopping district. "In Argentina we had all our relatives and so many friends. But when I was back visiting Argentina two years ago, Brian and I felt like we were tourists." Marcelo manages sports programs at a community center in Ashqelon, which is nearly identical to his old job in Buenos Aires. He is active in the synagogue in Israel, as he was in Argentina, and works with other Spanish-speaking Jews, including many from Argentina. "Coming to Israel," he says, "changed the place where we live but not the way we live. The Jew who lives in Argentina is not more or less of a Jew than the Jew in Israel."

Danny Lichter talks about Israel being a haven for Jews like his cousin Nicole, and loves visiting her in Paris. But he also admits he does not feel especially connected to the Jewish people or even the Jewish faith. His children are even less so. "I am not expecting support from anyone in the diaspora," says Danny, "but if it happens I think it's very good. Maybe people in the diaspora need to give that support more than I need to get it. My identity first is as an Israeli, then being Jewish. That I am Jewish is obvious. It is the reason I live here and not in Lebanon, not in Syria, not in the United States. I have given my children a connection to Israel, to the earth here, the mountains, the valleys, the fields. I have not made them feel connected to the bigger Jewish world beyond Israel."

Others, alarmed by the barriers that have slowly and almost unconsciously been erected between Israel and world Jewry, are working to find new ways of connecting. For Daniel Briscoe, those contacts take a very personal form. He and his wife, Nava, an Iraqi Jew, are trying to raise their three children to understand that although they are Israelis, they have ties to Iraq and Ireland. He plays for them his Irish drum and tells stories about his Irish upbringing. He has them spend as much time as possible with their Dublin grandparents, Joe and Debby Briscoe. "This is my home definitely," Daniel says, raising his hand to take in the horizon beyond his newly landscaped yard just outside Tel Aviv. "But I know that I also have a home in Ireland. It's two homes definitely. I think that Israel and the diaspora are inseparable."

The Rabinowitzes do not have to look far to keep alive their diaspora contacts. Their old Atlanta congregation of Temple Beth Jacob boasts the highest rate of aliyah of any synagogue in America, with a hundred families having moved to Israel with their southern accents and American style of Orthodoxy. Ben prays every day in a Jerusalem shul with other former Beth Jacob members and they gather as a bigger group for *brits* and bar mitzvahs, parties and funerals. Even their rabbi from their days in Atlanta, Emanuel Feldman, is there. "Most of the families who came did it because they wanted to grow more, Jewishly, than they could in the diaspora," says Feldman. "The next logical extension of growth was to move to the Holy Land."

Nathan Greenbaum admits that he is skeptical about the prospects for survival of much of the diaspora, and especially of Germany's Jewish community. He still refuses to buy German products and for years he refused to set foot in the country, despite invitations from his cousin Helen to visit Düsseldorf. But in the early 1980s he was driving through Scandinavia with Helen and others and "we were making our way back down south down Denmark toward Germany. My wife saw a sign saying, 'Berlin, 350 kilometers,' and she said she would like to visit Berlin. So we did." He returned later, for a professional meeting. He still doubts Germany's community of Jews will sustain itself over the long run, but his visit helped him understand why his cousin and others have opted to stay. In Düsseldorf, he says, "Helen finds she is somebody. If she came to Israel, she would be nothing."

Sima Greenbaum, Nathan's daughter, is more optimistic about the diaspora's future—and she is not trusting to chance or sentimental ties building her bonds to world Jewry. She works with teachers in Jewish schools from North America, South America, and Europe who come to Israel for two weeks. Rather than taking the standard tourist tours of the Western Wall, Masada, and other monuments, these visitors travel the country meeting Israeli teachers, talking to students, and, as Sima says, "seeing Israel as a resource that can help them improve their Jewish education in the diaspora." The same thing is happening with teenagers from the diaspora, with Sima and others helping set up five- to six-week trips where they meet their peers in Israel, sharing music and movies, computer games and Internet explorations, and generally coming to understand what it would be like to live in a Jewish state. And the exchanges are not just in one direction: Israeli teens and teachers take similar trips to America and other diaspora lands.

"There's a much more realistic view on both sides of the diaspora-Israel relationship than there was before. There's a sense that we can learn from each other," says Sima. "What is happening now is at the grass roots. Diaspora communities are seeing that Israel is where the Jewish story is happening. And Israelis are seeing that there is something to be learned from an American view of Judaism in how to be pluralistic, how to deal with things like conflict."

*   *   *

Projects like those are sprouting across Israel, offering a range of models through which Jews in the diaspora and Israel can share experiences. There are ones for the young and others for adults, some focusing on a single issue like the environment and others on broad issues like Jewish heritage. Israeli prototypes, like its "classrooms without walls," are being applied in places as remote as Buenos Aires, with Israel learning how the models flourish, or fail, in the faraway settings. Several of the programs were launched by big funders like the Bronfman and Steinhardt families, but there are lesser-known ones like the exchange under way between Jews who help battered women in Haifa and Jews who are doing the same in Boston.

It started in the old style, with the Jewish federation in Boston contributing $10,000 a year to a Haifa program that offers temporary shelter to women and children who were abused. But the program, part of a wider Boston-Haifa sister-cities network, has evolved from a donor-recipient, money-oriented relationship to a two-way exchange of ideas. Social workers and other professionals from Boston have come to Haifa to meet with their counterparts; the Israelis did the same in Boston. The meetings provided practical lessons on different ways to attack similar problems, with Boston learning from Haifa's strongly feminist approach and its wide array of social services, and Haifa seeing the way Boston focuses on victims' rights and builds impressive coalitions.

Even more important and unanticipated were the subtle messages that were conveyed. The Jewish community in Boston, like many across the diaspora, has had a hard time admitting it has a problem with domestic violence. Seeing that the Jewish state has the same problem and is doing something about it pushed the Jews in Boston to face their crisis. "We blew the whistle that Jewish men do indeed do wonderful things, but they also do not so wonderful things," explains Irit Umanit, director of the Haifa shelter. She and her colleagues were not just dispensing lessons in Boston, they also were learning them. They saw how U.S. synagogues could be vibrant, inclusive places, for women as well as men, the less observant as well as the pious. "It was not accidental that we saw that," Umanit says. "Boston leaders felt it was very important to give us the opportunity to go to different shuls. Our women were very touched. Pluralism within Judaism seems to us to be a very important issue that the American diaspora is pushing us to explore."

Rabbi Robert Samuels has been exploring such issues for forty years, ever since he arrived in Israel from Chicago. His Israel-diaspora exchange takes the form of the sprawling Leo Baeck Education Center in Haifa. More than 200 young Jews from abroad are studying there now, most from Ethiopia and the former Soviet Union, and 600 others have come over the years from America and Western Europe. There are 1,600 students at Baeck's highly esteemed high school, 100 young people participate in its early childhood education program, and thousands of adults come to swim or play tennis, learn languages or worship. Samuels is reaching out to the diaspora at the same time he is exposing Israel to a Reform Judaism that is almost nonexistent there. "I'm not one of those Israelis who believes the diaspora is dead," says the peripatetic rabbi, who looks like an aging Bohemian with his ridge of tumbled white hair, black jeans, white sneakers, and purple-and-white shirt with a "South of the Border" logo. "We should strive for Jews in lands of freedom to identify strongly as Jews, to be proud of their heritage. At the same time we must strive to make Israel so free, so democratic, so pluralistic, so egalitarian that such self-loving diaspora Jews will want to come to Israel as either their first or second home. Voltaire said that all cultured people have two fatherlands—their own and France. We must strive to get such a formula. All diaspora Jews have two motherlands, their own and Israel, and they can live in either or both."

Exchanges like those are precisely what Israeli leaders like Yossi Beilin have in mind when they talk about a new covenant between Israel and world Jewry. They want to demonstrate to diaspora Jews that Israel is not just a place in history books but a living, energized land, and to show Israelis that the diaspora is an equally dynamic place where Jews can and do feel at home. They understand the concern that led newly elected prime minister Sharon to call for all diaspora Jews to come to Israel, but they also understand just how outmoded that solution is for Israel as well as for the diaspora. In the process of forging their novel solution, Beilin and other young leaders hope to inject new meaning into a seemingly stale notion like "the Jewish people." Many of their programs are at an early stage, and too many focus only on the Israel-America relationship to the exclusion of flourishing Jewish communities like the one in Paris and struggling ones like Dnepropetrovsk. But it is a start.

To reach the next stage, Beilin and others are forming an Israel-diaspora forum that he calls a "coalition of the *macher*s." It would assemble leading businessmen, politicians, and intellectuals to craft an action agenda and eventually to supplant institutions like the Jewish Agency that were founded on the outdated donor-recipient relationship. At the heart of their agenda is Birthright Israel, a program that brings diaspora Jews aged eighteen to twenty-six on an all-expenses-paid ten-day trip to Israel. The $210 million initiative got going in 1998; is sponsored by Jewish philanthropists, the Israeli government, and Jewish communities worldwide; and includes everything from meeting Israeli youth to taking courses on topics like Jewish mysticism, Jewish wine, and Jewish sex. The hope is to involve nearly 100,000 young people a year, whetting their appetite for Jewish culture, getting many to come back to Israel on their own, and rekindling the diaspora-Israel romance.

The new partnership is also spawning a new language. In Israel, there now is a ministry of Israeli Society and the World Jewish Community, with a rabbi from Denmark fittingly serving as the first minister. The new agency is part of a trend that has many in Israel and elsewhere urging that the word "diaspora" be replaced by an expression that is less Israel-oriented and that acknowledges that Jews living in places like Dublin and Atlanta are as much at home as those in Tel Aviv and Haifa.

"Jews overseas" and "Jews elsewhere" are two proposed substitutes. Even the venerable Museum of the Diaspora in Tel Aviv now often refers to itself as the Museum of the Jewish People.

Whatever it is called, what matters is that confidence is growing in the diaspora that it has an existence worthy of celebration and preservation. Israelis are coming to understand that the diaspora matters to Israel at least as much today as it did in the country's early days. The more secure Jews become in Israel—and in communities from Paris to Boston—the more tempted they will be to look at the Jewish world the way I started out: as us and them. But that security also can encourage them to reach out to their cousins across the divide without fear of being overwhelmed or undervalued. History and reason argue that the more options Jews have, the more likely they are to survive and thrive.

Glossary

aleph-bet: Hebrew ABCs

aliyah: immigration of Jews to Israel

bet din: Jewish court of law

bimah: pulpit

bobbeh/bubbeh: grandmother

brit milah: ritual circumcision

brochas: blessings, such as over bread or wine

Chabad: popular name for Lubavitch Hasidic movement

challah: special bread for Sabbath and festivals

cheder: traditional Jewish school

chesed: kindness and charity

daven: pray

farfelach: little pasta squares typically served in soup

gefilte fish: boiled dumplings of chopped fish mixed with matzo meal, egg, onion, and spices

glatt: rigorous form of kosher

goyim: non-Jew, at times used disparagingly

Haggadah: text for Passover Seder

halakhah: Jewish law

Hasidism: Jewish movement founded in eighteenth-century Eastern Europe, stressing piety and mysticism

havurah: informal congregation or fellowship group

hazan: a cantor

JCC: Jewish community center

Judenrein: expression used by Nazis meaning "free of Jews"

ketubbah: Jewish marriage contract

Kiddush: Sabbath and holiday blessing over wine

kippah; kippot (pl.): scullcap

kishke: innards stuffed with matzo meal, then boiled and roasted

kollel: advanced school for Talmudic learning

kreplach: boiled dough filled with meat or cheese and served in soup

Lubavitch: branch of Hasidic Judaism

macher: political mover or shaker

Me'ah: 100

mentshlicheyt: decency or humanity

mezuzah: parchment scroll affixed to doorposts of Jewish homes

mikvah: ritual bath

Minchah: afternoon prayer

minyan: quorum of ten Jews required for prayer service

mitzvah; mitzvot (pl.): a good deed

mohel: religious authority who performs circumcisions

nudnick: pest

payess: sidelocks worn by Orthodox Jews

pushke: charity box

rebbe: Hasidic rabbi, sometimes used for other especially learned rabbis

rebbitzen: wife of rabbi

Shabbat or Shabbes: Sabbath

Sheeny: disparaging term for Jew

Shema: watchwords of Jewish faith, recited twice a day

shiddukh: arranged marriage

shivah: seven-day period of mourning

Shoah: Hebrew for Holocaust

shofar: ram's horn blown during Rosh Hashanah and Yom Kippur

shtetl: Jewish townlet in Eastern Europe

shukkle: to move up and down while praying

shul: synagogue

tallith: prayer shawl

Talmud: collection of ancient rabbinic texts consisting of Mishnah and
   Gemara

tefillin: small leather boxes containing scripture, bound to forehead and
   arm during morning prayers

Torah: five books of Moses

tzedakah: social justice and kindness

tzimmes: carrot stew

tzitzis: fringed undergarment worn as reminder to keep commandments

yarmulke: skullcap

yeshiva: religious academy

Yiddishkeyt: Jewishness

zeydeh: grandfather

References

Introduction. Charting the Journey

Council of Jewish Federations. *1990 National Jewish Population Study.* New York, 1991.

Dershowitz, Alan M. *The Vanishing American Jew: In Search of Jewish Identity for the Next Century.* Boston: Little, Brown and Company, 1997.

Eisenberg, Robert. *Boychiks in the Hood: Travels in the Hasidic Underground.* New York: HarperCollins Publishers, 1996.

Kamenetz, Rodger. *The Jew in the Lotus.* San Francisco: HarperSanFrancisco, 1994.

Rawidowicz, Simon. *Israel, the Ever-Dying People and Other Essays.* Cranbury, N.J.: Associated University Presses, 1986.

Reisman, Bernard, and Joel I. Reisman. *Life on the Frontier: The Jews of Alaska.* Waltham, Mass.: Brandeis University, 1995.

Singer, David, ed. *American Jewish Year Book.* New York: American Jewish Committee, 1998.

Wasserstein, Bernard. *Vanishing Diaspora: The Jews in Europe since 1945.* Cambridge: Harvard University Press, 1996.

Interviews with Steven Bayme, Yossi Beilin, Steven M. Cohen, Rachel Cowan, Sergio DellaPergola, Sherry Frank, Sidney Goldstein, David Gordis, David Harris, Sherry Israel, David Link, Diana Pinto, Shulamit Reinharz, Bernard Reisman, Herbert Rosenblum, Jonathan Sarna, Jeff Scheckner, Michael Schneider, Edward Serotta, Barry Shrage, Paul Spiegel, Henry Stevens, Dorothy Tye, Philip Warburg, Michael Williams, and Lenny Zakim.

Chapter 1. Düsseldorf: In the Land of the Murderers

Bodemann, Y. Michal, ed. *Jews, Germans, Memory: Reconstructions of Jewish Life in Germany.* Ann Arbor: University of Michigan Press, 1996.
Brenner, Michael. *After the Holocaust: Rebuilding Jewish Lives in Postwar Germany.* Princeton: Princeton University Press, 1997.
Brenner, Michael, and Derek J. Penslar, eds. *In Search of Jewish Community: Jewish Identities in Germany and Austria, 1918–1933.* Bloomington: Indiana University Press, 1998.
Encyclopaedia Judaica.
"Former Soviet Jews Find Uneasy Peace in Germany," *New York Times,* 6 August 2000.
Genger, Angela. *Jews in Düsseldorf: A Fotografic Memor Book.* Düsseldorf: Mahn und Gedenkstatte, 1998.
"German Police Focus on Far-Right Link to Bomb," *Jerusalem Post,* 30 July 2000.
"Germans Say Nine Wounded by Bomb Were Immigrants," *New York Times,* 29 July 2000.
"Germany as a Haven for Fleeing Jews," *Jerusalem Post,* 16 February 1999.
Rabinbach, Anson, and Jack Zipes, eds. *Germans and Jews Since the Holocaust: The Changing Situation in West Germany.* New York: Holmes & Meier Publishers, Inc., 1986.
Rappaport, Lynn. *Jews in Germany after the Holocaust: Memory, Identity, and Jewish-German Relations.* Cambridge, England: Cambridge University Press, 1997.
Serotta, Edward. *Jews, Germany, Memory: A Contemporary Portrait.* Berlin: Nicolai, 1996.
Stern, Susan, ed. *Speaking Out: Jewish Voices from United Germany.* Chicago: Edition Q, 1995.
"U.S. Eyes 50,000 Limit on Soviet Émigrés in '90," *Washington Post,* 12 September 1989.
Wiessmann, Hans. *From Horror to Hope: Germany, the Jews and Israel.* New York: German Information Center, 1997.

Interviews with Stefan Bajohr, Jeannette Barth, Michael Bleiberg, Arnold Blitzer, Marion Blitzer, Leonid Borissov, Eugenia Brecher, Esra Cohn, Anna Drosner, Adrian Flohr, Jaffa Flohr, Talli Flohr, Yoel Flohr, Angela Genger, Michael Goldberger, Burkhard Hirsch, Avner Horowitz, Isidor Israel Horowitz, Oded Horowitz, Helen Israel, Robert Viktor Israel, Judith Jacobius, Michael Jedwabny, Melike Karamustafa, Jan Katschko, Juergen Krueger, Orly Leventer, Eugene Mann, Salova El Mokhtari, Bella Monastirsky, Ludmila Monastirsky, Valery Monastirsky, Irvin Nagy, Daniel Padan, Jan Popp-Sewing, Tanya Rubinstein-Horowitz, Thomas Ruzicka, Bettina Schneider, Beate Schwammenthal-Zwecker, Marlies Smeets, Leonie Spiegel, Paul Spiegel, Vera Steyvers, Juan Strauss, Laura Strauss, Michael Szentei-Heise, Alexander Tamler, Dora Tamler, Ronald Tamler, Marcus Thill, David Zapesozke, Larisa Zapesozke, and Mara Zuckermann. Group interviews at Jewish nursing home and with classes at Jewish day school, public school, and Hebrew school.

Chapter 2. Dnepropetrovsk: Lifting the Iron Curtain

Abramson, Henry. *A Prayer for the Government: Ukrainians and Jews in Revolutionary Times, 1917–1920.* Cambridge: Harvard University Press, 1999.

———. "The Scattering of Amalek: A Model for Understanding the Ukrainian-Jewish Conflict." *East European Jewish Affairs* 24:1 (1994).

———. "Shouldering the Burdens of History: Aspects of the Ukrainian-Jewish Encounter since Independence," unpublished manuscript from a conference entitled "Problems of Development of Ukraine since Independence: A View from Canada" (University of Toronto, 1999).

American Jewish Joint Distribution Committee. *Snapshots: JDC Activities in the Former Soviet Union.* New York, 1999.

"Another Aim: The Health of Judaism," *Boston Globe*, 27 May 1998.

Aster, Howard, and Peter J. Potichnyj. *Jewish Ukrainian Relations: Two Solitudes.* Oakville, Ont.; Mosaic Press, 1983.

———, eds. *Ukrainian-Jewish Relations in Historical Perspective.* Edmonton, Alb.: Canadian Institute of Ukrainian Studies, 1988

Brym, Robert J. *The Jews of Moscow, Kiev, and Minsk: Identity, Antisemitism, Emigration.* New York: New York University Press, 1994.

"Down and Out in Ukraine," *Jerusalem Post*, 3 July 1998.

Encyclopaedia Judaica.

Gidwitz, Betsy. *Journey to Jewish Population Centers in Ukraine.* Chicago: Gidwitz, 1999.

———. *Post-Soviet Jewry: The Critical Issues.* Jerusalem: Jerusalem Center for Public Affairs, 1999.

Hamm, Michael F. *Kiev: A Portrait, 1800–1917.* Princeton: Princeton University Press, 1993.

Hanover, Nathan. *Abyss of Despair: The Famous 17th Century Chronicle Depicting Jewish Life in Russia and Poland during the Chmielnicki Massacres of 1648–49.* New York: Bloch, 1950.

"In Ukraine, the Diagnosis Is Faulty Care," *Boston Globe*, 27 May 1998.

Kaminetzky, Yosef Yitzchak. *The Cities of the Rebbe's Childhood: Nikolayev and Yakatrinoslav-Dnepropetrovsk.* Kfar Chabad, Israel: Maayanot, 1995.

Patkin, Judy, and Sheila Galland. *Trip to Dnepropetrovsk, Ukraine.* Waltham, Mass.: Action for Post-Soviet Jewry, 1997.

———. *Trip to Jewish Communities in Ukraine and Moldova.* Waltham, Mass.: Action for Post-Soviet Jewry, 1999.

Patkin, Judy, Sheila Galland, and Martha Moore. *Trip to Ukraine and Russia.* Waltham, Mass.: Action for Post-Soviet Jewry, 1993.

"Rabbi Schneerson Led a Small Hasidic Sect to World Prominence," *New York Times*, 13 June 1994.

"Rabbi Schneerson's Legacy," *New York Times*, 13 June 1994.

Reid, Anna. *Borderland: A Journey through the History of Ukraine.* London: Weidenfeld & Nicolson, 1997.

"Relighting Flame: Jersey Rabbi Rebuilding Religion in Soviet," *Newark Star-Ledger*, 31 March 1991.

"The Role of Politics in Contemporary Russian Antisemitism," *Jerusalem Letter,* 15 September 1999.

Solchanyk, Roman, ed. *Ukraine: From Chernobyl to Sovereignty.* New York: St. Martin's Press, 1992.

Subtelny, Orest. *Ukraine: A History.* Toronto: University of Toronto Press, 1988.

"Ukrainian Jewish Community Back on the Map," *Jerusalem Post,* 13 April 1999.

"Ukrainian KGB Head Apologizes to Rebbe," *Jerusalem Post,* 30 March 1992.

Weinryb, Bernard D. "The Hebrew Chronicles on Bohdan Khmel'nyts'kyi and the Cossack-Polish War," *Harvard Ukrainian Studies* 1:2 (1977).

Interviews with Henry Abramson, Elicha Baram, Yaakov D. Bleich, Karl Blyakher, Marina Brez, Vyacheslav Brez, Marx Chernostrik, Ted Comet, Sergio DellaPergola, Robert De Lossa, Alexander Dolnik, Yossi Drizin, Alexandr Abramovitch Fridkis, Barbara Gaffin, Betsy Gidwitz, Zvi Gitelman, Yosef Yitzchak Kaminetzky, Chany Kaminezki, Shmuel Kaminezki, Michael Karshenbaum, Nancy Kaufman, David Kolchinsky, Dina Kolchinsky, Grigory Korol, Uri Laber, David Link, Ksenia Lisovskaya, Larisa Lisovskaya, Vadim Mnushkin, Tamara Olshanytska, Judy Patkin, Scott Richman, Alexander Rivman, Sasha Rivman, Dmitry Rogovoy, Inna Rogovoy, Jakov Rogovoy, Malvina Ruvinsky, Benjamin Sachs, Jonathan Sarna, Aliza Shenhar, Mark Shlyak, Arkady Shmist, Yakov Sidelkovsky, Volodymyr Vynogradov, and David Wilfond. Group interviews with Hillel college students and Jewish community choir.

Chapter 3. Boston: Athens and Jerusalem

Congregation Beth El of the Sudbury River Valley. *Vetaher Libenu.* 1980.

Dershowitz, Alan M. *Chutzpah.* New York: Simon & Schuster, 1991.

Dinnerstein, Leonard. *Antisemitism in America.* New York: Oxford University Press, 1994.

Encyclopaedia Judaica.

Feig, Konnilyn G. *Portraits of the Past: The Jews of Portland.* Portland: Jewish Bicentennial Oral History Program/Jewish Federation of Southern Maine, 1977.

Gal, Allon. *Brandeis of Boston.* Cambridge: Harvard University Press, 1980.

Gamm, Gerald H. *Urban Exodus: Why the Jews Left Boston and the Catholics Stayed.* Cambridge: Harvard University Press, 1999.

"Great Fire of 1908 Was Third Largest in U.S. History," *Chelsea Record,* 4 February 2000.

Greene, Andrew, and Heather Greene. *Congregation Shaarei Tefillah: History.* 1997.

Hentoff, Nat. *Boston Boy.* New York: Alfred A. Knopf, 1986.

Israel, Richard J. "History of the Newton Centre Minyan." Web site.

Israel, Sherry R. *Comprehensive Report on the 1995 Demographic Study.* Boston: Combined Jewish Philanthropies, 1997.

"Jewish Faith Shows Signs of Renewal Despite Gloomy Forecast," *Boston Globe,* 20 February 1985.

Levine, Hillel, and Lawrence Harmon. *The Death of an American Jewish Community: A Tragedy of Good Intentions.* New York: The Free Press, 1992.

Linenthal, Arthur J. *First a Dream: The History of Boston's Jewish Hospitals 1896 to 1928.* Boston: Beth Israel Countway, 1990.

Pokross, David R. *Onward: Memoirs of David R. Pokross*, 1994.

Sarna, Jonathan D., and Ellen Smith, eds. *The Jews of Boston: Essays on the Occasion of the Centenary (1895–1995) of the Combined Jewish Philanthropies of Greater Boston.* Boston: Northeastern University Press, 1995.

Schick, Marvin. *A Census of Jewish Day Schools in the United States.* New York: Avi Chai Foundation, 2000.

Synnott, Marcia Graham. *The Half-Opened Door: Discrimination and Admissions at Harvard, Yale, and Princeton, 1900–1970.* Westport, Conn.: Greenwood Press, 1979.

Tye, Minnie. Taped interview by Dorothy and Mauray Tye, 1979.

Tye, Samuel. Transcript of interview by Phil Primack, 1974.

White, Theodore H. *In Search of History: A Personal Adventure.* New York: Harper & Row, Publishers, 1978.

Woodman, Bertha. *From the Hill to Main Street: Jewish Life and Work in Haverhill Massachusetts 1880–1940.* Haverhill: Trustees of the Haverhill Public Library, 1987.

Interviews with Susan Ansin, Jim Ball, Paula Brody, Samuel Chlel, Jason Chudnofsky, Judy Chudnofsky, Judy Corlin, Len Corlin, Lorie Corlin, Scott Corlin, Anita Diamant, Susan Ebert, Ruth Fein, Gerald Gamm, Andrea Goldberg, Norman Goldberg, Rachel Goldberg, Suzanne Goldberg, David Gordis, Irving Halpern, William Hamilton, Bernard Hyatt, Leora Isaacs, Richard Israel, Sherry Israel, Nancy Kaufman, Ira Korffnow, Larry Kushner, Daniel Lehmann, David Link, Larry Lowenthal, Bernard Mehlman, James O'Toole, Carl Perkins, David Pokross, Herbert Pollack, Michael Quinlin, Irving Rabb, Shulamit Reinharz, Herbert Rosenblum, Cindi Rubinoff, Stephan Rubinoff, Benjamin Samuels, Jonathan Sarna, Andy Savitz, Herb Savitz, Penelope McGee Savitz, Leonard Saxe, Marvin Schick, Barry Shrage, Ellen Smith, David Starr, Larry Sternberg, Steve Stone, Alan Temperow, Ariella Tye, Carol Tye, Donald Tye, Dorothy Tye, Eileen Tye, James Tye, Jerry Tye, Leslie Tye, Mark Tye, Randy Tye, Raymond Tye, David Wolfman, Arnold Zieff, David Zieff, Paul Zieff, Steven Zieff, and Sylvia Zieff.

Chapter 4. Buenos Aires: An Explosive Awakening

"Alongside the Dead in Argentina," *New York Times*, 2 August 1994.

"Argentina's Failure," *Jerusalem Report*, 4 September 1997.

"Argentina's Jews Cry for Their Torn Heart," *New York Times*, 21 July 1994.

"Argentine Bomb Trial to Begin Soon," *Jerusalem Post*, 18 July 1999.

"At Least 6 Die as Blast Destroys Israel's Embassy in Buenos Aires," *New York Times*, 18 March 1992.

Avni, Haim. *Argentina and the Jews: A History of Jewish Immigration.* Tuscaloosa: University of Alabama Press, 1991.

Beller, Jacob. *Jews in Latin America.* New York: Jonathan David Publishers, 1969.

"Deadly Blast and an Itinerant's Tale: Hazy Figure May Hold the Key to Anti-Semitic Bombings in Argentina," *Los Angeles Times*, 17 April 1999.

Elazar, Daniel J. *Jewish Communities in Frontier Societies: Argentina, Australia and South Africa*. New York: Holmes & Meier, 1983.

Elkin, Judith Laikin. *The Jews of Latin America*. New York: Holmes & Meier, 1998.

Encyclopaedia Judaica.

Gerchunoff, Alberto. *The Jewish Gauchos of the Pampas*. New York: Abelard-Schulman, 1959.

"Islamic Jihad Claims Attack in Argentina, Israel Vows Reprisal," *Washington Post*, 19 March 1992.

Kiernan, Sergio. *A Glimmer of Hope: The AMIA Bombing, Five Years Later*. Buenos Aires: American Jewish Committee, 1999.

Mirelman, Victor A. *Jewish Buenos Aires, 1890–1930: In Search of an Identity*. Detroit: Wayne State University Press, 1990.

Timerman, Jacobo. *Prisoner without a Name, Cell without a Number*. New York: Alfred A. Knopf, 1981.

Weisbrot, Robert. *The Jews of Argentina: From the Inquisition to Perón*. Philadelphia: The Jewish Publication Society of America, 1979.

"What Would Evita Say?" *Jerusalem Report*, 20 July 1998.

Zemer, Moshe. "The Rabbinic Ban on Conversion in Argentina," *Judaism* 37:1 (1998).

Interviews with Yitzhak Aviran, Haim Avni, Alejandro Avruj, Lydia Azubel, José Barbaccia, Gabriel Berger, Sergio Bergman, Alfredo Berlfein, Aida Bortnik, Enrique Burbinski, Rogelio Cichowolski, Daniel Colodenco, Sergio DellaPergola, Lili Esses, Isidoro Felcman, Martin Feldman, Laura Ginsberg, Daniel Goldman, Raul Gulman, Beatriz Gurevich, Pablo Klersfeld, Gilbert Lewi, Cipe Lincovsky, Natali Lisman, Naomi Meyer, Alfredo Neuburger, Daniel Oppenheimer, Isidoro Perelmutter, Marcos Perelmutter, Debi Pinson, Horacio Carlos Pinson, Liliana Pinson, William Recant, Brian Reznik, Mario Ringler, Mario Rojzman, Yaacov Rubel, Herman Schiller, Angel Schindel, Diana Sperling, Jacobo Timerman, Eliahu Toker, Mario Trumper, Anita Weinstein, and Mauricio Wior. Group interviews at Temple Bet El's day school and elderly study group, and with members of Memoria Activa.

Chapter 5. Dublin: Who Ever Heard of an Irish Jew?

Briscoe, Robert, with Alden Hatch. *For the Life of Me*. Boston: Little, Brown and Company, 1958.

Encyclopaedia Judaica.

Forde, W. P. *A Case Study of the Hebrew Community in Cork City*. Cork: University College Cork, 1985.

Hyman, Louis. *The Jews of Ireland: From the Earliest Times to the Year 1910*. Jerusalem: The Jewish Historical Society of England and Israel Universities Press, 1972.

Keogh, Dermot. *Jews in Twentieth-Century Ireland: Refugees, Anti-Semitism and the Holocaust*. Cork: Cork University Press, 1998.

Lentin, Ronit, and Robbie McVeigh. *Racism and Anti-racism in Ireland*. Dublin: Irish Academic Press, 1999.

Nolan, Christopher. *Under the Eye of the Clock: The Life Story of Christopher Nolan*. New York: St. Martin's Press, 1987.

Interviews with David Abrahamson, Maurice Abrahamson, Colin Acton, Ronnie Appleton, Asher Benson, Ben Briscoe, Brian Briscoe, Carol Briscoe, Daniel Briscoe, David Briscoe, Debbie Briscoe, Joe Briscoe, Robert Briscoe, Gavin Broder, Carolyn Collins, Alexandra Crivon, Louise Crivon, Quentin Crivon, Zvi Gabay, Gerald Goldberg, Ida Gressis, Robert Gressis, Howard Gross, Nick Harris, Pamela Harris, Chaim Herzog, Esther Heselberg, Dermot Keogh, Sandra Leventon, Maurice Manning, Nick Miller, Norine Miller, Cleo Morrison, Joe Morrison, Carmel Niland, Joan Briscoe O'Reilly, Brian Quinn, Fred Rosehill, Cyril Rosenberg, Adam Ross, Colin Sheena, Raphael Siev, Martin Simmons, Marie Smyth, Jacqueline Solomon, Michael Solomons, Amelia Stein, Mervyn Taylor, David Warm, Hubert Wine, and Natalie Wynn.

Chapter 6. Paris: Getting Along, Getting Ahead

Adler, Jacques. *The Jews of Paris and the Final Solution: Communal Response and Internal Conflicts, 1940–1944*. New York: Oxford University Press, 1987.
"1895 Cover-up Reveals Lessons for Today," *Orlando Sentinel*, 7 April 1999.
Encyclopaedia Judaica.
"A French Embarrassment Even after 100 Years," *Jerusalem Post*, 19 October 1994.
Golub, Jennifer. *Anti-Semitism in France: Recent Trends*. New York: American Jewish Committee, 1994.
Graetz, Michael. *The Jews in Nineteenth-Century France: From the French Revolution to the Alliance Israelite Universelle*. Stanford: Stanford University Press, 1996.
Hyman, Paula E. *The Jews of Modern France*. Berkeley: University of California Press, 1998.
"In Paris, Tracing the Roots of the Jewish Community," *International Herald Tribune*, 12 June 1993.
"J'accuse—The Article That Altered the Course of History," *Financial Post*, 16 January 1998.
"Paris' Jewish Quarter Thrives Despite Change," *Denver Post*, 23 May 1993.
Pinto, Diana. *Beyond Anti-Semitism: The New Jewish Presence in Europe*. New York: American Jewish Committee, 1994.
———. *A New Jewish Identity for Post-1989 Europe*. London: Institute for Jewish Policy Research, 1996.
"A Shadow on the Soul of France," *Los Angeles Times*, 12 May 1992.

Interviews with Alexandre Adler, Sophie Aizenfish, Marilyn August, Mendel Azimov, Stephanie Azoulay, Yvonne Baby, Antoine Bebe, Beatrice Birnbaum, Henry Bulawko, Anne Bunde-Birouste, Moise Cohen, Eliane Corrin, Marc Danzon, Sergio Della-Pergola, Elaine Ganley, Henri Hajdenberg, Stella Kac, Nicole Kac-Ohana, Serge Klarsfeld, Nathalie Levy, Felix Mosbacher, Benjamin Ohana, Karen Ohana, Michael Ohana, Sydney Ohana, Diana Pinto, Eric de Rothschild, Olivier Rubinstein, David

Saada, Roger Salloch, Max Sarcey, Paulette Sarcey, Alberto Senderey, Maurice Szwarc, Myriam Szwarc, Huge Tannenbaum, Simone Veil, Jean-Jacques Wahl, and Michael Williams.

Chapter 7. Atlanta: Hebrew with a Southern Accent

"After 69 Years of Silence, Lynching Victim Is Cleared," *New York Times*, 8 March 1982.

Atlanta Historical Journal, special issue on History of Atlanta's Jewish Community (Fall 1979).

Bauman, Mark K. *Harry H. Epstein and the Rabbinate as Conduit for Change*. Rutherford, N.J.: Fairleigh Dickinson University Press, 1994.

Bauman, Mark K., and Doris H. Goldstein. *The Jews of Atlanta: 150 Years of Creating Community*. Atlanta: William Breman Jewish Heritage Museum, 1996.

Birnie, Joseph Earle. *The History of the National Bank of Georgia*. Atlanta: Conger Printing Co., 1978.

Blumberg, Janice Rothschild. *One Voice: Rabbi Jacob M. Rothschild and the Troubled South*. Macon, Ga.: Mercer University Press, Inc., 1985.

Dinnerstein, Leonard. *The Leo Frank Case*. New York: Columbia University Press, 1968.

Encyclopaedia Judaica.

Eplan, Elise R. *The Early Years of The Atlanta Jewish Community: The Ordeal of Settlement*. Waltham, Mass.: Brandeis University, 1982.

Eplan, Samuel L., as told to Leon S. Eplan. "Biography of Eplan Family and Sidelights of Early Atlanta," 1971.

Evans, Eli N. *The Provincials: A Personal History of Jews in the South*. New York: Atheneum, 1973.

Feldman, Emanuel. *Tales out of Shul: The Unorthodox Journal of an Orthodox Rabbi*. New York: Shaar Press, 1996.

"Frank Case Still Painful for Atlanta's Jews," *Washington Post*, 27 March 1982.

Gettinger, Max C. *Coming of Age: The Atlanta Jewish Federation 1962–1982*. Hoboken, N.J.: KTAV Publishing House, Inc., 1994.

Golden, Harry. *A Little Girl Is Dead*. Cleveland: The World Publishing Co., 1965.

Goldstein, Doris H. *From Generation to Generation: A Centennial History of Congregation Ahavath Achim 1887–1987*. Atlanta: Capricorn Corporation, 1987.

Greene, Melissa Fay. *The Temple Bombing*. New York: Fawcett Columbine, 1996.

Hertzberg, Steven. *Strangers within the Gate City: The Jews of Atlanta 1845–1915*. Philadelphia: Jewish Publication Society of America, 1978.

"In *Parade*, Lynch Mob Meets Love Story," *San Francisco Examiner*, 18 December 1998.

"Jews of the South: The End of an Era," *Globe and Mail*, 9 August 1999.

Metro Atlanta Chamber of Commerce, demographic and economic growth data.

Schick, Marvin. *A Census of Jewish Day Schools in the United States*. New York: Avi Chai Foundation, 2000.

Sheskin, Ira. *Atlanta's Growing Jewish Population*. Atlanta: The Atlanta Jewish Federation–Ukeles Associates, Inc., 1999.

————. *The 1996 Jewish Population Study of Atlanta*. Atlanta: The Atlanta Jewish Federation-Ukeles Associates, Inc., 1996.

"You Will Find Him on Mary Phagan's Grave," *Newsday*, 25 November 1998.

Interviews with Cecil Alexander, David Alexander, Elaine Alexander, Kent Alexander, Miles Alexander, Joel Babbit, Sandy Berman, Sherry Blanton, Marvin Botnick, Gerald Cohen, Jay Davis, Daryn DeVille, Elise Eplan, Harlan Eplan, Jana Eplan, Leon Eplan, Madalyne Eplan, Gil Eplan-Frankel, Gail Evans, Emanuel Feldman, Ilan Feldman, Sidney Feldman, Cheryl Finkel, Robert Franco, Sara Franco, Sherry Frank, Craig Frankel, Tim Funk, Carolyn Goldsmith, Arnold Goodman, Mark Greenberg, Melissa Fay Greene, Shira Grossman, Leora Isaacs, Randy Karesh, Don Kent, Danica Kombol, Stephen Kutner, Joshua Lesser, Larry Levin, Elliott Levitas, David Lewis, Robert Marcovitch, Sam Massell, Ellen Mazer, Yossi New, I. J. Rosenberg, Molly Samuel, Belinda Sandalon, David Sarnat, Marvin Schick, Lori Kagan Schwarz, S. Stephen Selig III, Marvin Shoob, Alvin Sugarman, Ozell Sutton, Toni Troop, Margaret Strauss Weiller, and Erwin Zaban. Group interviews with youth leaders of Atlanta chapter of the American Jewish Committee, and with second and eighth grade classes at the Epstein Solomon Schechter School of Atlanta.

Epilogue. Israel: A Partnership of Equals

American Jewish Committee. *American Jewish Year Book*. New York, 1998.

Beilin, Yossi. *On Unity and Continuity: A New Framework for Jewish Life in Israel and the Diaspora*. Jerusalem: Institute of the World Jewish Congress, 2000.

Cohen, Steven M. *Religious Stability and Ethnic Decline: Emerging Patterns of Jewish Identity in the United States*. New York: Florence G. Heller–Jewish Community Centers Association Research Center, 1998.

Council of Jewish Federations. *1990 National Jewish Population Study*. New York, 1991.

Shenhar, Aliza. *Shenhar Report on Jewish Education in the Non-Orthodox Public School System in Israel*. Haifa, 1994.

Interviews with Haim Avni, Mordechai Bar-On, Yossi Beilin, Daniel Briscoe, Marcelo Burdman, Virginia Burdman, Joel Cahen, Steven M. Cohen, Sergio DellaPergola, Lauri Friedman, Nomi Friedman, Nurit Friedman, Victor Friedman, David Gordis, Nathan Greenbaum, Sima Greenbaum, Yosef Yitzchak Kaminetzky, Grigory Korol, Eli Lederhendler, Danny Lichter, Michael Melchior, Ben Rabinowitz, Sonya Rabinowitz, Shulamit Reinharz, Robert Samuels, Jonathan Sarna, Aliza Shenhar, Yuli Tamir, Irit Umanit, Philip Warburg, and Tamar Warburg.

Acknowledgments

When I began to think about writing this book most of those I asked for advice politely suggested that I think again. The topic was too controversial, they said, and I was too much the novice on matters of Jewish community and continuity. Luckily, I also asked Lenny Zakim, head of the New England office of the Anti-Defamation League, who urged me to push ahead. To show he meant it he offered to write the book with me, a proposal I jumped at. That was shortly before Lenny was diagnosed with cancer. Even as he fought to ward off the disease he was generous with his advice and support.

So were Barry Shrage and David Gordis, who had helped set the vision for the Boston Jewish community and endorsed my thesis that something equally inspired is happening across the diaspora. Barry, a master fund-raiser as head of Combined Jewish Philanthropies of Greater Boston, convinced me I could raise any money I would need to travel around the world. David, president of Hebrew College, steered me to sources who helped select my diaspora cities and let me work through his Wilstein Institute of Jewish Policy Studies. Leaders from the American Jewish Committee, the American Jewish Joint Distribution

Committee, and other organizations also weighed in with valuable advice on communities to target and people to talk to.

All I needed then was a publisher. Jill Kneerim, the best book agent there is, believed in this book even before I did. She edited and reedited my proposal, and landed me a good contract. She also matched me up with Deborah Brody, whose incisive mind, agile editing, and total enthusiasm for the project made our interaction more enjoyable than any author has the right to expect. She demonstrated that commitment when, months after we had signed a contract, she took the book with her to Henry Holt when she accepted a job there as senior editor. Thanks to Holt publisher John Sterling for having the faith in Deborah and me to take it on and to Muriel Jorgensen for gifted copyediting. None of this would have been possible, of course, unless I got time away from my job at the *Boston Globe*. Editor Matt Storin, who already had given me two leaves in the six years he had been back at the paper, said yes again. I am grateful to him, to managing editor Louisa Williams, and to my health/science section colleagues who had to work even harder because I was gone.

Philip Warburg, Sally Jacobs, and Andy Savitz were there when I was deciding whether to do this book, when I was frantically trying to get all my reporting and writing done during my year's book leave, and when I was working to make sense of things at the end. Each read the entire book, offering advice that I at times complained was a bit too candid, and each helped substantially in making it better.

I had at least one additional reader for each chapter, all experts on that Jewish community or topic and all exceedingly helpful. Jonathan Sarna of Brandeis University reviewed the introduction. My reader for Düsseldorf was Michael Szentei-Heise, chief administrator of that city's Jewish community, while for Dnepropetrovsk it was Robert De Lossa, director of publications at the Harvard Ukrainian Research Institute. Ellen Smith, curator of the American Jewish Historical Society, carefully critiqued and edited the Boston chapter. Doing the same for Buenos Aires was Anita Weinstein, who runs the Federation of Jewish Communities of Argentina and the Documentation and Information Center on Argentine Jewry. For Dublin my reader was the husband-wife dynamic duo of Quentin and Louise Crivon, and for Paris it was Jean-Jacques Wahl, general director of the Alliance Israélite Universelle. Ellen

Mazer and Sandy Berman of the Jewish Federation of Greater Atlanta reviewed the Atlanta chapter, and David Gordis read the concluding one on Israel and the diaspora. Credit for things I got right goes partly to those specialists but blame for anything I got wrong is mine alone.

Even with a generous contract from my publisher, I needed more money to finance my travel and that of Ilene Perlman, the ace photographer who worked with me. Dorothy Tye, my mother and great friend, got things started as always. My uncle and confidant, Ray Tye, opened his wallet and his Rolodex, neither of which I could have done without. Others who gave, and thereby made this book feasible, were the Stone Charitable Foundation, Steve Grossman, Harold Burson, Sir Maurice Hatter, Ted Benard Cutler, the Irwin Chafetz Family Charitable Trust, Harold Grinspoon and Diane Troderman, the Savitz family, Leonard Florence, the Sidney and Esther Rabb Charitable Foundation, Roberta and Maxwell Burstein, Alan and Susan Solomont, the Casty-Dunn families, and Richard and Carol Bendetson. Thanks to you all.

Thanks also to my family, for many things. My father and mother sparked my interest in things Jewish from a very early age, and supported all the writing and other adventures that led me to this one. The rest of my immediate family, and nearly all of my extended family, let me violate their privacy in researching the Boston chapter. I was perpetually on my computer to Judy Corlin, on the phone to Sylvia Zieff and Leslie Tye, and interrupting family gatherings to ask my sister and her family, or my brother and his, "just one more question."

You expect your own family to indulge you like that, but not all the other families that let me into their lives and may well have regretted it afterward, when I would not let them alone. Thanks to the Briscoes and the Ohanas, to the Kaminezkis, Eplans, Israels, Avrujs, and all the others. I now count you as part of my family.

Marc Shechtman offered the same brilliant research assistance he always does, Susan Ebert helped me raise my money, Lois Goldberg masterfully managed it, and Ken Whitney picked out my desktop and laptop computers, set them up, taught me how to use them, and steered me through endless crises in Boston and abroad. In each city there were people who did what Vyacheslav Brez did so patiently in Dnepropetrovsk, and Tanya Rubinstein-Horowitz did in Düsseldorf, which was think they had answered all my inquiries only to have me call or e-mail with more. And across the diaspora there were experts like Rabbis Herbert Rosenblum and Ira Korinow, and Professor Sylvia Fuks Fried of Brandeis, who helped me translate Hebrew and Yiddish and sort through ancient Jewish texts and modern Jewish practice. All told I interviewed more than 500 people, all of whom were gracious in giving me their time and sharing their often painful tales, and most of whom were not quoted by name. Your stories *are* here, and I truly am grateful.

Last I want to thank friend and restaurant critic Alison Arnett for sustaining me with all those great meals, and Billy and Sally Connolly for all their encouragement. Robin Romano was an inspiration and I wish she were here to see the book published. Thanks to old friends Anne Bernays, Beryl Ann Cowan, Miranda Daniloff, Carolyn Hine, Claudia Kalb, Justin Kaplan, Sheila Rauch Kennedy, Mary Keogan, Bill and Lynne Kovach, Steve Kurkjian, Dick Lehr, Larry Lowenthal, Tom Palmer, Judy Rakowsky, Marianne Sutton, David Watson, and all my Nieman buddies, and to new friends Nancy Cahners, Barbara Gaffin, Nancy Kaufman, David Link, Bernie Reisman, and Ben Sachs.

Index

in Germany, 14, 30–42, 44–45, 46–47,
49, 52, 55, 60, 75, 92, 184
in Ireland, 196, 209
in Israel, 33, 35, 60, 61, 75, 76–77,
284, 297–98
poverty of, 32, 44
in United States, 33, 34, 60, 75, 92,
108, 126
see also individual cities

"Sabbath goy," 122, 197
Sachs, Dr. Benjamin, 89
Samuels, Rabbi Benjamin, 138
Samuels, Rabbi Robert, 301–2
Sandalon, Belinda, 258
Sarcey, Max, 228
Sarna, Jonathan, 91, 102–3
Sarnat, David, 245
Savannah, Georgia, 265, 275
Savitz, Noah McGee, 144
Savitz, Andy, 144–45
Savitz, Herb, 111
Savitz, Penelope McGee, 144
Saxe, Leonard, 143
Schachter-Shalomi, Rabbi Zalman, 43
Schindler, Rabbi Solomon, 119
Schneerson, Rabbi Menachem Mendel,
62–63, 74–75
Schneider, Bettina, 47–48
schools, Jewish day, see day schools,
Jewish
Second Temple, 1, 8–9
Seders, 140, 150, 152, 209, 257, 259
Selig, S. Stephen, III, 242–43
Senderey, Moises, 173
Sephardic Jews, 126, 222
and Ashkenazic communities in Paris,
6, 220, 221, 231–33, 237, 238
in Atlanta, 268
in Israel, 238
of North Africa, 219
Shaarei Tefillah, Newton, 137–38
Shabbateanism, 85
Sharon, Ariel, 284, 302
Sharon, Massachusetts, 111

Shenhar, Aliza, 92, 97–98, 290
Shlyak, Mark, 98
Shoah, see Holocaust
Shoob, Judge Marvin, 246
Shrage, Barry, 129, 141–42
Simchas Torah, 45–46, 136
Sirota, Graciela Narcisa, 168
Sitruk, Rabbi Joseph, 238–39
Slaton, John M., 271
social and sports clubs:
in Argentina, 166–67
in Atlanta, 265, 267, 268, 273, 275
in Ireland, 196, 198, 206, 211
socialists, Jewish, 164, 165, 268
social justice, 168, 191, 277
new Jewish identity and, 102, 139–41
Social Justice, 107
Sociedad Hebraica, 166–67, 180, 182
Solomons, Dr. Michael, 207
Solomon Schechter Schools, 151, 152
Soloveitchik, Rabbi Joseph B., 101,
120–21
South African Jews, 211–12, 213
Souviens-toi de ton Futur (Remember
Tomorrow), 220, 239
Soviet Union, former, 9, 170, 301
conditions for Jews in, 34, 38–39, 60,
64, 78–82, 86, 97–98
migration of Jews from, see Russian
Jews
during World War II, 33
Spanish Inquisition, 1, 11, 16, 22
Spiegel, Hugo, 22–23
Spiegel, Paul, 13–17, 22–23, 51, 57–58
Spiegel, Rosa, 15
Spiegel, Ruth, 15, 16
spirituality, new Jewish identity and, 102,
133–39
Spolsky, Sergio, 178
Spolsky family, 178
sports and social clubs, see social and
sports clubs
Stalin, Joseph, 34
Standard Club, Atlanta, 265, 268, 273
Starr, Rabbi David, 130

About the Author

LARRY TYE is a journalist with the *Boston Globe*, where he has won numerous awards. He was a Nieman Fellow at Harvard University and is the author of *The Father of Spin*, a biography of public relations pioneer Edward Bernays.